MORE POST BIOGRAPHIES

More Post Biographies

*Articles of Enduring Interest about Famous Journalists
and Journals and Other Subjects Journalistic*

Edited by JOHN E. DREWRY

*Dean, Henry W. Grady School of Journalism, The
University of Georgia; formerly President,
American Association of Teachers of
Journalism*

THE UNIVERSITY OF GEORGIA PRESS

ATHENS

PRINTED IN THE UNITED STATES OF AMERICA

Contents

Introduction

SOME four years ago, the first edition of a book known as *Post Biographies of Famous Journalists* was published. The critical response (and sale) more than substantiated the editor's pre-publication faith in the entertaining and enduring qualities of the articles therein preserved. "An extremely merry, irreverent, and informative volume"—so reads *Book-of-the-Month Club News* appraisal. "I can hardly praise this book . . . too highly," wrote the late lamented William Lyon Phelps. "A survey of modern journalism by some of its ablest practitioners. . . . Those who shaped our copy made good copy themselves"—said Jonathan Daniels in the *Saturday Review of Literature*. "A major contribution to biographical literature," commented the Portland (Me.) *Sunday Telegram*. "Their private lives have remained somewhat more private than those of Hollywood actors and actresses, but are certainly no less interesting, and many will doubtless find them considerably more interesting"—that is the California touch from the San Francisco *Chronicle*.

Poor Richard, yonder in some journalistic Valhalla, must have been greatly cheered by the enthusiasm of such reviews. He had reason to believe that his successors on Independence Square in Philadelphia are pretty good journalists themselves, for they—George Horace Lorimer, Wesley Stout, Ben Hibbs, Robert M. Fuoss, and others—are the ones who deserve the credit for this book. They first assigned or accepted these articles, and without their work this book would not have been possible. It is in tribute to them that the foregoing extracts are here reproduced, because these favorable reviews are, after all, but testimonials to their editorial perspicacity.

vii

The success of *Post Biographies of Famous Journalists* has led to this *More Post Biographies*. In the language of Mr. Fuoss, the *Post's* managing editor, "the consensus here seems to be that the first edition of *Post Biographies* was a good job and that it would make good sense to try another edition . . ." Since the publication of the first book, a dozen or more of the country's most colorful journalistic figures have been treated biographically by the *Post*. These sketches, like those in the other volume, merit longer life and greater permanence than is afforded by single periodical publication. Hence, this second collection.

More Post Biographies differs from *Post Biographies of Famous Journalists* in several minor details:

For one thing, some of the subjects in this collection are less well known than those in the first book. They are no less colorful and worthy of treatment, however.

A few of the present group are no longer living. Dead physically, they are, none the less, very much alive in the memories of all those who will be attracted to a book of this kind, and will likely continue to be so for years to come. An Ernie Pyle or a Raymond Clapper—to name but two—are not likely soon to be forgotten, and their lives, as herein depicted, are both a memorial and an inspiration.

For each of the sketches, there is an Editor's Preface, a device which has been employed to supplement data in the articles, to bring them up to date, and to provide pertinent comment.

The last difference in this and the other *Post* collection is that the roster has not been restricted to "famous journalists." There are also articles about famous *journals* and other agencies of journalism. We have in this country certain newspapers which have, during the years, acquired or created for themselves such a distinctive flavor that each is as much a personality as any individual connected with it. They are, for want of a better term, institutional personalities, or personified institutions. As such, these papers merit a place in a collection such as this. To be more specific, for many Americans, the

Philadelphia *Bulletin,* and the *Christian Science Monitor* are more readily recognized journalistic entities or personalities than some of the individuals herein treated. And, of course, in the story of each of these papers, there appear a number of individuals responsible for or associated with the publication. Great newspapers inevitably are but the lengthened and continuing shadows of great men and women, many of whom make their contributions to institutional prestige anonymously.

As for the other agencies of journalism herein represented, there are the story of the newsreels ("Headlines in Celluloid"), a report on women in journalism ("Paper Dolls"), and a piece about the journalistic relationships, uses, and methods of the *Encyclopaedia Britannica* ("160 Miles of Words") an article on *Who's Who in America* ("How to Get Your Name in *Who's Who*"), another indispensable tool of the working newspaper man or woman—all subjects very much at home in a collection such as this, and altogether worthy of preservation in book form.

Much water has passed over the dam since some of these sketches were first written. Yet these biographies are today almost as fresh—certainly as vital—as when they first were given magazine publication. They possess a kind of timeless timeliness. Glenn Frank, as editor of *Century* Magazine, once said that American journalism is too timely. "There is something essentially unsound in the editorial race for timeliness," he wrote. "Editorial timeliness is not primarily a matter of the calendar; it is determined by how quickly interest . . . spreads far enough to insure that the maximum number of persons will turn to a discussion . . . with genuine interest."

This book possesses the kind of timeliness about which Mr. Frank was speaking. There has been enough time for a maximum number of people to hear about and to become interested in the persons herein discussed. Individually and collectively, they are very much a part of the American scene. And like any other part of the American scene, there are small changes, year by year. Grand Canyon is not the same today as it was ten years ago. But it is still Grand Canyon. The same thing can be said about these "famous journalists." There may be new facts here and there, but, like a good portrait, these sketches have caught the true likeness and will not soon fade. Indeed, some of them, again like a good canvas, will enhance in value with the passage of time. All of which is said in explanation of an editorial decision against making any changes in tenses in any of these articles. The date of original publication of each is given, and each should be read with this date in mind.

A word should be said about the growing demand for stories about journalists. Public interest in articles about the men and women who make our public press is "at the highest peak in the history of U. S. journalism," according to a recent item in *Editor and Publisher,* leading newspaper and advertising trade journal. *Post* Associate Editor Jack Alexander is quoted in this connection as follows:

"There is no doubt the public likes to read newspaper stories. We have the evidence to prove that. Letters pour in here every time a newspaper article appears. The curiosity seems not to be confined to any particular region, but to be typical of the entire country.

"The curiosity seems to revolve around such points as how the news is collected and presented, who collects it and who edits it—particularly the men who make the newspapers. We have arrived at the point where people are writing, not merely to register their approval of a particular article, but to suggest that a particular paper apparently long a favorite with them should be done by our staff writers.

"We find the newspaper article a good and staple product. The best answer probably is that we have more articles of this type already in hand, and more planned for the future."

Some may wonder why two *Post* collections should be edited by someone as far removed from Philadelphia as Georgia. The explanation is two-fold:

First, both books have been an outgrowth of a quite ordinary pedagogical practice—the preservation of clippings for illustrative purposes in teaching. For many years, the editor has collected distinctive periodical biographies, especially of journalists. The *Post* biographies, by number, quality, and enduring qualities were a pressing argument for book publication. Editor and publisher simply acceded to what the articles themselves suggested and made possible.

Second, there is a kinship between the *Post* and the University of Georgia in that both, in a sense, stem from the same illustrious sire. The *Post* has for years featured the statement, "Founded in 1728 by Benjamin Franklin." When the University of Georgia, oldest chartered state university (1785), came into being, its liberal arts division was known as Franklin College—named, of course, in honor of wise old Benjamin. Some little historical interest attaches, therefore, to the fact that more than two hundred years after Franklin established his *Pennsylvania Gazette,* of which the *Post* is an outgrowth, his name, and possibly his spirit, are indirectly associated with and partially responsible for two new journalistic creations— this book and its predecessor.

Matthew Arnold has written that "journalism is literature in a hurry." Lawrence Martin has said that "literature . . . is simply journalism that has showed lasting interest—journalism with staying powers." Both of these statements are applicable to the sketches which have been chosen for preservation between these covers. They may have been hastily done—there is almost as much pressure in the preparation of the content of a weekly such as *The Saturday Evening Post* as in the city rooms of some metropolitan dailies. But however much of a hurry may have marked their preparation and publication, they have "staying powers." Professor Martin has said that "the literature of today was the journalism of yesterday; and the best of journalism of today will be the literature of tomorrow." This statement too is largely applicable here—so much so that it is in this spirit that these *Post* biographies have been selected and are here offered for a new and wider reading and a more readily accessible and more enduring preservation than is possible in the scattered issues of a magazine.

xii Introduction

For assistance in transforming the idea of this book into a reality, credit and appreciation are due Robert M. Fuoss, managing editor, and Glenn Gundell, advertising and promotion manager, *The Saturday Evening Post;* Frazier Moore, director, and Ralph H. Stephens, assistant director, University of Georgia Press; and Miss Miriam Thurmond, secretary of the School of Journalism.

J. E. D.

Rip-Roaring Baillie

(HUGH BAILLIE)

By JACK ALEXANDER

EDITOR'S PREFACE.—This article about Hugh Baillie has a double significance: (1) it delineates, with the verve and gusto of all Mr. Alexander's sketches, an unusually colorful personality; and (2) it provides high points in the story of press association development, particularly that of the United Press.

Both as an individual and as the head of the UP, Mr. Baillie is the kind of person who is an ideal subject for biographical treatment. Just as he has always demanded that news be written so as to be forceful and dramatic, so has his own life been dynamic, forthright, aggressive. He is, as Mr. Alexander notes, "a simon-pure extrovert," and as such has been *making* copy as well as writing copy ever since he has been in the newspaper business. As one of his co-workers put it, "Nowadays with newspaper men getting more scholarly and aiming for Harvard Fellowships in subjects like municipal government, Hugh is a wonderful shot in the arm to the whole trade."

Thomas Carlyle once wrote that "the history of the world is but the biography of great men." Ralph Waldo Emerson said, "There is properly no history; only biography." Thomas Heywood has noted that

> "The world's a theatre, the earth a stage,
> Which God and nature do with actors fill."

All of these quotations are suggested by and applicable to this sketch of Mr. Baillie. His biography is history—especially so since he has directed the reporting of so many important stories that since have become history. The late Dr. John H. Finley, when editor of the New York *Times,* often referred to the newspaper as *the historian in the present tense.* This would be even more true of the press

1

association. Through his own reporting, interviewing, and writing, and also by direction of bureau managers and correspondents in almost every land, Mr. Baillie has for years been a living epitome of Dr. Finley's concept of the newspaper man in his highest and most enduring role. And not only has Mr. Baillie recorded history; in not a few instances, as Mr. Alexander reports, he has made history.

In thinking of an appropriate title for this article, the *Post* editors first chose, "The World, the Press, and Hugh Baillie." In view of the subject's global sweep, both contemporaneously and as a present-tense historian, this would have been very fitting. No less so, however, as a reading of the following piece will substantiate, is the heading, "Rip-Roaring Baillie."

I

June 1 and 8, 1946

A FEW weeks after Japan's surrender, two highly dissimilar men wearing cropped haircuts sat at tea in a cottage on the bomb-scarred Imperial Palace grounds. In this testy meeting of the East and the West, it is a question which man found the other the more baffling. The host, Emperor Hirohito, was dressed in a morning coat, striped trousers and patent-leather shoes, and he wore steel-rimmed glasses. He looked like a skinny recluse professor tricked out for his daughter's wedding, and was just about as uncomfortable about the business at hand, which was an interview. The other man was Hugh Baillie, the president of the mighty United Press, one of America's world-wide news services. Baillie, an erect, scowling man with the bearing of a Prussian general, looked bulky in a correspondent's uniform and field jacket.

Dissimilar as they were, the two men at Tokyo had two things in common besides the way they wore their hair; each was a minor-league divinity—Hirohito had not yet applied for membership in the human race—and each was, in his own way, an anachronism. Baillie was a successful anachronism, like the rubber hot-water bottle, and was at the very peak of his success. Thirty years earlier, when he had first joined the

United Press, it was almost as shabby as the Emperor's domain is today, and its future seemed just as threadbare.

From the beginning of his United Press career, Baillie, a simon-pure extrovert, took the godlike view of himself, and through his own efforts he was able to make it stick. The most difficult years of his life came in the early 1930's when, having risen to an acknowledged eminence as the organization's crown prince, he was kept waiting while the president, Karl A. Bickel, dawdled over his retirement plans. Bickel talked a good deal about retiring, but, having had a strong hand in building up the United Press, hung on and on for sentiment's sake. By the time he finally did make his exit, in 1935, Baillie, a man of impressive dynamism and impatience, had all but exploded into bits.

In his frustration he clamped his jaws with such energy that he wore the surfaces off some of his teeth and had to have them recapped. When a telephone connection went bad, he might rip the instrument from its moorings and throw it into the wastebasket, depending on his mood. He trumpeted like a love-sick moose when his subordinate rank prevented him from instituting reforms he felt were necessary, or he crushed a fountain pen into his desk pad as a child crushes a cockroach into the floor. He sought relaxation on the golf course, but found himself, as usual, swinging the clubs as if they were axes. In an attempt to simplify the game, he had a professional make him a sturdy all-purpose club. It broke when, according to office mythology, he tried to chop down a tree that had him stymied. Anyway, he gave up golf for a while.

When Baillie and the United Press were growing to manhood, it was a rip-roaring individualistic era, and Baillie, in his approach to news coverage today, retains the era's fiery stamp. His attitude toward events is that of an old-fashioned fire-engine-and-police-raid reporter. He is an incurable seeker of the spectacular and of the human-interest angle, and he cares little for the profounder implications of world news. The United Press, in supplying its subscribing newspaper clients, does carry its share of the more solid news, such as complicated reports on labor-employer disputes, social legislation and the hagglings of the chancelleries, but Baillie has to be sold on them first by other executives.

Inwardly, he isn't really sold at all. He simply gives in grudgingly here and there to a trend of reader interest of which he does not approve, as the late John Barrymore would have given in to a bit of flat dialogue. Unless a story thrills him personally, he rates it as a flop. "A lot of people have got to die," one of his co-workers says with admiring cynicism.

One of Baillie's great worries, in the present highly organized state of the news services, is that the United Press will lose the intense competitive instinct of its earlier days. It is this instinct, carefully nurtured by those in charge, which has raised it during Baillie's lifetime—he is now fifty-five—from a struggling brat to a colossus rivaling the older and better-established Associated Press. Baillie feeds on competition and dreams about it at night.

"I am by nature one hell of a competitor," he explained a few weeks ago to a visitor in his New York office, "and that is what keeps me going. My work keeps me gigged up all the time."

Baillie rides herd imperiously on his army of correspondents and bureau chiefs. His roars of anguish over a poorly handled news story can be heard with equal vehemence—by telephone, telegraph, cable or radio—in New Orleans, Shanghai, Kansas City, London or Calcutta. By some odd twist of mind, he regards a failure on the part of one of his men as a personal affront. "I'm just not going to sit here and get beaten!" he yells in a harsh strident voice as he prepares to dictate a reprimand. "We're not going to have any more of this! He can't do this to me!"

Baillie's impatience with sloppy work extends to the illnesses of the human body, particularly his own. His remedy for indigestion is to punch himself in the abdomen. A few years ago he woke up one morning with a side of his face paralyzed. Standing before his bathroom mirror, he landed several right hooks on his jaw. The net effect of this therapy was to cause one eye to stick open. Baillie then set out to assign medical specialists to the job, in much the manner a city editor would use in deploying his reporters to cover a murder story. For a few days he went from one specialist to another comparing notes, arguing about treatment and driving them half crazy. One of them, probably a pioneer in psychosomatic medicine, rigged up Baillie's face in a leather harness and put a black patch over the eye that refused to shut. The patient's morale soared. He wore the patch and harness about the office with unconcealed pride and was openly triumphant when the paralysis ultimately went away. Actually, it was a type of ailment that disappears in a few weeks anyway, if let alone.

Baillie's innate sense of drama, and his continuing appetite for it, are a living legend around the United Press. He can't stand a dull performance, by himself or anyone else. One of his associates, discussing him recently over a highball, said wonderingly: "Nearly everything that happens to Hugh or has ever happened to him is cloaked in the radiance of high adventure. Even a cold in the head, to hear him tell it, is accompanied by nosebleed and 'large clots of blood that came cascading down my necktie'; he licked pneumonia in three days, and a strep throat in two—and that was before the sulfa drugs were invented. When he gets a group of people together to tell about a flight over the ocean, you'd be convinced it was the most hazardous adventure a man ever went through; the whole plane was shuddering as the de-icers got to work shaking off the icicles, and all that. He always comes through alive though." He paused and sighed, then added, "I guess he is just what you would call a forceful man."

The president's conception of the ideal foreign correspondent is that of an animated newsreel camera equipped with gadgets for conveying sound, taste, touch and smell to the newspaper reader. This conception, throwback though it is, is regarded by many as a refreshing influence in an age when so many correspondents have become twisted up in the toils of interpretive reporting. Anyway, it makes for absorbing reading.

During the recent war Baillie came back from a visit to the

North African and Sicilian fronts tremendously stimulated by what he had seen, and settled down for a rest in a house he owns in La Jolla, California. His rest was a brief one. As he read the press-service dispatches from Europe in the newspapers, it seemed to him that they bore no relation to what he had seen in the field. He began bombarding the New York office with telephone calls in which he demanded more brutal realism.

"Tell those guys out there to get the smell of warm blood into their copy," he ordered. "Tell them to quit writing like retired generals and military analysts, and to write about people killing each other." United Press war dispatches soon conformed to these instructions. When they were published by UP newspaper clients throughout the country, papers subscribing to the other services began demanding the same kind of coverage. As a result, painful realism infused the war news, and civilians got to know fairly well from their newspapers what war was like, up close. As a reminder that there was to be no letup on the blood-and-guts theme, Baillie got up a booklet of dispatches which he himself had filed from the front, and mailed copies of it to his war correspondents. The models he chose were competent, earthy reports on battles, written in somewhat the style of the late Arthur Brisbane's lurid speculations on a putative fight between Gene Tunney and a gorilla. In discussing the booklet at the time, Baillie explained simply, "I am naturally dramatic, and that is why I write such damned dramatic copy." He didn't know at the time that some of his Sicilian dispatches had not reached UP clients precisely as he had written them. Someone, regarding them as too ornately colorful, had toned them down a bit. When Baillie did find out about this, he put on a brilliant show of transatlantic fireworks.

Even Baillie's personal memorandum pad is dramatic. Its sheets, which are captioned "Memo from HB," are of a striking shade of red, a color reserved for Baillie's use. The pads of less dramatic executives run to drab shades. Although he is sometimes referred to around the New York office as Flat Top, a

nickname apparently based on his spiked hair and low forehead, Baillie is regarded with reverential awe by United Press
men, all of whom admire his vivid nature and like to talk
about it. "During the war, Hugh liked nothing better," one of
them says, "than to wear a uniform and helmet, and bounce
around an active front in a jeep, especially when the racket
was real loud and everyone was ducking for cover. He was so
wrapped up in the spectacle that he forgot danger. The front
was a hell of a fine show—that's the way he looked at it. Nowadays, with newspapermen getting more scholarly and aiming
for Harvard fellowships in subjects like municipal government, Hugh is a wonderful shot in the arm to the whole trade."

Baillie's contempt for a dull news performance transcends
the personnel of the United Press and covers anyone who is
involved in the news anywhere in the world. Unless the news
has what is known as a high startle value—that is, unless it is
thrilling or shocking—he usually loses interest in it. Sometimes, if a situation has unrealized dramatic possibilities, he
attempts to bring them to life, as he did during the 1944 Republican convention in Chicago. The United Press was represented by a large staff which was faithfully recording every
development as the delegates dallied with their beloved tribal
preliminaries. Baillie was disgusted. He got United Press convention headquarters on the telephone and was full of suggestions about what the party leaders ought to be doing to pump
life into the proceedings. One suggestion was to have Dewey
flown secretly from Albany and released upon the convention
at the first night session, like a mustached jinni from a jug, for
a rousing speech.

The suggestions were relayed, but the uninspired party
hacks ignored them all, and nobody was less surprised than
Baillie was when Dewey was snowed under in November. The
Democrats put on a much better convention show, and Baillie's often-expressed admiration for Franklin Roosevelt after
the election had no political significance; it was just a low bow
in the direction of a master showman. Baillie has no political
affiliations.

One thing that Baillie is thankful for in reminiscent moments is the fact that he escaped being born in Australia, where the United Press would have been just a name to him, and his aggressive talents would have been cooped up in a remote continent. It was a fairly narrow escape. His father, David Gemmell Baillie, was a journalist who got his start on a paper in Dumfries, Scotland, and later worked on a paper in Birmingham, England. Looking for new fields, the elder Baillie set sail for Australia in 1887 and stopped off in New York, en route, to see the town. New York held him, as it has a way of doing with tourists. He got a job as a reporter on the *Tribune,* later moving over to the *World,* then to the *Press.*

David Baillie, who had once been a divinity student at the University of Edinburgh, was a spare, quiet man, well-grounded in classical learning. He amused himself by composing poems in Latin and Greek, and he devised his own system of shorthand, which he found useful in reporting political speeches. In the dignified manner of the political reporters of the day, he wore a frock coat and a high hat, and carried a cane. His work brought him in contact with John B. Hays, a veteran reporter who was of Scottish lineage. Hays was the *Tribune's* political star. Baillie married Hays' daughter. The couple lived in Brooklyn and there, in 1890, Hugh was born.

From the time Hugh was able to get around, he was immersed in a newspaper atmosphere. His maternal grandfather sometimes took him to City Hall, where he was dandled on the laps of other political reporters. When Hugh was six, his father, assigned to Canton, Ohio, to cover McKinley's "front-porch" campaign, took his family along, and there the boy was introduced to a man who was about to become President. After these exciting experiences, he never considered being anything but a newspaperman.

A part-time job the elder Baillie had—that of writing speeches for Andrew Carnegie—came close to sidetracking the boy though. Carnegie offered to pay his speech writer in securities of his steel company. Item No. 2 on Hugh Baillie's thankfulness list is the fact that his father had the wisdom to take cash instead of securities. Had he accepted stock, he might have become a rich man and Hugh would have been turned into a rich man's son.

When Hugh was thirteen, his father pulled up stakes once more and moved to Los Angeles, where he joined the editorial-page staff of the *Herald*. Academic learning held little interest for the son. At nineteen, after boggling through sophomore year at the University of Southern California, he resolved that the time had come for him to break into the newspaper business. He had a talent for drawing, and one day he bundled up some of his work and tried to persuade the managing editor of the Los Angeles *Record* to hire him as a cartoonist. The editor, unimpressed by the cartoons but deeply impressed by an unearthly confidence his visitor exuded, tried him out as a sports reporter. Baillie turned out to be a colorful writer, and the *Record,* a minor paper willing to gamble, let him try anything he wanted to.

With a police press badge pinned to his vest, Baillie covered fires, murders and court trials, and was vastly stirred by the drama of what he saw. He carried a revolver, a privilege accorded journalists by the liberal-minded city police. On a juicy story he let himself go in an orgy of self-expression. Typical of his rather Byzantine style was one crime story which began: "Lurking in the shadows with bloody knife and the gore of three victims staining his hands, Juan Soto, a murderous maniac who escaped from Patton Asylum and killed two women Monday night a few hours after gaining his liberty, is today at large in this city. The 'leopard man,' as Soto is known because of his mottled flesh and savage instinct, was sent to Patton after, in cold blood, murdering Ralph Gallardo, of 363 N. Main St. . . ." The inflation of a punk criminal's repute for literary purposes by inventing a shuddery nickname for him such as "leopard man," as Baillie did in this instance, is a city-room liberty which is infrequently granted to young reporters. When the police and the rival newspapers take up the nickname, as they did in Los Angeles, the reporter's fame as a creative genius is made.

A versatile performer, Baillie would shift his gears after unloading imperishable prose about a murderer, and compose humorous verse, which the *Record* published. He also found time to turn out a local gossip column. It lacked the bite of its present-day counterparts, but it had a homey touch. "Sorry to hear that my old friend, Joe Ford, candidate for district attorney, broke his arm cranking his auto," the columnist would write, or, "Saw Bugs Goodenow at the football game." At times the column got highly moralistic. "Some of those drunks, dead beats and professional alcoholists who have been landmarks at First and Main for 20 years should be destroyed," the columnist once wrote. The verse and the gossip column were published under pen names. Baillie saved his real by-line for the crime articles. He was immensely proud of any contact he had with violence in eruption.

His biggest chance came when a naïve national magazine published in New York came out with an article titled "Los Angeles, the Chemically Pure." The *Record* management, anxious to warn maidens against local seducers, and also worried about a declining circulation, assigned Baillie to the task of proving that the city was anything but pure. Baillie came through in melodramatic fashion. Using the pen name of John Danger, he aroused *Record* readers one afternoon with a curtain raiser which led off with: "Two hundred and seven young girls were stolen from good homes in Los Angeles during the five months ended June 1 and consigned to lives of shame!"

His article inspired a torpid police vice squad to bestir itself and descend upon the segregated district. Baillie accompanied the raiders, throwing himself wholeheartedly into the moral spirit of the crusade. He carried a small ax or a maul up his sleeve and helped to crash in the bordello doors with all the fervor of a probationary patrolman trying to impress his superiors. After seeing the inmates safely to a station house, he would return to the office and write a John Danger story for the next day's paper.

When the articles had been running for a few weeks, characters with tough voices began telephoning the *Record* and demanding to know who John Danger was. Baillie got a bodyguard, a retired prize fighter, and kept his revolver oiled. When abroad on the streets at night, he ducked into motion-picture theaters and left by a side exit to shake off ugly looking men who, he was convinced, were following him. One night after dismissing his bodyguard, he got a chance to use his revolver. Two men who had followed him out from town tried to assault him near his suburban home. Baillie fired a wild shot and they fled.

After that, he left town for a week to let the situation cool off. No count was kept of the young women who were saved from lives of shame, but during the crusade the *Record's* meager circulation had doubled.

Baillie had started at twelve dollars a week on the *Record,* and within a few action-crammed years his salary had risen meteorically to thirty dollars. On the side he made money by promoting semiprofessional baseball, football and boxing exhibitions, and he owned a piece of a lightweight boxer who, unfortunately, never amounted to much. It was a full and active life, but a comparatively restricted one for one who longed, as Baillie did, to see the exciting world outside. When the United Press, in 1915, offered him a job in its San Francisco bureau at the salary he was getting on the *Record,* he took it. Baillie knew nothing of the technique of press-service work, which differs considerably from that of straight newspaper work.

The United Press was still in its pinfeather stage and, although it was financially undernourished, it made a great show of scratching around busily and squawking like a full-fledged, world-wide news service. A brash, quick-thinking youngster like Hugh Baillie, who didn't mind living in rooming houses on a soup diet, was a welcome addition. The founder of the United Press, E. W. Scripps, operated on a theory that the good newspaperman was the hungry newspaperman. Scripps, a raffish titan who made newspaper history, established the United Press in 1907 by buying the Publishers' Press and merging it with two services he already owned, the Scripps-McRae

Press Association and the Scripps News Association. These services had been separately supplying telegraph news to newspapers on the Atlantic Coast, in the Middle West and on the Pacific Coast, respectively.

At the start of its career the United Press' assets consisted of the battered furniture and office equipment of the three regional services, a file of a few inherited newspaper contracts and the belligerent attitude of an intoxicated field mouse squaring off against an elephant. The elephant was the Associated Press, which for ten years had enjoyed a virtual monopoly as a nation-wide service. It was, as it is now, a nonprofit-making, co-operative league of newspapers financed by annual assessments levied against its members. Nonmember publishers who wanted to obtain Associated Press franchises often found the going as difficult as a tramp would encounter in trying to gain entrance to a gentlemen's club. Scripps, as a publisher of the Scripps-McRae chain of papers, which editorially championed the cause of the sweaty masses, knew what it was to be denied a franchise. His United Press was intended to break this monopoly. It was also intended to make money. It sold its news to whoever would buy it, as button shoes were sold in department stores.

The San Francisco bureau had quarters in the building of the San Francisco *Daily News*. The *Daily News* was a Scripps-McRae paper—as was the Los Angeles *Record*. Scripps had a custom of starting up his papers in ratty structures in low-rent districts, and the *Daily News* building ran true to form. It was a ramshackle, one-story brick barn in a drayage district, and the United Press bureau occupied a cubbyhole in one corner of the barn. In winter the only heat came from a small, potbellied stove. The *Daily News* building had no central heating, a Scripps tenet being that men who were impervious to hunger should likewise be impervious to cold.

The bureau operated in an almost continuous state of bedlam created by the racket of typewriters, the jangling of telephones and cries of "Flash!" whenever an important news bulletin began coming in. Added to this was the clacking of four telegraph sounders, to which the Morse operators, in their immemorial way, had attached empty tobacco cans for amplification.

Baillie found the noisy atmosphere invigorating and his new duties a challenge to his versatility. His first task, writing for the pony wire, took restraint and a knack for condensation. The pony was a brief budget of world news prepared for a dozen or more small papers in the San Francisco area which couldn't afford all-day service. It was sent in three installments daily—at 10:30 A.M., 1:00 P.M. and 2:00 P.M.—in time for each installment to catch the various editions of the subscribing clients. The pony's total length was restricted to 500 words, and the chief problem of an eager newcomer was to keep from blowing in too much of his 500-word allowance on the early installments. If he allowed himself to do that and a big story broke later on in the day, the words he had left would be insufficient to do justice to it, and the clients would complain. Pony work, which called for concise, clear English, took a lot of the fat off Baillie's florid Los Angeles *Record* style.

After graduating from the pony wire, Baillie was assigned to a task which called for the opposite knack—that of expanding skeleton bulletins of world news for the Pacific Coast leased-wire service. This service was kept operating continuously and it supplied newspapers in urban centers all the way from Seattle to San Diego. The Coast clients didn't know it at the time, but the United Press' system of leased wires from the East stopped on its way west at Denver. The Denver bureau bridged the gap by sending San Francisco a 1500-word condensation of the news each day by regular Western Union commercial service. By using his imagination, but keeping within the bounds of credibility, Baillie quickly learned the high art of enlarging bare items to many times their original size. A year later, a full leased-wire service from Denver completed the circuit from New York, and it was considered a tribute to Baillie's talents that the West Coast clients never noticed the difference.

One of the more attractive features of toiling for the United Press was the way in which it fed young men's sense of identity by carrying their by-lines on the bigger stories—a policy which the Associated Press was to adopt some years later. The neophyte was told, when he felt low about his income, that he was becoming a world figure. When Baillie got a copy of an Eastern newspaper and saw his name at the top of a front-page column, he was ready to believe this. To a world figure slaving twelve hours a day or more, as United Press men habitually did, prominence gained 3000 miles away was medicine for an ailing ego. It was almost as good as a steak dinner or a new suit.

Baillie often got away from the office to report local events of national interest, and he was ingenious in dreaming up ways to beat competing reporters. Once when assigned to cover an intercollegiate shell race in the Oakland estuary he insisted on taking along a roughneck hanger-on around the bureau known only as Mert. Mert had a motorcycle, and Baillie rode out with him to the race course, but the free ride wasn't what he had in mind. At the point where the race was to end, only one telephone was available—a public booth in a grocery store. Baillie stationed Mert at the booth with a handful of nickels and instructed him to get in touch with the bureau when the shells were nearing the finish line and to keep the line open by dropping in nickels.

When the race was finished, Baillie sprinted for the booth. He elbowed his way past his rivals and took over the telephone wire. While Mert, who was a preliminary prize fighter, took a Horatius-at-the-bridge stance outside the booth and fended off the other reporters, Baillie dictated his story of the race to a rewrite man. Then he stayed in the booth for another half hour, dropping nickels lavishly, and thus won for the United Press a clean beat on sports pages all over the country. This was probably one of the earliest versions of a simple, though effective, competitive stunt that later became a standard practice wherever telephones were scarce. Subsequent innovators improved on it by going outside, after turning in their stories, and snipping the lead-in wire.

Baillie had made his mark in San Francisco, which was the

principal United Press bureau on the Coast, and in 1916 he was offered a small bureau of his own, in Portland, Oregon. Eager to keep moving, he said he would take it. Then he stepped across the hall into the *Daily News* office and held a short conference with a girl reporter named Constance Scott whom he had been taking to movies on his evenings off. Miss Scott had just finished typing a story about a young "typewriter girl" who had escaped the clutches of a Barbary Coast white slaver and had turned to a quieter daily chore of hers, writing the advice-to-the-lovelorn column. Baillie described his new assignment and suggested forthrightly that they get married.

If Anxious Brown Eyes or Disturbed Nob Hill Debutante had asked for Miss Scott's advice on a similar problem, she would doubtless have counseled caution. But a few weeks later she was a bride setting up housekeeping in Portland.

The Portland bureau was typical of the smaller United Press outposts of the day. The backbone of the smaller bureau was the Morse telegraph operator. Bureau managers came and went with discouraging rapidity, but the Morse man stayed on. He was a substantial member of the community and he got more pay than the itinerant managers did. He trained green newcomers and, if no one else happened to be around, he could and did run the bureau.

Baillie, who had a staff consisting of one reporter besides himself, had to lean heavily on the Morse man because the United Press expected him to scratch for new clients in addition to covering the news in his area. The dominance of the Associated Press was hard to buck. The best deal the United Press could get in many towns was to sell its service, for supplementary use, to a newspaper proprietor who already had an Associated Press franchise. This was unsatisfactory because it meant only an infrequent appearance in newspapers of the United Press credit line.

As the Associated Press member in any town was almost invariably the leading paper, the United Press chose to gamble on the smaller, or "dog," papers whose editors made up in com-

petitive spirit for the small price they were able to pay for
pony-wire news. In return for a contract, the United Press plas-
tered the town's billboards with posters chanting the praises of
the "dog" paper which, by a gracious act of Providence, had
been selected as the local outlet for the United Press' enlightening accounts of what was going on around the world.

In Portland, Baillie found himself in the thick of the uneven
fight to gain a foothold in the kingdom of the Associated Press.
He was buoyed up to some extent by a strange rah-rah conviction shared by all the United Press men of the day that they
were part of a significant progressive movement. The feeling
of fraternity was so strong that the lowliest novice, in talking
about the future, identified himself with the organization. Instead of saying, "I'm going places," he would be more likely to
say, "We're going places." The young news service would have
foundered early without this strange spirit of loyalty. It drove
young men like Baillie sometimes to forget sleep, and to work
all night to develop local stories.

Life was easier for their rivals. A newspaper which was a
member of the Associated Press was required to make all its
news promptly available to the nearest AP bureau. A United
Press subscriber could either do this or not, as it wished, and
often when it was perfectly willing to do so its local coverage
was so poor as to be useless to the UP bureau chief. The resultant scramble for stories by the United Press men had the effect
of hardening their muscles, and in the long run this proved to
be an advantage. The Associated Press' conservative method of
handling its news gave the younger service another opportunity; United Press copy was deliberately made smart and
bright, and this style, in an age when newspapers had relatively few entertainment features, gradually caught on. Today,
all the news services use the light touch when it seems even
remotely appropriate to the subject matter.

A revolution took place in United Press' missionary pony
service while Baillie was still in Portland. The management in
New York decided that the slowness in selling the 500-word
pony traced back to the inability of many small papers to pay

for it. As a confectionery-store proprietor breaks open a package of gum and sells single sticks to school children, the United Press now put on the market a miniature pony of 100 words a day and called it "The Century." A system-wide contest, known as the "Century Handicap," was held over a period of a month among the bureau chiefs. Baillie hit the tank towns in his bailiwick and made his first sale, at $12.50 a week, to the Bend, Oregon, *Bulletin*. When the month was up, he was discovered to be the winner of the contest, and he received a small cash prize.

More important to Baillie than the cash was the notice he had attracted among the United Press executives in New York, into whose ken had swum a new star of considerable magnitude. In 1917 they began moving him eastward, town by town. Just twenty years after breaking in on the San Francisco pony wire, Baillie was president.

Both Baillie and United Press have come a long way since his novitiate. The gamble on the dog papers turned out handsomely; most of them grew as encouragingly as the United Press did, and became leased-wire clients. In addition, many of the largest newspapers in the country came into the fold.

Baillie himself has become the world figure he erroneously thought himself to be when he scooped the opposition on the Oakland estuary shell race. A world figure, however, is not necessarily a celebrity. Baillie had always expected that when he attained to his present eminence other world figures would beat a path to his door. They do to some extent, but with discouraging frequency in the hope of using the United Press to further their personal ambitions, a trick Baillie refuses to have played on him. As a result, he lives in a sort of resplendent anonymity, like a Tibetan lama.

Baillie has seen the United Press grow from a pygmy to a giant and, although he is proud of the giant and his mastery over it, he deplores the effects that have come with giantism, particularly the numerous changes that have come over newspapermen since giantism has set in. In nostalgic moments he draws a bitter contrast between the United Press men of the

old days, who worked long hours at small pay for the excitement of it, and the present crop, protected, as it is, by glasses
and by a Newspaper Guild contract guaranteeing minimum
wages and an eight-hour day.

When working in his New York office, in the *Daily News*
Building on East 42nd Street, Baillie frequently steps across
the hall into the big United Press newsroom in search of inspiration. More often than not, he is depressed by what he sees.
The old Morse operators have long since given way to impersonal rows of teletypewriters which emit a muffled thumping
noise instead of a pulse-raising din like that of machine-gun
slugs striking a bulletproof dishpan. Much of the thumping
is blotted up by a soundproofed ceiling. Nobody vaults over
desks to get bulletins to outgoing wires, and the yell of "Flash!"
survives only in vestigial form. Desk men cry it out as a gesture
to tradition, but it doesn't carry far; the soundproofing absorbs it.

Looking upon this efficient, uninspiring scene, Baillie
growls, with profane trimmings, "What a bunch of drones and
copy shovelers!"

II

Hugh Baillie, the dynamic Brooklyn-born Scot who is president of the United Press, lives as close to his job as a battalion
fire chief. Relaxation, or an attempt at it, acts upon him like
a slow poison on a guest of the Borgias. He has always talked
about getting a rest, and once he went so far as to buy a beautiful home, suitable for idling purposes, at La Jolla, California,
with a view of the Pacific from a high hill. He spent little time
in it, and much of the time he was there he was in more or less
constant communication by direct telephone line with the San
Diego bureau of the UP.

He was vacationing briefly at La Jolla in his own distinctive
way not long after the war in the Pacific began. The panic
which the Japs caused on the Pacific Coast was considerably
more of a tonic to Baillie than the surf bathing. He got himself

appointed a special deputy sheriff, so he could carry a pistol, and conferred with similarly armed members of the gentry on plans for repelling an amphibious assault on the Beach and Tennis Club. Soon, however, he was en route to New York by airplane to show the opposition news services how to cover two wars at once. Until peace came, he rarely got back to La Jolla.

Once, when asked if he ever had introspective moments, Baillie, without hesitating, answered a flat "No." He is, however, a global worrier, but not in the Walter Lippmann sense. Baillie's worries about the world are directed solely at trying to divine where the next big news story is likely to break. All day and in his wakeful hours at night, which are frequent, he brings his knowledge and hunches to bear on the planet the way a scientist bombards an atom with neutrons. The flashes which are the end result of this process are not always blinding in their intensity, but they do cast a light which United Press men on far away continents follow . . . if they know what is good for them.

When Baillie is in residence at his New York apartment, which overlooks the East River at 52nd Street, he awakens abruptly around two or three o'clock in the morning and reaches for a bedside telephone. The telephone connects directly with the United Press home office in the *Daily News* Building, ten blocks to the south. He may have a full-blown idea to communicate about something that needs doing in some such place as Cairo or Sydney. More often, merely restless, he wants to know what is going on, and the man on the night news desk gives him a summary of late developments around the world. One news-desk man, not sufficiently aware of Baillie's instinct for the dramatic, got in the habit of replying: "Nothing much doing, Hugh. Everything is under control." After a few such experiences, Baillie, infuriated at the man's lack of perception, had him transferred to other duties.

After Baillie has received his briefing on the state of the world, he may, if he deems a crisis ominous enough to call for his personal attention, get dressed and take a taxicab to the office, where he assumes command and barks orders like a top sergeant. If the world is in only a minor stew, he lights a cigarette and gets himself tied in simultaneously through the United Press switchboard with four or five night-shift department heads. In a round robin dominated by Baillie, the impending day's schedule of special foreign coverage is worked out.

Baillie's job, as he sees it, is not solely to sit in New York and command his legions by wire or radio. More than any other news-service chief, he rambles around the globe, alone or accompanied by whatever United Press men happen to be stationed in the areas he visits. Actually, at fifty-five, he is unable to overcome the habits built up during an unusually strenuous life, and after sitting around the office for a couple of months, he gets cabin fever.

The travel which he subconsciously prescribes for himself happily works out to the benefit of the organization. Baillie always talks to high officials in the countries he visits and keeps them aware of the United Press' existence, thus planting the flag where it should be planted, as his subordinates describe it. Also, by keeping his eyes and ears open and by putting two and two together, Baillie is often able to guess where events of high news value are about to occur and is able to deploy his men advantageously, like cats at ratholes.

Baillie began his globe-trotting shortly after becoming president of the United Press. His first trip was to Rome, where he attempted to interview Mussolini about his widely reported intention of invading Ethiopia. As Baillie walked the length of the dictator's imposing office, Mussolini gave him what Baillie described later as "the full treatment," standing at his desk with arms folded, chin elevated and eyeballs rolling until the whites showed prominently. The pair never did hit it off. While Baillie was trying to explain the purpose of his call, Mussolini kept interrupting to ask, "Are you for us or against us?" He wasn't satisfied with Baillie's reply that he was impartial, and no interview was granted. However, the trip to Rome proved to be worth while.

Baillie, convinced by what he saw that war was imminent, telephoned dispatches to London, for relay to New York, describing the martial display that was going on in Rome— Capronis buzzing the housetops, troops marching through the streets and crowds cheering warlike balcony speeches. Meanwhile, he assembled some of his best correspondents from other places on the Continent and assigned them to sit in Djibouti, Addis Ababa and other potentially explosive spots. The rival Associated Press took the optimistic view that Mussolini was bluffing, as usual. As a result, it found itself at a disadvantage in the early days of the invasion.

In 1936, Baillie learned of the underground crisis a Mrs. Simpson was creating in England when he was discussing business matters with some United Press clients in Holland. He hastened to London, took over control of the United Press bureau and established contacts with members of the royal household. Because of his spade-work, the United Press was able to score a beat on the impending abdication of Edward VIII. In 1938, Baillie was in Munich handling coverage of the appeasement crisis, and he stayed on to watch the German divisions roll to the border of Czechoslovakia. In 1939, after England had declared war on Germany, he sat before a fireplace at 10 Downing Street and listened in incredulous silence while Prime Minister Chamberlain expressed the confident opinion that German bombers could never penetrate to London through the east-coast antiaircraft batteries.

Baillie refrained from suggesting that perhaps the bombers would approach from a safer angle, and left Downing Street with plans for covering the bombing of London already rolling around in his head. He was impatient with Chamberlain, not because of his military obtuseness, but because he was unable to discern that a big story was about to be dropped on his doorstep.

Baillie's unique conception of his duties, especially after the

United States got into the war, involved living abroad under varying conditions of danger and discomfort that would appeal to few men of his age. Occasionally it got him into painfully embarrassing positions. In 1943, while he was traveling from Sicily to England in a Flying Fortress, one of the engines failed over the Bay of Biscay. Two Junkers 88's followed the crippled plane for a time but for some reason did not close in. The bomber arrived over an English airdrome during a night visit by German intruders, and it was rocked by antiaircraft fire, but managed to land safely.

Later, on the Continent, a Cub plane in which Baillie was making a hop near Brussels was chased by a Messerschmitt. The German pilot didn't get close enough to deliver an effective squirt and the Cub pilot shook him off by ducking down over a wooded section and skimming treetops. Subsequently, while Baillie was returning from a visit to the Siegfried Line in a jeep, he was thrown through the windshield when the driver, in turning off a narrow road to avoid hitting an Army truck, crashed into a tree. His injuries were minor ones.

His closest shave came, oddly, when he was riding luxuriously back toward Paris one night in a chauffeur-driven staff car after having paid a call at General Spaatz's headquarters. His companion in the back seat was a French air commodore. They were speeding through a forest which was policed by trigger-happy Maquisards when they were halted by a sentry with a tommy gun in the crook of his arm. The challenge would have been satisfied in routine fashion, except that while the commodore was offering his credentials, Baillie removed his correspondent's cap to scratch his head. The beam of the Maquisard's flashlight was turned upon Baillie, who sits erect, looks like a man who expects obedience and wears a crew haircut.

"Zut alors! Le Boche!" screamed the sentry. He swung his tommy gun in Baillie's direction and held it there while other Maquisards popped up out of the bushes and surrounded the car.

The commodore saved the situation with a freshet of French

in which he affirmed that his friend was, in all truth, *un Américain*. Baillie, annoyed at the whole business, dug his papers out from under his overcoat and satisfied the Maquisards. For the rest of the trip, at the commodore's urging, he kept his cap on.

Early last August, when Baillie decided that the war in the Pacific called for his expert attention, it was whispered around United Press headquarters, where he is regarded with sardonic reverence, that he was going out to show MacArthur how to mop up on the Japs. Baillie was disappointed when the Japs surrendered while he was flying the Pacific, but he recovered nicely by getting an interview with the Emperor, and he flew to Chungking and interviewed Chiang Kai-shek.

It is no trick at all for the president of a powerful news service to get a private audience with a foreign monarch who is anxious to have his views published abroad. Baillie's prize performance in the Pacific was in dealing with General MacArthur. He pointed out to the general something the general already knew and was worried about—that his occupation policies were under severe criticism by segments of the American press—and suggested that the atmosphere should be cleared. MacArthur agreed that it should, but, being anxious as the next general to keep his correspondents happy, wanted to call them all in for a mass interview. Baillie registered polite amazement, then became eloquent.

"Mass interviews," he said, "are a dime a dozen. The only way to meet this situation is to give me an exclusive interview. As president of the United Press, I'm the ranking press-association correspondent on the scene." He paused for effect, then played his ace. "I've got prestige. You've got prestige. We'll send this interview out under my by-line and we'll get a big play all over the world."

MacArthur, weakening, said the interview might be more effective if it came from one of the generals on his staff. Baillie smiled depreciatingly.

"You, sir," he said, "are the one the people want to hear from."

It was perhaps the first time MacArthur had met his match, theatrically, at least. Anyway, Baillie got his exclusive interview.

On the way home, in a C-54 of the Air Transport Command, Baillie got caught in a typhoon between Guam and Kwajalein and he arrived in San Francisco badly beaten up and moody. Here, just thirty years before, he had started his United Press career as a minor bureau hand; here he had early resolved that he would one day become president of the organization and, automatically, a world figure. Yet no committee was on hand to welcome him back to San Francisco; he was just another digit in the ATC's passenger report.

This anonymity bothered his sense of importance. He kept the wires hot for several hours in an attempt to wangle a Superfortress which would take him East in appropriate style. The attempt failed and he boarded an ATC plane with no more fanfare than a buck general would get.

No one in the United Press begrudges Baillie his sense of importance. Through his personal forcefulness, his vanity is pumped throughout the UP's global system as pressure is transmitted through an enclosed hydraulic system by force exerted at its head. Baillie's vanity seems to infect his men despite an old United Press tradition described by one of its correspondents as "getting them young and keeping them lean, tough and hungry." Baillie demands top-notch performance from his men, and he usually gets it.

Working for Baillie, on Baillie's terms, sometimes gives a young man a benign form of split personality. A United Press correspondent, recently returned from London and points east, summed it up in stream-of-consciousness fashion over a beer, as follows: "It is a strange and wonderful outfit, and it has a peculiar effect on you. You grumble about the dough, yet you have a lovely, unreasoning loyalty to Baillie and the UP. It is a communion of penury, I guess—or at least relative penury—and I suspect that there is something spiritual about it.

"You wash your own underwear and socks to save enough to take a news-counter girl to a third-class food trap in Soho while your AP opposite number is dining with a lovely at Claridge's. He's getting two hundred and seventy-five a month for living expenses, and your allowance is eighty-eight. So what? So you're probably younger than he is, and he's mixed up with a more hierarchical outfit than you are. You know that you can start as green as grass in the UP and really advance on your own merits. But after you've advanced, where are you? It's all very contradictory."

He sighed, sipped his beer and continued, "Here is what I mean: Say you have just nicked the AP with a pretty good exclusive story. You are relaxing in your low-priced flat and dreaming of what a fine party you could throw if you had an extra shilling, when the charwoman brings you a cablegram from Baillie. It is an inspiring pep talk urging you on to even greater efforts to skin the nefarious AP. You know that you're being conned, but you don't mind being conned by such an expert con man, and you go forth armed to perform miracles."

Conceivably, the contagious enthusiasm which Baillie is able to stir up in his men stems partly from the fact that his own United Press career has been a starve-and-succeed epic. The organization was much hungrier than it is today when Baillie was transferred East in 1917 after creating a minor flurry on the Coast. Veteran United Press men recall that even then he had what they call "a presence." "He was a slugger and you always knew when he was around," one of them explains. After two years of slugging in Chicago, New York and Washington, Baillie, at twenty-eight, was made manager of the Washington bureau, one of the key points of the system.

He left Washington to report President Wilson's tour in behalf of the League of Nations, and found the trip vastly exciting. After every small-town speech, there was a mad rush by the reporters to get to the local telegraph office and back to the station before the presidential train pulled out. The secret-service men helped them to plunge through the crowds, half carrying them some of the time. The crowds almost tore their clothes off.

At the 1920 Republican National Convention in Chicago,

Baillie's pugnacity brought him afoul of the chairman, Senator Lodge, and made him a figure in the convention news. The convention was getting ready to nominate Harding. Lodge had called a private huddle of party leaders on the platform. Baillie climbed up onto the platform to find out what was going on. Lodge ordered him to leave. Other reporters were on the platform, too, but a loud silk shirt which Baillie was wearing, or perhaps it was his "presence" or his crew haircut, caused Lodge to single him out. Baillie replied that he would leave if the other reporters did. Lodge waved his gavel and yelled that Baillie would have to go first. Baillie stood his ground. Lodge called for the sergeant at arms. Baillie threw a punch at the sergeant at arms, who cagily backed away.

Other United Press men finally persuaded Baillie to climb down and let the convention proceed with its task of nominating a President. In the press row he was surrounded by reporters who wanted to publish his version of the squabble. Among them was the late Arthur Brisbane, whose massive intellect was always stimulated by physical violence. Brisbane devoted part of his column next day to a panegyric of Baillie.

In 1924, Baillie's president, Karl Bickel, suggested that he go out on the road as a salesman and get acquainted with the business side of the United Press. For a reporter, this was equivalent to exile into some dim shadowland, but Baillie, vain about his versatility, accepted the challenge. As a salesman he burned up the South and Midwest. Up to that time the Associated Press had a rule requiring a member paper to give six-months notice when it wanted to relinquish its membership. Baillie weaned so many papers away that the AP extended its notice period to two years. This caused Baillie to work all the harder. If he couldn't wean a paper away, he would try to sell it the United Press service for supplementary use.

The general business manager, who was also a vice-president, resigned in 1927, and Baillie got the post. This break put him for the first time in the high-executive bracket, where salaries were good and the privilege of stock ownership was accorded. Baillie now came to the office in fancy suits and haberdashery. He carried a cane and wore a carnation in his lapel as outward symbols of the crown-prince status which he had achieved in the organization. In 1931 he was moved up to executive vice-president and general manager. In 1935 Bickel resigned the presidency and Baillie at last took over. Having achieved his long-sought goal, he dropped the fancy sartorial accessories and took to wearing conservative business suits.

It was apparent from the beginning of his tenure as president that a long-pent-up force had been released. With distaste, Baillie looked over the office which Bickel had vacated. It had stucco walls and an artificial fireplace, and the furniture was of ornate, cumbersome Spanish design.

"Looks like the lobby of a Bessarabian bordello," Baillie remarked. He assigned the office to someone else and continued to occupy his old office, which had cork-lined walls and was furnished with leather-upholstered divans and chairs.

Then he moved promptly into a confused relationship which then existed between the press associations and the radio newscasters. Newspaper proprietors and the press associations were slow to recognize the competition of radio. For a time they had kept the broadcasters happy by doling out bulletins on news of special import, and in 1934 they had formed a Press-Radio Bureau which supplied the material for two five-minute newscasts a day. But radio's appetite was more voracious than that, and several independent news-gathering associations had sprung into being to cater to it. They were strong competitors and, what was galling to Baillie, they were gathering in money while the United Press, which had retrenched for the depression, was scratching for it.

Baillie pulled the United Press out of the Press-Radio Bureau and began selling news to radio stations. So did the management of the International News Service. The Associated Press published an advertisement in *Editor & Publisher*, the newspaper trade organ, which was captioned: IN THIS CHANGING WORLD—ONE THING AS YET UNCHANGED. The thing that remained unchanged was the AP, sticking to its exclusive function of supplying news to newspapers. Five years later the AP changed, too, and established a subsidiary to market radio news.

Always conscious of the fact that he is in the business of merchandising, Baillie is quick to apply any good merchandising technique he happens to run across. He picked up one when he drove his car into a filling station one day. The station was a well-managed chain unit. Baillie asked the proprietor how it worked.

"I'm in complete charge here. I've lived in this town all my life and everybody knows me," the proprietor replied. "I keep the ladies' room in good shape. I hire the help and meet the customers. I run the place as if it were my own."

Within a few months Baillie had applied this decentralizing principle to the United Press. Up to then, its coverage had been master-minded in New York and its news reports had taken on an Eastern emphasis. Baillie reorganized the system into divisions. He made Chicago the central division for domestic coverage, and set up other divisions in San Francisco, Kansas City and Atlanta, with a manager in charge of each. In the foreign field he set up divisional managers in London, Tokyo, Buenos Aires, Berlin and Sydney. Each divisional manager was an archduke wholly responsible for keeping in touch with events in his archdukedom, aided by occasional suggestions from the king. The reform had the effect of encouraging local initiative and of broadening the tone of United Press news.

From the filling-station visit Baillie drew another moral. The UP had kept its bureau managers moving from city to city, on the theory that a man grew stale if he stayed in one place more than a year or so. Baillie, impressed with the contacts the filling-station proprietor had built up from long residence in his home town, modified the bureau-manager policy drastically. The managers stay put now for a reasonable length of time and are able to build up their news sources and particularly to keep in close contact with the public officials from whom so much of the news flows. They are able, too, to educate their children the way bookkeepers and bankers do.

Baillie also terminated a practice his predecessors sometimes employed of going outside the organization to find a man to fill a choice vacancy. Today, when such a vacancy occurs in, say, Washington or Paris, it goes to some promising United Press youngster in Columbus, or Seattle, or Houston. The effect of Baillie's reforms on organizational morale has been noticeably good.

Few persons familiar with the growth of the press associations would deny Baillie his right to a Herculean view of himself. He has had much to do with the rise of the United Press, and the impact of the United Press has, in one way or another, had much to do with freeing world news substantially from the blight of governmental propaganda. The first press associations sprang up on the Continent in the middle of the nineteenth century. Subsidized by governments from the start, they were looked upon basically as weapons for maintaining diplomatic and commercial prestige abroad, and were so used in a rather bald fashion.

Paul Julius Reuter, a Prussian bank clerk who had been using carrier pigeons to speed market quotations to German bankers, saw his big chance in the newly invented telegraph and in the first underwater cables. In 1851 he abandoned his pigeons, moved to London, took up British citizenship and organized the famous Reuter news agency. Victorian England was in a period of expanding prestige. As its prestige spread and its dominance over wire communications grew, the Reuter agency spread and grew with it. Before long, the powerful Reuter was able to bring the continental agencies into a vast cartel and to parcel out spheres of influence. Reuter took the United States, Japan, China and most of the Far East; the Havas Agency, of France, got South America. Separate spheres were awarded to Rosta, of Russia; Stefani, of Italy; Wolff, of Germany, and a dozen or so others.

The news that was sent out to the spheres of influences was

colored in favor of the nation of origin. The United States was depicted in an unfavorable light by emphasis upon its murders, riots, floods, tornadoes and railway accidents, with favorable news played down to a minimum. A South American merchant, reading the Havas news, could well get the impression that if he dared to go to New York on a buying trip he might be scalped by a red Indian. The American of the day, not being very global-minded, didn't seem to care.

In the United States, press associations got a later start. After a few decades of vicious competition among various services, the Associated Press, in approximately its modern form, was organized in 1892. In 1893 it negotiated an exclusive tie-up with the Reuter cartel and, thus armed, drove its last competitor to the wall in 1897 and had a clear field.

The Associated Press traded its domestic news for the cartel's news of the outside world, and the trade was an uneven one for AP. It was able to squeeze some of the propaganda out of the cartel's incoming dispatches, but outbound news of the United States, funneling through London, as all cartel news did, was shaded before being passed on to other countries. The exchange arrangement saved the AP the heavy expense of maintaining foreign correspondents of its own. But for some years thereafter it was in the compromised position of a respectable maiden who has married into a family of bootleggers, and, for economic reasons, is afraid to pack her grip and depart. It took the competition of the United Press, founded in 1907, and, to a lesser degree, that of the International News Service, founded in 1911, to jar her loose.

The United Press first scratched the cartel by making exchange contracts with independent news agencies in England, Germany, Australia and Japan. The Japs, disbelieving the Reuter news of America, had sent a delegation to UP headquarters to ask for unbiased reports. Then the UP began stationing its own correspondents in foreign capitals. The extent to which the AP was handcuffed was illustrated in 1914, when one of the largest newspapers in South America asked it for the text of the Central Powers' war communiqués. Lacking distribution rights in South America, the AP had to refuse. The UP was able to supply the communiqués, and it did. It followed up this advantage by selling its news service all around South America, and eventually drove Havas out.

All of this angered Kent Cooper, a young AP executive, and under Cooper's goading the AP began to sever its cartel connections gradually. The last vestigial strings were cut less than a decade ago.

Today the Reuter cartel no longer exists, most of its European members having failed to survive the second World War. The Reuter agency is now a co-operative which has been reorganized along AP lines, and its managers are quick to deny imputations of lack of objectivity. In most countries today the ideal of objectivity in news reporting, which is an American contribution to journalism, is honored, at least by protestation. Perhaps the outstanding exception is Soviet Russia, where objectivity in the news is defined as that quality which enables it to serve the interests of the Communist Party and of the working class.

Both Hugh Baillie and Kent Cooper, who is now executive director of the AP, have busied themselves in recent years working to assure free access to news sources all over the world. As neither is afflicted with the curse of modesty, the contest for the role of plumed knight has taken on certain amusing aspects. A few years ago, Cooper published a book, *Barriers Down*, in which he described his intramural fight to shake the AP loose from the old Reuter cartel. In the process he virtually canonized himself as the patron saint of the free and untrammeled press. In Baillie's view the book proved merely that Cooper was the Martin Luther of the AP. It is a matter of interpretation. Anyway, when the book came out, Baillie published an *Editor & Publisher* advertisement suggesting sourly that the AP was taking credit for every improvement in news transmission since bulletins were chiseled in stone.

Sometimes the Cooper-Baillie warfare takes the form of ostensibly private messages which the senders are careful to broadcast over their own teletypes. Each message has its own little bite. In September, 1944, Baillie was in London obtaining assurances from exiled governments that freedom of the news would reign in their countries after the victory, and the United Press duly chronicled its president's activities. Cooper, who was in New York at the time, cabled Baillie that he was "personally enthusiastic" over the fact that "at long last" the UP had joined in the great crusade. The cablegram stung Baillie, particularly that phrase "at long last," and he stung back. He replied, in a cablegram dripping the sirup of friendliness, that he was only carrying on the campaign for the unimpeded flow of international news "on which we of the United Press have been engaged in ever-increasing scope for thirty-seven years." He registered his gratification that the AP had "apparently" revised its agreements with the foreign agencies "so that it may now join us in this field on a bigger scale than ever before." The parting crack, in which Cooper's most telling phrase was thrown back at him, was: ". . . and we welcome you most heartily as a great associate *at long last* in this high cause."

On his return from abroad Baillie felt the need for robust entertainment, and bought a single ticket, on an aisle, for a rowdy Broadway musical show. He waited in the rear until the house was darkened for the opening curtain, and then slunk down the aisle to his seat. As the curtain was rising, another man with the same idea in mind slunk down to a seat across the aisle. Baillie, peeking sidewise, saw that his neighbor was Kent Cooper. Cooper peeked, their eyes met and they both grinned. Between the acts they had a drink together. But the warfare may break out again at any time.

Baillie, like most blustery men, is incurably sentimental. The chief objects of his sentiment are his ancestral land, Scotland; the University of Southern California, where he attended college; and the great reporters of past days, who would naturally include himself. He has worn the kilt to fancy-dress parties and has eaten the horrible haggis at Saint Andrew's Day dinners. His apartment is hung with paintings of Scottish scenes, and the draperies bear the design of a tartan. The tartan happens to be that of his wife's family; the Baillies were lowlanders, and the lowlanders didn't have tartans.

One of Baillie's heroes is Jean Froissart, a fourteenth-century war correspondent—and perhaps the first of his breed—whose collected works he often dips into when depressed by the intellectual trend of news writing today. Froissart led a merry life. He followed the wars of England, France and Spain, and was a hearty lover of music, wine, women and feasts. "It was a romantic era," Baillie says enviously. "Lots of color, blood and adventure. Froissart was a regular firehouse reporter." Baillie has one son, Hugh Scott Baillie, who recently got a newspaper job on the Coast after being discharged from the Army Air Forces. It is unlikely that young Baillie will ever enter the United Press. The UP has always discouraged any relationship that might give rise to a suspicion of nepotism, and an office joke is that it even discourages reproduction.

The end of the Second World War came as a letdown to Baillie because it removed his chief excuse for hopping airplanes and sticking his head into dramatic situations. His office is littered with war and occupation souvenirs, among them a Jap battle flag. Over his water cooler hangs a sign which says, WATER UNFIT FOR DRINKING. It came from a Tokyo hotel where Baillie stayed. On the walls hang autographed pictures of generals whom Baillie met during his wartime travels. "Ike gave me this one just before the Sicily landings," he will say with pride in showing a caller around, or, "Monty gave me that one just after the Arnhem mess." An itchy restlessness seems to dominate him today. During a lull, when not discussing the wars, he sometimes entertains a visitor by running up and down his office in delineation of great U.S.C. football plays—"Baillie's sole interest in higher education," according to one authority.

Baillie rates as the greatest news story of the war one which was written by a UP correspondent about the entrance of Allied troops into El Alamein headed by bagpipers in full cry. When the correspondent came home, Baillie took him to his apartment, where the correspondent delighted him by doing a Scottish sword dance. Around the United Press it has become a kidding tradition that the way to get a raise is to work a Scottish angle into a dispatch under any pretext whatever. A young newcomer to UP who hadn't been apprised of the boss' pet enthusiasm, reported to him during the war at the Hotel Savoy in London, after an airplane trip which had landed him at Prestwick. "And how did you like Scotland?" Baillie asked cordially.

"What a jerk joint!" the youngster replied. "Clammy weather, porridge, bagpipes——"

An older UP man who was present tried to signal him to shut up, but the distress sign was misinterpreted, and the youngster raved on. United Press men consider it a tribute to Baillie's self-control that he didn't send the youngster home on the earliest plane.

Baillie takes a paternal interest in his correspondents, and he becomes very angry when anyone expresses a doubt about the accuracy of their reporting. Even a slur upon newspapermen in general can get him worked up. He was sitting in the steam room of a Manhattan athletic club one afternoon, wrapped in a sheet and cleansing his pores of battlefield grime, when he heard someone remark, "There's a war on and the damned newspapers don't tell us the truth about it." Dropping his sheet, Baillie roared and went after the voice. The voice ran and eluded him in the thick, warm fog, and he never saw the face to which it belonged.

On returning to his office, he swore loudly about the bloated leeches who infest steam rooms, and sighed for a newspaper of his own in which he could expose them. At times like this, his inborn crusading instinct suffers from the restrictions of press-service objectivity.

Papa's Girl
(HELEN BONFILS)

By Mary Ellen and Mark Murphy

EDITOR'S PREFACE.—In spite of the many charges of standardization that have been made against the American press, the fact remains that there is such a thing as newspaper individuality. Papers do differ, and the bases of individuality are sufficiently objective to permit actual measurement of differences. As Prof. L. N. Flint of the University of Kansas notes in his *The Conscience of the Newspaper* (Appleton-Century), there are at least four of these yardsticks of journalistic individuality:

(1) Appearance (cheap, flashy, smashing, refined, sleek, mild, chaste, vulgar, ornate, sensational, conservative, somber, monotonous, diversified, slovenly, neat, harmonious, orderly, dignified).

(2) Intellectual qualities (dull, serious, sane, ponderous, flimsy, penetrating, high-brow, low-brow, sparkling, keen, interesting, stimulating, bigoted, brilliant, pale, clever, smart, powerful, weak, cosmopolitan, exhaustive, intensive).

(3) Tone or spirit (dynamic, pugnacious, optimistic, staid, serene, dictatorial, calm, tolerant, arrogant, placid, oracular, dogmatic, satirical, vehement, scolding, nagging, hysterical, impassioned, jovial, cultured, whimsical, severe, rough, lively, aggressive, enterprising, independent, fearless, militant, subservient, commercialized, visionary, practical, easy going).

(4) Moral character (yellow, reliable, honest, fair, venal, obstinate, tolerant, persistent, decent, truthful, sincere, considerate, kind, clean, generous, brutal).

Nowhere is newspaper individuality better illustrated, especially as regards appearance, than in the case of the Denver *Post,* the newspaper which serves as the background for the following sketch of Miss Bonfils. The *Post* has, at various times and by various persons, been described as flashy, vulgar, sensational, cheap, and smashing —to use but a few of the words in the foregoing list. The authors of this biography of Miss Bonfils themselves refer to "the relentless use of big type which made its front page one of the curiosities of the American press." The editors of the *Post* sounded the same note in their boxed comment which accompanied the article when it first appeared:

"Since the death of domineering F. G. Bonfils, his sheltered daughter, Helen, has blossomed into a serious actress, but has meanwhile kept his gaudy Denver *Post* looking like an explosion in a type factory."

Since the appearance of this article, the Denver *Post* has acquired a new publisher: Palmer ("Ep") Hoyt. Reporting this significant change in an article entitled "Ep Hoyt and the Hussy" which reviewed the *Post's* past, *Time* magazine commented (February 18, 1946):

"The rich and rowdy Denver *Post* is a lady with a shady past. For most of her 53 years she was the gaudy consort of a river gambler and a barkeep, helped make them both multimillionaires. But for the last 13 years, having outlived them and their time, she has found life dull. Last week the aging hussy of Champa Street took a tardy fling at respectability, snatched herself a new kind of man.

"From the eminently respectable Portland *Oregonian,* the *Post* stole solid, affable, eminently respectable Publisher Edwin Palmer ("Ep") Hoyt, who at 48 is still the white-haired boy of Western journalism. The lure: around $52,000 a year. Though friends of both asked what they saw in each other, Ep Hoyt and the *Post* were sure it was a fine match.

"Last week in Denver, *Post*men held their breaths. Their paper-with-a-past might have a future after all."

Here then is a study in journalistic individuality—a most unusual daughter and father and their equally unusual newspaper.

December 23, 1944

GOD knows what the late Frederick G. Bonfils, who, with his partner, Harry Tammen, built the Denver *Post* into one of the most raucous and annoying newspapers in the country, would think of his paper and his favorite daughter, if he could see either of them now. Along the front of the *Post* building on Champa Street, there is still a sign which, in weak gilt on faded black, reads, O JUSTICE, WHEN EXPELLED FROM OTHER HABITATIONS, MAKE THIS THY DWELLING PLACE. Near the entrance to the building are two other announcements which Bonfils also put up, 'TIS A PRIVILEGE TO LIVE IN COLORADO, and ONE MILE ABOVE SEA LEVEL. But things haven't been so exciting on Champa Street or in Denver since the old man died more than a decade ago.

The paper continues the relentless use of big type which made its front page one of the curiosities of the American press, but the reading matter beneath the raging headlines is little different from that appearing in any other undistinguished newspaper in any other American city.

Bonfils and Tammen ran a hard, greedy sheet; it was often called a blackmailing rag, and both it and the men who ran it could inspire admiration and hatred. They had loyal friends as well as bitter enemies, and a lot has been told about this in a book called *Timber Line,* written some years back by Gene Fowler, the noted obituarist. The paper makes no local enemies now, though, saving its squeals—which once were roars—for such menaces as the Japanese in internment camps and the Democrats in Washington. Old Man Bonfils would approve of the paper's policies toward the Japanese, rationing, labor and Democrats, although he would never understand its coziness with the Denver Chamber of Commerce or its continuing failure to interfere in the lives of Denver citizens.

Helen Bonfils would startle her parent somewhat too. She has married a man connected with the stage, has become an actress, lives a good part of the time in New York and gives a lot of Bonfils money away, sometimes without even getting a receipt. She runs the paper, or at least controls it, in a way that he could never understand. She is satisfied to see that it comes out a least once a day, and she leaves most of the editorial and business control to her employees. She has a tremendous income, which she spends on her own church, the Roman

Catholic, and on a lot of others of various denominations; her gratuities to impoverished friends run high, and the money she gives away on other things is amazing.

The town looks upon her with pride and affection. She has gained this respect through effort and a genuine graciousness and charity. As an angel of bounty, she looks like a super-annuated chorus girl, having that sort of taste in clothes and a similar manner. "My dear," she is likely to say in describing an episode (or maybe "Darling" or "Honey"), "it was brutal." A lot of people can't figure her out, and one of the town's games of an evening is guessing her age. The guesses run from forty to sixty. Her manner and style of dress mislead some people too. She neither drinks nor smokes, and is easily shocked by what other people regard as rather mild facts about life. People who bump suddenly against this Puritan outlook some-times wonder if she reads her own newspaper.

Miss Bonfils, now a tall, handsome woman somewhere in late middle age, with bright blond hair and gray-blue eyes, which she inherited from her father, is a person who always had money, clothes and a certain beauty, and yet was a Cinderella anyway. Her father kept her in gentle seclusion. Her cocoon stage lasted well into her thirties, and she became a butterfly—a sedate butterfly—at an age when most women are worrying about what colleges to send their children to. She and her husband, George Somnes, live in the old Bonfils home when in Denver, and their listing in the telephone book is under her father's name. To some people, the influence of Helen's father upon her is that of a persistent old ghost, a situation not unlike that in *Hamlet*. Others think that Helen's graciousness and the extent of her charities represent some form of family atonement. Helen seems to remember her father as a great, proud man who lived to improve the world as well as his own fortunes. She speaks of him often, reciting little axioms of his which, she gives one to think, guide her life. She introduces the maxims usually with, "Papa used to say——"

Papa was an ex-West Pointer who ran some lotteries, worked some fairly ripe land promotion in the Southwest, and in the

1890's bought the *Post*. With Tammen, he built it into the most powerful paper in the Rocky Mountain area. Both made a lot of enemies as well as money. Tammen was a generous, laughing fellow, who described himself quite accurately as a rascal; he was capable of great, undemanding affection.

Bonfils was a complex man, hungry for money and power, which he got, and for honor in the world, which he received only from politicians and employees. He was rapacious and cunning, and he had a great pride. He was brilliant in his knowledge of what people would read and of how to make a paper a part of a region's life, and, although the *Post* was one of the most monstrous efforts in American journalism, no competitor could come close to it. He was a showman with great personal charm and a fine presence, and he wore bright clothing, which, on him, seemed elegant.

He made it a policy to see anyone who came into his office to talk to him, and he had people near him who were fanatically loyal for years and years. Among these were his wife, Belle Bonfils, and his daughter, Helen. His only other child, May, was a rebel, as well she might have been.

Helen remarked recently, "Papa used to say that a woman should have a good education and a good speaking voice," which caused some wonder as to where he expected a woman to use either. He was a disciplinarian and he was jealous of his family. He loved its members—at one point he had his mother and father and a sister and a brother living with him—and he believed their regard for him could be shown by complete deference to his whims. His secretary, Anne O'Neill, in trying to make him understandable to people who hadn't known him, once said, "He would have been happiest living in the time of feudalism."

Lights went out in his house at nine or nine-thirty at night, and all beaux were discouraged because Bonfils was convinced that men who paid any attention at all to his two quite attractive daughters were after the Bonfils money.

May eloped, with unhappy results, but Helen stayed at home, occasionally going with her mother to New York, where

they would be entertained by representatives of news and
feature services which numbered the *Post* among their clients.
In Denver, the family didn't go out much, partly because
Bonfils didn't believe in displaying his women and partly
because the established families of Denver wouldn't invite
the Bonfilses anywhere, considering them upstarts who ran a
paper which gave Denver's men of wealth ulcers. Denver in
the 90's and the first part of this century was rich, and its
climate and mountains attracted a number of affluent Euro-
peans and members of the British aristocracy.

The town called itself "The Newport of the West," and its
snobbery was breath-taking. There was a bluebook called
Who's Who in Denver Society, a quite serious little publication. In the edition of 1908 there was a picture of Mrs. Crawford Hill in the front, over a caption, THE ARBITER OF COLO-
RADO SOCIETY. She was the daughter-in-law of Sen. Nathaniel
Hill, who published the Denver *Republican,* a faint rival of
the *Post.* Among the sections of the book were "The Smart Set,"
sometimes called—and still mentioned in nostalgic Denver
newspaper columns—the "Sacred Thirty-Six," which was led by
Mrs. Hill; "Pioneers in the Social Field," "The Married Set,"
"The Younger Married Set," "The Younger Set," "Prominent
in Various Fashionable Sets," "Types of Denver Beauty" and
"Suggestions on How to Go Into Society." The Bonfils family
was mentioned only once—under "Worth Over a Million."

Helen, a bright, pretty, yellow-haired child, went to public
school at first and then to private schools, dressed a bit more
fancily than the other girls, and was snubbed often by her
schoolmates, who were only aping their elders. Helen went
away to finishing school, and, when she returned, did as much
as she could with her singing and charitable work and
had as much social life as the town and her father would
allow, which wasn't much. A woman recalled not long ago,
"I never saw her at the Cotillion Ball, the Club Ball, the
Charity Ball, the Denver Club or at the New Year's Eve
party at the country club—the big social events of the year.
In the first place, no one liked old man Bonfils; in the second

place, he wouldn't have let a boy take Helen to a party if she had been invited; and in the third place, there was her chorus-girl appearance. She was really a sweet girl, and she was as gracious then as she is now, but she did, the Lord knows, dress dramatically."

Helen did, however, occasionally go to the annual press ball in the company of some young man and a married couple, and when her father was out of town, she and her mother would entertain with small dinners at home.

After Tammen's death, in 1924, Bonfils, without the watchful, biting humor of his partner, became fond of the encomiums which might accrue to a millionaire and an owner of a powerful newspaper. He talked with Presidents and elder statesmen, and even Denver society paid some attention to him. Mrs. Crawford Hill, the arbiter, led off in inviting Bonfils around, and Helen was finally invited to join the Junior League. But she still didn't get out much at night. In the early 1930's, she began taking an interest in the Denver University Civic Theater. She was of an age where she was considered best suited for character parts, and her father, who in a careless youth had acted in amateur minstrels, saw his daughter in one or two productions, and was pleased. He took to calling her "Helen Bernhardt Bonfils." He probably would have disapproved of her later acting in New York and in stock in Denver as being for money and therefore unladylike.

When Bonfils died, on February 2, 1933, a number of merchants and politicians of the town attended his funeral, to make sure he was dead and also buried deep, they said. The *Post* used so many black margins that day that people thought something had gone wrong with the presses. Except for the weather and Arthur Brisbane's column on the first page, an editorial on Government spending on the second and a few advertisements and news stories, the first seven pages were on Bonfils—stories, pictures, testimonials.

Bonfils left a number of annuities to his family, including $50,000 to his wife and $25,000 to each of his daughters, and the bulk of an estate of many millions to an entity of vague functions called The Frederick G. Bonfils Foundation for the Betterment of Mankind.

At the time of Bonfils' death, the foundation had long been holding out a couple of standing offers for cures for cancer and influenza. Mrs. Bonfils and her two daughters, loyalty aside, broke the will, and Mrs. Bonfils elected to take the widow's half of the estate. When she died, in 1935, May and Helen had some unamicable disputes, and settlements were arrived at. One of the provisions of Bonfils' will had been that May would get $25,000 if she divorced her husband, $12,000 if she didn't.

The courts found this to be conrtary to the public interest, and gave May the $25,000; although later, in her private interest, she shed her husband anyway. He began bothering her for money in court actions. The *Post* dutifully reported all the Bonfils litigation.

A newspaper, like most corporate enterprises, is able to live a life of its own, going on its way, its decisions made by men who actually are its employees. Helen adored her father, and she let the paper proceed under his—and her own—Bourbon ideas. Without Bonfils to scheme and make money and enemies, the paper became even more prosperous than it had been. Helen found a good personal adviser in Anne O'Neill, her father's secretary, one of the few women in whose good sense he ever believed, and in William C. Shepherd, a capable editor who has a profound respect for money. Helen watched the *Post,* attended to her own affairs, and, freed from unreasonable restrictions, started emerging into the woman she is now.

She had been working for several years with the Civic Theater, a group of moderately gifted amateurs under professional direction, and she showed definite talent as an actress. In 1934, a year after Bonfils' death, she went out to Elitch Gardens in Denver and got a job with the stock company that was playing there that summer. Elitch's, as it is called in Denver, is a lovely amusement park of pastel buildings, fine gardens and a neat, graceful, Old World air. It is considered a choice summer spot by people of the stage, and many famous stars have played there. Adison Pitt was the stock-company director at the time and needed a player for the part of an Italian woman in *Men in White*. Pitt, the story goes, was not told who Helen was, yet he picked her from about a dozen women who applied.

"I wasn't at all nervous or frightened," Miss Bonfils says of her early work at Elitch's. "I wore a wig and old clothes, and it wasn't at all like playing oneself."

Miss Bonfils played bit parts at Elitch's in the summers of 1934 and 1935, and in the winters worked with the Civic Theater, which she still underwrites to a large extent, and for which she is planning to build a theater in downtown Denver after the war. In 1936, George Somnes, a pleasant, quiet-voiced man with a reputation as an actor and a director in stock, came out to handle Elitch's productions. It wasn't long before Somnes and Miss Bonfils fell in love. They were married in a Catholic ceremony at the home of the Elitch Gardens impresario, Arnold Gurtler, an old schoolmate of the bride's.

The rival *Rocky Mountain News* covered the story as a big news event, giving a long description of the wedding and short biographies of the bride and groom. The *Post,* which was at a high pitch of excitement over a parade and convention of the Veterans of Foreign Wars that day, mentioned the wedding on the society page.

It is, to all appearances, a quite happy marriage. The principals were well into middle age when it began and they had much to offer each other. Somnes, who had been in comfortable circumstances, found himself able, if he wished, to live lavishly, and Helen found herself working seriously with and on the stage. Helen and George, in the order that people talk of them, work hard both in New York and, each summer, at Elitch's, where Helen's best parts are considered to have been in *Whiteoaks,* in which she played the 101-year-old matriarch; in *Call It a Day, Morning's at Seven, The Royal Family* and in *Murray Hill,* in which, during a drunk scene, she crawled about on her hands and knees and awed Denver. Her wardrobe and her home, both magnificent, have helped outfit productions at Elitch's and at the Civic Theater. Her fur coats, jewels, silver, furniture and rugs have appeared in more scenes than she has.

They set up an office in New York, under the firm name of Bonfils and Somnes, and produced a number of plays, in some of which Helen had small—very small—parts, but until 1944, when they had an investment in *Helen Goes to Troy,* they didn't have much luck. At first, Broadway was a little suspicious of them; press agents, producers and actors looked upon them as amateurs in a professional's business. By now they are reckoned as a reasonably solid outfit.

Helen Bonfils and George Somnes—they never go as Mr. and Mrs. Somnes—live in a duplex apartment in River House when in New York. River House is a fabulous building on the East River, and the Bonfils-Somnes apartment is one of the most remarkable in it. Somnes has spent a considerable part of his life acquiring French and Italian Renaissance furnishings. Great, intricately carved, aged pieces of wood are all over the place, and, oddly enough, the general effect is fine. Somnes has a good sense of color, and there is a lot of it to bring out the splendor of the furniture.

Except for occasional trips to Denver, the Somneses live at River House from November until June. They have several servants, and a poodle and a toy bulldog. The Bonfils family has always been very fond of dogs, and the *Post* is continually running long stories about them, especially lost ones. Helen and George go out in New York some, but not excessively, and they make it a point to entertain any people from Denver.

In Denver, they live in the old Bonfils mansion, a big stone museum piece, with period rooms, fountains, gardens and more dogs. Strangers visiting the Somneses in the living room of this house quite often get a vague feeling of apprehension which they usually find is caused by a constant drip, drip, drip from a feeble fountain on a porch. Helen's mother's and father's rooms are much the same as when they were living.

George's bedroom is yellow and blue, and Helen's is almost

precisely as it was when she was a girl. There are twin beds
with woven-cane headboards, a dresser, a small dressing table,
another table littered with books and magazines, and an oval
mirror, all in the neutral cream color so many parents pick
for a girl child's room. It is quite a contrast to the appearance
of Helen. Mrs. Somnes, although her imperious face shows
some strain and age, has a young neck and a young, full figure,
which isn't corseted as much as some Denver women would
like to believe.

Although Helen gets a lot of honest admiration from Denver,
she does draw some arch descriptions from a few women. One
matron explained the detractors, saying, "Every woman thinks
she could have been a great actress, and a lot of women here
who had everything—husband, children, money, social position—when Helen had nothing, are jealous of her now. They
think she's leading a glamorous life, living in New York and
going out with theater people. And I don't blame Helen one
bit for lording it over them a little. Here she is with a New
York apartment, a cultured, handsome husband. And, remember, she's an actress."

When in Denver, Helen is an excellent mark for churchmen and other people who want money for meritorious needs.
Helen is a strong Catholic, and has built the Church of the
Holy Ghost in pink marble and lovely Spanish architecture.
Gurtler, her friend at Elitch's, is convinced she has given electric organs to half the churches in Denver, no matter what
denomination. Some of her contributions come out of her
pocket, others from the ubiquitous Foundation for the Betterment of Mankind.

One day a friend met her and mentioned how she seemed
to be all dressed up—she always looks dressed up, but this
day it was more evident than ever. "I've just had lunch with
the clergy," Helen explained. "I asked Fanny, my maid for
years, what I should wear. Should I be humble and go in rags?
Fanny growled and said, 'No, they probably want a donation,
so you might as well dress up and have some fun.'" Helen
was wearing a black, low-necked dress, a flower hat with a

purple veil, purple gloves and a light fur jacket. She tries to make it a point of buying most of her clothes from Denver merchants, although she does get some of her things for the stage in Chicago and New York. Helen, who wins hands down as the most dressed woman in Denver, if complimented on a hat or gown, is likely to say, "This old thing," and, if luck is with her, rather ostentatiously show you a worn-out elbow.

She supports a number of old ladies for various reasons, and they line up outside her office on certain days. When she sees one, she will call, "Come right in, honey," and give her a check.

Her secretary, Henry Meier, who used to work in the box office at Elitch's, finds the best part of his time occupied in opening mail, most of it requests for money. Helen, in some of her personal charity for old friends, shows traces of her father, and there is one woman in Denver, living on Bonfils bounty, who, after a couple of drinks, has sobbed, "Helen won't let me pick the drapes for my own house." The Bonfils attributes also show in a conversational trick she has of popping out with flat contradictions. An acquaintance, while walking with Helen and one of Helen's close friends one day, is fond of telling of a rather odd exchange of remarks which took place in front of a store.

"Aren't those blouses cute!" cooed the close friend.

"No, they're foul," said Helen.

"Yes, they are, aren't they?" said the friend.

The *Post* for years sponsored a number of events for children and grown people, such as egg rolling, circus parties, trips to Holy Cross Mountain and the Frontier Day festivals at Cheyenne, a juvenile rodeo, a mutt show, an ice-cream day, and a number of others, most of which *Post* promotion men managed to get someone else to pay for. Some of these are being curtailed by the war, and much of the wild, free activity of the F. G. Bonfils days is being dropped because the present management doesn't like to spend money at all.

Al Birch, a dapper old-timer on the paper, is in charge of such events as the *Post* and Helen keep up. Birch, of a diminishing breed, is a stunt promotion man with one of the most extensive wardrobes west of Lucius Beebe. He speaks reverently of a public-park opera whose deficits Helen meets. "It is strictly noncommercial," he says. "We don't sell any peanuts, popcorn or Denver *Posts*."

The *Post* still has a few of its old staff around, most of them, like Al Birch, acutely nostalgic for the more rollicking days. They no longer feel a part of a paper "with a heart and a soul," as Bonfils used to describe it, but merely cogs in a well-paying, soberly run investment. Their regard for the past is even stronger than that of most old newspaper people. Among the most noted members of the staff are Lord Ogilvy and Frances Wayne. Lord Ogilvy, who is really the second son of a former Earl of Airlie, is an uncle of Mrs. Winston Churchill, and it pleases him that she still has nice legs. He came out to Denver in the last century, farmed for a while and then lost his money, and was working as a night watchman in the freight yards of the Union Pacific when Harry Tammen, who had found Ogilvy an entertaining customer during his bartending period, gave him a job on the *Post*.

Ogilvy is one of the best writers in the country about cattle and sheep. A tall, straight old man with intense blue eyes, he wears the same clothes winter and summer and the same kind of khaki tie. As the tie soils, he keeps snipping the end off it, and, when it is about an inch or so long, puts on a new one. Mrs. Wayne, who appears to be in her forties and is at least twenty years older, is a crisp woman and one of the paper's top reporters. She has short, faded red hair, which gives her the nickname of Pinky. Once she was interviewing some visiting dignitary in the Brown Palace Hotel when he said, with a show of modesty, that he didn't know why she should want his opinions. "After seeing you and talking to you, I don't know either," she said, and walked out, thereby fulfilling a reporter's dream.

William C. Shepherd, a pink round man with white hair, which seems to have been cut with the aid of a bowl, and with a vague resemblance to W. C. Fields, runs the paper now.

His managing editor, Lawrence Martin, is sometimes credited
with maintaining the *Post's* low salaries to its general help,
but people who have worked with Shepherd contend he never
relinquishes actual control to anyone. "I've been here as long
as the foothills," he tells people. He came with his parents
from New York in 1885, and still has an accent redolent of
Brooklyn. Helen says of him, "The hiring and firing on the
paper is up to Shep. We couldn't have people coming to me,
and to Mrs. Tammen when she was alive. That would be
terrible."

Shepherd says that a good paper is one that is successful,
and by his standards the *Post* is wonderful, making, as it does,
more than $1,000,000 a year. Shepherd is pleased to say, "We
have the lowest overhead in the country for a paper this size,"
and his staff agrees. Some of its old members are paid as high
as $150 a week, but its average wage is low, as compared with
the salary scales of many major newspapers.

Shepherd says that the *Post* follows the policy of the New
York *Times* in respect to news, a statement which must make
the *Times* proprietors wince. To the relief of Denver merchants in these days of paper shortages, the *Post* runs nearly
all the advertising it can get, including columns of patent-
medicine copy, and the news gets in somehow. The *Post,* however, does not encourage any free advertising, and the use of
names of hotels, theaters and exhibits in reporting the activities
of Denver notables is frowned upon. The paper buys an awful
amount of columns and features, and runs them when it
pleases. Shepherd, wiser than many editors in some respects,
says that no columnist is good six days a week, and so he runs
the columnists' stuff only when he likes it. On the grounds that
he buys the United Press wire service and that the U.P. and the
Rocky Mountain News are Scripps-Howard owned, he often
doesn't put credit lines on U.P. copy.

The *Post* has one of the neatest city rooms in the world.
It is large, with a great deal of space between departments,
sterile and astringent. Women are not allowed to smoke, and
the cuspidors, placed near the men's desks, have the appear-

ance of being unused. With local news coverage only moderate, the most professional work on the staff is that of the copy-readers who write the headlines. The *Post* loves headlines. It has more of them, and bigger ones, than any other paper. Its front page is a puzzle which Denver people have somehow mastered over the years. They look upon the readers of normal papers as double-acrostic fans do on persons who work only crossword puzzles. The *Post* has headlines in colors, and one edition in red. Even in days of peace, one look at the *Post* gave a stranger a feeling of panic and impending doom.

With all of this fireworks Helen agrees. Her father started it, and she believes in his newspaper and his ideas. The paper has attacked all phases of the New Deal, and many of the war, as F. G. Bonfils certainly would have done. Japanese-Americans, interned in Colorado and helpless to retaliate, were blasted miserably a year and a half ago. It was just the *Post* yelling about something rather aimlessly.

Few of the people of Denver any longer look upon the name of Bonfils with any anger or loathing. F. G. Bonfils has been taken up in Denver legend, and Denver keeps bright its past, its memories of wild, lusty days, and the only emotion they cause is pride that all these things happened in the town.

Helen keeps busy brightening up the name, and she is liked and admired by the town, and occasionally people remember that she was her papa's daughter.

"The *Post* is papa's monument," she said not long ago of the most tangible influence the Bonfils family has on the town. "It is like he was, dynamic, protean and strong with the strength of a virile man. You think of other people's families dying, but never your own. I judge my life by my father's. I don't think mine has been much; I haven't done much or accomplished much. I'll always live in my father's shadow."

And so will her newspaper.

She Didn't Write It for Money, She Says

(MARY COYLE CHASE)

By WALLIS M. REEF

EDITOR'S PREFACE.—Everybody by now knows about *Harvey*—both the play and the rabbit—the first being the most delightful entertainment to appear on Broadway in many a year, and the second being a character more real and likely to be remembered longer than many of the flesh-and-blood big names that illumine the marquees of the gay white way. Less well known, however, is the ex-reporter who is responsible for this charming bit of whimsicality. In the following article, Mr. Reef delineates the personality and gives the background of the attractive Denver newspaper woman and playwright whose *Harvey* won the 1944 Pulitzer prize ("thereby pleasing a lot of people"), and who is just superstitious enough (as all those connected with the theatre are supposed to be) to admit that she felt sure that her play would succeed when a passing truck driver said, "Hello, Love."

For those who have seen *Harvey*, a particularly significant part of Mr. Reef's article is that brief paragraph in which he quotes Mrs. Chase's mother as telling her daughter years ago:

"Never be unkind or indifferent to a person others say is crazy. Often they have a deep wisdom. We pay them a great respect in the old country, and we call them fairy people, and, it could be, they are sometimes."

As Mr. Reef comments, and as all those who appreciated the fey quality of *Harvey* will also say—"Mary remembered."

Just as *Harvey* is good entertainment, so is Mr. Reef's profile an engaging revelation of a charming, talented, and original writer—and, from what he says, a grand person.

September 1, 1945

A WONDERFUL thing happened in New York last fall. It was a play named *Harvey*, which the Pulitzer Prize Committee later chose as the best play of 1944; thereby pleasing a lot of people. It is an ironic and witty story about a man who has acquired for a friend a rabbit that is six feet, one and a half inches tall, and invisible, except to the man himself. A few reviewers saw in it a dexterous plea for alcoholism, but, to most people who saw the play, this seemed to be a summary piece of thinking. The majority feel that the show makes a great case for understanding, decency and friendliness among humans. Besides, it is a very funny play.

The woman who wrote the play, Mrs. Mary Coyle Chase, is is in many ways as unusual as her script, and the life she leads is several shades more vigorous, although just about as bizarre, as that of Elwood P. Dowd, the drinking man who has Harvey, the tall rabbit, for a steady companion. Her work is accomplished under conditions which would drive the average writer crazy, and yet she manages to do much very nice writing in a house crowded by her husband, three sons and assorted friends of the Chases, most of whom expect a drink and some talk.

The Chases live in Denver, a town with a long theatrical and literary tradition, and a place of strong friendships. Friends are often the greatest hindrances to a writer's chances of getting any writing done. Though not many persons would think of walking into a friend's office, chasing his stenographer away with a few cute words and spending the rest of the day in desultory talk, anybody at all will drop in at a writer's house to cheer him up. The fact that writers often are despondent and work in frivolous surroundings and circumstances, such as living rooms and no money, makes many people feel missionary toward them. Mary Chase never hides or pleads her children's illnesses; she likes callers. The noise of talk and argument provides a background for her thinking something like the sound of water which sea captains are said to miss so much when they retire.

The money from *Harvey,* which in time will run up pretty high despite taxes and a series of new hats for Mrs. Chase, is a stuff which the author has been shy of, and somewhat flippant about, all her life. "I didn't write *Harvey* for money," she has said. "Around my house, money has never been anything you made; it has been merely something you owed."

She has had a long experience with bill collectors, both those who shout and pound on doors and the letter-writing kind that first send a hurt note, then a series of nasty ones. Once, before she was recognized nationally as what her friends have known her to be for a long time, she said that whenever she was lonely she would get invariably a letter from a Denver bank which would cheer her immensely. The salutation, "Dear Madam," would sound warm-hearted, and the text concerning money she had borrowed for household and hospital bills would have an intimate touch.

Her friends around town think it is wonderful that she now has all that *Harvey* money; they remember the times when she was called a dangerous radical because of fervent and able fighting on behalf of labor and mistreated minorities. They can't see how the money will make much change in Mrs. Chase, but they can see how mighty respectfully some of her old disparaging critics look at her now.

What Mary Chase's life lacked in ready cash was made up probably by warmth, pride of family, a talent for fighting and a nature, common in the Irish, which is given to both gaiety and melancholy. She managed always to eat and dress well, and to pour a drink, even for a bill collector, and, in some ways of thinking, nobody can do better than that.

She was born in West Denver, two blocks from Dooley's saloon. Her birthplace was not quite on the wrong side of the tracks, but the noise of trains reached it. Her mother, whose maiden name was Mary McDonough, came from Ireland to Denver when she was sixteen, to keep house for her brothers, Peter, Timothy, James and John. The brothers in the 1880's and 1890's had been trying their luck in the Colorado gold camps. The luck wasn't good. Mary McDonough went to St.

Mary's Convent, and while there met Frank Coyle, who, some time before, had sought his fortune in the Oklahoma land rush and hadn't done too well.

He was delivering groceries at the time Miss McDonough met him, and after they were married he became a salesman for a flour mill.

Mary was the last child Mary McDonough Coyle bore, and the baby got gay and reverent attention from her father, her mother, her four uncles, her sister and her two brothers. Peter, Timothy, James and John, born in Ulster, were men with talk and long memory, especially Timothy, who had attended Trinity College in Dublin. Timothy talked a long tongue about the wrongs done Ireland and they all talked rhythmically and poetically of banshees, leprechauns, cluricaunes and pookas, the last being a large mischievous goblin of the Harvey sort. Timothy McDonough carried an I.W.W. card, too, and knew Joe Hill songs as well as Irish fairy tales.

Once Mary's mother chased away several boys for tossing snowballs at a tiny old woman who walked with the aid of a cane.

"Never be unkind or indifferent to a person others say is crazy," Mary McDonough Coyle said to her daughter. "Often they have a deep wisdom. We pay them a great respect in the old country, and we call them fairy people, and, it could be, they are sometimes." Mary remembered.

"I got the highest grades for studies and the lowest for deportment," Mrs. Chase recalls of her childhood. "I had a reputation for physical daring and some notoriety for getting other children into mischief. Mother tried to hide the gamin qualities of her child with bonnets of feathers and ribbons, but they didn't hide anything at all; just made the combination confusing, although certainly arresting."

The Coyle household needed all the money it got. Mary's clothes were from bargain basements and her underwear often was fashioned from flour sacks trimmed in the beautiful hand embroidery her mother had learned from the nuns of Londonderry. Occasionally the legend "Pride of the Rockies" was exposed on Mary's backside as she skinned the cat on the bars in the schoolyard.

Recently the family found a copy of *A Tale of Two Cities* in which was scrawled on the flyleaf, "My name is Mary Coyle. I am eight years old. I have just read this book. Don't you think that I am smart?" She never lost this particular confidence, and through her childhood and youth retained her advanced reading tastes. At ten she was reading De Quincey, picking out his volumes in the public library because his name looked attractive. One of Mary's brothers turned out to be a reckless, adventurous kid, running away from home and hopping freight cars, a common custom among high-spirited boys in Western cities. One Saturday afternoon a policeman found him and two other boys shaking a gum machine.

The boys ran, and the cop, with excessive zeal, shot and wounded Mary's brother.

The story of the shooting appeared in the Sunday papers the next morning and, on the way to church, Mary could see mothers warning their children not to play with her. They didn't look into the facts of the story; the name of the Coyle boy had been in the paper, in some tale having to do with a fracas with a policeman; that was enough. The policeman was later discharged, but, because the incident and the dismissal were far apart, it was not soon enough to vindicate Mary's brother. The ostracism which started that Sunday grew during the week and had a bitter effect on the girl which has never been quite erased. However, she was normally vigorous, and she had the biggest tricycle in the neighborhood. She would speed around, ribbons flying in the breeze, and occasionally peg a rock at some neighbor's windows.

Probably the tragedy made Mary spend more time with books than ever; in any case, the quality of reading and studying she did was amazing for a pretty, quickly intelligent child in an American town. At eleven, she began slipping away to Denver's excellent theaters; often in this truancy walking more than five miles. The first play she saw was *The Merchant of Venice* with Robert Mantell. She wished to be something like De Quincey, and came quite close to it when she entered the University of Denver at fifteen and began reading Xenophon's *Anabasis* in the Greek. During summer vacation she talked the city editor of the *Rocky Mountain News* into giving her a job. Her "wages" consisted of carfare.

Mary McDonough Coyle, an indomitable woman, had saved carefully through the years, and with some of the money, Mary moved on to the University of Colorado, at Boulder. By this time she was beautiful, with wide gray eyes, rich brown hair with hints of red in it, and a white, imperious face, scarred expertly with lipstick. She was not invited to join a sorority, a fact which inspired one of her plays later, and after completing a major in the classics in two years, she left college and returned to the *News;* this time at a salary which included carfare and money.

Denver throughout the '20's had a rowdy, competitive, wonderful journalism. The *News* and the Denver *Post* of F. G. Bonfils and Harry Tammen were startling sheets, and the pages were loaded with gang killings, love nests, intimate pictures of chorus girls, paeans to virtue and the home, and accounts of the various effects of prohibition on society. Mary Coyle got along very well. She was curious, dressed in the flapper styles of the period, had good-looking legs and a fine face, and possessed, too, the bland, amoral effrontery of a good, aggressive, cityside reporter. She would perch on the rim of the copy desk and give translations of unusual Latin authors, and, after the paper had gone to press, would sit around the office and drink quick ones with the fellows on the late trick. She had a flip, sharp tongue which contrasted nicely with her Madonna appearance.

Once this writer was riding with her in a notably unstable airplane on an assignment to cover a mine explosion. The crate's one motor died, and Mary said, "Why didn't he do this before? Now we can talk without all that noise." The pilot, Cloyd Cleavenger, flipped the plane into two screaming dives. The motor caught, and life for Mary and me went on. She thought it was great fun. Later that night, returning alone with pictures for the *News*, Cleavenger made a forced landing in the foothills and the plane caught fire. He persuaded a farmer to drive him to Denver, and the pilot's story of the plane trip, with photographs of the principals, got as much space as the story of the explosion.

Once Mary was in the middle of a personal telephone conversation just as a verdict was to be read in a murder trial. She cut the conversation short, returned to the courtroom and got the verdict. As she was going into her office, another reporter asked about the call. "Oh, that was dad," she said. "Our house is on fire." She turned in her copy, then went home and wrote a story about the fire. The paper bought her a new dress to replace one that was burned up.

Although she nurses her own superstitions, she violated one of the strongest ones of hard-rock miners when she entered the Moffat Tunnel. These men believe it is the worst kind of luck to allow a woman to enter a mine or a tunnel when they are working. Mary, in a howling blizzard, talked a male reporter into taking off an extra pair of trousers he was wearing, and, adding the pants and a miner's cap to her attire, she went inside and was there for the dramatic hole-through. After the final blast had ripped away the last core of rock separating the two entrances, she stumbled through smoke and fumes and crawled up the mount of broken granite to grasp the hand of a reporter who had come in from the other side.

Once, in the later stages of her newspaper career, she took truth serum at a public demonstration. The then chief of police tried to make her confess an incident of years before when she had tossed a rock through a window of a house, climbed inside, and beat detectives to a picture of a couple wanted for murder. This was one time the truth serum failed. Mary didn't confess.

Mary, these days, isn't particularly interested in talking of those hectic times. They seem overdrawn, filled with futile tenseness and action. From them she got possibly a greater understanding of people than she might have had otherwise, and she learned the glib incisiveness and the ability to discover—

and dislike—sham, which most good reporters have. At night, after the sunrise edition was rolling, people like Clyde Brion Davis and Mary would sit around and talk over a pint of Leadville moon about writing. Libbie Block, whom she met at a short-story class, talked her into doing some short stories, which sold without any trouble.

Denver has turned out a number of distinguished magazine writers and newspapermen, most of whom did their best work after leaving the town. Even in those days, Mary intended staying in Denver and writing plays. She developed about this time, too, an affection for a type of practical joke worked with telephones. One day, for instance, she telephoned a local auto dealer and, imitating the soft speech of a woman she knew—who runs an orphanage—said that the orphanage was having a picnic, and would the dealer supply her with a dozen automobiles to transport her charges? The dealer—for such things are considered good public relations—said he would like to help, but he had only six cars available. "Oh, well, if that's the case, we'll take them," the motherly voice said resignedly, adding, "But I think you're the cheapest —— in town."

One Saturday afternoon, the late Eddie Day, an editor with normal courtesy to persons outside his business and a short temper around his shop, was trying to get out a sports extra—a mean technical job, involving game scores, unhappy printers, and, as always in the newspaper business, time. The *News,* at the time, promoted a Christmas Good Fellow Club which distributed food to the poor. Mary watched Day work for a while, and then went into a telephone booth in the building and telephoned him.

"Them apples you handed me got worms in them," she said, as soon as Day picked up the phone. "That's a fine Christmas present. Did you keep all the good apples yourself?"

"I'm sorry," Day said. "We buy them wholesale, and they are supposed to be the best——"

"Don't give me that. These'd turn your stomach. Do you want my kids to eat them and all get worms?"

"I'm very busy, lady. If you'll give me your name——"

"My name's O'Hanrahan. Mrs. Beatrice Lillian Gwendolyn O'Hanrahan. What's yours?"

Day told her his name, and asked for Mrs. O'Hanrahan's address.

"I live at Fourteen-forty Blake. Where do you live? And I got seven children. How many you got?"

"That doesn't matter!" Day screamed. "I'll have somebody check on your basket!"

"I want to know how many kids you got. You know how many I got. You ashamed? You trying to hide something?"

It went on and on, Day screaming, Mrs. O'Hanrahan relentlessly talking. Finally, she said, "Oh, so you won't talk, won't even talk about them lousy apples. Well, let me tell you—let me tell you what I think: You're a cheap, lying, apple-stealing, penny-pinching rat. Now what do you think?"

Other reporters heard of the gag, and most of them tried variations on Mary's theme. It got so Day could hardly bear to look at a telephone. He finally found out that Mary had started the thing, and he fired her. He tried later to get her to come back, but she wouldn't. She was busy doing all the things she wanted to do—bearing children, reading plays, writing, seeing people and fighting for causes of the moment. Before leaving the *News* she had married Robert L. Chase, a tall, serious-minded reporter, who is now managing editor of the *News*. With time at home, Mary indulged her liking for extremes, even in foods. She will get a liking for something, eat it three times a day for a week, and then never taste it again. Once, in an afternoon, she baked twenty-four banana cream pies.

Despite the quick writing habits she had developed on the *News,* Mrs. Chase found that plays took time and labor. She developed a knack for an almost trancelike concentration, which would be unaffected by her husband, her children or the always increasing number of friends. Her first play, *Me Third,* was completed about the time her third son, Barry, was born. Mary showed the play to this writer and his wife, a first-reading custom she has followed in all her work. We thought it was fine. It was a rowdy tale of a political candidate and the ex-cashier of a genteel bordello. It was presented by the WPA theater, and Denver critics thought it excellent. Brock Pemberton bought the play, and five weeks after the arrival of Barry, Mary went to New York on her first trip east of Colorado.

The name of the play was changed to *Now You've Done It,* and the whole thing was rewritten. The opening-night audience registered 220 laughs, but very few of them came from the critics who were present. It lasted seven weeks and cost Pemberton money.

Mary's next play was *Sorority House,* a play which she probably just had to get written—about a poor girl snubbed in college who comes out, of course, on top. Then came *The Banshee*—about a sorrowful fairy—which may be produced on Broadway someday. Following that was *Colorado Dateline*—about a girl reporter and a murder trial—and then *A Slip of a Girl,* a comedy which played Army camps around Denver until the Federal Theater folded.

While all her writing of plays was going on, Mrs. Chase managed to stay involved in about a half dozen occupations, each of which would have been full time for almost anyone else. She aided in forming a chapter of the American Newspaper Guild, she handled publicity for the NYA, and, with Mrs. Edward P. Costigan, widow of the late senator from Colorado, fought for the rights of the Spanish Americans in Denver, who had been getting kicked around. All this was done with a gaiety that astounded some of her dead-serious associates. She was likely to show up in a picket line wearing a fifty-dollar hat, fantastic earrings and a dress best described as slinky. The effect on employers was amazing. At one time she was writing a weekly radio program for the Teamsters' Union and running a quiet and effective lobby for an oleomargarine concern.

The group of people whose activities seem to revolve about Mrs. Chase would, on a chart, be a sort of vertical section of

Denver's social and economic life—labor organizers, Junior League charity workers, grocery boys, bankers, teachers and newspaper people. The conversation is expert, and apt to be on any subject.

Mary, who at first seems abnormally self-reliant, has a tendency to depend upon somewhat mystic influences. She lies in a warm bath and ideas come to her, from outside, she says. Fortune telling is a serious, desperate business with her, and she often gets out a deck of cards and finds out what's going to happen to her or her friends.

The idea for *Harvey* came when she was told about a woman across the street who had lost her only son in the Pacific. Mary, heartsick, would watch the woman from a window, and then one day she dusted off a four-foot miniature stage she works with, and, in two years marked by periods of trancelike concentration, wrote a cheering play. She called it *The White Rabbit*, and sent it to Pemberton, who decided to gamble on the oddity. Everything was right except the title, and it was soon changed to *Harvey*. Even the rehearsals under Antoinette Perry's direction were friendly, because no one wanted to hurt the spirit of the play. Somebody thought of Frank Fay for the part of Elwood P. Dowd, a perfect piece of casting.

By the time of the tryout opening in Boston, Mary was dead sure she had a success. "Just before we left New York for Boston, a member of the cast gave me a two-dollar bill," she explains. "He got it in change someplace and asked me to keep it for good luck. Then, a short time later, Josephine Hull gave me a four-leaf clover. Then, as I was walking to the theater on opening night in Boston, a huge truck drove slowly next to the curb. The driver turned his head and said casually, 'Hello, Love.' It wasn't an attempted pickup; he didn't even smile. I noticed he wore a dirty leather jacket and his face was solemn and well shaped under the grime, and his eyes were dark and thoughtful. He didn't stop, but drove on without another glance. Somehow, it seemed like benediction, and it was the third sign."

Everything was right, and life goes on for the Chases despite all that nice fresh money.

People crowd the house; Mary forgets to order soda, and you drink plain water with your bourbon. She says she is going to write another play, and her husband groans. The three boys announce loudly that they want to go East and see *Oklahoma!*

The Christian Science Monitor

By Marquis W. Childs

EDITOR'S PREFACE.—"Published under the creed established by Mary Baker Eddy—'to injure no man, but bless all mankind'—*The Christian Science Monitor* has confounded and surprised the newspaper craft for 37 years. Refusing to notice crime, accepting no tea, coffee, liquor, tobacco, or health advertising, covering world news better than the average daily, the *Monitor* is perhaps the world's unique example of idealistic journalism." So commented the *Post* publishers when this article by Mr. Childs first appeared.

The *Monitor,* in addition to the distinctions noted in the foregoing quotation, is one of the few American newspapers whose circulations are national. As has been stated elsewhere in this book, most of the newspapers in this country are local or regional in appeal and distribution. Not so, however, in the case of the *Monitor.* Published in Boston, only about 15 per cent of its 155,000 subscribers are in the New England area. The remaining 85 per cent are scattered throughout the country—and world: 22 per cent on the Atlantic seaboard (other than New England), a little over 30 per cent in the Middle West, 22 per cent on the Pacific coast, and the remainder in Canada and foreign countries.

Another important point of distinction which Mr. Childs mentions, but which could be treated at much greater length, is the *timeless timeliness* of the content of the *Monitor.* As he says, "the fact that so many *Monitor* readers receive their papers long after the news has been recounted elsewhere necessitates an entirely different type of news treatment." Actually, the *Monitor* is, in a sense, a daily magazine in a newspaper format—just as *Time* or *Newsweek* are weekly newspapers in a magazine format. Among the things which are supposed to distinguish a magazine from a newspaper, other than format, are (1) more time for preparation, (2) more space for theories and expositions, and (3) a much longer period of usefulness than a newspaper which is read hastily one moment and used for fire-making the next. All of these are, of course, applicable to the *Monitor,* and enter the explanation of its wide appeal—both as to space and time.

Is such a paper profitable? Yes and no. As Mr. Childs explains in greater detail in the piece which follows, "In bad years the Publishing Society absorbs any deficit, and the high standard of the *Monitor* is maintained regardless of losses. In some years, though, the paper makes a handsome return."

September 15, 1945

THE hushed cathedral quiet of *The Christian Science Monitor* newsroom in Boston would give an ordinary newspaperman the screaming meemies in no time at all. There is nothing like it in the United States, and it just doesn't seem natural. Most of the typewriters are noiseless and the others seem strangely muted. The whole place is bright and shiny and clean. No haze of tobacco smoke hangs over the copy desk. So far as can be determined, no one has ever smoked in the *Monitor* newsroom, or in any other department of the paper, for that matter.

Not long ago Col. Evans Carlson, of Carlson's Raiders, came to call on the editors of the *Monitor,* on the invitation of a *Monitor* correspondent whom he had met in the Pacific. During the conversation, the colonel pulled out a cigarette and struck a match. But for some reason he hesitated.

"It's all right if I smoke in here, isn't it?" he asked.

"Oh, certainly," said Charles Gratke, the foreign editor, adding, "of course, no one ever has." Colonel Carlson blew out the match and put his cigarette back in the package.

The *Monitor,* which is the property of the Christian Science Church, is a daily newspaper with excellent coverage of the news of the world. It carries, in fact, more news of world events than an ordinary daily. Christian Science itself is discussed in only one article each weekday—the *Monitor* is not published on Sunday. This article appears on the Home Forum page in English and also in one of fifteen other languages. A national newspaper, the only one of its kind, the *Monitor* has many readers who are not members of the church, although no poll has ever shown the exact ratio between sectarian and nonsectarian circulation.

Of the honors which have come to this unique paper in the thirty-seven years of its existence, none has been more gratifying to the editors than an award it got last year from the University of Missouri for "fulfillment of the difficult assignment given to it by its founder, Mary Baker Eddy." In an editorial published in the first issue of the *Monitor*, in 1908, Mrs. Eddy, who also founded the religion, gave orders for a daily newspaper that should "injure no man, but bless all mankind."

Newspapermen of the time mistakenly regarded her benevolent injunction as an impossible handicap. Even the New York *Times*—"All the News That's Fit to Print"—predicted failure for this venture in idealistic journalism. Mrs. Eddy did set a very tough task. To keep within the spirit of her instructions and yet bring out a daily which does not entirely exclude human frailties and follies is a problem that has plagued the editors from the beginning. As if to compensate *Monitor* readers for the absence of the more highly seasoned fare, the editors have encouraged the light touch in the writing of feature items. There was a period when Editor Erwin Canham kept a basket of apples beside his desk. At the morning editorial conference, the news editor producing the snappiest anecdote to enliven Page 1 was given an apple as a reward. This cheery ceremony took place in Canham's private sanctum, a spacious book-lined study with high windows.

There is more than good cheer behind the *Monitor's* news policy. The fact that the paper has behind it a definite religious viewpoint has led to an unusually conscientious attitude toward reporting the news. *Monitor* correspondents are held accountable for a balanced insight into the situations they are assigned to cover. Dispatches that give only one side of a controversial situation are sometimes held up, so that a parallel dispatch from some other source may be obtained to round out the picture. In short, the paper's basic standard has been "responsibility." News beats and sensationalism have taken second place to balance.

Today, few religious inhibitions prevent the *Monitor* from reporting the important news of the world. There is, of course, a special policy with respect to crime. No word of Errol Flynn's legal troubles appeared, nor has the *Monitor* published a single line dealing with the sordid Chaplin affair. But if a crime is considered to have national significance, it is briefly reported. Thus, for example, terse accounts of the Lindbergh kidnaping and its aftermath were carried in the *Monitor*.

It was not always so. The news policy today represents a striking evolution from a period when the most narrow taboos were enforced.

Twenty-five years ago, the first that *Monitor* readers learned of a disastrous New England flood was when the paper reported collection of a Red Cross fund to aid the families of victims (in the Christian Science doctrine, death is not recognized). The inhibition extended to the weather. An adverse phenomenon, such as a heavy snowfall, could not be reported. In fact, snow itself was considered pretty unfortunate and, if it had to be mentioned, it was referred to as a "blanket of white." One occasional contributor recalls reviewing a book with the title, *Apple Tree Insects and Diseases*. The review appeared more or less as he had written it, except that the words *and Diseases* had been stricken from the title of the book.

These taboos derived, in the view of the men responsible for the paper's present standing, not from the founder herself, but from overscrupulousness among some of her followers. Searching for precedents for realistic reporting, Canham found that Mrs. Eddy, in the *Christian Science Sentinel,* another church publication, had included a news summary with reports of the Spanish-American War that gave totals of the dead and wounded. So war is reported realistically in the columns of the *Monitor*. The Jap atrocities practiced on American prisoners were recounted in some detail.

Most of the curious prohibitions once prevailing were gradually eliminated after a bitter row that was finally concluded in the highest court of Massachusetts. The storm center was Frederick Dixon, who had been brought from England at Mrs. Eddy's direction and eventually made editor. Dixon joined with the three trustees of the Christian Science Publishing Society to ignore the authority of the five Directors of The First Church of Christ, Scientist, known as The Mother Church. Both sides cited chapter and verse in Mrs. Eddy's *Church Manual* to support their arguments. The overwhelming majority of church members through the country was on the side of the Directors, and the circulation of the *Monitor* shrank decidedly.

Basing an opinion on an independent reading of the *Manual,* the Supreme Judicial Court of Massachusetts in 1922 ruled for the Directors. Dixon and the trustees were dismissed.

An editorial hailing the end of this "unrighteous factional disturbance" declared that in the future the *Monitor* and the other periodicals put out by the publishing society should have "the fostering care and loving guidance of the Board of Directors of The Mother Church."

The board named Willis J. Abbot, C. S., LL.B., of New York, as editor of the *Monitor*. In many ways the genial, positive, persuasive Abbot, who was descended from New England scholars and divines, set the paper on the path it has followed ever since. After Abbot gave up the editorship and became a sort of roving correspondent and columnist he set the tone, too, for later *Monitor* correspondents. A shrewd observer, Abbot, who "passed on" in 1934, was also an apostle who practiced his cheerful religion before the world. He loved to bring back tales from remote places of the influence of the *Monitor* and Christian Science. He used to take pains to see that the paper was available in the writing rooms of all the principal hotels in world capitals, and once, while thus engaged, in Athens, he observed a scholarly gentleman who came each day to pore over the *Monitor's* columns. Interviewing him, Abbot discovered that he was a professor from a near-by university who obtained from the paper's financial pages material for his course in economics and finance. This was reported with due pride to Boston.

Even more gratifying was a discovery he made at a small railway junction in the course of a journey between Peiping and Shanghai. Hounded by a persistent newsboy, he finally bought a local sheet printed in Chinese. To his amazement, the entire last page was given over to Abbot's own column, "Watching the World Go By"—in English, and with due credit to the author.

Monitor foreign correspondents work hard to maintain the Abbot tradition of poking into odd places. Often their zeal sets them a little apart from the ordinary, vulgar breed of reporter. The *Monitor's* Latin-American specialist, Roland Hall Sharp, was one of a group of correspondents who made an inspection tour of the Amazon rubber country under the tutelage of the Government's Rubber Development Corporation. I happened to be along on the trip, and am ready to testify that there has probably been nothing like Sharp's jungle equipment since Stanley went to Africa to find Doctor Livingstone.

His equipment included a portable distilling apparatus for producing fresh water, a portable mosquitoproof tent with hammock, and a complete outfit for developing and enlarging films. Once off the beaten path of civilization, Sharp pulled out of his voluminous luggage a pith helmet, and put on white drill riding breeches and black leather boots that—most wonderful of all—were especially equipped with flypaper tops to stop the bugs from crawling up any higher.

The name applied to him by his fellow reporters was Frank Buck, Jr. Rarely has anyone been so kidded. People practically paid for the privilege of watching Sharp operate his still in his room. Sharp had a perfect answer for the kidding—he intended to stay on at least five months after the rest of the party had returned to North America, and visit all sorts of strange and out-of-the-way places. Sharp's plan was to travel on native river steamers, with stops in small country hotels where the facilities are most primitive.

Another of the *Monitor's* far-roving correspondents is R. H. Markham, now on loan to the Office of War Information. Covering the Italian conquest of Ethiopia, Markham found it necessary to buy a mule, with a red saddle and trappings. No other means of conveyance was available, he explained to his home office, when he put the mule on his expense account. Moreover, he wrote a story about the mule and how much it had cost and how he was charging the expense to the paper. There has always been a certain chagrin in the *Monitor* office that this particular story caused more comment than the more serious news dispatches which Markham sent back to Boston. Markham used the light touch with a vengeance.

Monitor men have ranged all the attainable fronts of World War II. Joseph C. Harsch, who went across the Pacific with the first convoy to reach New Zealand, followed the grim retreat of the British and Americans before the Jap conquests. Ronald Stead was with the task force that went ashore at Oran. Gordon Walker flew with a dive bomber on a mission at Munda. John Beaufort was with the landing party at Kiska. Edmund Stevens followed the Finnish, Norwegian, Greek, Abyssinian and Libyan campaigns.

The stories that these men and their *Monitor* colleagues wired back to Boston were free of the flamboyant adjectives and the exaggerated optimism that have marred much of the reporting of World War II. They were as close as possible to realism—to the discoverable meaning of what had happened.

Under the direction of Canham and Gratke, coverage of the Allied invasion of Europe was carefully planned. And plans were worked out, too, for covering Europe after the reoccupation. *Monitor* men who had been in France and in Germany went back to report one of the biggest stories of the war—the changes that have come with years of occupation.

Editor Canham is widely regarded as one of America's most capable newsmen. Canham's earliest recollection is of riding in the family buggy on news-gathering expeditions with his father, who was editor of the Lewiston (Maine) *Sun-Journal*. His entire formal education was combined with practical experience in newspaper work, and he joined the *Monitor* staff as a cub reporter in 1925, on graduation from Bates College.

This apprenticeship was followed by three years at Oxford as a Rhodes scholar, mixed with foreign correspondence for the *Monitor* from Geneva. Service in Europe was followed by a term as chief of the *Monitor's* Washington bureau, lasting from 1932 to 1939. It was in Washington that Canham acquired the nickname of "Spike," which has stuck ever since. In 1939, at the still youthful age of thirty-five, he was called to Boston to assume the then top editorial post of managing editor. In January, 1945, his title was raised to editor.

Foreign Editor Gratke is completely in the *Monitor* tradition. I traveled with him in Sweden a year or so ago. It was not alone his energy and zeal that impressed the Swedes. At one point—and this was in May, when the water is still icy cold—Gratke put on swimming trunks, plunged into the Baltic and swam for three quarters of an hour while the stalwart Swedes watched from the shore in awe.

Besides having international coverage, the *Monitor* has international circulation. Before the war, more than 10 per cent of its subscribers lived outside the United States. The overseas circulation is now only 5.5 per cent, with British readers rationed on a basis of three papers a week.

Though the *Monitor* circulation list has never been large—it is today about 155,000—its influence is disproportionately great, partly because of its widespread distribution. A little more than 15 per cent of the total is in the region in which it is published—New England. Twenty-two per cent is on the Atlantic seaboard other than New England. Slightly more than 30 per cent is in the Middle West, 22 per cent is on the Pacific coast and the balance is accounted for by Canada and countries overseas.

The fact that so many *Monitor* readers receive their papers long after the news has been recounted elsewhere necessitates an entirely different type of news treatment. *Monitor* correspondents, both abroad and in Washington, write interpretive news stories pointing up the significance of events and shrewdly forecasting their probable effects. They are given a great deal of leeway, without the hampering qualifications which clog the conventional news story.

Monitor editors feel that they have worked out the pattern of the kind of postwar national newspaper that is believed likely to develop here.

The *Monitor* has regularly published advertising not only from American firms but from firms in the various world capitals. Women readers are sometimes bemused to discover that the little bargain which looks so attractive is on sale not on Boylston Street, but in Wellington, New Zealand. This advertising derives in part, of course, from faithful Christian Scientists. Then, too, other advertisers have discovered that a small ad in the *Monitor* has exceptional pulling power precisely because members of the church take their paper with unusual seriousness.

Except through the Board of Directors, there is no direct relation between the church and the paper. The back copies that travelers see offered free in railway stations are provided not by the publishing society, but by Christian Science churches in local communities. Members bring copies they have read to a special collection place and they are then given free distribution where, in the view of the church, they will do the most good.

Infrequently, Christian Science doctrine influences the treatment of the news. For example, *Monitor* articles on compulsory health insurance are likely to be critical.

Having the solid support of a body of readers with a deeper tie than is owed to an ordinary newspaper gives the advantage of a definite head start. Moreover, the fortunes of the paper are not dependent on the up-swings and down-swings of business. In bad years, the Publishing Society absorbs any deficit, and the high standard of the *Monitor* is maintained regardless of losses. In some years, though, the paper makes a handsome return.

Consistently, the *Monitor* has kept to a higher ratio of news to advertising than the average secular daily. In prewar times, it ran about 20 per cent advertising to 80 per cent news. The paper shortage reduced this to 30 per cent and 70 per cent. And news in the *Monitor* means news. There are only three so-called comic strips, one of them a humorous comment on current events. All are by *Monitor* artists.

At least as much advertising is turned down because of the principles of Christian Science as is accepted. The schedule of prohibitions as set out in the *Monitor's* rate sheet would horrify the ordinary advertising manager. Listed as "not acceptable" are: "Tea and coffee; tobacco; liquor; medical, surgical or hygienic articles; food products, soaps or other commodities when advertised on a health basis; hotel, resort or travel advertising employing a health appeal; schools, camps, travel agencies, financial institutions established less than two years; firearms; complexion preparations claiming medicinal qualities; hair dyeing; face or body massage; tombstones; undertakers; cemeteries; chiropodists; dentists; oculists, opticians, optometrists; hearing aids; lawyers, including patent attorneys; collection agencies; oil or mining propositions; political; adoption of children; animals in captivity; illustration or text representing life or health as dependent upon weather; securities of promotional enterprises or of firms engaged in business of tobacco, liquor or health products; partnership or investment of capital wanted; illustrations showing use of tobacco or liquor; the abbreviation 'Xmas.'"

Over both the business and the editorial departments the five Directors at the top of the Christian Science church maintain a close watch. Every Wednesday morning, Editor Canham walks across the street to a Board of Directors' meeting in the offices of The Mother Church. And if he has any doubts on matters of policy during the day, he consults the Directors by telephone. Present business manager of the *Monitor* is John H. Hoagland, who meets with the Directors once a week and with the Board of Trustees four days weekly. Hoagland, like Canham an experienced newspaperman, received his early training on the Louisville *Courier-Journal* and the old Louisville *Herald*.

The *Monitor's* editorial policy has generally been on the conservative side. In presidential elections the paper has invariably swung to the Republicans. The New Deal has come in for some sharp criticism that occasionally strains Mrs. Eddy's benevolent injunction. At the same time, however, in foreign policy it has been consistently internationalist and even on domestic issues there is liberal expression in the *Monitor's* columns. One of the paper's ablest reporters is Richard L. Strout, of the Washington bureau, who customarily takes the liberal view in writing of events in the capital. Strout, incidentally, is not a Christian Scientist. The unwritten rule, however, is that only members of the church advance to the higher posts.

The chief of the Washington bureau is five-foot Roscoe Drummond, better known as Bulldog Drummond, who was once executive editor of the paper. Possessed of a droll sense of humor, Drummond has contributed several amusing skits to dinners of the Gridiron Club. Being a good Christian Scientist, he is a teetotaler, but this has never prevented him from taking a full, though nonalcoholic, share in the revels of the club. Perhaps the ablest woman reporter in Washington is Mary Hornaday, of the *Monitor's* bureau. Happily for her, she is not confined to the "woman's angle," but is permitted to play her dispatches straight.

At least two members of today's staff come down from the time of Mrs. Eddy. One is Paul S. Deland, the managing editor. Deland once encountered a burglar in his house in Boston. Although he is a slight man and the burglar was husky, he captured and subdued him before the arrival of the police. The news, since it dealt with an ordinary crime, did not appear in the *Monitor.* Another veteran is Ernest C. Sherburne, the paper's dramatic critic in New York. In his youth, Sherburne used to go to Mrs. Eddy's home to get the articles she wrote for the *Christian Science Sentinel,* before the *Monitor* was established. Covering the openings on Broadway for more than twenty years, Sherburne has become a fixture on that mercurial street.

One thing the *Monitor* editors take particular pride in is the cartography that has been used to illustrate war stories. The paper has its own staff of map makers headed by Russell H. Lenz, who began as an office boy and worked up through the art department, perfecting his special ability through courses at Harvard. Lenz's maps have shown simply and clearly the far-flung course of global war.

The *Monitor's* home-office mapparium is a favorite with visitors. It is a huge glass globe with the countries of the earth painted on in color. The visitor walks through the middle of the globe on a glass bridge, so that, in effect, he stands inside the middle of the earth and looks out, upward or downward, at a translucent crust. Cleverly illuminated, the mapparium provides a unique visual concept of the earth on which we live.

Many attractions of the *Monitor* building were contributed by faithful Christian Scientists in distant lands. German Scientists, for example, could not send money because of currency regulations in force when the building was erected. Instead, they sent the special ornamental windows in the second floor of the lobby. Some of the ornamental metalwork came from Czechoslovakia.

But, as Christian Scientists themselves are well aware, it is not the mortal shell which makes the institution; it is the institution itself that has influenced the ways of man. Members of the faith have a very real sense that the paper is theirs. Partly by way of encouraging this, the *Monitor* frequently publishes special regional sections. Christian Scientists painstakingly contribute articles about their localities to these special editions.

The editors like to tell stories of their volunteer contributors' zeal for accuracy. In a special edition devoted to the Northwest, a *Christian Science Monitor* reader sent in an article on the work of the Girl Scouts in her area. It was set in type and placed in one of the special pages. Just before the edition was to go to press, the contributor telegraphed: "Please hold up story on Girl Scout activities. Error discovered. Letter follows."

The editor in charge of the edition, rereading the article, was puzzled; he could see nothing that would justify such drastic action. To make sure, however, he had the article withdrawn and the special edition went to press without it. In an air-mail letter that arrived a day later, the contributor explained that in her copy she had written that the cookies sold by the Girl Scouts were round, whereas actually they were oblong. That, the *Monitor* editors knew, could happen only on the *Monitor*.

Average Man's Columnist

(RAYMOND C. CLAPPER)

By OTTO FUERBRINGER

EDITOR'S PREFACE.—To the great loss of the profession of journalism—and the emphasis is on the word *profession*—and to the grief of the thousands who had come to rely on his unpretentious but usually sound reportorial and interpretative articles, Raymond Clapper was killed in an airplane crash during the invasion of the Marshall Islands early in 1944.

The official announcement of the death of the then 51-year-old correspondent, who had left his Washington headquarters in January, 1944, for a first-hand view of the Pacific war, as released in the New York *Times* of February 4, 1944, read:

"The Commander in Chief of the Pacific Fleet has reported that a plane, in which Raymond Clapper was a passenger, engaged in covering the Marshall invasions, collided with another plane while forming up. Mr. Clapper was in the plane with the squadron commander. Both planes crashed in the lagoon. There were no survivors."

Essentially a political commentator, Mr. Clapper, as the war progressed, de-emphasized politics in his writing so as to focus his commentaries increasingly on the human side of the war. Before going to the Pacific, he had spent a part of 1943 in the Mediterranean theatre and was aboard an American plane in the first bombing of Rome. This particular mission carried him to Sweden, England, and the battlefields of Africa and Sicily. Mr. Clapper's first trip overseas during World War II was to England before Pearl Harbor. Shortly after the United States entered the war, he flew to Cairo, Calcutta, and Chungking.

Mr. Clapper was the sixteenth American correspondent to lose his life in World War II. When news of his death reached this country, many in high places paid tribute to

him both as a man and as a reporter. President Franklin
D. Roosevelt, in a personal letter to Mrs. Clapper, said:

"The tragic event which has brought such sorrow to you
and the children emphasizes once more the constant peril
in which correspondents do their work in this war. It was
characteristic of Ray's fidelity to the great traditions of
reporting that the day's work should find him at the scene
of action for first-hand facts in the thick of the fight.

"I share personally the grief which has been laid so
heavily on you and yours and offer this assurance of heartfelt sympathy, in which Mrs. Roosevelt joins."

The secretary of state, Cordell Hull, issued the following statement:

"I have just learned of the tragic death of Mr. Raymond
Clapper. I was privileged to know Mr. Clapper as a friend
over a long period of years and held him in the highest
esteem. He was one of our most eminent and distinguished
journalists who earned the confidence and respect of the
American people."

Other public officials and many newspapers and newspaper men were high in their praise of the departed columnist. The New York *Times* said that he "contributed in
his widely syndicated column what were generally accepted as among the most objective, tolerant and understanding views on national and foreign affairs of any of
the political writers."

One of Mr. Clapper's last columns, dated "Somewhere
in New Guinea, January 26," contained the following
which some will regard as a premonition and others simply as a good human interest paragraph:

"Just about every individual has some religious charm
or other good-luck token. I'm not a religious man but I
find myself frequently taking out a tiny brown bear which
my daughter gave me as I was leaving last year for the
European theatre. Over here seven war correspondents
have been killed, most in the last few months, and I never
get in a plane any more without checking with the little
brown bear."

Although much of the following article is in the present
tense, it should be remembered that the present in this instance is 1943. From an editorial standpoint, it seemed best
not to tamper with tenses in reprinting this particular
biography, the chief significance of which now is as journalistic history.

November 6, 1943

A LANDMARK in the history of American journalism was reached in January, 1942, when columnist Raymond Clapper told his readers that he knew nothing about military affairs. This was a rank violation of the unwritten canons of columning, which require that a columnist, at all times and on all topics, be infallibly wise. Had there been a Columnists' Guild, the miscreant would unquestionably have been summoned before a board of inquiry and given, at the very least, a stiff warning never to do it again.

The column in which Clapper had the temerity to declare his ignorance concerned the Owen J. Roberts' report on the unpreparedness of Pearl Harbor. Clapper rarely gets more than mildly ruffled in print. This document made him boil. "As I read the report," he wrote, "I keep thinking that would be a hell of a way to run a newspaper. I don't know anything about military affairs. But I have been around a newspaper office all my life, and I never saw a newsroom that was as slack or sloppy as the Roberts report shows the Navy and Army to have been at Pearl Harbor."

This talent for freely admitting the gaps in his knowledge, but writing warmly or informingly about what he does know, has lifted Clapper to top rank in the chancy business of columning, given him an income very near six figures, and recently enabled him to pass his colleague Westbrook Pegler in both the number of papers and the readership of the papers in which their respective columns are published. Clapper appears in 180 papers with a circulation of 10,000,000; Pegler in 175 with a circulation of 8,800,000. As a "think" columnist, Clapper surpasses all his rivals in the extent of his audience. Closest to him is Walter Lippmann with 138 papers. Clapper's added appearances on the radio make his total potential audience far greater than that of any other columnist commentator except those who deal in gossip and chitchat.

The Clapper technique, permitting him to carry on his education in public, appeals particularly to those who dislike the thundering omniscience of other columnists. Reasonably well-informed readers can feel that Clapper is telling them something they should know largely because he has the same curiosity as they, but is closer to the sources of information. The personal observations he makes on the news are grounded on an upbringing in a thoroughly devout Baptist home in Kansas plus years as a conscientious newsman in Kansas City, Chicago, Minneapolis and Washington. He has been called "the average man's columnist" and he rather likes that appellation.

Another axiom of columning, almost as strong as the tenet of infallibility, is that a columnist should not change his habits of thinking, at least not too violently. Faithful readers of a columnist have a right to foresee how he will react to a given topic, just as these readers could once demand the same from newspaper editorial pages—which the columnists have made the great unread section of American journalism. But Clapper, again throwing tradition aside, made reams of copy out of his conversion from an isolationist to an interventionist. True to his Midwestern background, he had taken a rather sour view of Europe's troubles, until Munich changed his mind. Long before Pearl Harbor, he was writing pieces which only the most devout interventionists could applaud. Chided for the change, Clapper admitted his dereliction in public. "Yes, I have switched," he wrote. "I try to learn from events. Events have not been consistent, so why should I?"

Clapper has always shied away from doing his punditing in an ivory tower. Unlike gossip columnists, he has no list of tipsters who pass along choice items to him, for either a fee or a favor. Since he hews to no special political line, he is not the recipient of special bits of news from Washington bigwigs, either in or out of the Administration. A Clapper column never floats a trial balloon.

Clapper does more of his own leg work than any other columnist, and he finds out what he wants to know rather than what people want to tell him. This applies to Washington as well as to other parts of the world. Since 1937, Clapper has made four extended trips outside the United States: to England and Russia in 1937, again to England in 1941, to the

Middle East, India and China in 1942, and, most recently, to Sweden, England and the battlefields of North Africa and Sicily. He has seen more of the world in recent years than any rival columnist. Each trip has been followed by a substantial boost in the Clapper clientele.

Clapper is a newspaperman's newspaperman. Washington correspondents, who are not given to log-rolling, voted him their favorite columnist in a poll taken by Sociologist Leo Rosten for his book, *The Washington Correspondents*. Their verdict was that Clapper is the "most significant, fair and reliable" among the columning fraternity in the nation's capital. The late Heywood Broun once nominated him as the man he would like to see as head of a School of Practical Politics. Columnist Pegler, never prodigal with nosegays, has several times anointed Clapper as the most intelligent of Washington reporters. And Quincy Howe, a rival radio commentator, gave him the ultimate accolade: "He does not believe that God has summoned him personally to save the American people."

Such praise has its basis in the fact that Clapper is an acute, hard-driving reporter who does not over-dramatize himself or his work. American reporters are apt to look with a slightly jaundiced eye upon those of their number who always tell, or attempt to tell, the inside story. Too often, the inside story is offbeat, and none know it better than the other reporters. Clapper has never attempted to give his readers the hot lowdown; in fact, he probably has fewer outright scoops to his credit than any other top reporter. Yet his critics cannot say that he has ever been behind the news.

Clapper's popularity with members of his own craft was directly responsible for his branching out on a national scale. In 1933, when he was night manager of the United Press Bureau in Washington, he decided that any further rise in journalism he could make would be as a writer, not as an executive. He had begun some free-lance writing for magazines, and was working on a book based on a series of stories he had written for U. P. about petty graft in the capital, such as nepotism among Federal officials and absurd padding of expense accounts. His subordinates in the U. P. office recall that Clapper, conscientious about his job, never worked on his book on company time; he returned to the office each night after dinner and pecked away at his typewriter.

The book had the misfortune to be published late in 1933, at a time when the New Deal had begun throwing out billions for relief and rehabilitation. No one seemed to be interested in reading about a mysterious five dollars in a senator's expense account. The book, although it had the come-on title *Racketeering in Washington,* brought Clapper the handsome sum of sixty-five dollars. And a sharp notice from higher-ups in the U. P. that United Press men were to do no outside work. Clapper, who is the mildest of souls, was also disturbed because a general U. P. retrenchment forced him to fire a half dozen of his staff. Banker Eugene Meyer had just bought the moribund Washington *Post* and was looking for talent. Clapper went to him and was hired at $12,000—$2000 more than his U. P. salary—to head the *Post's* capital bureau.

Within a year, at the suggestion of Assistant General Manager Mark Ethridge, now general manager of the Louisville *Courier-Journal,* Clapper began writing a column on national affairs. It was called "Between You and Me," and for several months it got no noticeable response at all. Finally, Clapper returned home one night with an appreciative fan letter from a person who obviously understood what he was trying to do. He read it aloud at the dinner table, but his wife and two children seemed embarrassed rather than pleased. Clapper learned he was the victim of a hoax. His daughter Janet, then ten, was the understanding letter writer.

Clapper's superior knowledge of Washington soon made itself felt, however, and before his two-year contract with the *Post* had run out, the Scripps-Howard organization, which controls United Press, was begging him to return to the fold. He did, at $15,000 a year, and began writing a daily column for the twenty-four papers in the Scripps-Howard chain. A year later George Carlin, a hardheaded character who runs the United Feature Syndicate, suddenly realized that the columnist he was reading most often was Raymond Clapper, a writer who did not happen to be in his or any other syndicate's stable. Carlin sought to sign Clapper up.

Carlin, who sells comics as well as columns, looks at writers with a strictly commercial eye. His first thought when he appraises a prospective addition to his stable is, Does he have box-office appeal? Carlin thought that Clapper lacked this quality, but felt confident that it could be built up with a battery of press agents. When he approached Clapper with this plan, he found him eager to expand his column, but insistent that he not be exploited as a hot tipster or one who would give the lowdown. Carlin added Clapper to his list anyway.

The column had slow going at first, but it built itself up gradually. From a commercial viewpoint, Clapper is looked upon as a steady article, not a flash or quick seller, but one which will return profits over the long pull. That is what Carlin felt, and he turned out to be right. The success of Clapper is the triumph of the solid, unspectacular man.

As an apprentice in a Kansas City, Missouri, print shop some thirty years ago, young Ray Clapper felt, as has many a dreaming and ambitious reporter before and since, that he would like to own his own small-town newspaper and say what he pleased. The success of William Allen White, Henry Allen, and Ed Howe, all owners of small-town Kansas newspapers with an influence far beyond their own confines, was strong upon the young printer. Somewhere along the way, Clapper discarded this project. But he feels now, with some justification, that he has achieved his aim in double measure. He can say what he pleases to a ready-made national audience, and without the bother of worrying about the ads, getting the linotype machines fixed and keeping a paper alive.

Clapper has been censored only once. When debate over the New Deal's reorganization bill was hot and heavy, he wrote a column plainly showing his disgust with the fight being made against the bill on the ground that it would entrench President Roosevelt as a dictator. Clapper, plainly in favor of the bill, pointed out that it was but a slightly warmed-over proposal from the Hoover Administration. When his column appeared in the New York *World-Telegram,* fountainhead of all Scripps-Howard papers, which were hammering away at the bill, it had been edited to such an extent that it gave the impression that Clapper, too, opposed the measure. Clapper promptly wrote another column for the following day, restating his position in terms no less strong. The *World-Telegram* just omitted that column. Proponents of the bill began circulating photostatic copies of the first Clapper column as it had appeared in other papers and as it had been edited by the *World-Telegram.* The futility of the censorship soon showed itself, and the incident passed over without further public quarrel. Clapper and Roy Howard, the diminutive head of Scripps-Howard, by no means see eye to eye on all questions. Howard has gulped mightily at Clapper approval of some New Deal measures. Relations between the two men, however, except for the one instance, have rarely been strained. Howard respects Clapper as a searching reporter who says what he thinks; Clapper respects Howard as a publisher who, more than many another, permits his columnists free rein.

Clapper was born of parents of Pennsylvania-Dutch stock on a farm near a small Kansas town which some pioneer with a little knowledge of French had misnamed La Cygne. There was no swanlike beauty about the town, or about the Clapper farm, for that matter. The elder Clapper promptly failed at farming and moved to Kansas City, Kansas, where he worked first in a slaughter house and then in a soap factory.

Young Ray, like any other son of poor parents, went to work early, selling the old Kansas City *World* on street corners. Kansas was then, as now, a dry state. But Kansas City, catering to the drovers and livestock men, had its share of saloons. Clapper recalls that most of his newspaper earnings were spent in these saloons, not for beer, but for choice hamburger sandwiches, made from freshly killed Kansas City steer.

By the time he was in high school, young Clapper had a job as delivery boy for a grocery run by a Mr. Ewing. The grocer, who lived above his store, had a daughter, Olive, who used to annoy Clapper by playing the piano. The Ewings, like the Clappers, were strict Baptists. Young Clapper and Olive Ewing finally met at Christian Endeavor. Ray was twenty, Olive seventeen. Their respective parents had strong objections to their going together. Once, when Ray and Olive came to the Clapper home to play an innocent game of checkers, they found that the checkers had been burned in the kitchen stove. Finally, Olive's parents laid down the law: one more date with Ray Clapper and she would be packed off to visit a maiden aunt.

The next morning, Olive, accompanied by her younger sister, met Ray on the streetcar going to high school. She communicated the ultimatum; whereupon the young couple gave Olive's sister the slip, hopped off the car, and scoured around for a justice of the peace. Almost at the altar, Ray suddenly discovered that Olive still had her schoolbooks under her arm. She hastily dumped them on the public-library steps. Years later, she found that they had duly been made part of the library's collection.

Ray had been working after school at a print shop in Kansas City, Missouri, run by two elderly ladies who published a weekly paper patterned after William Marion Reedy's *Mirror*. He and his wife now quit school and Ray took a full-time job at the print shop, working up to a journeyman printer. The Clappers moved to a two-room apartment, where their most treasured piece of furniture was a small filing cabinet in which Ray had already started to keep notes. He longed to be a writer, but as a responsible young husband felt he should settle down at a trade. He used $200 of his savings to make a down payment on a bungalow, which he bought from a contractor's blueprint.

But before the house was finished, Ray had misgivings about the printer's trade. Coming home one afternoon from work, he announced to his bride that the thing to do was for both of them to go to college. They let the contractor keep his $200 and hitch-hiked sixty miles to Lawrence, seat of the state uni-

versity. Although neither Ray nor Olive had been graduated
from high school, they wangled their way into college as special students. Ray entered the journalism department, which
was then headed by Merle Thorpe, now editor of *The Nation's
Business*. Thorpe got Ray a job as campus correspondent for
the Kansas City *Star*. Olive did her share toward household
expenses by traveling back to Kansas City every week end to
give piano lessons. At the university, Clapper is best remembered for having yanked the chancellor out of bed at two
o'clock one morning to ask his comment on a news story.

Three years of college were enough for Clapper. He was
anxious to get into full-time newspaper work and took a job
with the *Star*. Covering police stations, fires and hotel lobbies
was fun, but when he saw Roy Roberts, then the *Star's* Washington correspondent and now its managing editor, come
home for vacation, he knew what he wanted. Being a Washington correspondent seemed the best job of all to Clapper.
Although he liked the *Star's* progressive attitude and clublike
atmosphere, he knew that staying with the *Star*, which had one
Washington correspondent, and a healthy one at that, was not
the way to get to the nation's capital. He signed up with
United Press, which sent him to Chicago.

The Clappers were a deadly serious young couple and
thought solemnly about remaking the world. In Chicago,
Mrs. Clapper enrolled for training as a social worker. Before
she had completed the course, Ray was transferred to Minneapolis. Finally, in 1917, came the break to go to Washington.

Clapper, who on some occasions describes himself as a 75-
per-cent New Dealer and on others as a progressive Republican, owes a good deal of his success to such an Old Guard
Republican as Warren G. Harding. It was on Harding's nomination for President in Chicago in 1920 that Clapper got his
first big scoop. Prowling around the corridors of the Black-
stone Hotel at three o'clock one morning, he ran into Charles
Curtis, then a senator from Kansas, who had just emerged
from George Harvey's now-famous smoke-filled room. "They're
going to try to put over Senator Harding," Curtis told Clap-

per. When the U. P. morning wire opened a few hours later, Clapper had a clean beat, although the story went out, as was the custom, under the by-line of the top U. P. man covering the convention.

Clapper's reward was an assignment to cover Harding's front-porch campaign, a task which required little work but an acute skill at playing pitch. Harding, he recalls, was the world's worst pitch player. Two nights before the election, Clapper received an order to get a final election statement from Harding for the United Press. He took the request to "Dutch" Welliver, Harding's publicity director. Welliver was up to his ears in work and told Clapper to write it himself. Having listened over and over to Harding's two or three stock campaign speeches, Clapper found this an easy task. He dashed off a brief statement exuding confidence, ending with the phrase: "The heart of the nation is sound." This bit of ghost writing, the only Clapper has ever done, endeared him to Harding for the rest of the President's life. Harding's first official dinner after he entered the White House was for the correspondents who had covered his campaign. The twenty-nine-year-old Clapper sat at the President's left.

Today, at fifty-one, Clapper is slightly paunchy, slightly stoop-shouldered, but as energetic a leg man as the campus correspondent who roused the chancellor in the early-morning hours. He has a large head and thick tousled hair, which, together with his sloping shoulders, gives him the appearance of a bear. Pictures taken with a flash bulb, which accentuate the dark circles under his eyes, give him somewhat of a panda look. He spends most of his mornings traipsing around Washington, interviewing officials, looking in at press conferences, checking his sources. His column is written between two and five in the afternoon in the office of the Washington *Daily News,* a Scripps-Howard paper. Used to working under pressure, he writes quickly and easily, once he has settled on his topic. He doesn't torture his phrases.

Almost his only recreation is taking long walks on Saturdays, when he has no column to grind out for the following day.

Like most Washingtonians, he spends some time at Delaware's Rehoboth Beach; and it was here, one summer day in 1941, that he got a call from Mutual Broadcasting Company asking him to take on a twice-a-week news broadcast. Mutual wanted him to step into Raymond Gram Swing's place, as Swing was shifting to the Blue Network. He took the job and also the usual short, intensive course in voice training. After a year of broadcasting, with a short humming period preceding each microphone appearance, his voice now comes out as a pleasant Kansas twang, which in a way is a bit of an asset. Clapper's radio sponsor is the White Owl Cigar Company, a fact which has subjected him to a certain amount of ribbing ever since he stopped smoking. At a recent dinner tendered by the White Owl company, he got a series of dirty looks when he refused the after-dinner cigar. He explained it by saying he wanted to keep his voice clear for the broadcast.

The radio program brings Clapper in the neighborhood of $40,000 a year. Earnings from his column, made up of his base pay from Scripps-Howard, bonuses from Scripps-Howard and commissions from United Feature Syndicate, about equal the radio salary. Checks for articles and reprints of his column send his income close to $100,000.

Just before the war stopped home-building altogether, the Clappers completed a new house in the Spring Valley section of the District of Columbia. Like many suburban developments, Spring Valley is a restricted section, in which the original promoters exercise the right to pass upon every new dwelling. Until then it had had nothing more than the usual conglomeration of eclectic architectural styles. The Clappers gave the promoters quite a start by proposing to build a "modern" home, costing $50,000. The Clappers won out, but they have had to take considerable abuse from the neighbors, who consider the house an unsightly box. To Alf Landon, it looked "New Dealish." After further needling, Clapper finally set down his thoughts about his home. As well as anything, they express the Clapper philosophy:

"It seemed silly to waste money in useless gables and

dormers when we could square the house out, take full advantage of all space and get a more livable house for our money. We have no plantation nor any slaves, so it hardly seemed appropriate to imitate Mount Vernon. We have no personal roots in New England, so there was no urge to copy a colonial design from the North. We both come from Kansas, like wide-open spaces, and, since we had a lot which gave us that, we thought it appropriate to place a house on it which gave us room, light and air in full measure. It just seemed common sense.

"I am naturally conservative, but neither of us has any undue respect for traditions that seem no longer to serve a useful purpose. That is my viewpoint about public affairs and it is the viewpoint with which we went into house-building. The results have been much to our satisfaction."

How to be a Cartoonist

(JAY NORWOOD "DING" DARLING)

By TOM MAHONEY

EDITOR'S PREFACE.—The value of the cartoon as a means of journalistic interpretation is very great, and the place of Jay Norwood ("Ding") Darling among the cartoonists of his time is very high.

The potency of the cartoon has been the subject of comment and praise by many high in journalistic, academic, and political circles. Dr. Albert Shaw, whose *American Review of Reviews* featured a regular department called "Cartoons of the Month," said that these cartoons were used "not merely because they are diverting and amusing, but chiefly because they express so much fact, sentiment, and point of view in such telling and convincing ways. . . . Cartoons (reflect) the opinion of the world . . . more briefly and more vividly than words." C. R. Ashbee, in his *Caricature,* notes that "the cartoon tells us what that important fellow, The Man in the Street, is thinking about. Moreover, it tells The Man in the Street himself what he is thinking about. Kings, priests, and press may fail in the interpretation of the moment to the ordinary man, but not the great caricaturist. . . . [He] can therefore play a large part in forming public opinion." Abraham Lincoln is credited with saying that Nast was his "best recruiting sergeant."

Two recent books and their commentaries on the cartoon should be mentioned and recommended here: *A Century of Political Cartoons: Caricature in the United States from 1800 to 1900* (Scribner's) by Allan Nevins, professor of American history, Columbia University, and Frank Weitenkampf, curator of prints, retired, New York Public Library; and *Cartoon Cavalcade: A Collection of the Best American Humorous Cartoons from the Turn of the Century to the Present* (Simon and Schuster) edited by Thomas Craven, assisted by Florence and Sydney Weiss.

Both of these contain much shrewd analysis of the appeals and values of the cartoon. Messrs. Nevins and Weitenkampf, for example, think that the requirements of a really good political cartoon are these:

1. Wit and humor—"This should be smart and flashing, not a mere broad comic effect obtained by exaggeration. . . ."

2. Truth—"or at least one side of the truth. The characters depicted must be instantly recognizable likenesses, personal idiosyncrasies not too heavily distorted. The situation presented must possess at least a rough fidelity to fact. . . ."

3. Moral purpose—"The monarchs of British and American caricature . . . were all men of strong convictions. It is such men who in the end have the deepest, most convincing influence. . . ."

The word *caricature,* Mr. Ashbee says, "comes from the Italian *caricare*—to overload or drag a weight just a little heavier than our vehicle can carry. Here we have the very essence of the method of caricature—exaggeration which, with simplification, brings home the point."

Both the Nevins-Weitenkampf and the Craven books speak in praise of the work of "Ding." In the first, he is mentioned among the moderns referred to in the following passage:

"Into changing times the great tradition of caricature marches on . . . and will doubtless die only when the human race dies. We have American cartoonists today who need take no shame in comparison with their predecessors. . . ."

Mr. Craven has several references to "Ding," one of which places him among "the old-timers [who] stuck to the newspapers, creating an art of and for the people."

October 19, 1940

IF A Yankee genius named Lamarcus Thompson had not invented the roller coaster, Jay Norwood ("Ding") Darling might not be a famous cartoonist today. Thompson and Jay's father, the Rev. Marc Warner Darling, a Congregationalist minister, were friends a generation ago. When the inventor went to England to build Europe's first roller coaster, he mailed back a "Pat and Mike" card.

The Irishmen were drawn as ditch diggers, and Mike said:

"Pat, I wish I was a bishop. It's a clane, easy business, I'm thinkin'." As the inventor had long called the minister "the bishop," the latter laughed at the drawing. He laughed so much that his younger son, Jay, who witnessed the mirth, decided that there must be something in cartooning, and began to draw.

He has been drawing ever since, for forty very full years. But cartooning is not his only distinction. He is also noted as the foremost defender in America of the wild duck, a friend of six Presidents, a man who has read his own obituary, and an individual who prefers to live in Des Moines, Iowa, when he could live in New York City. He is further remarkable as the only editorial cartoonist to earn something like a million dollars with his pen.

Jay was only eight when he copied the "Pat and Mike" sketch, and neither he nor anyone else sensed the significance of the step for many years. He regarded drawing as a hobby to be pursued between periods of pipe-organ pumping, which today makes him a member of the Guild of Former Pipe Organ Pumpers, and other chores of a small-town minister's son. Jay started, but did not complete, a correspondence-school course in art and, though he filled his books with them, his drawings were not deemed of enough merit to revise the plans for his becoming a doctor like his red-faced Uncle Frank, of Jamestown, New York.

His first cartoon to gain notice outside the Darling family was drawn in the Beta Theta Pi fraternity house during Jay's junior year at Beloit College, in Wisconsin. It was an innocent representation of the school faculty as a line of ballet girls, but its appearance in the *Codex*, the school annual, caused Jay's suspension for a whole year and delayed his graduation until 1900.

This Beloit drawing was signed "Ding," which disproves the story that this signature resulted from a printer's abbreviation. His father and brother Frank were called "Ding" before him and the nickname became his in college. After some experimenting with longer forms of his name, he made it famous as a cartoon signature.

After graduation Ding went to work as a combination reporter, photographer and cartoonist on the *Journal* in Sioux City, Iowa, where a change in pastorates had shifted his father. It was supposed to be a temporary job before medical school, but fate in the form of an irate lawyer ruled otherwise. The lawyer caned an opponent in the courtroom and, when no photograph was available, Ding turned out such an effective drawing of the incident that the managing editor decided to let him draw a daily cartoon.

As local subjects became exhausted, Ding began to cartoon national events, state politics and human-interest subjects. He recorded the first airplane flight with a cartoon of the Wright brothers soaring past two eagles. When George D. Perkins, publisher of the *Journal,* ran for governor, Darling valiantly supported him with cartoons and, though Perkins was beaten, the Ding cartoons won fame beyond Sioux City.

A lack of faith in the idea that two can live as cheaply as one caused Darling, then thirty, to think of a wider field. The girl was Genevieve Pendleton, a judge's daughter; and, while they were honeymooning in the West Indies in 1906, opportunity knocked in the form of a telegram from the Des Moines *Register & Leader* offering him a job on the paper now famous as the Des Moines *Register.*

Darling took the job, and for the subject of his first Des Moines cartoon chose the city's smoke. He drew a fat monk, labeled Des Moines, puffing clouds of black smoke from a pipe marked soft coal, being sketched by a long-legged artist. A line announced: "Ding begins his work of cartooning Des Moines." The cartoon provoked a storm of protest.

Those who failed to object to the drawing of the priest on the ground of taste assailed it as a matter of accuracy. Darling had been under the impression that the name Des Moines was derived from the French word meaning monk. Better authorities say that the name of the Iowa capital came from an Indian word meaning salt.

"Des Moines still hasn't learned anything about abating its smoke nuisance," mused Darling recently.

America's social and political history can be traced in Ding cartoons as well as history books. Early telephone service was ridiculed with drawings of masked robbers who took away a householder's furniture and residence before he could obtain the police number. Another depicted the frailty of early automobile tires with a motorist trading his tires for cantaloupes and rolling happily away on the latter.

There was a light series of drawings titled "The Education of Alonzo Applegate." Alonzo was a long-haired farm youth who had college experiences like those of Darling at Beloit. Cartoons showed Alonzo being hazed, failing examinations, suffering in football, and joining a fraternity. Alonzo was interested for a time by boys who sang, "You must be a loyal Sigma Chi or you won't go to heaven when you die," but the college widow pledged him for Darling's fraternity by saying: "You are too nice a man to be anything but a Beta Theta Pi."

Darling's character, "the Iowa farmer," was discovered in this period. The cartoonist looked up one day to see Samuel H. Cook, of Van Meter, Iowa, a farm-implement dealer, standing in the door. Cook had never been a farmer, but he was a commanding figure, six feet tall, and looked more like a farmer to Darling than any farmer he knew. Cook died in 1932, but still lives in Ding cartoons.

By 1911, Darling's work was being reprinted all over the country and he was offered a job in New York by George Matthew Adams, who was forming a syndicate connected with the now defunct New York *Globe*.

The Darlings moved to New York and Ding joined a rare collection of geniuses in the syndicate's art department in the Singer Building. Darling and H. T. Webster, creator of "The Timid Soul," reported for work the same day. The staff included Percy Crosby, producer of "Skippy"; Frank Moser, famous as an animator of movie cartoons, and Harry Baker, an office boy who grew up to be an editor of International News Photos and more recently picture editor of *PM,* the new New York daily.

To the office also came one day an awkward nineteen-year-old boy fresh from San Francisco in an army shirt and trousers cuffed halfway to the knee. Distrusting subways, he had trudged many blocks with a bundle of sports cartoons. These impressed no artist in the office except Ding, who was enthusiastic over a certain boldness of stroke in a sketch of a baseball player. "The boy's got something," Darling told the syndicate manager. "Hire him for six months and I will guarantee his salary," Darling did not have to pay. The youth was Robert L. (Believe It Or Not) Ripley, destined to become one of the highest paid newspaper artists of all time.

A now forgotten tragedy descended on Darling. Soon after the birth of his second child, a daughter, who is now Mrs. Richard Browne Koss, he began mysteriously to lose the use of his right hand. Doctors were baffled, but Darling refused to give up. When only the fingers were affected he put the pen in them and pushed his right hand over the board with his left. He then discarded the pen in favor of a brush. As the right arm became completely useless, he began to draw with his left hand. After two years of struggle, a surgeon solved the mystery. As a boy, Darling had broken a bone in his elbow in a fall and it had been set improperly, years later causing the ulnar nerve to be pinched. An operation, moving the nerve from one side of the arm to the other, almost miraculously restored the use of the hand.

The experience soured Ding on New York and, a failure in the eyes of metropolitan journalism, he moved back to Des Moines in 1913 and, except for brief excursions, has lived there ever since. His restored right arm and the opportunities afforded the cartoonist by the World War soon caused New York to revise its estimate of Ding. While some diplomats were still vacationing, he forecast the conflict in a cartoon showing a hunter labeled Austria aiming a gun at a Serbian rabbit in front of a dynamite storehouse. This and other war cartoons so impressed the late Clinton W. Gilbert, then an idea man on the New York *Tribune,* that, in 1917, though still allowed to live in Des Moines, Darling became editorial cartoonist for the *Tribune* and its syndicate.

A few days after Darling signed this contract, he produced

one of his most famous cartoons on the death of Col. W. F. "Buffalo Bill" Cody. The frontiersman was depicted bidding three little children good-bye while a long wagon train rolled into the clouds. The caption was "Gone to Join the Mysterious Caravan." On the death of his personal idol, Theodore Roosevelt, Ding produced his most famous cartoon to date. The Rough Rider was drawn as a shadowy, mounted cowboy waving his hat in a farewell salute as covered wagons rolled into the distance. The caption was "The Long, Long Trail," from the title of the song then on the lips of America. This cartoon is still reproduced on Roosevelt anniversaries. Bronze reproductions of it hang in Roosevelt High School of Des Moines and in the lobby of the Roosevelt Hotel in New York.

During the jazz age Darling drew some cartoons deriding elders who criticized the young, but some antics of prejitterbug youth did not please him. Thus was born the cartoon "In Good Old U. S. A." Strips illustrated these captions: "An orphan at eight is now one of the world's greatest mining engineers" "The son of a plasterer is now the world's greatest neurologist" "A printer's apprentice is now chief executive of the United States." A final strip said: "But they didn't get there by hanging around the corner drugstore." The fact that Ding was in error by two years as to the orphaning of Herbert Hoover, who was drawn in the first strip, did not prevent the cartoon receiving the Pulitzer Prize as the best American cartoon of the year.

Darling received more proof of the country's regard in 1925, when he collapsed in his office and lay for a month at the point of death with peritonitis. His family was summoned. Newspapers everywhere set his obituary in type, obtained comments from notables, and awaited the fatal bulletin.

But Darling refused to die. On the day that the Iowa Senate passed a resolution wishing him a speedy recovery, he began to get well and was soon laughing over proofs of his own obituaries. Some of the material that had been prepared was of much interest to him.

Herbert Hoover, for example, said: "Mr. Darling's death takes from us a great contributor to our daily life. His insight into national life lifted his cartoons into the high rank of great and trenchant editorials. His kindliness and humor were but the reflections of his own character." Among other things, President Coolidge, whom Darling has already outlived by many years, said: "The country has sustained the loss of a lovable personality and an outstanding figure."

Ding's illness softened Beloit College, which had suspended him as a student, into giving him an honorary degree of Doctor of Letters as "a son of Beloit, cartoonist, journalist, national interpreter of current events, bringing to play upon the shifting developments in public affairs the kindly satire of his discerning mind, a loyal upholder of the best in American traditions." The Beloit chapter of Phi Beta Kappa, a body quite remote from Darling as a student, elected him to honorary membership. More important, only one of the 100 newspapers for which he drew canceled his cartoon during his illness.

Income-tax litigation at this time revealed that Darling was receiving an annual salary of $26,000, plus a 50 per cent commission on sales of his cartoons over $11,700 a quarter, which worked out to a total of nearly $100,000 for many years. In addition, he has income from stock in the Des Moines *Register and Tribune,* one of the Iowa insurance companies and other enterprises.

Though all Presidents from Roosevelt to Roosevelt, inclusive, have been sensitive to Ding cartoons, the cartoonist enjoyed unique distinctions during the regime of his friend, Herbert Hoover. President Hoover asked for many of the originals and actually had the White House placed on the syndicate's mailing list, so that he could see cartoons without waiting for newspapers. The fact that Darling was then training his understudy, Tom Carlisle, and sometimes completed cartoons started by the latter bothered President Hoover. He asked Darling to place a special mark on the cartoons that he had conceived and drawn entirely by himself. This resulted in a little *x* after the Ding signature. Though Hoover has long since left the White House, his *x* survives in the cartoons.

So intimate had Darling been with Hoover that it was one of the surprises of the New Deal when Pres. Franklin D. Roosevelt named the cartoonist Chief of the Biological Survey, and Darling accepted the post. Though some saw in this a sinister Democratic move to stop a critical Republican pen, Darling regarded it, at least at the start, as an opportunity to do something for a cause in which he is deeply interested.

"The cartoonist's best friend," he once explained, "is any animal—dog, wolf, or what have you. There's the Republican elephant, the Democratic donkey, the Tammany tiger, the American eagle, the Russian bear, the dry camel, the pessimistic buzzard sitting on a fence, the rats of corruption, the gorilla of ignorance, the wolf at the door, the cat with the nine lives, the hare and the tortoise, the British lion, the mouse that gnawed the rope, and the goose that laid the golden egg."

But Darling has more than a drawing-board interest in wild life. He hunted and fished as a boy and thinks that future generations should have a chance to do likewise. Since the World War he has fought actively for game preservation and restoration. His work as chairman of the recreation committee of the Des Moines City Planning Commission won him the city's 1929 Community Award as its most useful citizen. He headed the Iowa Conservation Association, served on the Iowa Fish and Game Commission and gave $9000 to Iowa State College for the study of wild-life conservation.

"Ducks can't lay eggs on a picket fence," says Darling. "There should be a puddle for every duck."

With this as his program Darling took charge of the Biological Survey, refurnished the office at his own expense, and fought for the ducks. For converting submarginal farm land into wild-life refuges, he obtained first $1,000,000 and later $8,500,000, largest appropriations in the history of the Biological Survey. To provide additional funds, he designed a one-dollar duck stamp, showing two mallards in flight, which hunters were required to affix to state hunting licenses before shooting migratory wild fowl. The migratory season was cut from sixty to thirty days. Live decoys were barred, a three-shell limit was placed on repeating shotguns, and shooting over baited ground was prohibited. Darling had to convince some sportsmen of the wisdom of the regulations with personal letters, often illustrated by a special cartoon.

Darling's ducks, however, had many rivals for the Administration's attention. Lands which he wanted to flood, somebody else wanted to drain. Streams like the Columbia River, which he believed should be preserved for fish, were chosen for what he called "cockeyed water-power projects." Meanwhile, the $8000-a-year salary of the job did not replace the money that he was losing by neglecting his cartooning. In 1935 he resigned.

Darling continued his role as "the prophet, Nestor and evangelist" of conservation by uniting, in 1936, representatives of America's 36,000 wild-life societies in a national body, the General Wild Life Federation, of which he was unanimously chosen president.

Darling draws cartoons and has headquarters for his wildlife campaign in an unmarked office on an upper floor of the *Register and Tribune* Building, in Des Moines. A reception room outside in which two secretaries work is decorated with the original drawings of John T. McCutcheon, Rollin Kirby and other cartoonists. On the basis of a poll conducted by *Editor & Publisher,* the newspaper trade journal, as part of the celebration of its fiftieth anniversary, Darling's popularity with newspaper editors exceeds that of any of these rivals. Asked to name their favorite cartoonist of the last half century, the country's editors put Ding at the top of a list of twenty-seven cartoonists.

"I fancy," Darling has said in explaining his art, "that in its inception, the cartoon set out to be a sort of humor-coated capsule, by means of which the sober judgments of editorial minds might be surreptitiously gotten down the throats of an apathetic public. In other words, the cartoon was the applesauce in which political pills were buried and fed to unwilling children.

"The cartoonist absorbs all of the information, facts and emotions of passing events he can hold and daily puts himself in the stewpan, starts the fire, and boils and boils, in the hope that out of the concentrated solution he may coax a little crystal which, while embodying the ingredients of the whole, will catch the eye with its glint and be picked up and carried home."

When he has a cartoon idea visualized, Darling works rapidly, making faces as he draws. When giving shape to a laughing character, he laughs himself. If a figure on the drawing board leers, Darling leers too. Like an actor, he throws himself into the task of the moment without bothering much with minor details and technicalities.

"I was rebuked for putting teeth in the mouth of a vegetarian whale," Darling recalls. "Carpenters write in when I leave floor girders unsupported, and if I have the sparks flying the wrong way from a grindstone, the whole machinists' union protests."

Boners would be more numerous in the cartoons but for the vigilance of Earl J. Beeson, an extremely well-informed engraver, who for years has been turning the drawings into metal. Beeson takes keen delight in tossing back inaccurate panels.

Darling finds the public today is more tolerant and broadminded than formerly. Cartoons are applauded now which could not have been published in the past. Darling turns out, like most cartoonists, a cartoon now and then that he considers too rugged for publication. This sort usually go to New York on the backs of other cartoons and are highly prized by *Herald Tribune* Syndicate men.

Darling drew, solely for the eyes of his New York friends, he thought, a cartoon titled Halloween, 1936. It showed President Roosevelt, James Farley, and Harry Hopkins as young pranksters carrying away an old-fashioned out-house tenanted by John Public and labeled "private rights." This figure, inci-

dentally, is that of a choir leader Darling knew as a boy in
Sioux City. The cartoon impressed Harry Staton, *Herald Tribune* Syndicate manager, as so funny that he annexed the
original for himself and serviced the cartoon to the syndicate's
clients. Some *Herald Tribune* editors were less enthusiastic.
According to a widely told story, it was not used until Mrs. Ogden Reid threatened to publish it on the woman's page. To
Darling's surprise, it was one of the most acclaimed cartoons
of the year.

Besides letters praising and denouncing his own cartoons,
and having to do with his duck and political affairs, Darling's
mail includes a stream of letters, often accompanied by drawings, from boys asking how they can become cartoonists. For
these he has a stock reply which goes about like this:

"If you want to be a cartoonist, get a lot of pads of white
paper. Put them in both pairs of trousers and make five or six
sketches a day from life. Any boy with the average amount of
intelligence who will do this for five years will develop enough
skill to fill a minor position as a cartoonist. And his success
after that will not be slow if he continues to work hard. Cartooning is not an art. You need not be talented to do it."

As Darling has strong convictions, some of them quite bitterly held, and is allowed to draw as he likes, some unusual
situations have developed. As early as 1915, he was convinced
America would be drawn into the World War and should prepare. The editors of the Des Moines *Register* did not agree.
He presented his arguments in his space and the editors con-
tradicted them in editorials, to the amusement of Iowa. The
editorials argued that armament bred war. Darling retorted
with cartoons showing that fire escapes don't cause fires and
doctors don't cause sickness. The cartoonist regarded the
dream of the League of Nations with the United States as a
member as the brightest of all hopes for world peace. The New
York *Tribune* fought the League, but, to the confusion of
many readers, also published the Ding cartoons expressing the
opposite view.

After turning out what he considers a particularly crushing

cartoon, Darling is disconcerted now and then by the supposedly crushed victim begging for the original of the cartoon. This has happened with Alfred E. Smith, Gen. Hugh Johnson and several times with John L. Lewis. The more brutal he is depicted, the more Lewis seems to want the cartoon.

On the other hand, there is evidence that the cartoonist's pen, if not exactly mightier than the sword, is not without influence. Mrs. Franklin D. Roosevelt has said that she will never forgive Darling for depicting the President as Little Lord Fauntleroy. A New York lawyer has confessed that a Ding cartoon titled "Give Until It Hurts" caused him to give $5000 to the Red Cross.

In 1935, Darling drew a cartoon titled "The Fates Are Funny That Way." Panels showed persons being killed by auto crashes, earthquakes, lightning and poisonous food. At the end, John Public said to Mrs. Public: "But nothing ever seems to happen to Huey Long." Three days later, Long was assassinated. In the *Spokesman-Review* of Spokane, Washington, the account and the cartoon ran for an edition in adjoining columns.

Darling makes it a rule to stay away from his drawing board when angry. He regrets cartoons in which there is more venom than humor.

The sixty-three-year-old cartoonist, who is a grandfather and has a son following the medical career he missed, has no accurate idea of the number of drawings that he has produced. In addition to doing his cartoon, Ding illustrated a daily poem by Helen Cowles during his first years in Des Moines. He has written and illustrated two books, *Ding Goes to Russia,* his unfavorable impressions of the Soviet Union, and *The Cruise of the Bouncing Betsy,* an account of his trip by auto trailer from Iowa to Florida. Of some 12,000 Ding cartoons of the last four decades, the cartoonist's brother, Frank, has assembled the largest single collection, with the idea of eventual book publication.

Lamarcus Thompson, the Indiana roller-coaster inventor whose comic drawing launched Jay's cartoon career, it can be noted, had an equally decisive role in his brother's life. Thompson employed him to install roller coasters throughout the world and, after the inventor's death, Frank Darling became president of the vast Thompson Scenic Railway Company.

When asked his business, Frank once answered: "My brother is the greatest cartoonist in the world. I make roller coasters."

Panhandle Puck

(GENE HOWE)

By JACK ALEXANDER

EDITOR'S PREFACE.—In *Post Biographies of Famous Journalists* there is a sketch of Ed Howe by his son, Gene A. Howe. It bears the title, "My Father Was the Most Wretchedly Unhappy Man I Ever Knew." In the present volume, immediately following, is an article about Gene Howe by Jack Alexander. It will be noted that the title of this piece is "Panhandle Puck." There is food for thought in the difference of spirit and implication of these two titles. As the editors of the *Post* pointed out at the time of publication of this profile, "Gene, son of the great and sardonic Ed Howe, reversed his family pattern and found that kidding accomplished more in Texas journalism than masterful cynicism did in Kansas."

January 1, 1944

WITH one or two conspicuous exceptions, Gene Howe probably is the only man who ever made a success of newspaper publishing by being a buffoon. Howe's clowning, unlike that of the exceptions, is not of the unconscious type; it is as carefully calculated as the arch of a lady's eyebrow. His tendency toward buffoonery is something of a genetic aberration, for his father, Ed Howe, an Atchison, Kansas, editor with a world-wide renown as a sage, was one of the most painfully serious of men. And Grandfather Howe, a circuit rider with a sadistic penchant for giving five-hour sermons and whipping his children, was a psychological study in deepest black. That is as far back as genealogical research goes on the paternal side, and it is far enough.

Ed Howe, who influenced Gene more than anyone else, was a brilliant cynic who spent a good part of his life and his great

102

genius in trying to convince his fellow man that religion was evil and that women were crazed with power. It was a challenging thesis, but, on the whole, his fellow man refused to accept it—openly, at least—and the elder Howe, famed as the Sage of Potato Hill, died in 1937, embittered to the last over the failure of his crusade of enlightenment.

By that time his son, who had started off unpromisingly as a lad, had established himself joyously as a publisher in Amarillo, Texas, a town well removed from Atchison and connected with it, impersonally, by the Santa Fe Railroad. He had done this without capitalizing on his father's reputation; in fact, one of the toughest obstacles he had to surmount was his status as Ed Howe's boy. That the Amarillo *Evening Globe* and the Amarillo *Morning News* are today among the best known and most influential of small-town American newspapers is the result of Gene Howe's good sense in refusing to imitate the Ed Howe pattern, as people expected him to do, and in creating a Gene Howe pattern of editing instead. It is a screwball pattern, but it works.

He accomplished this minor marvel by resolutely being himself. It was a course which demanded self-confidence and, in the absence of this quality, Howe fell back on desperation, which sometimes works just as well. The desperation was an outgrowth of his experiences with his father. No family relationship was ever more grimly fascinating than that of the Howes of Atchison. The great Ed Howe was lean, cadaverous, and saturnine in appearance, an effect which was heightened by an addiction he had to string ties and somber black fedoras. His intense disposition matched his façade. Most of the time he was steeped in a Stygian gloom. Sometimes for months on end he would refuse to speak to members of his family. Once he snubbed a relative permanently because she suggested during a casual sidewalk conversation that he was wearing the wrong kind of tie.

He never recovered from the paradox that, although he was one of the most widely quoted editors in the United States and his sayings were published abroad in translation, the human race lagged discouragingly behind his deepest beliefs. The paradox seemed to have a deleterious effect on his behavior.

Gene Howe, on the other hand, is proud of the membership card he holds in the human race, and loves every member of it, including the female. He also loves ducks, skunks, fish, deer, and any other type of being God has seen fit to create. He thinks churches and clergymen, on the whole, are wonderful; he occasionally goes to Presbyterian services, and he contributes money to all denominations. Nothing pleases him more than to see a lot of people having a good time, and his papers are always promoting laugh fiestas of various kinds, getting jobs for the unemployed, finding lost dogs, helping to place litters of kittens, staging mother-in-law festivals and rejoicing generally over the wonders of living, particularly in the Texas Panhandle, of which Amarillo is the metropolis.

He is a stocky, baldish, gregarious man of fifty-seven, and is a devotee of good food, good company, good government, good hunting and good fishing. His eyes are squinty, partly from being out in the Texas sun, partly from laughing, and he has a catfish-size mouth which, even in repose, turns up puckishly at the sides as abruptly as his father's used to turn down.

In a sense, Gene Howe dominates Amarillo and the Panhandle, but not in the way his father dominated Atchison. Ed Howe ran Atchison. As long as he was editor of the Atchison *Globe,* the town had no golf club, Rotary or Kiwanis club, or Y. M. C. A. It wanted them, but Ed Howe considered them nonsensical, and his powers of ridicule were so strong that the community didn't dare oppose him. As soon as he retired from the paper, Gene, who took over the editorship, contributed $1000 toward the founding of a Y. M. C. A., and a long-suppressed community spirit spurted forth in a golf club, a Rotary, a Kiwanis, and other back-slapping institutions dedicated to convincing ordinary human beings, by a benevolent mass hypnosis, that they are quite all right, really.

Strangely, Ed Howe did not object when he heard of this, and later, when Gene took the same aggressively warm spirit to Amarillo, Ed followed his progress closely and with a good deal of wonderment. There was even approval in his attitude as his life drew near its close, possibly because he saw that, though his son was his temperamental opposite and not a great writer, he had the Howe knack of getting people to read what he wrote and of making a newspaper pay its own way. Journalistic tradition could hardly ask for more.

Gene Howe has an awed respect for the memory of his father. He feared and obeyed him when he was alive and, now that he is dead, he is still afraid of him and says he expects never to shed this feeling. Ed Howe is always popping into his everyday conversation.

In the midst of a talk session he will suddenly furrow his brow and launch into an anecdotal discussion of his queer Atchison days, as if trying dutifully to take care of some business that will never be finished. He is perpetually trying to relate his own career to that of his father, and somehow is never able to feel that he has turned out properly.

Once he wrote a revealing article about his father, thinking it would get the matter completely off his chest. It was titled "My Father Was the Most Wretchedly Unhappy Man I Ever Knew," and it appeared in the *Post* of October 25, 1941. But, aside from being one of the most entrancing human studies ever published, the effort was about as effective as a dose of bicarbonate of soda would have been. The memory of his father still won't let him rest. It has given him chronic insomnia.

"My father was an intense genius," he will say, rationalizing. "He influenced people by his sheer brilliance. Now, you can't inherit genius; at least, I didn't. And you do have to go your own way, don't you? Well, I discovered a long time ago that I could clown around and kid people into doing things, so I did it that way. I couldn't have cake, so I took corn bread."

It has been substantial corn bread. Howe is chief owner of the Amarillo Globe-News Publishing Company and receives, besides income from his stock, a salary of $20,000 a year. In addition, he is part owner of radio stations in Amarillo, Lubbock, Weslaco, and San Antonio, and of the Lubbock *Ava-*

lanche and the *Journal*. He is chief owner, too, of his father's *Globe* back in Atchison, and his income from all sources runs to well over $60,000 a year.

Howe lavishes most of his time upon the Amarillo *Globe*, and his bible has been an old precept of his father's: "In writing an item or an article, always get in something that will make the reader exclaim, 'Well, for heaven's sakes!' " The *Globe*, which has a circulation of 43,000, looks like any other competently edited newspaper outwardly and its well-for-heaven's-sakes department is a column on an inside page called "The Tactless Texan." At the top of the column is a photograph of the late cross-eyed comedian, Ben Turpin, and the contents of the column are just as surprising and often as loony.

Howe writes the column and submits copy each day to a committee of *Globe* staff members to make sure he has struck just the right note of looniness. If the committee thinks he hasn't done this, he solemnly rewrites and rewrites until it approves. Then the copy goes to the composing room to be set into type. Howe does not sign the column with his own name. When he refers to himself in his writings, it is as Erasmus R. (for Rookus) Tack, and is more often called Tack, or Old Tack, than he is Gene Howe. Erasmus R. Tack is, of course, a phantom.

The column's humor is of the hearty, kindly variety and is based largely upon exaggeration, a device that is popular in the Panhandle. The Panhandle, an oil-and-cattle country, has no reason for considering itself a special region, other than the fact that on the map it has a certain geographical unity. It looks like a pan of fudge perched on the roof of Texas. But Howe, through persistent flattery, has just about convinced his readers that, as residents of this happy region, they are a sort of super race—the finest, tallest, handsomest, cleverest, healthiest, fightingest people in the world. He has driven home this gospel so effectively that when the county hospital was refitted a few years ago, Supt. Harry Hatch had the new beds made a foot longer than standard hospital size. "Tack says to make things big," Hatch explained.

Howe "makes everything big." An editor of his who orders a photograph published in one-column width, instead of two or four column, is in for a rebuke. If something is good or bad, Howe wants it to be superlatively so. He insists, for instance, that Panhandle skunks are noticeably more offensive than the skunks elsewhere. During the dust storms he bragged in his column that the Panhandle had the most beautiful and destructive dust storms on the globe. Moreover, he said, the Panhandle dust contained a vitamin of its own that actually made the clouds healthful to inhale, and added that that was one reason the girls of the Panhandle had such shapely legs.

From the beginning of his stewardship of "The Tactless Texan" column, Howe beat the drum for Amarillo as America's most beautiful city and put a line in his editorial masthead calling it "the city of roses." Soon the townspeople were trying to make the boast come true by planting flower gardens in their yards. Howe imported carloads of rose plants, and the staff of the *Globe* knocked off work to sell them at cost to crowds of garden-conscious citizens. The roses had barely bloomed when a wind came whistling in off the prairie, scattering the petals and whipping the plants to a frazzle. Tulip plants were substituted, and they stuck. But Howe kept calling Amarillo "the city of roses" until the dust storms came, at which time, taking advantage of the coughing and the low visibility, he quietly removed the legend from his masthead. The net effect of all the hullabaloo was that Amarillo was changed from an ordinarily drab town into a rather pretty and well-groomed one, and everyone had a fine time while the change was being wrought.

In writing his column, Howe takes another leaf from his father's book and plays up the local items, which, in a small town, are the vertebrae of any paper. Back in Atchison, Ed Howe, in the strolls he took about town, always made a point of keeping close tab on front-porch courtships. When one got to a stage where the girl's dog followed her swain down the street, the editor reasoned that if the dog so approved the suitor an engagement was not far off, and he sent a reporter around to demand first break on the news. Amarillo, which now has a population of around 65,000, is too large for such close scrutiny, so Gene Howe gets his items on engagements, surgical operations, and other intimate happenings chiefly by paying his readers from two to five dollars for news tips. "Nothing can happen in Amarillo without the *Globe* knowing about it," he says with pride.

Howe is especially proud of the pulling power of the *Globe* as it was depicted in a private reader-interest survey of American newspapers made in 1941 by a New York advertising agency. When the *Globe* scored a rating of well over 90, the agency, which considered 70 to be an excellent rating, refused to believe its figures and ordered a resurvey. On the resurvey, the score was just below 90. Still a third survey was made, and the result was in the high 90's again. At this point, the agency gave up.

The answer to the mystery lay in "The Tactless Texan" column, whose conductor, by unorthodox methods, had established himself as jester, father confessor and friend to the whole Panhandle. Howe's readers often do not know whether to take him seriously or not. Once he wrote that on his own ranch, which he has appropriately named The Big Bull, he had provided a bull for every cow, in order to give his female cattle freedom of choice in their home life. The result, he wrote, was greater happiness all around and a super race of cattle. This drew a number of letters from ranchers, who are inclined to be literal-minded, asking for the privilege of breeding their cattle to Howe's stock. Howe's reply was that outside breeding would wreck the monogamic system which he had set up on his land and suggested that the ranchers establish their own bovine democracies.

Howe's office door is always open and there is no receptionist present to stand off unwanted callers. There is a constant stream of visitors. One day an agitated insurance collector, whom Howe had never seen before, sat down beside the desk and blurted, "Tack, I'm just a——thief! I'm short twelve hundred dollars in my collections—gambled it all away—and the auditors are coming in tomorrow. I've got a family of kids, and I promise to go straight if you help me. If you don't, it's Katy, bar the door!" Howe gave the collector his personal check for $1200, and didn't see him again for several months, when he returned with a sizable part of the borrowed money. Since that time, the whole debt has been retired.

Panhandle cow hands regard Howe as a great white father who can do almost anything, and when one stands hesitantly in his office doorway, shuffling and blushing, Howe knows before a word is uttered that he is looking for a wife. He writes out a matrimonial advertisement for his inarticulate visitor, giving all specifications, and afterward arranges meetings between the cow hand and the girls who write in indicating a maidenly interest. He has managed upward of 200 legal matings in this way, and he insists that only one of his marriages has ended in divorce. He attributes this glorious fact, if it is a fact, to the superior climatic and economic attractions of the highly favored Panhandle, where the worst-tempered persons invariably find domestic happiness.

Occasionally his faith is shaken. Recently a woman with a discolored eye hove to in front of his desk and poured forth a tale of husbandly drunkenness and brutality. Fifteen minutes after the woman had left, the husband came in and confided to Howe that his wife was a heavy drinker and a lazy doxy. Howe got the couple together on neutral grounds and, after much soothing talk, brought about a reconciliation. The couple kissed and went home. A week later they put on a real brannigan and broke up permanently.

"That old boy and girl," Howe explains in the idiom of his adopted state, "were recent arrivals in this area and the Panhandle didn't have time to work its wonders. If they had stuck it out a little longer, they would have turned into a couple of sweethearts."

A sure-fire human-interest technique which Howe uses from

time to time is that of creating a furor of jovial misunderstanding, which is ultimately resolved by Howe apologizing, after which there is emotional handshaking all around. Panhandle folk seem never to tire of this one. Last year Howe ran across a joke book consisting of stories in which one of the characters is made to look stupid. He published one joke as a true incident, embellishing the story so as to make the bright character a Panhandle resident and the lackwit an Oklahoman. Oklahomans with nothing better to do sent in demands for an apology. The apology was made with sweeping bows and the column formally acknowledged that Oklahoma residents were fine people, indeed, and no harm intended. Old Tack was terribly, terribly sorry.

As an experiment, he published a similar chestnut as an incident purporting to have happened in Maine, which seemed to be far enough away from Amarillo for safety. According to the story, the eleven-year-old daughter of a small-town Maine mayor complained that her teacher was nagging her. The mayor's wife called at the school for an explanation, and the teacher, who was a Texas girl, denied the charge. It was the child's turn to recite, and the teacher asked her to add two and two. "What did I tell you, mamma?" cried the pupil. "She's commencin' again."

Weeks went by and Maine disdained to notice the slight, so Howe had one of his staff write a letter of protest to the *Globe* and sign it "A Man From Maine." The letter stated that the writer was in Amarillo on a business trip, looking for a site upon which to erect a factory which would employ 500 persons; naturally, he was now disgusted and was going home. Howe really wept in public this time. Under a black two-column headline asking WHAT HAS TACK DONE NOW? he reprinted the letter and appended an abject retraction beginning: "Help! Help! I'm sorry, I'm sorry. I apologize, I apologize. I'm sorry, I'm sorry. I apologize so completely and deeply and genuinely. Oh, what have I done? Oh, what have I done now? . . . The finest people in the world live in Maine. They are smart, intelligent and cultured and handsome, and stand

for the best in everything. . . ." This qualifies as the all-time
high, or low, in Tack's apologies. Of such corn is his corn
bread made.

Despite Howe's horseplay, or perhaps because of it, the
Amarillo *Globe* exercises a hefty influence with the Panhandle's voters. And people living within a radius of 150 miles
—in Texas, Oklahoma and New Mexico—quote Old Tack
as if he were the only man in the world who had feedbox information. In every election since Howe came to Amarillo,
the Panhandle has supported the candidate of his choice, even
when the rest of the state was voting the other way.

Once, a decade ago, Howe dabbled in criminal investigation
with detective-novel results. The wife of an Amarillo lawyer
named A. D. Payne had been killed by a planted explosive
when she stepped on the starter of her automobile. Howe was
at his ranch at the time, and when he got back to town he
found his friends divided fifty-fifty on the question of whether
or not Mrs. Payne had been done in by her husband. Howe
ran a paragraph in his column addressed to Payne, in which
he rashly promised to catch the murderer within ten days if
the lawyer would come to his office and talk over the case.
Payne, an earnest middle-aged man, accepted. He told a
plausible story, but Howe's suspicions were aroused at his
constant reiteration of affection for his dead wife. When Payne
tearfully related that he used to drive home from the office
every time he got fifteen minutes of spare time, just to be with
his wife, Howe made a mental note to the effect that such
devotion was unnatural.

Then he telephoned his friend Roy Roberts, who is the
managing editor of the Kansas City *Star*, and Roberts sent one
of his sharpest reporters, the late A. B. MacDonald, to Amarillo. Howe and MacDonald scurried about town, talking to
Payne's associates, and on the fourth day tricked Payne into
signing a confession by telling him that a woman with whom
he had been friendly had told all. MacDonald won a Pulitzer
Prize for his share of the solution, and Howe got a letter from
Payne stating that whenever the publisher was around him, he

had difficulty restraining himself from blowing him to glory. Howe didn't take this seriously until Payne blew himself to bits one day with a bottle of nitroglycerin which he had secreted in his jail cell.

Gene Howe's boyhood was, by his own description, a nightmare because of his father's moods and stern prejudices. The youngest of Ed Howe's three children, he got along with his father for a time by being submissive. His brother, Jim, resisted and was occasionally whipped. Their sister, Mateel, also snapped back at her father, and the family became divided into two camps. When Gene was about eleven years old, he and his father moved into a cottage in the yard, and Mrs. Howe, Jim and Mateel continued to hold forth in the main house. Diplomatic relations were severed and after a few years Mrs. Howe got a divorce. Jim ultimately became a correspondent for the Associated Press in Russia, possibly to get as far away from Atchison as he could manage. Mateel is now Mrs. Dwight Farnham and lives in Connecticut. She is a novelist and has had a number of books published. Some traits have died out in the Howe line, but not the habit of writing.

During the divided-home period, Ed Howe took Gene with him on a round-the-world trip. In the course of the railroad trip back to Atchison, after the voyage had ended in New York, the pair stopped off at Sedalia, Missouri, for lunch. The elder Howe, without consulting his son, ordered two No. 1 lunches. Gene protested that he wanted the No. 2 lunch and, after an argument, got it. For this insubordination, his father didn't speak to him for the rest of the trip and for three months thereafter. That was Gene's first taste of insurrection, and he liked it. He was sent to high school and was expelled within two months for impudence to a teacher. His father, without comment, made him a reporter and typesetter on the Atchison *Globe*.

When Gene was sixteen, he lost his father's blessing completely. During a steamboat excursion to Leavenworth, Gene and two other Atchison boys got drunk before the eyes of some of Atchison's leading families. The *Globe* next day reported curtly: "Three Atchison young men disgraced themselves in Leavenworth yesterday. The publisher's son was the drunkest of the bunch."

For punishment, Gene was dispatched to Emmett, Idaho, where his brother Jim had a weekly newspaper. Gene stayed at Emmett for a year, at the end of which trial period Jim reported to his father that Gene was hopeless. Ed Howe mailed Gene a check for fifty dollars and told him that he was on his own. Gene went to Portland, Oregon, and got a job as reporter on the *Oregonian*. He thought at the time that he had talked his way into the job, and didn't learn, until a couple of decades later, that his father had written the editor asking him to give the boy a chance. Nevertheless, Gene turned into a good reporter and stayed in Portland for four years. Shortly after he had turned twenty-one, Ed Howe ordered him to return to Atchison to work on the *Globe*. When he got home, Gene showed his father his bank book, which had a balance of more than $1000. Ed Howe never mentioned the steamboat ride to Leavenworth again; nor did he ever say another unkind word to his son. He had a firm belief that the only worthwhile people in the world were those who made money and held on to it.

By this time, Gene had decided that for his own peace of mind, if for no other reason, he would never try to imitate his unhappy zealot of a father. Ed Howe sent him to New York State to register in William Muldoon's health camp and write a series of articles about his experiences there. Muldoon had a waspish habit of insulting his clients on every possible occasion, and Gene, in his dispatches home, detailed his misadventures with Muldoon. They were popular articles and their success set the pattern for the rest of the correspondent's writing career. Ever since then, Howe has kidded himself in print.

The first paper Howe got to own was his father's Atchison *Globe,* and this came about because of what he calls his father's "December mood." "He was the unhappiest, wretchedest and most uncivil man in the world around Christmas," Gene says. Ed Howe's temper was at its worst at that time of the year because December was a poor month for news. People were looking forward to Christmas and behaving themselves. Such newsworthy social events as wife beatings, knifings and burglaries were postponed until after the holidays. The *Globe* was therefore dull, and the editor, disgusted with his staff and his business, would walk the floor at night, ranting and swearing. One Christmas he tried to sell the *Globe* to outsiders for $50,000. Getting no takers, he offered to give Gene a $25,000 equity in it on condition that he raise the other $25,000. Gene did it, and got the paper, and Ed Howe devoted the rest of his life to writing books and magazines articles.

The *Globe* continued to prosper, and in 1924 Gene Howe founded another *Globe,* in Amarillo, placing an editor in charge. The editor started "The Tactless Texan" as a serious feature and got in bad with the Ku Klux Klan, which promptly began waging a boycott. Howe hurried down from Atchison and took over the editorship himself. The going was hard. After two years, the Amarillo *Globe* was still trying to make headway against the long-established *Morning News.* The *News'* owner offered to sell for $235,000, and Howe went to Kansas City to meet his Atchison backers. He didn't go to Atchison, for fear of letting his father know he was in straits. Ed Howe heard about it, however, and sent word that he would be glad to lend his son $200,000. He was worth about $400,000 at the time. Not wishing to risk losing his father's money, Gene got the funds from his backers and bought the *News.*

The consolidation of the *Globe* and *News* took place in January, 1926. Three months later, the Panhandle was in the midst of a wild oil-and-natural-gas boom. The population of Amarillo, which was 16,000 when Howe arrived there, doubled in less than half a year. The *Globe* and the *News* had to turn away many full-page advertisements because of lack of printing facilities. Nevertheless, they printed enough advertising to retire the $235,000 purchase price of the *News* in eleven months. Not until 1937, when the tabloid Amarillo *Times* was founded, did Howe have any competition. The *Times* has never bothered the *Globe-News* combination appreciably.

Before the lucky oil boom got under way, Howe had already

swung his circulation into a mild upturn. He did it by taking over "The Tactless Texan" column, planting Ben Turpin's picture at the head of it and converting it into a burlesque of the more dead-pan columns; instead of setting himself up as an authority, he paraded a spurious ignorance. The intellectual and social set of Amarillo was disgusted and said he was a disgrace to his great father and a crude carpetbagger from Kansas, but the lowbrows were delighted. Howe cast in his lot with the lowbrows, which was smart circulation tactics, as they were much more numerous than the highbrows.

Howe lives in a medium-priced house in Amarillo with his wife, who before her marriage was Miss Gale Donald, of Atchison. Their house is a few blocks away from the home of their daughter, Jeanne, who is the wife of Shelby Kritser, a former Pan American clipper flight engineer who has recently returned to his family's profession of ranching.

In order to devote more time to his column, Howe resigned as editor in 1936, but he still hangs around the *Globe* office a lot, figuring out new ways to create a pleasant hullabaloo of some kind. The hullabaloos invariably attract so many telephone calls that Howe flees to his ranch, near Canadian, about 125 miles from Amarillo, and stays until the excitement blows over. The ranch is equipped with a telephone, but the connection is along fence wires, and the cattle can be depended upon to butt the fences and destroy a connection at the right time. Howe says he has bred them to do this. He raises purebreds and range cattle, and says he is a sucker at ranching, as most businessmen-turned-cattlemen are. If he loses less than $7500 on the ranch, he considers it a good year.

Talk at the ranch always comes around to Howe's favorite subjects, one of which is a belief he has that too many newspaper publishers underpay their editorial workers and stifle their talents by restrictive rules. Howe encourages his own men to write for outside publications and helps them to get jobs on papers in larger cities, if they seem to be qualified. He pays unusually generous salaries and gives out a bonus at Christmas amounting to about a month's pay. Most of the employees are stockholders, and through sales to them Howe's own shares have gradually dwindled to about 22 per cent of the total.

Another favorite topic is a theory Howe has that the fish-and-game laws of the various states are ruining game fishing by requiring sportsmen to throw back their small-sized catch. In characteristic fashion, he appropriated the theory from some-one else whose identity he has forgotten. Four lakes on the Big Bull ranch are dedicated to proving the theory, which holds that tossing back the little ones destroys Nature's balance in the lake; that the hordes of midgets denude the feeding grounds, stunting the growth of the larger fish and making them so list-less they won't strike. Periodically, Howe stocks his lakes with bass, and later has them drained to prove his theory. When the bass are seined up from low water, Howe is always on hand. He holds a bass aloft, shakes his head disapprovingly, and with the apostolic zeal of the conservationist carries on a running fire of comment. "Look at that fish," he will say, with horror in his voice. "That's a runted fish. Ought to weigh twice as much. That's a sick fish. That's awful. That's terrible."

At night the coyotes squat around the ranch building and howl dismally. Howe, a poor sleeper anyway, rolls out of bed and sits on the porch in his pajamas. For a while, he will rub the ears of Charlie, a tame deer who is the ranch pet, and maybe feed him a couple of cigarettes, a delicacy for which Charlie has an avid appetite. Afterward he will go inside and awaken the guests, demanding that they get up and talk. Then, when the bleary-eyed guests have gathered around a wood fire, Subject No. 1 will crop out.

"My father," Howe will begin, "never wrote a dishonest word in his life." Or, "Genius is wonderful, but it is damned hard to live with. Now, my father——" And so on and on, until the embers are cold and the coyotes fade away into the dawn.

Up From Akron

(JOHN S. KNIGHT)

By JACK ALEXANDER

EDITOR'S PREFACE.—With the possible exception of Marshall Field (and he is of a different genre altogether), John S. Knight, as the author of the following article points out, is "the only new entry to appear in major-league journalism for many a year." Inheritor of the Akron *Beacon Journal* from his father, he has successively acquired the Miami *Herald,* Detroit *Free Press,* and, most recently, the Chicago *Daily News.* In a sense, Mr. Knight now controls one of the most potent newspaper groups in the country, and (in the language of Mr. Alexander) "with his relatively small number of papers . . . has become a challenge to the larger and longer-established newspaper chains, such as Hearst and Scripps-Howard." Actually, however, Mr. Knight does not think of his papers as members of a chain, but as separate units, each independent of the other. "His local editors enjoy a greater share of autonomy than do those of most chains." This new type of journalistic entrepreneur admits that he may not have made his last newspaper purchase. "I am interested only in large-city papers now," however, he adds. Indicative of the esteem in which his contemporaries hold Mr. Knight is the fact that at this writing (1945), he is president of the American Society of Newspaper Editors, the best-heeled and most influential editorial group in this country—or any other country for that matter. Here, then, is the story—the success saga—of one who has combined sound publishing sense with a shrewd gambling instinct to build up a powerful newspaper empire.

August 18, 1945

JOHN SHIVELY KNIGHT, who last October became proprietor of the Chicago *Daily News,* one of America's most respected newspapers, is fond of saying that he is the best

117

crapshooter in the world. When well-meaning friends try to convince him that the prideful remark does not befit his new dignity, he replies with a directness that is typical of him, "But I am the best crapshooter in the world."

Conceivably, Knight may overrate his dicing skill. However, he is actualy a formidable man when he kneels on the floor of a golf-club locker room in front of a few $100 bills. His virtuosity is not with the dice themselves; it lies in his scholarship of the mathematical theory of probability. Knight is what is known in gambling circles as a percentage player, which is what all smart gamblers are. He can recite the odds against the probability of any point being made— 2 to 1 against a four, 3 to 2 against a five, 6 to 5 against an eight, and so on— and he never bucks the percentages.

He learned his lesson as a sergeant in training with a motor-transport unit during the first World War. Most of the men in his platoon were ex-taxi drivers, a segment of the population that ranks high in the dicing science. After losing his pay regularly for a while, Knight, suspecting crooked manipulation of the dice, insisted that his opponents toss them out of a soup bowl on the concrete floor of a latrine. They still won his money. He studied their mathematical system, and it repaid him later when, in France, he was transferred to the infantry, and subsequently to the Air Corps. Knight slaughtered the reckless innocents of these branches and came home with more than $5000 in winnings.

The parallels between scientific crapshooting and newspaper ownership are not dwelt upon in colleges of journalism, but Knight, who never attended one anyway, has since applied crapshooting principles to publishing with high success. He started off with the Akron *Beacon Journal,* which he inherited in 1933 from his father, the late Charles Landon Knight, a brilliant editor who made and broke Akron mayors for two decades with his sulphurous editorials. Because of the depression, the *Beacon Journal* was pinched for ready cash, and its profits declined, but its prestige was still strong enough to tempt anyone of true gambling instinct. Instead of selling it to an outside adventurer, which would have been an easy way out, the younger Knight held on.

The *Beacon Journal* recovered healthily, and in 1937 Knight was able to borrow enough on it to buy the Miami (Florida) *Herald*. The *Herald* was a percentage player's dream, prosperous and solid. Knight improved it and made it more prosperous, and in 1940 he moved on into his first big city, Detroit, purchasing the *Free Press,* an ancient and honored paper which had bogged down. The *Free Press* generously repaid his judgment of its capacity for rejuvenation by winning a Pulitzer prize last May "for the most distinguished and meritorious public service rendered by an American newspaper during 1944"—the exposure of graft in the Michigan legislature. By that time Knight was well into his second big-city venture, in Chicago.

In corroboration of his judgment of percentages, all four of the Knight papers are making profits. It is likely that Knight will take on other newspaper properties eventually—if the percentages are right—and, if he does, they won't be small-city papers. "I am interested only in large-city papers now," he said recently. He has come a long way since Akron.

Those who think he will go a lot farther, which includes almost everyone who knows him, like to talk about his icy toughness of character. He will toss a coin or turn a card for $1000 without a flicker of expression. A tautly strung man, he is apt to be abrupt and jumpy in the early stages of any venture, but when the pay-off comes he is purposeful, cold and efficient. In a golf game he is an extremely bad man to be even up with on the eighteenth tee and, although a rather weak putter normally, he is a dead shot on the last green if someone on the clubhouse veranda shouts a fifty-dollar bet that he won't hole out in one stroke.

Knight has been champion six times of his home club, the Portage Country Club, of Akron—on which he once shot a 67—and has taken part in a number of amateur-professional matches. He plays his best after having stayed up late the night before, and he revels in the added stimulus of side bets. A few

years ago he was teamed up with golf pro Jimmy Thomson in
an amateur-professional medal-play competition at the Indian
Creek Country Club, in Miami. Before the match began, the
teams were auctioned off to the highest bidders in the clubhouse, and Knight bought his own team for $150. The Thom-
son-Knight team was a late finisher and the issue hung on the
last hole. Thomson's drive was out of bounds, but, recovering
in machinelike pro fashion, he scored a good par five. Unfortunately, it wasn't good enough to win. Knight was on the
green in two and took two putts, for a birdie four. As an
amateur, he received an added discount of a stroke, which
made his score for the official record a three. His skillful finish
won him a pot of $1200.

One day last May, when he was playing the same course, he
reacted to a far graver emotional crisis in a similar way. He
had just driven off the tenth tee with a foursome of friends
when a messenger came over from the clubhouse with the news
that his eldest son, Lt. John S. Knight, Jr., a paratrooper, had
been killed in Germany. The other players wanted to abandon
the game, but at Knight's request the foursome played on. The
game was completed in grim silence. Knight's score on the
par-3 tenth hole was a five, but after that he tightened up and
finished the round just a few strokes off his usual game. "I
felt," he explained afterward, "that I just had to keep going.
It's just the way I do things." For a month or two thereafter,
he was unable to go near any of his newspapers.

As a boy, Knight was unusually shy, and he has never entirely broken out of his shell. At fifty, he is still reserved and
aloof, except when with his family or among close friends. He
has on several occasions gone out of his way to apologize for
this. Once, when he was managing editor of the Akron *Beacon
Journal,* he was disturbed to learn that the city-room employees thought him standoffish; this was a view that was
shared in the composing room, where Knight, wearing his
vest well buttoned up, coolly directed the make-up of page
forms while the shirt-sleeved compositors were wilting in the

summer heat. Knight called a special staff meeting. He explained gravely that he was not the back-slapping type and expressed the hope that no one would think he was being deliberately rude.

Already, with his relatively small number of papers, Knight has become a challenge to the larger and longer-established newspaper chains, such as Hearst and Scripps-Howard. Except for Marshall Field, he is the only new entry to appear in major-league journalism for many a year. Knight and Field differ widely. Field, because of the immense inherited fortune he has at his disposal, doesn't have to worry about percentages. He has lost millions on his *PM,* of New York, and his Chicago *Sun,* without suffering undue pain.

Knight has a passion for solvency, not only for Knight Newspapers, Inc., which is the name of his group, but for each member of the group. His insistence that each paper pay its way is a fairly radical concept in multiple-newspaper operation. Both Hearst and Scripps-Howard have in the past kept papers alive in some communities long after they had become money losers, apparently in order to retain regional political influence. Knight is content to let political power develop as it will. His purchases have, nevertheless, been spotted cannily. In Akron, which is the center of the rubber industry and a turbulent meeting ground of capital and labor, the spotting, of course, was done for him. But he chose the other locations himself: a great air-transport terminal and chief hopping-off place for Latin America; the heart of the automotive industry and another turbulent capital-labor metropolis; and the Middle West's greatest railroad and industrial city.

Knight insists that his papers do not constitute a chain in the accepted sense, and his mode of operation seems to bear out his contention. His local editors enjoy a greater share of autonomy than do those of most chains. He sends them no daily message from headquarters telling what position to give selected news stories or how much of them to publish. Knight's view is that a story that calls for prominent front-page space in Chicago may not appeal to readers in, say, Akron or Miami, and that the local editor is the best judge of what space to accord it or of whether it ought to be thrown in the wastebasket. And, except for one long editorial which he writes over his own signature each week and which is carried in all his papers, there is no flood of canned manifestoes to pre-empt editorial-page space which ordinarily would be used for discussing community problems. Knight's weekly editorial has the effect of setting the policy of his papers on national and international issues. His editors and their staffs formulate their own city and state policies independently, and decide, in meeting, what local political candidates to support.

Thus, Knight feels, each of his papers, free from dictation in local matters by a central authority, is able to function as a community organ. His hope is that they will choose their local candidates in such a way that no one will be able to remark, as his father once did in Akron, "Why should the public go to the polls when there is nothing to vote for except a jackass and another bond issue?"

In reporting touchy labor-employer news the Knight papers steer an objective course. Some union officials have gone so far as to issue public statements praising Knight for his impartiality. Employers are less inclined to rush into print with hosannas. Once, in Akron, before Knight had begun to expand his holdings, the management of a struck tire plant refused to bargain with its strikers. After the plant had been locked for some time, Knight walked through the picket line and warned the management that its no-bargaining stand might have disastrous results. Making no headway, he published a front-page editorial in the *Beacon Journal* next day entitled "WE'VE HAD A BELLYFUL," which excoriated the management. The result was a boycott which cost the *Beacon Journal* several thousand subscribers, but Knight persisted in his stand and the bargaining ultimately took place. In the end, the paper gained more subscribers than it lost.

Classifying Knight politically is an adventure in choosing among badly shopworn labels. Although an enrolled Republican, he is often spoken of at Akron's Portage Country Club as a traitor to his class. A journalist of pinkish coloration who once worked for Knight describes him as "a hard, sincere man who got his liberalism synthetically, but who is, nevertheless, an enterprising liberal." An Eastern newspaper publisher who is a devout supporter of the New Deal says: "He is a liberal much of the time, but when a national election rolls around and the chips are really down, you will always find him on the conservative side. He is, however, a fine type of conservative and if we had more conservatives like him we'd have more intelligent elections. But if Jack Knight is a liberal, I am a ballet dancer." The Eastern publisher weighs about 200 pounds.

Knight inherits both his temper and his gambling instinct from his father. The elder Knight, who was something of an autocrat, was an inveterate poker player. He was also a connoisseur of bourbon whisky, a status he achieved by assiduous study after the beginning of the dry era, prior to which he had been a teetotaler. He held a poker game each Friday night in his home, sometimes wearing a red-lined opera cape which he fancied. When the cards ran against him, he would jump up, knock cards and ash trays off the table and stamp into an adjoining room, where he would puff his pipe and read the Bible for half an hour before returning to the game.

It was perhaps the overshadowing influence of his father that drove Jack Knight inward and caused him to keep his temper under wraps. This suppression gave him an underlying spirit of restlessness which in his boyhood broke out in numerous fist fights. When the United States entered the war in 1917, Knight was a junior at Cornell with an indifferent campus and scholastic record. Dropping his books promptly, he went home and argued an old grade-school chum into joining the Cornell Ambulance Unit with him. Outfitted in sky-blue French uniforms by an Akron tailor, they went to

Cleveland to entrain for Ithaca, but slept late after a farewell party with Cleveland friends and missed the train. On Knight's suggestion, they sent their French uniforms back to Akron and enlisted, in civilian clothes, at the nearest Army recruiting station.

After spending eight months in France as a sergeant in an ammunition train, Knight, impatient of what he considered slow promotion, went to the infantry officers' school at Langres. He emerged a lieutenant and put in a few months in a quiet sector with the 113th Infantry. Then a transfer to the Air Corps, for which he had applied back in the States, came through, and when the war ended he was in training at Tours as an aerial observer and machine gunner.

The war had proved frustrating to Knight. His most gratifying memory of it was that of a boxing match at Langres in which he had volunteered to defend the honor of his battalion without knowing who his opponent was to be. The opponent turned out to be a former professional prize fighter. Knight was well cut up, but he took deep satisfaction, and still does, in the fact that he was on his feet at the end of the sixth and last round.

Knight was a reluctant convert to journalism. When he got back from France, he wanted to go into business or cattle raising, but at the persistent urging of his father he joined the staff of the *Beacon Journal* in 1920. His reluctance was well grounded. The *Beacon Journal* was a one-man show. Since 1910, when the elder Knight had become its editor and publisher, it had ridden to prosperity on the rubber boom and on the editor's vehement editorials, which were directed mostly at reformers, machine politicians, censorship, child labor and the foibles of the human race. Although an agnostic, the elder Knight was an assiduous student of the Bible; he also studied such authors as Gibbon, Aristotle and Plato, and tried to relate their teachings to Akron and the rest of contemporary America. It was a great act, but the lessons failed to make much of an impress, and Knight once gave vent to this Olympian sigh on his editorial page: "Socrates spoke the truth and was given hemlock. Jesus Christ spoke the truth and was crucified. Then who are we pygmies that we should complain because the people will not understand?"

It was understandable that such a self-conscious star actor should be, as the elder Knight was, contemptuous of the syndicated entertainment features which were beginning their invasion of American newspapers. He grudgingly bought a few comic strips, but looked upon them as filler material and often omitted them for days at a time to make room for textual matter. In disgust, he wrote of the trend toward standardization: "Where we once, as in the old days of Dana, had the journalistic gem casket, we now have the garbage cart of flotsam and jetsam which neither amuses nor instructs an understanding mind."

The elder Knight probably had good taste on his side, but the days of one-man journalism were dying, and his son, who spent his first year in the office poring over newspapers from other cities, clearly perceived the trend toward entertainment. This led to hot disputes during daily seminars at which the veteran tried to instruct his pupil in the intricacies of newspaper publishing. Jack Knight, advancing his arguments with frigid desperation, gradually won out, and the *Beacon Journal* began to sprout syndicated columns and more comic strips.

With a sense of inevitability and ultimately one of resignation, the elder Knight watched his son take hold of the paper and make it over. He himself had become politically ambitious and was away from the office a great deal, making speeches. He served a term in Congress, an experience which deepened his conviction that the world was going to pot, and spent $200,000 in an unsuccessful attempt to win the Republican nomination for governor.

Meanwhile, his son moved up to city editor and, in 1925, to managing editor. In that year, the Scripps-Howard chain, which owned the *Akron Press,* bought in the town's third paper, the *Times,* and merged the two into the *Times-Press.* In the shrunken Akron journalistic world a struggle for circulation began. A new editor, imported for the *Times-*

Press, was quoted as saying that he had come to town to take the swaddling clothes off of Akron journalism. Whether he actually said it or not, Jack Knight took up the challenge implied by his arrival on the scene. He fed more features into the *Beacon Journal,* raised salaries and watched for breaks.

He got one when the *Times-Press* relinquished an Associated Press franchise which it had acquired along with the other assets of the defunct *Times.* Jack Knight, without consulting his father, grabbed up the loose franchise and, with the aid of its comprehensive coverage, instituted a special late-afternoon edition whose outside sheets were printed on green paper.

His father scoffed at the gaudy novelty, but when the *Beacon Journal's* circulation rose sharply, he remarked, "Son, for all I care you can make the damned thing red, white and blue."

After that the son was monarch of the *Beacon Journal.* His father continued to write his editorials, but spent less and less time around the paper and more time with his poker-playing, bourbon-drinking cronies. Most of these were politicians, whose works he hated, but whose characters he loved. He objected only weakly when his son proposed building a new plant for the *Beacon Journal.* When the building was being finished, he was vacationing in Florida. On his return he was shown to his new office. For a while, there was a flare-up of the old rebellious spirit. Nobody had consulted him about the furniture or draperies, he protested, and he would perish in hell before he would work amid such Oriental surroundings. He walked out, and sulked in a disordered cubicle he had long occupied in the old building; he had a messenger deliver his editorial-page copy, which he scribbled left-handed in hieroglyphics that only one veteran linotyper could decipher. After his rebellion had lasted three weeks, he capitulated and moved into the new building.

When he died, in 1933, his son, who succeeded him as editor, was in the thick of another fight to keep the *Beacon Journal* from going under. Heavily loaded with debt, the paper was muddling through depression times. Word reached the *Beacon Journal* office that at the rival *Times-Press* office the slogan was: "Now that the old man is dead, let's take Jack."

Few Akronites would have bet on the *Beacon Journal's* chances to survive, for Jack was looked upon around town as a rich man's son who was coasting on his father's reputation. Actually, the elder Knight wasn't very rich. He left an estate of $515,000, but most of it was in *Beacon Journal* stock, and if the paper had gone under, the new editor would have been broke. As it was, he had to borrow money to pay his inheritance tax.

The *Times-Press* met the depressed economic situation defensively, by retrenching. Knight became more aggressive. He spent more money on new features and on his staff, and the *Beacon Journal* pushed ahead. Knight reached the height of his prestige in Akron during a protracted strike in one of the town's rubber factories in 1936. Violence seemed imminent when a former mayor organized something he called a Law-and-Order League and publicly urged citizens and nonstrikers to assemble outside the factory and forcibly break through the strikers' lines.

Knight wrote and published a front-page editorial in which he denounced the ex-mayor's invitation as "deliberately provocative and inflammatory" and added, "We need no vigilantes here." The *Times-Press* paid him the unusual compliment of reprinting the editorial on its own front page, and the vigilante movement was broken.

Afterward the *Times-Press,* either in honest admiration or in order to get Knight out of town, proposed him as a candidate for governor. By this time, Knight had well-defined ideas about newspapermen entering politics. His father had tried to get him interested, and to please him he had served a term as president of the Young Republicans Club. But he had no liking for politicians. He had noticed, too, that when his father was running for public office the *Beacon Journal's* ostensibly impartial news columns took on a partisan coloring. His conclusion was that newspaper publishing and politics mix poorly, and he has never altered this opinion.

Instead of going out for the governorship, Knight kept slashing competitively at the *Times-Press,* and in 1938 it collapsed. Knight bought in the body, and the *Beacon Journal* has had a monopoly in Akron ever since. At the time of the merger, leading citizens held a public meeting at which the monopoly was denounced as unhealthy for a community the size of Akron. Knight attended and surprised everyone by admitting that the citizens were right. He offered to sell the old *Beacon Journal* plant and equipment—the paper had moved to the *Times-Press* building—at a reasonable price to any citizen or group of citizens who wanted to set up another paper. There were no takers.

For several years prior to the downfall of the *Times-Press,* Knight had been under the approving observation of a brassy and mysterious character named Smith Davis. Like Knight, Davis was an Ohioan, and he was also a young man on the way up in the newspaper business. An ex-stockbroker turned financier, Davis in 1937 had just finished refinancing the Brush-Moore newspapers, a small Ohio chain, and was rapidly gaining a reputation as rainmaker among publishers who wanted to buy or sell properties. Davis called on Knight and advised him to buy the Miami *Herald,* whose aging founder and owner, Col. Frank B. Shutts, was in a mood to sell. Knight demurred, saying that he didn't want to buck up against the late Moses L. Annenberg, of Philadelphia, who owned the tabloid Miami *Tribune* and had once been a moving figure in the old Chicago circulation wars. Besides, he said, he had no ambitions outside of Akron. Davis knew Knight too well to believe the latter statement.

To overcome Knight's fear of Annenberg, Davis took him to New York, where they were luncheon guests of a friend of Davis', J. David Stern, who was then publisher of the New York *Post.* The luncheon was held in Stern's penthouse atop the *Post* building, a circumstance which greatly impressed

Knight, who then had a midlander's awe of New York. During the meal, Stern kept assuring Knight that Annenberg, with whom he had competed in the Philadelphia area, was by no means invulnerable. Stern continued to orate on Annenberg's supposed weaknesses at dinner, which was held in the Stern apartment on Park Avenue. Knight began to warm up. When Stern proposed that they all go up to the Joe Louis-Tommy Farr championship fight, which was being held that night, Knight suggested that it was too late to obtain tickets. He was pleasantly flabbergasted when Stern, by merely putting in a telephone call, arranged for ringside seats. Plainly, Stern was a man of substance whose opinion was not to be discounted. By the time the fight was over and a few plushy night clubs had been visited, Knight was ready for Annenberg and Miami.

On the plane trip home, he underwent a violent renewal of his Annenberg fears, and argued with Davis all the way. A few days after getting to Akron, he went to the Mayo Clinic, in Rochester, Minnesota, hoping that the doctors would advise him that his heart would not stand up under any added strain. The clinic verdict was that his heart was perfectly sound. He bought the Miami *Herald* for $2,000,000. Next, he sought out Annenberg and eliminated him from the Miami newspaper scene through shrewd dickering, an art at which Knight is adept when he wants something badly. Annenberg handed over his Miami *Tribune,* which had been losing money, in exchange for cash and for a paper which the elder Knight had bought years before, the Massillon, Ohio, *Independent.* Knight then suspended publication of the *Tribune.* This cut the Miami field down to Knight's *Herald,* a morning paper, and the *News,* an evening paper owned by former Gov. James M. Cox, of Ohio. Under Knight's management, the *Herald* paid off the $2,000,000 loan in a few years. The *Herald* now has about twice the circulation of the *News.*

Knight made no attempt to eliminate the *News.* His days as a saber-toothed tiger were fading. He was mellowing a little and, as he drew nearer to the major league, his approach became more dignified and conservative. One reason for this was that he seemed to be attaining a status as an heir apparent in the newspaper field. The Miami *Herald* had fallen to him partly because Colonel Shutts, who wanted to retire, had seen in him a young, vigorous successor who could be depended upon to keep the property alive. In 1940, Knight fell heir to the Detroit *Free Press,* in much the same way.

Edward D. Stair was eighty-one, and had been publishing the century-old *Free Press* for thirty-four years. He, too, was ready to retire, and he was anxious to find a successor whom he considered worthy. Stair particularly wanted to avoid passing on his paper to a politician publisher. Smith Davis heard of this and took Knight to Detroit for a series of talks with Stair. Knight's dislike of political maneuverings pleased Stair. He heard with satisfaction that Knight had made the Miami *Herald* politically independent and that he had passed up an an opportunity to run for governor of Florida. He sold the *Free Press* to Knight for $3,200,000, taking his notes for all but a down payment of $100,000.

Knight made over the *Free Press* from a rock-ribbed conservative paper into one marked by his own brand of liberalism. In less than four years the notes he had signed were retired from earnings, far in advance of maturity. The *Free Press* is now setting an aggressive pace for its rivals, the *News* and the *Times.* Its week-day circulation, which stood at 293,000 in 1940, is now around 400,000.

The heir principle, now well established, worked its best favor for Knight when Secretary of the Navy Frank Knox died in April, 1944, and his Chicago *Daily News* went on the block. Knox's death precipitated one of the biggest gold rushes in the history of American journalism. The *News* had run down and become stodgy during Knox's long absence in Washington, but it retained enough of its original luster to attract offers from more than a score of publishers and would-be publishers. In anticipation of just such a rush, Knox, in his will, had instructed his executors that they were under no obligation to accept the highest bid; the will charged them simply with passing on the paper to the bidder whom they considered best qualified to preserve the paper's character and traditions.

Over a period of six months, the executors narrowed down the field. Some applicants were eliminated because they were straw men for anonymous bidders; some because the executors were not satisfied with the sources of the proposed purchase money. Others plainly wanted the *Daily News* for prestige purposes only, and still others lacked experience in metropolitan publishing.

Knight appeared before the executors and underwent an examination which lasted two hours. As examples of his political independence, he cited the records of his papers in municipal affairs, his Detroit *Free Press'* support of Sen. Prentiss Brown, a Democrat, for re-election, and his Akron *Beacon Journal's* support of the candidacy of Democratic Mayor Frank Lausche, of Cleveland, for governor of Ohio. One of the executors asked Knight if he didn't think the *Daily News* should go to a Chicagoan. Knight surprised him by replying that he thought it should, if a qualified operator could be found. When asked if he would become a Chicago resident if he obtained control of the *News,* Knight frankly replied that Akron was his home and that he proposed to keep it his home.

When the interview was over, the executors checked on Knight's statements through leading citizens and politicians in Detroit, Akron, and Miami, and were convinced of their accuracy. Word got around that the executors were favorably inclined toward Knight. At this point, Knight began playing hard to get. He left Chicago and holed up in Detroit. A group of civic leaders who had long taken an interest in the *Daily News* tried to get him to come back. Failing, they enlisted the services of Gordon Lang, a Chicago jeweler who was a life-long friend of Knight's. Knight told Lang he was washed up with the deal. But after Lang had harangued him by long-distance twice a day for ten days, he returned to Chicago and bought the *Daily News*. The price he paid for a controlling interest,

$2,300,000, was well below the bids of several other applicants.

Those who expected Knight to enter the Chicago newspaper jungle with his fangs dripping were let down. One of his first acts as publisher of the *Daily News* was to drop a series of cartoons in which the military pretensions of Col. Robert R. McCormick, the publisher of the *Tribune,* were bitingly lampooned. This disappointed the *Daily News* staff. Further shock was suffered when Knight livened up the physical make-up of the paper.

"He has put bobby socks on the madonna," one editorial executive said sourly, and resigned. Most of the staff, however, were willing to string along. There had long been a saying around the office that the *Daily News,* which traditionally was a stronghold of the substantial folk of Chicago, lost a reader every time it printed an obituary. Knight deliberately aimed at attracting more younger readers, even down to those of high-school age, by shortening his news stories and having them written with less circumlocution and ponderous phrasing.

This policy created a small revolt among the *Daily News* foreign staff, which, in its unique task of writing interpretive dispatches, had formerly been allowed all the space it wanted. Knight, convinced that some members of the foreign-news staff had got into a rut of punditry, ordered the dispatches written concisely and in such a way that the man-on-the-street could understand them. Two of the foreign correspondents resigned. The rest, numbering around twenty, are now engaged in trying out the Knight formula, some with their fingers crossed. Meanwhile, Knight is enlarging his foreign staff and is putting into operation a rotation plan under which correspondents will be brought back to this country every year or so. This is designed to give them a refresher course on what is going on in the United States, and is expected to serve the secondary purpose of keeping their wives reasonably familiar with what they look like. Wife trouble is one of the major hazards of a roaming correspondent's life.

It is too early to assess Knight's impact on Chicago. The circulation of the *Daily News* has gone up, but great news breaks, such as President Roosevelt's death and the close of the German war, have thrown calculations off. The *Daily News,* as an evening paper, competes directly with the *Herald-American,* a Hearst paper which makes generous use of red ink, and the *Times,* an intelligently run New Deal tabloid. As Knight is not out after red-headline readers, his chief fight for circulation is likely to be with the *Times.* In the morning field, Marshall Field's *Sun* is still outnumbered, by about three readers to one, by McCormick's giant *Tribune,* a circumstance which gives Knight little concern.

Except for a couple of winter months which he spends in a rented home in Miami, he divides his time among Akron, Detroit and Chicago, and occasionally makes a trip to New York in his capacity as president of the American Society of Newspaper Editors.

The business worries of Knight Newspapers, Inc., are handled capably by a man named John H. Barry, whom the elder Knight brought to the *Beacon Journal* in 1912. The elder Knight, who was an easy touch for friends in need, had an informal habit of extracting two or three hundred dollars at a time from the cash drawer and leaving an IOU. Barry put a stop to that and also to another informal custom the editor had of burying bills in a drawer of his desk and forgetting them. Jack Knight and Barry often have loud, acrimonious fights over finances, which Barry invariably wins, after which they become friends again.

Knight maintains hotel apartments in Detroit and Chicago, and when in Akron lives in the home he grew up in. It is a rambling gray-brick house on a slightly run-down section of Portage Path, the town's best residential street, which the elder Knight used to refer to disrespectfully as Mortgage Heights. It has a formal English garden and a swimming pool, and is close to the Portage Country Club. His family's stage of development makes him comparatively foot-loose. Of his two surviving sons, one is a cadet at Culver Military Academy and the other is a reporter on a paper in Port Huron, Michigan. A married stepdaughter lives in Honolulu. Knight is often accompanied on his trips by his wife, Beryl, an attractive, prematurely gray woman, whom he married in 1932, after her divorce from Jackson Comstock, a rubber manufacturer. Knight's first wife died in 1929.

Knight has shown no striking originality in making his way to the first rank of American publishers, a fact of which he is acutely aware. In his early days he freely borrowed ideas from the out-of-town newspapers which he read while occupying the *Beacon Journal's* exchange desk, and he later introduced these ideas into his other properties. He is equally ready to borrow an idea today. He has been an adapter, rather than a pioneer, and has operated largely as a salvager and renovator of established journals.

He has, however, helped to restore a semblance of personal journalism in a field which has grown more and more impersonal with the years. His weekly editorial, to which he signs his name, is a talky discussion of whatever subject happens to be stirring in his mind at the moment. Its chief virtue is what is known in sports as a change of pace, and it usually has a fairly high indignation content. It may be a discussion of foreign policy or it may be a criticism of such wartime gaucheries as Elsa Maxwell's "victory" festival in Hollywood celebrating the liberation of Paris.

Today, less than a decade after stepping beyond the Akron horizon, Knight exercises an unusually strong influence upon public opinion. Because of the financial solidity of his growing empire, he is in a position to be an independent voice limited only by his own philosophy and prejudices. He intends to widen his influence further by adding radio stations to his holdings, if allowed to by the Federal Communications Commission.

Friends of Knight say that the only interest that could conceivably deflect him from newspapering is diplomacy. During the European war he put in a stretch in London as liaison man for the United States Office of Censorship with the Ministry of Information. His task was to smooth out some difficulties that had arisen between the two agencies, and during his mission, which turned out amicably, he came to like and admire the English. On returning to this country, Knight, who was always a dapper dresser, took to lounging around the house in a silk dressing gown and an Ascot tie. From his talk about the English, his friends gathered that nothing would please him more than to be appointed ambassador to the Court of St. James's. When asked about this, Knight smiles and says, "Nobody would think of giving me a diplomatic job. I'm too outspoken."

The Talleyrand of the Times
(ARTHUR KROCK)

By MATTHEW JOSEPHSON

EDITOR'S PREFACE.—American newspapers are largely local. Some, especially those published in capital cities, have state coverage, and a few of the larger ones are regional in circulation. We do not, in this country, however, have national newspapers in the sense that the London *Times* or the Manchester *Guardian* may be so regarded. There are several reasons for this, among which are these:

(1) The territorial size of the United States has made it difficult for a daily newspaper anywhere to seek a nation-wide circulation.

(2) Local newspapers, by means of the press association and syndicate services, can provide adequate coverage of national and international news, which will (and possibly *should*) always be but an adjunct to locally written news, features, and editorials which, theoretically at least, are the mainstay or chief stock in trade of the community newspaper.

(3) The news magazines such as *Time, Life,* and *Newsweek,* have a natural advantage—partially as a result of their own efforts—in the realm of national circulation.

There is one newspaper in this country, however, which comes very near to being national in character. That paper is the New York *Times.* Certainly, as the following article suggests, it is read as carefully by those in high position in the national capital as any paper published there—more so by many. It is also read by persons in key positions in the professions and business throughout the country. During the United Nations conference in San Francisco, it even printed an edition in the California city which was distributed free to the delegates, who were high in their praise of the *Times* for this journalistic enterprise.

All of which is said to emphasize the importance of the position occupied by Arthur Krock, the subject of this biography. As Washington correspondent of the *Times*, he can (and does) interpret the capital both to those who compose the government, and to the nation at large. When this article originally appeared, the *Post* editors chose as the title, "Typewriter Statesman." Presidents (now that Mr. Roosevelt has passed on to his reward) may come and go, an old Congress may die and a new one may convene, bureaus may be created, consolidated, and eliminated, but the Washington correspondent of the great *Times* endures—a kind of super-statesman or external conscience, sphinx-like, whose words are weighed carefully by those whose actions are being reported and interpreted, whose praise is as nectar from the gods, and whose criticism is to be avoided as the plague. Mr. Krock has been a statesman in this sense. But Mr. Josephson prefers "The Talleyrand of the Times." "Talleyrand," he notes, "used to change sides and liked to overthrow persons in power. Such is Mr. Krock also."

I

July 29 and August 5, 1944

ONE of the seven wonders of newspaperdom has certainly been the spreading power of today's crop of Washington correspondents and columnists. As our national politics has become more complex, the public has come to depend more and more on the journalistic oracles who unfailingly expound its mysteries. One syndicated prophet is published in 622 newspapers reaching 21,000,000 readers. Others appear in papers with combined circulations of from 6,000,000 to 10,000,000. Hence, statesmen, lobbyists, and the presidents of labor unions in Washington bow low before the big columnists, almost as low as the maîtres d'hôtel in Hollywood bow to the movie peerage. The men who were once reporters have become commentators, and sit in the tents of the mighty. Well they might say, paraphrasing an old English poet: "Let others make the laws of the nation, if we may but write its Washington columns."

Relatively far down the list, in point of reader circulation, stands Arthur Krock, the chief Washington correspondent of the New York *Times,* who, since 1934, has been turning out a deceptively quiet and reflective article. Entitled "In the Nation," it appears three times a week as a signed piece filling column five of the *Times'* dignified editorial page, and once a week in a part of the Sunday section which is devoted to national and foreign news. Jealously, the *Times,* a newspaper of strong traditions, refuses to sell or syndicate Krock's column, though it is constantly being invited to do so. Thus, Arthur Krock, who would also like to be syndicated and earn $100,000 a year instead of a third of that sum, is confined to what seems a mere handful of 440,000 readers weekdays and 805,000 Sundays. Yet partly owing to the prestige of the *Times,* which approaches the status of a national newspaper—with 100,000 out-of-town circulation daily and 400,000 Sundays—and largely owing to the special, patented qualities of his products, Krock wields an influence that is like nobody else's in his business.

For long years, small-town editors throughout the United States have formed the habit of guiding their opinions by the *Times'* editorial page, in which Krock holds down such a prominent position. On a number of occasions, recently, out-of-town publishers arriving in Washington have been heard to say that the two men they wanted to meet most of all were President Roosevelt and Arthur Krock. In Washington itself, people who must follow the political news for their living read Krock's column more closely than any other comment, and they read it between the lines.

"The first thing we members of Congress do when we get up in the morning," says Sen. Harry F. Byrd, of Virginia, formerly a reporter himself, "is to reach for the New York *Times* and read Krock. He is by all odds more alert about what is going on in national affairs than anyone else." On any morning, a trip through what Bernard M. Baruch has fittingly called the "political jungle" of Washington might show Mr. Baruch himself, an old friend of Arthur Krock, presiding as an unofficial elder statesman on his bench in Lafayette Park and beginning the day by reading the same column. Continuing through the many newspaper bureaus, in the neighborhood of 14th and Pennsylvania, one would find the other capital correspondents studiously occupied with the same literature.

About five years ago, a poll of 200 correspondents indicated that more than 70 per cent of them read four or five of the big Eastern morning newspapers each day, including the New York *Herald Tribune,* the Washington *Post* and the Baltimore *Sun,* but 100 per cent of them read the New York *Times* and Arthur Krock. Their favorite columnist was, up to the day of his death in the Pacific war front, Raymond Clapper; the most respected, because of his learning, Walter Lippmann. But Krock, though distinctly less popular among his fellow workers than was the breezy Clapper, is the one who, in their opinion, follows the game most sharply and calls the plays signaled by the great quarterback with an insider's knowledge.

During the long Roosevelt tenure, the *Times'* Washington bureau, headed by the fast-moving Krock, has compiled an outstanding record in scoops, or exclusive stories—though no count has been kept of the journalistic extra-base hits and no one paper has had a monopoly of them. In any case, the *Times* runs the largest special news bureau in the capital— aside from the leading national press services—and its chief has had entree to the highest political, military and business circles. He writes, as the other reporters say, "from a thorough background knowledge of the news." He knows where the news is being made, and sometimes even helps to make it. For Krock, his colleagues believe, is something of a politico himself.

At fifty-seven, dignified and self-confident in manner, Arthur Krock looks a good deal like a successful doctor. His hair is iron-gray over a high, square forehead, his features are sharply cut, his bespectacled glance is keen. A stocky, middle-sized man, he has grown lately a little rounder and ruddier than he used to be, though his movements are still abrupt and quick. Nowadays, Krock is never seen running into the Government offices, or going to White House press conferences, or mingling with the leg men who try to pick up off-the-record stories from one another at the convivial bar of the National Press Club. He is well past that stage. "Krock used to be a good reporter," the other newspapermen say with a certain edge, "but now he's a journalist."

During the day he is usually to be found in his private office in the *Times* bureau, quietly hewing to his line, with the typewriters and telegraph instruments going like mad outside his door. Richard Oulahan, his predecessor as chief of the *Times* bureau, was a handsome, lovable giant of a man who, during long years of distinguished service, carved out for himself an imposing social rank in Washington, somewhere between that of an ambassador and that of the mythical senator at large. Krock, less impressive physically, has inherited or taken over the decorum that goes with his key post, and he walks with the deliberate stride of outward self-assurance. The twenty-three reporters who work under his direction always address him, by request, as "Mr. Krock," and he misters them in turn. This usage is something of a cold douche to the shirt-sleeved democracy of the press, in which everyone is called by his first name after five minutes. On a few occasions, men coming to the *Times* from other newspaper shops, and being unaccustomed to such protocol, have protested. One of them asked Krock, "How long does a man have to work around here before this 'mister' business stops?"

"As long as you care to stay here," Krock answered firmly. "I'm sorry, that's the way I am."

Krock's method is, literally, to make the news come to him, instead of running after it. Some years ago he bitterly offended Thomas G. Corcoran, when that high-spirited young barrister was acting as the President's intimate White House assistant. Calling up Corcoran one day, Krock expressed a desire to see him about some story.

"Delighted," answered Corcoran hospitably. "Any time you say."

Krock then suggested, "Won't you come down to my office tomorrow morning at eleven?"

Corcoran, after struggling for some moments with the expletives that surged to his lips, finally blurted out that the *Times* correspondent could damned well come over to the White House to see him, and he hung up.

Undisturbed by such rather rare reverses, Krock has persisted in his methods, and has long made the insiders of politics and big business either talk over the telephone, see him at lunch or come to his desk with their stories and with the documents backing them up. They not only come to him, but sometimes senators or heads of Government departments like to ask him for his advice. And why not? His experience of professional politics runs back thirty-seven years, during which he has been at the top or near the top of three famous newspapers—the Louisville *Courier-Journal,* the old New York *World,* and the New York *Times*. He has covered national party conventions since he was a cub reporter, and he saw Bryan nominated at Denver in 1908. When, late in 1932, Cordell Hull was first offered a cabinet post by Roosevelt—that of Secretary of Commerce—he consulted Arthur Krock, long known to him, and was advised to hold out for the Secretaryship of State.

Mr. Hull, a tight-lipped old recluse, has a habit of retiring regularly at nine P.M. Krock is probably the only newspaperman who ever succeeded in having him called to the telephone late at night, as he once did, during an international emergency, by sending a reporter to slip a note under the secretary's bedroom door. The not so "dear Alben" Barkley, of Kentucky, a compatriot who has known Krock since the days in Louisville, has also benefited from the brilliant political reporter's advice.

Newspapermen get an intoxicating sense of power when statesmen, sometimes letting them in behind the scenes, ask them what they think will be the public effect of certain measures that may be tomorrow's news. Under the New Deal, the astute Arthur for years has enjoyed such a relationship, par-

ticularly with some of the key members of the so-called Minor
Cabinet, such as former Budget Director Lewis Douglas,
former Under Secretary of the Treasury John H. Hanes, and
the former chairman of the SEC and Ambassador to England, Joseph P. Kennedy. In this way he has been able to have
a Justice of the Supreme Court nominated by the *Times,* a
month before the President actually sent his name to the
Senate—which happened in the case of Mr. Justice William O.
Douglas. Krock, learning from Douglas himself that he was
being considered for the place by Roosevelt, simply fell in
with the plan of Douglas' friends, who aimed to emphasize
the young jurist's availability as a Westerner, hailing from the
state of Washington. In the same way he got the *Times* the
first news of the coming appointment of Joe Kennedy as
ambassador to England at the end of 1937. The then incumbent, Judge Robert W. Bingham, for whom Krock had worked
on the Louisville *Courier-Journal* twenty years earlier, and
whom he no longer liked, lay dying at the Johns Hopkins
Hospital in Baltimore. When the news about Kennedy's suc-
ceeding him was scooped, Bingham had not yet resigned, the
British had not been consulted. The President grumbled something about Arthur Krock's not even waiting until Bingham
was in the grave before making Kennedy ambassador.

In the autumn of 1937, all Washington, and, in fact, the
whole steel, shipbuilding and aircraft industry awaited the
forthcoming report on the merchant-marine program being
prepared by Joe Kennedy, then chairman of the Maritime
Commission. It was due to be released on November tenth, but
more than two weeks before that date, Arthur Krock, in his
column, gave, in general terms, a quite accurate forecast of its
policy and scope. Even as the fertile-minded Krock wrote, a
considerable portion of that "closely guarded" report—so the
Times man laughingly described it—reposed in a drawer of
his desk. His friend Kennedy had come to him for advice and
obtained some expert assistance. In fact, Kennedy, an open-
handed man, was so fond of Krock and so grateful to him that
when he went off to England a little later he lent him his

luxurious villa in Palm Beach for a short winter vacation. However, the newspaperman afterward admitted ruefully to friends that the bills for Scotch and tips to servants made the thing costlier than a suite at The Breakers and spoiled his suntan a bit.

During the day, Krock is kept busy contacting his live sources. At night, he puts on his dinner suit and with his handsome, fashionably dressed wife, the former Martha Granger Blair, of Chicago, who is something of a socialite, dines out at the smartest dinner tables in Washington. The capital's society columns regularly carry the traces of his movements in the purlieus of ambassadors, assistant department secretaries and dollar-a-year men. Washington hostesses have reported his table talk as "brilliant," but "barbed." For Krock, as his polished newspaper articles show, is given to irony and indirection rather than to the battering tactics of a Westbrook Pegler. He favors what wily old Mr. Baruch calls "the oblique attack." Even if he felt himself overwhelmed by dislike for President Roosevelt, he would not say, as Pegler might, that the President had gangsters and brothel keepers in his labor-union following. He would, in florid phrases, describe the President as so overloaded with responsibilities that, unknown to him, elements poorly regarded by the business and financial community had introduced themselves into his entourage. Of Harry Hopkins, whom he has reproached for excessive loyalty to his chief, he has said, "Mr. Hopkins may, at times have thought that something the President said or did was not perfect. If so, he suppressed the unworthy thought with ease."

At late parties, Krock has been seen standing with his back to the fireplace, laying down the law in a fatherly way to a circle of men whose names make headlines. But thanks to his instincts as an old reporter, he also knows how to listen, question and prod. On quitting his office, he usually leaves the telephone number of his hostess for that evening; there may be a story by another reporter whose facts need checking. "I may be able to confirm that story at dinner," he sometimes says.

Up to a late hour, he is always in touch with the night staff at the *Times* bureau, telephoning in tips for stories or confirmations he has received for stories already in the works. Among the capital's correspondents there is a tradition that Krock, a light sleeper, works almost twenty-four hours a day.

An example of what Senator Byrd calls Krock's extreme political alertness was to be seen last February, and it indicated how much more valuable the *Times* Washington column was than some of the costly dope services issued as inside stuff. On February eighth the Senate, after three months of bitter debate, passed a compromise bill providing for ballots for absent soldiers, sailors and marines. It was a bill that was very disappointing to the Roosevelt Administration, leaving the ballot mainly under state control, with some provisions for a Federal ballot—which Roosevelt desired—to be used only under severe restrictions. The House had meanwhile passed a somewhat different bill, and the next move was to send both measures to a joint conference between the two branches of Congress in order to work out a common bill. However, there was still some faint chance that Roosevelt's clever ideologists—as Arthur Krock calls them—might somehow, at the eleventh hour, amid the intricate machinery of joint-conference debate, slip over a combined bill that still contained some of the Federal-ballot features favored by Roosevelt.

But Krock is quite an ideologist himself. In his column the next morning he gave the alarm at once, urging that the anti-Administration senators work for further delay and prevent the soldiers'-vote bill from going to joint conference "immediately" because "the Administration has ways to pack the conference committee." That day, Senator Byrd took the floor and aroused the Senate against possible eleventh-hour packing efforts by the Roosevelt men. Delay killed the last chance for a simplified Federal-ballot bill for the servicemen. Byrd, complimented on his foresight, said later that he had got his idea from reading Krock's column in the *Times*.

In lending expert assistance to the hardened opponents of the New Deal, such as Senators Byrd, George and Bailey, working in combination with the Republicans, Vandenberg and

Taft, Krock, of course, was scarcely befriending the Roosevelt Administration. By now, it looked as if he had given up just calling the plays from the press stand, and, after catching on to the signals, was passing them over to the team opposing the great quarterback.

The truth is that Krock has been doing this sort of thing very cleverly for six or seven years, but has recently grown bolder. In Washington, it is an open and somewhat diverting scandal that the chief representative of "America's most distinguished newspaper," the New York *Times*—Independent Democrat—is frankly *persona non grata* at the White House. On the other hand, the correspondents of regular Republican newspapers, such as the *Herald Tribune,* continue in good standing as amiable members of the loyal opposition. Napoleon I used to say that the defiant tongue-wagging of Madame de Staël in Paris was as much of a menace as a couple of enemy divisions. Roosevelt would probably be willing to lose a state or two to the Republican side if that would eliminate Arthur Krock's "sniping," as he has termed it, from Washington. Discreet complaints to Publisher Arthur Hays Sulzberger, of the *Times,* have done no good, as Krock, by a long-standing agreement, has a free hand over his bureau and over his colunm. Krock, in very good measure, determines the policy of the New York *Times* on national affairs. He is a member of its executive committee of editors, an informal policy-making group, presided over by Sulzberger, that meets only once in a couple of months.

However, the regular editorial writers of the *Times* on several occasions have tilted a lance directly at Krock himself—a fact which constitutes one of the major mysteries surrounding this great and slightly bureaucratic newspaper institution. Arthur Krock had reason to congratulate himself when the compromise servicemen's-vote bill, on March fourteenth, was finally passed in the form he had desired. But on March fifteenth the *Times'* leading editorial attacked the bill as an ineffectual measure that would sorely disappoint our soldiers and sailors.

"I have been a nail in the side of the gentle Arthur Hays Sulzberger many times," Krock laughs; but he adds, "I don't really abuse my power."

A different view of Krock's use of his power is held in the precincts of the White House, in Elmer Davis' OWI, and in the big Government departments, such as the Treasury and the Interior, where the faithful Morgenthau and Ickes, respectively, preside. There, the New Deal lieutenants indulge in puns about "sounds from an empty Krock," but show pretty plainly how much he has got into their hair.

The President hates to have his hand tipped in advance—as has been done repeatedly by Arthur Krock beats—and you can hardly blame him. On one occasion, long ago, in the summer of 1933, when premature news of the approaching international economic conference in London was given by the *Times* correspondent, Roosevelt, unusually irritated, denounced him as one who purveyed falsehoods. Krock prides himself on his accuracy, and also happens to be a very touchy fellow. Once, in his boyhood, a friend of his suddenly stole up behind him and threw him into a swimming pool. Krock, very frightened and angry, never spoke to him again. Today, he is still apt to be moody, and sulks up in the *Times* bureau, avoiding White House press conferences, when Roosevelt denies one of his stories. His younger colleagues appear in his place, but when they ask some too-pointed question, the President, peering suspiciously over his pince-nez, remarks: "I suppose Arthur told you to ask that one."

"There's a barb or a hook at the end of everything li'l' Arthur writes," the President has said. And it is true that, though Krock seems to confine himself to reporting and discussing the news of the day objectively, and with an air of science and learning, the significant thing about his articles is the angle, or slant, he gives them. As a scholar of professional politics, he knows the little tricks and political subterfuges used by Franklin Roosevelt. If some young New Deal lawyer, after coming under attack in the press or in Congress, were to be suddenly removed by the President to a post in the rear,

Krock would find out quickly where he had been removed to and inform his readers that the obnoxious man in question could now be found somewhere on a shelf in what used to be Stettinius' Lend-Lease Administration—now FEA—or in the basement of the RFC, which he has amusingly called "Jesse Jones' oubliettes." The oubliettes were the dungeons employed by the Bourbon kings of France for troublesome subjects before the French Revolution.

The chief complaint of the New Dealers is that Krock for some five years has taken or tried to take the scalps of some of Roosevelt's most devoted aides, such as Morgenthau, Harry Hopkins, Corcoran, Leon Henderson and others. Meanwhile, according to these complaints, he has tried to arouse jealousies among big officeholders or build up their opponents within the palace, especially the "moderate" or conservative Democrats of the type of Joe Kennedy and John W. Hanes.

Among his rounded, well-bred periods, there have been mingled occasional sentences touched with arsenic, such as: "Assistant Secretary of War Louis Johnson is widely credited with confidential designs on the job of his boss, Secretary Woodring."

Morgenthau has been put into rages because the *Times* columnist has suggested from time to time that the conservative commercial interests of this country would prefer to see a man like Kennedy, or Jesse Jones, or Hanes in his place as Secretary of the Treasury. Morgenthau has muttered darkly about the "intrigues" directed against him by Arthur Krock. Harry Hopkins, too, has considered himself victimized.

During the so-called purge elections of 1938, Hopkins was often accused in the press of trying to defeat Roosevelt's Democratic opponents in Congress by the use of WPA relief money. Various gossip columns quoted an indiscreet remark attributed to him: "We will tax and tax, and spend and spend, and elect and elect!" But when Arthur Krock published these words in the New York *Times*, the affair was taken seriously and led to a Senate investigation of this episode during a hearing on the nomination of Hopkins as Secretary of Commerce, at which the correspondent was called to testify. Following the newspaperman's code, he refused to reveal his source of information. As the clandestine and anonymous witness remained in hiding, the charges against Hopkins were dropped. But Hopkins, who denied everything, bitterly assailed Arthur Krock and the high-minded New York *Times* for publishing anonymous accusations against him. Partly because of ill health, but partly because he had been made a political liability, Hopkins remained Secretary of Commerce for only a few months, then resigned.

In short, Krock's cool sniping at the New Dealers has sometimes sown a certain confusion in their ranks. If half the things they say of him are true, Krock will have earned a large debt of gratitude, perhaps an embassy or two, if and when the Roosevelt Administration is turned out of office. The very extremes of *lèse majesté,* according to the men around the President, were reached by Krock last summer, when he enlisted himself and the *Times* in an alleged cabal to drive Under Secretary of State Sumner Welles out of office. Mr. Welles himself, according to Krock, believes that the *Times* columnist set in motion the whole train of events that led to his downfall.

Krock has long known and felt the tenderest regard for the venerable Secretary of State. "Mr. Hull was under attack," he maintains. "I defended him and let the chips fall where they might."

The not-too-well-hidden "battle of the State Department" was brought into the open through the normally discreet news columns of the *Times,* which, on August 4, 1943, printed a front-page story signed by John H. Crider, a very able member of Krock's staff. Crider reported the continuing clash of the Hull and Welles factions within the department, and described the confusion over policy and the bad administrative practices that resulted from this. The story was not pegged on any interview, but is believed to have originated from the Executive group in the White House, and was so thoroughly informed, so authoritative in tone, that it had the effect of suddenly opening a door on a closet drama. The public generally interpreted the story as putting the blame for the reported inefficiency of the State Department upon Secretary Hull, who was, after all, its official head, yet was described as not even knowing what was going on.

Three days before this story appeared, Arthur Krock and his wife had left town for a vacation in Hot Springs, Virginia, and Krock received the *Times* a day late. He had known that the Crider story was coming in, but hadn't expected it would contain reflections so unfavorable to Secretary Hull. As soon as he read it, he got on the long-distance telephone and raised Cain. Then he sat down and in warm blood wrote a sermon ostensibly using the New York *Times'* own news story as its text, entitled: "The Situation in the State Department." For the troubles that had multiplied there, Krock bluntly placed the blame upon President Roosevelt himself. It was the President, he charged, who had, in the first place, prevented Secretary Hull from choosing his own chief administrative aides. After appointing Sumner Welles as under secretary, the President had permitted him to go over Mr. Hull's head and handle matters of paramount policy himself, as if he were Secretary of State, Krock wrote. Thus Roosevelt had prevented Cordell Hull "from having an administrative officer in whom he is willing to rest full faith." The conflicts that had arisen over the "two State Departments" could be settled only by having one or the other man go. Krock ended by urging that Secretary Hull be permitted "to be the real undisputed head of a loyal staff." He had, in the course of his article, done everything but call Sumner Welles a disloyal officer in so many words. After reading the article over the telephone, Krock hurried back to Washington to take charge of the battle.

The August fourth story on the State Department had placed Cordell Hull in a painful enough dilemma. But Krock's blast of August sixth left him no alternative but to go to the President and force a showdown between himself and Welles, which is what he did. All through the month that followed, when the outcome was uncertain, Arthur Krock, with whom politics can sometimes be used as a brutal sport, took pot shots

at Mr. Welles and his faction, while a powerful journalistic
rival of Krock's, Drew Pearson, in his widely syndicated Washington Merry-Go-Round column, came to Welles' defense.
From time to time, Krock took a sideswipe at Pearson, so that
the duel between the rival columnists provided a side show
for the bigger internal conflict in the Administration and enlivened the torrid summer weeks in Washington. A good many
of the men in the *Times* organization itself believe that, putting it most charitably, Krock's loyalties to his friends create
the most serious mote in his eye. Occasionally, Krock was ad-
monished by Mr. Sulzberger, who felt that his violently partisan methods were out of keeping with the *Times'* style. But
Krock evidently managed to carry his publisher along with
him.

Early in September, the resignation of Sumner Welles was
announced, and at last a troubled peace returned to the banks
of the Potomac. It was an event that the *Times* commentator
signaled correctly as a serious defeat for Roosevelt, who, he
said, feared Hull's power of political reprisal on the eve of
another presidential election. The unhappy Welles had gradually been worked into a most precarious position, but, undoubtedly, Krock had given him the *coup de grâce* and had
good reason to sound notes of triumph in his column. Although Krock talks much of principles, to him the political
drama has been largely an affair of personalities who were
either devils or angels.

II

Arthur Krock, the fertile-minded Washington correspondent and columnist of the New York *Times,* who has spent all
but twenty of his fifty-seven years in the newspaper profession,
assumes toward the world in general a somewhat firm and authoritative tone. Toward his fellow journalists his manner
now approaches aloofness, and this, it is confidentially reported, is really but a mask for a kindly though sensitive and
unhappy soul. "Arthur is always eaten by about seven devils,"

whisper his old acquaintances. For instance, he despises politicians, yet it has been his fate to spend most of his life almost in bed with them, or even under the bed. "I have no feeling, one way or another, about men who occupy public office," he has said as if holding his nose. Krock dislikes Washington—"a one-industry town, full of envious conflicts"—yet finds himself still stationed there, aiming his putty blower every day at the politicians in office, though he wishes he were somewhere else. A waspish critic of President Roosevelt—for whom, incidentally, he feels a secret admiration—he has been forced to devote himself to writing Roosevelt history since 1932 in some two million words, which will provide rich source material on our inner-circle politics to future generations of scholars. He knows that many members of the ruling party dislike him, yet he is a man who longs to be loved.

Arthur Bernard Krock, unlike most Americans of the great middle class, looks back at the years of his boyhood and youth as a period of frustration and insecurity, all of which helped to put a little iron into him. He was born on November 16, 1886, in the small market town of Glasgow, Kentucky, the only child of Joseph Krock, a bookkeeper, and Caroline Morris Krock, daughter of one of Glasgow's leading drygoods merchants. His father was Jewish, while his mother was not. He was brought up outside the Jewish faith. His father he describes as "an impractical dreamer with a yearning for culture," who, in his spare time, wrote verse that was published occasionally in the local gazettes. Krock speaks with great affection of his mother and of his maternal grandparents, the Morrises; it was with them that he lived during most of his boyhood, after his father had gone off to Chicago to seek the better fortune that somehow always eluded him. At fourteen, however, Arthur also went to Chicago to study in high school. Four years later, aided by his grandparents, he entered Princeton with the class of 1908. However, financial reverses also overtook his grandfather, and Arthur despondently left Princeton in midcareer. "I had a sort of false pride in me in those days," he recalls, "and I hated to stay on at Princeton without money."

Returning to Chicago, he worked his way through Lewis Institute and earned the somewhat illusory degree of Bachelor of Associated Arts. At this stage, a friend gave him a pass on a railroad day coach headed for Louisville, and Krock, a skinny, eager and nervous little man, sat up all night, talking to no one on the train, looking out the window and worrying all by himself. Having earned his tuition in Chicago by running the school paper, he had applied for a job he heard was open on the small Louisville *Herald*. He got the job and, as a cub reporter, covered the police stations, earning fifteen dollars a week for about a year; then he moved over to the Associated Press office, where he spent two years editing the night wire out of Louisville. Through a helpful older friend, the Louisville political reporter, John D. Wakefield, Krock was introduced to the wealthy publisher, William B. Haldeman, and won a job as Washington correspondent for the Louisville *Courier-Journal* and its afternoon version, the Louisville *Times*. There he worked under the orders of the swaggering, walrus-mustached Henry Watterson, founder of the *Courier-Journal,* whom Krock has called "the last of the great editors." Watterson wrote in a leisurely, full-blown style that carried, as Krock has said, plenty of "poison arrows" when he needed them. Watterson had a profound influence on the younger man.

In 1915, after four years in Washington, Krock returned to Louisville as editorial manager of both the Louisville *Times* and *Courier-Journal*. The turbulent politics of Kentucky became his school. Once, serving as a chief deputy sheriff, he carried around with him a six-shooter that he prayed he wouldn't have to use. Another year, as editor, he played a strong role in a hot municipal campaign, but on the last night before the elections, his candidate for office, together with all the candidate's party workers, was hustled off to jail by the police chief of the ruling party, on a charge of traffic violation. The elections took place as usual, but Krock's candidate came out a poor second.

At Louisville, an aggressive young newspaperman, Arthur

Krock knew editorial power. In 1911, at the age of twenty-four, he had married Marguerite Polleys, daughter of a Minneapolis railroad official. A son, Thomas Polleys Krock, was soon born to them. Krock now earned enough to rent a nice house in Louisville at seventy-five dollars a month and felt himself ready to climb the social ladder to a place fitting the brains and talent that everyone knew were brimming in him.

However, Louisville society up to those days had been ruled by the legendary "first hundred families," some of them, it must be said, quite poor and decayed as well as proud. Louisville recalls that the pushful, fast-talking young editor tried to break into its charmed circle, but was never really accepted, and that this gave him a certain grief.

On occasion, Krock played at crusading, and boldly cocked a snoot at the politically influential Louisville Gas & Electric Co. Whereupon, Executive Vice-President Donald MacDonald was heard to remark, "That Arthur Krock is a coming young man. I think we ought to invite him to dinner." The Krocks came, were kindly received at MacDonald's big house, and met his three handsome daughters. After that, Krock was on a friendly footing with the MacDonalds, who were leading members of Louisville's upper crust.

In 1917, a bitter feud broke out between Watterson, a minority stockholder, and the Haldeman family, majority owners of the *Courier-Journal* papers. Krock engineered a deal by which the property was sold to Judge Robert W. Bingham—the future ambassador to England—who had lately inherited $5,000,000 in Standard Oil shares. Under Bingham, Krock was editor in chief of the Louisville *Times* from 1919 to 1923, when the judge put another man over him, thus giving the brilliant Arthur the finger. Promptly, Krock left for New York, where he had wanted to go all along, and wound up, in October, 1923, as an editorial writer for the *World*.

In Louisville, it was his fate to have been overshadowed by the formidable Watterson. In New York, he worked for a while under Frank Cobb, another famous editor, and side by side with such journalistic stars as Walter Lippmann, Laurence

Stallings, F. P. Adams, Heywood Broun, and Rollin Kirby. Krock enjoyed most of all the happy lunch table of the old *World,* which he believes had some of the best talk of the age. Once more, however, he edged over toward the managerial end, becoming assistant to Ralph Pulitzer, the president and publisher of the *World.* Part of his duty was to do the "breakfast editing" of the news—that is, read over the news stories after the paper came out and tell Pulitzer whether the *World's* reporters had covered their assignments as fully as those of the *Times* or *Tribune.* This made him fairly unpopular with the hired hands. When Lippmann, after Cobb's death, became editor, Krock, who disagrees on almost everything with Lippmann, retreated to the more flourishing *Times,* to which Adolph Ochs had already called him. It was a lucky move; the *World* was to die a few years later.

On the *Times,* from 1927, Krock wrote editorials and also traveled about the country as a political expert, doing signed articles. On the night after an election he would always be called in, as is still the custom, to write the leading story interpreting the results at the polls. But at forty-five, Arthur Krock, esteemed by rich newspaper publishers for his astuteness and news sense, was little known to the general public. When, late in 1931, Richard Oulahan, the long-established *Times* representative in Washington, died, and the post was offered to him, Krock hesitated a long while before he accepted. He thought it was like being sent to Siberia, and agreed to go only for a limited time, in order to reorganize the Washington bureau. But soon Washington became a great stage upon which Krock also had his hour of glory—especially, after 1934, when his signed column, "In the Nation," began to appear on the editorial page.

Like many other newspapermen, Arthur Krock admired Franklin Roosevelt, when he first took office, as a combination of Machiavelli, Mark Hanna and William Jennings Bryan. "We must support Roosevelt; it is the only line we can take," he used to say to his staff in 1933. Furthermore, no President had ever shown so much courtesy to the press. At the start of his Administration, Roosevelt inaugurated regular biweekly press conferences at which he himself read the news release of the day, and held a friendly and informal question-and-answer period with a hundred or more reporters. Franklin Roosevelt, as a rule, played no favorites in handing out the news, as some of his predecessors had done. He enjoyed, for a while, a honeymoon with the men of the press.

However, no reporter can manage to get a beat at a general White House conference. The news of those times was all "money and statistics," as Krock says, and so he decided to fortify his own working knowledge of politics with "a smattering of economics."

On April 14, 1933, Krock scooped the nation's press with a front-page, signed story giving accurate advance news of the coming NRA laws. He got this story not from the White House but, as reporters define it, by working on the fringes of the Administration. One day he happened to take lunch with a prominent businessman he knew and Senator Wagner of New York. With wide-open ears he listened to the senator's somewhat indiscreet talk about the new plan for industry and labor, then he filled in the rest of the story. This brought down upon him the first of a series of denials by Roosevelt.

Five days later he was able to publish an advance story of the coming embargo on gold exports from the United States, which was news of world-shaking importance. This news had leaked to Krock through a telephone conversation with a seemingly unwary official of the Treasury Department, who asked, "Don't you think it's fine what the President has decided to do about the gold?" Krock, who is always careful never to give the impression of being surprised by anything, thought quickly and guessed, "You mean the export embargo?" "Certainly," was the reply. Krock then called kindly old Secretary Woodin, who was not used to the harriers of the press, and bully-ragged him into giving a confirmation.

This time Roosevelt did no denying, and Krock always suspected that he knowingly permitted the leak, possibly to prepare the public for coming events.

After Roosevelt's first re-election, by a record-breaking majority in 1936, The New York *Times* home office put through an inquiry regarding his second-term policies which were to be the subject of a Sunday magazine article. Krock, taking the assignment, had the benefit of a long private conversation with the President, and brought back a story that seemed to him so important that it was run on February 28, 1937, as a front-page, exclusive interview, signed by himself.

Roosevelt later complained that he was given to understand only "background information" was wanted. The story announced the President's determination to go forward with his plans of reform, his scheme to pack the Supreme Court, and—amusingly enough, as it seems in 1944—his intentions to retire at the end of his second term, in January, 1941. At the time, Arthur Krock's story seemed to tell the whole world what it was panting to know about the President's future intentions.

The other newspapermen protested at the special favor to the *Times,* and the President said ruefully, "My head is on the block; I will never do it again." In 1935, the *Times* Washington correspondent had been awarded the Pulitzer Prize for journalism; in 1938 he was given the Pulitzer Prize a second time, for his exclusive interview with the President. After that, Krock was credited with knowing more about the President's mind than any other newspaper correspondent. Krock, as early as January, 1935, in a speech before the Republican Club of New York, said, "I deeply suspect this Administration of more ruthlessness, intelligence and subtlety in trying to suppress unfavorable comment than any other I have known." A while later, Krock wrote in his column that Roosevelt loved to "hoodwink" the press and sometimes tried to "channel" publicity through chosen newspapers. When, on February 9, 1938, Krock's comment in the *Times* in a round-about way gave out inside information on a rumored secret naval understanding between the United States and Great Britain—by which the two navies, in case of need, were to aid each other in the Atlantic—the British Foreign Office complained through diplomatic channels and Roosevelt was embarrassed. Before a full press conference, the President denounced Arthur Krock roundly, saying that he had informed all foreign embassies that the *Times,* once regarded as reflecting accurately our State Department policies, was no longer to be considered in that light.

Although the New Dealers treated him with increasing suspicion, the crafty Krock once more, in March, 1939, bobbed up with another "exclusive story" that seemed to come right through a pipe line from the White House. Published at a nerve-racking moment in international affairs, the story described a supposedly cherished plan of Roosevelt's to hold a parley at sea with Hitler, Mussolini, the King of England and various presidents and dictators, in order to bring about a general understanding that would save the world's peace.

Krock claims that he had heard of the President's plan as early as August, 1936, but had been unable to confirm it. Such ideas he usually preserves carefully in a sort of card index he keeps, and he waited with this one until the winter of 1939, when an American financial agent who had important connections in Europe brought him a memorandum on the plan. After verifying it through certain sources in Wall Street, Krock went to the White House, where, he says, he "sold" the idea of publishing such a story to Miss Le Hand and the President, as something that might do great good. Roosevelt, according to the *Times* correspondent, likes to send up trial balloons; if they work, all is well, and if not, he denies having sponsored them—as so many other politicians have done. This one, when it appeared, may have seemed ill-timed, for the President said of it, "very interesting and well written, but untrue." Of another exclusive affair by Krock, a little earlier, concerning a reported plan of the President's to forgive British and French first World War debts, he had said, "A pure fabrication, with some doubts about its purity." But Krock no longer showed himself at the White House.

The President spoke of him as the Cassandra of the press

and, in this connection, used to tell a typically cute Roose-
veltian anecdote which Krock himself repeats, though he
thinks it is pretty flat.

"Li'l' Arthur"—it runs, for that is what the President now
calls him—"once made a trip to Paris and wanted to see the
sights. He asked for a guard of honor and was given the president of the republic and the commander in chief of the Army,
for that is the way he likes to do things. By and by, they came
to the Louvre Museum, and there they saw the Venus de Milo.
'Ah!' exclaimed li'l' Arthur. 'What grace, what classic beauty,
what form divine! But'—approaching nearer—'alas, alas! She
has halitosis.' "

The Roosevelt honeymoon with the press had ended some
years before, as long ago as 1935, and in the case of Krock even
earlier. The *Times* political expert, who declared himself thoroughly disillusioned about the New Deal, lampooned the
President's personal friends and aides most bitterly. He would
liken the former social worker, Harry Hopkins, to Boies Pen-
rose, the machine-manipulating Republican boss. The New
Dealers, he said, had formed one of the ugliest, most menacing
political groups ever seen in our history and were determined
to use the Federal Treasury to perpetuate themselves in office.
On the other hand, he eulogized "moderate" Democrats like
Joe Kennedy or John W. Hanes, and repeatedly urged that
they be given jobs, calling them the "brilliant unemployed."
Although he believes that he is an objective commentator who
carries no torches, Krock's partiality for his personal friends in
politics and his solicitude about getting them Government
jobs is a byword among the men of the New York *Times* organization, and he himself has confessed to the "human failing" of leaning over toward his friends. His attacks on the
Administration had made Roosevelt's brain trusters eager for
vengeance, and when, early in 1940, Krock took up the cause
of Hanes, one of his social friends, not wisely but too well, he
opened himself to their reprisals.

Hanes, a Democrat from North Carolina, but more lately a
Wall Street investment banker and man of independent

wealth, had served as a member of the SEC and then had become Under Secretary of the Treasury, which office he resigned on December 28, 1939. Actually, he served, as Krock wrote, as a sort of liaison officer between the New Deal and the business community, but after fighting within the palace against the current spending-and-borrowing policies, he had been ignored and treated as a hostage.

Two weeks after Hanes' resignation from the Treasury post, the one-billion-dollar Associated Gas & Electric, one of those holding-company "monstrosities" around which financial scandal had raged since 1929, filed a petition in bankruptcy. Then, on February 13, 1940, Krock, in his column, came out with an appeal that John W. Hanes be appointed sole trustee in receivership for Associated Gas, a job bringing fees of around $70,000 a year. The amended Federal Reorganization Act of 1938 now gave the Government considerable control over such situations, in which many investors had lost money. In addition the Public Utility Holding Company Act of 1935 permitted the SEC to act as trustee. But Krock gave warning that Tom Corcoran and Ben Cohen were scheming to take over the Associated Gas, and he warmly recommended Hanes as a conservative choice for trustee, arguing that "all parties in interest, save the Government Mr. Hanes has recently served, united to ask the court to appoint him."

It happened that the existing Federal Bankruptcy Law expressly forbade the appointment as trustees in receivership of any persons even *indirectly* connected with interested groups among the stock or bond holders. Yet Krock, in his story, had reported that somewhat earlier such groups had met informally and selected Hanes as their choice. It was known, as Krock also reported, that Hanes had considered their proposal favorably and discussed it with Secretary of the Treasury Morgenthau—to whom $5,000,000 in back taxes were owed by the bankrupt.

However, all this proved to be an uncomfortable business for Arthur Krock to be mixed up in. Three days after the column on Hanes appeared, the New Dealers moved to the attack, Senator Norris sending a petition to the SEC and a letter to the *Times* in which he charged that Krock's recommendation of Mr. Hanes was improper under existing law. The article itself, according to the senator, indicated that interested financial groups had chosen Hanes as their man "in advance of the filing of the petition in bankruptcy"—which was specifically forbidden.

In other words, Hanes, a likable and honest man, through the unfortunate terms in which his friend Krock espoused his cause, was brought under suspicion of heading special interests who might be unfair to the small security holders involved. Indeed, Senator Norris threatened to force an investigation in Congress.

Norris' charges, though probably inspired by some New Deal brain truster, gave the sedate New York *Times* quite a turn, but its editors saw fit to print them—together with Krock's answering statements that he had been misconstrued—back on Page 34 in the financial section. Hanes, in some embarrassment, dropped out of the contest. In Washington, where the affair caused a ripple of amusement among the well informed, some newspaper wag coined a phrase about "The New York *Times* having gone off half-Krocked."

Arthur Krock's devoted first wife, to whom he had been married happily for twenty-seven years, died, after a long illness, in September, 1938. Nine months later, on June 15, 1939, he was married to Martha Granger Blair, then aged thirty-seven, a handsome Chicago divorcée who had two children of her own. She had recently come to Washington to try her hand at running a society column herself for the Washington *Times-Herald*. Krock had met her socially at the salon of her editor, "Cissie" Patterson, and at embassy parties. As it happens, Mrs. Blair once wrote a little pen portrait of him in the Washington *Times-Herald* for February 15, 1939, placing him among the Washington Glamour Boys and describing him as a man who tried very hard to be charming to the ladies and "thinks he has a deceptive charm, but hasn't." However, he possessed "enticement," she said, and this lay in the fact that "he looks so fierce, takes everything so seriously that, to quote Ralph Pulitzer's couplet about him,

> *"Krock has a tongue as sharp as emery*
> *And a heart as soft as hominy."*

Six months later, after Arthur Krock had looked at her fiercely enough, she yielded to his enticement, and they were married. Krock is obviously proud of his wife. The second Mrs. Krock, unlike the first, does not hold her husband in awe, nor does she read many of his stories or fetch his warmed-up carpet slippers for him. For a while, her husband, in addition to his own work, struggled to help her get out her society column, but some months after they were married, he finally persuaded her to drop the thing.

The Krocks now live in a four-room apartment in Washington, and they also use an all-year country home called Limestone, placed in a 170-acre farm fifty-five miles out of the city, near Berryville, Virginia. The Limestone place dates from 1804 and is built of yellow brick. The decoration and furnishings of its nine rooms—not to speak of bathrooms with fireplaces in them—are expensively simple, in accordance with the taste of Mrs. Krock, whose father was an architect. On week ends and during vacations Arthur Krock farms the place seriously, keeping two men who raise hay and livestock. He enjoys being a landowner and often rides around the circumference of his property on a gentle nag. A close neighbor, within ten minutes' drive, is Sen. Harry F. Byrd.

The political commentator usually rises at eight, breakfasts in bed on a cup of tea and a raw apple, and reads right through five newspapers—the New York *Times,* from cover to cover, the New York *Herald Tribune,* the Baltimore *Sun,* the Washington *Post,* and the Washington *Times-Herald.* By eleven A.M. he reaches his office, runs through his mail and goes over the press-service dispatches. Ordinarily he leaves the details of story assignments to Luther Huston, the assistant chief of the *Times* bureau—unless there is some special story that either he or the New York office is interested in.

Krock watches carefully over the work of his reporters and pounces upon them for using old newspaper clichés. However, he appreciates the presence of good brains in his staff, and is proud of having developed a number of protégés into star reporters, like Turner Catledge and young Felix Belair, who is now head of the Washington bureau of *Time* magazine.

Crusty though he seems in manner, Krock is by no means unkind to the people working under him. Nobody he doesn't want can stay on his staff, but once he is satisfied that a man is doing good work, he lets him largely alone, rarely censuring or praising.

When he does want to praise a man for an unusually smart piece of work, he writes him a little note and has it delivered by his secretary. To keep himself informed, he often picks the brains of the able and experienced reporters on his staff.

At one o'clock he usually takes lunch, not at the crowded National Press Club, where the boys-with-dirty-fingernails noisily congregate, but at the exclusive old Metropolitan Club, where he now has the privilege of sitting at the table reserved for long-standing members, along with political and financial big-wigs and occasional generals or admirals who make news. He is also a member of the select Gridiron Club.

For covering the Treaty of Versailles in 1919, he was made an Officer of the Legion of Honor. Princeton, which he had quit for want of money, awarded him an honorary M.A. degree, almost thirty years later, in 1935.

By four o'clock in the afternoon, Krock is pretty clear about what he is going to write that day. Puffing rapidly at a cigar, he pounds a large typewriter with two rigid fingers, going at high speed. As he writes, he gets up quite a head of steam, and no interruptions are permitted. Within forty-five minutes, more or less, he has written his regular stint of 700 words, and he stops within a line or two of the exact space requirements for his column. At the home office in New York, no one has the right to change his copy, even though it may sometimes differ slightly in style or orthography from that of the rest of the paper. This is a most unusual privilege for a correspondent.

Some years ago, after Adolph Ochs died and Arthur Hays Sulzberger replaced him as publisher of the New York *Times*, Krock was seriously considered for the job of editor. At that time he still kept an apartment in New York, to which he longed to return. But finally he was persuaded to stay at the key post in Washington, which no one else, it was believed, could fill as well as he. In recompense, he was given a remarkably free hand to write as he pleased, which has sometimes brought headaches to the editor, Charles Merz; the Sunday editor, Lester Markel; and the managing editor, Edwin L. James. With these men, Krock sits on the policy-making Executive Committee of the *Times,* an informal body that meets once in a few months.

Krock has often written signed comment at right angles to the news and editorial policy of his own paper—acting as if a man with a by-line is responsible only to himself. In the huge *Times* organization the big shots rattle around in their own orbits a good deal, and when they sometimes collide the good Mr. Sulzberger usually comes in and keeps the peace.

For some years it piqued Krock that Arthur Sears Henning, the veteran Washington correspondent of the Chicago *Tribune,* was the highest-salaried man in the game, at $22,000 a year. But in 1936, following an offer from Hearst and a fast round trip by air to San Simeon, California, Krock was raised to $25,833. Since then his salary has gone "above $30,000."

In addition to this, he can call occasionally upon an expense account which permits throwing dinner parties at the Carlton Hotel for forty to fifty guests at a time.

In Washington's somewhat fluid society Arthur Krock has gained the social rank toward which he aspired. For years he has dined at embassy parties and with the higher officials of the State Department, such as the Thomas K. Finletters, the

Pierrepont Moffats and the James Clement Dunns, with whom the Krocks have sometimes combined to give large lawn parties.

Krock is probably the only newspaperman who is close to Secretary Hull. But if you can't reach Mr. Hull, Mr. Dunn, a career official, Hull's closest adviser on European affairs, is the next best thing. Other extracurricular connections of Krock include Robert A. Lovett, Assistant Secretary of War for Air, John McCloy, Assistant Secretary of War, and James Forrestal, Secretary of the Navy.

For company in the evening, he also enjoys the more intellectual type of financier, such as Lewis Douglas, who has been back in Washington lately, Joe Kennedy, and Bernard M. Baruch, with whose bench in Lafayette Park he is also in close communication during the day. Krock entertains his friends sometimes by standing at the piano and singing old-fashioned barbershop songs and rare old darky tunes, such as "The Warmest Baby in the Bus," which he remembers with a photographic memory.

Something of a phrasemaker, he has been heard in trials of wit with men like Sir Willmott Lewis, the old raconteur of the London *Times,* in the parlor of Mrs. Alice Longworth, the acerb cousin of the President.

Once after seeing the play *Harriet,* in which Helen Hayes recites a long monologue concerning the trials of President Lincoln, Arthur Krock observed, "Well, tonight we had Harriet Beecher Hayes electing Franklin Delano Lincoln for another term of office."

Though he still longs to run a great newspaper of his own, preferably in New York, Krock today, grown ruddy, gray-headed and a trifle jowled, is reconciled to life in the capital. He says a little grimly, "I like Washington the way a chemist likes his laboratory—in spite of its smell—because it has the materials with which he must work."

Up Front with Bill Mauldin

(SGT. WILLIAM HENRY MAULDIN)

By FREDERICK C. PAINTON

EDITOR'S PREFACE.—Since the appearance of the following article about Bill Mauldin, he has written, as well as provided the pictures for, a book which has been a national best-seller, and has won a Pulitzer prize. The book, *Up Front* (Holt), was the July, 1945, selection of the Book-of-the-Month Club. The particular panel which won Sgt. Mauldin this distinction appears on page 21 of the book, and will be remembered by the thousands who follow his cartoons in more than 100 American newspapers, not to mention *Stars and Stripes,* as the one carrying this caption: " 'Fresh, spirited American troops, flushed with victory, are bringing in thousands of hungry, ragged, battle weary prisoners'—news item."

The cartoons in *Up Front* were no surprise to those who have followed this feature in the press. They understood why 23-year-old Bill Mauldin's pictorial record of battle-weary Joe and Willie were the doughboys' favorite. They knew that the popularity of *Up Front* was well founded. It had mordant humor, and it also portrayed army life realistically, with all its jokes, gripes, and tragedy.

That Sgt. Mauldin was a great war cartoonist—in a sense the pen and brush counterpart of Ernie Pyle—is not news. But it probably did surprise some of his fans to discover through this book that Mauldin is also quite a good writer. His textual commentary is in keeping with the spirit of his drawings. It reveals him as a close observer and a discerning thinker. And what will especially appeal to many, he is very modest.

"My business is drawing, not writing, and this text is pretty much background for the drawings," he writes. ". . . I haven't tried to picture this war in a big, broad-

165

minded way. I'm not old enough to understand what it's all about, and I'm not experienced enough to judge its failures and successes. My reactions are those of a young guy who has been exposed to some of it, and I try to put those reactions in my drawings. Since I'm a cartoonist, maybe I can be funny after the war, but nobody who has seen this war can be cute about it while it's going on. The only way I can try to be a little funny is to make something out of the humorous situations which come up even when you don't think life could be any more miserable. It's pretty heavy humor, and it doesn't seem funny at all sometimes when you stop and think it over."

Looking at these cartoons and reading Sgt. Mauldin's text will give one a better understanding of the life and the point of view of the fighting man. It will also help in the readjustment of returned veterans. "They don't need pity, because you don't pity brave men—men who are brave because they fight while they are scared to death," writes this first-hand observer. "They simply need bosses who will give them a little time to adjust their minds and their hands, and women who are faithful to them, and friends and families who stay by them until they are the same guys who left years ago. No set of laws or Bill of Rights for returning veterans of combat can do that job. Only their own people can do it. So it is very important that these people know and understand combat men."

March 17, 1945

SGT. WILLIAM HENRY MAULDIN is twenty-three years old and when he's tired he looks all of sixteen. He has jughandle ears, big brown eyes with a satyr expression, and a boyishly smooth complexion that only requires a razor—to his secret sorrow—about once a week. His uncombable shock of black hair, his youthful grin and his slim eager walk make him appear some high-school kid not quite dry behind the ears. But nonetheless, history will reckon him the greatest cartoonist of World War II, and among the combat men his memory will linger when many a multistarred brass hat is catching dust on some museum wall.

For in the cartoon "Up Front," which appears in the many European editions of the doughboys' newspaper, *The Stars and Stripes*, Bill Mauldin has created G.I. Joe and Willie. In these two hollow-eyed, unshaven infantry characters he has immortalized the misery, the grandeur and the godlike patience—as well as the grim humor—of the front-line fighting man. Most of us in Italy and Southern France knew long ago that Bill was a top-drawer cartoonist, but recently on a day in Northern Italy, watching the Yanks slug their way through the Gothic Line, I realized that Bill is among the great of this earth.

It was raining, this day I'm telling you about; but then, it always rains in Italy in October. It was a driving, ice-cold rain, whipped by a biting wind that made the drops sting like a whiplash. Up here in the high Apennines, the rain had turned to sleet, and the pound of the bitter wind made a man gasp.

My jeep had crossed a lateral road from Firenzuola westward, and we had turned north toward Bologna. This ground had been captured for only a few hours, so now we were in the midst of the back-breaking drudgery of getting it organized, so we could get set for a new attack against another mountain peak rain-hidden somewhere ahead.

Engineers were splashing through molasses mud to make a by-pass. Signal Corps men laid telephone wires with blue, numbed hands to an installation that hadn't even as yet arrived. Tank destroyers and self-propelled guns inched forward, spraying mud and water. Just ahead of us, a traffic jam had formed where a new barrel for a 155-mm. rifle had slid off a truck, and men were cursing and sweating to get it back on the vehicle.

Men miserable and wet risked German shells to build a fire in a patch of field. Antiaircraft crews were not above firing a few rounds from their .50's to heat the barrels and gain a little warmth. Everybody shivered in the cold and wet, and listened to the slamming crump of German 88-mm. shells hitting in the smashed village just ahead.

Toward this mess of misery, evenly spaced out on each side of the road, slogged a battalion of the 91st Infantry Division. These men had been fighting for sixteen straight nights and days. Finally, the survivors had gone out for forty-eight hours of sleep, a bath, dry uniforms; and now, with replacements, were going forward to assault the next mountain.

Their faces were masks of fatigue, their eyes dull; their movements were slow, like tired men on a treadmill to nowhere. Their bodies were wet and cold, and in their hearts the knowledge that when they took the next mountain, there'd be one just like it across another valley to attack again. The lines of doughboys reached the traffic and fell out for a brief rest. One of them pulled out of a hiding place next to his skin a paper pamphlet, a copy of Bill Mauldin's book of cartoons, *Mules, Mud and Mountains.*

Cigarettes going, others gathered around him. Suddenly, through those cold and muddy men passed a cackle of laughter as harsh as the snicker of a cocking machine gun. They were looking, I discovered, at a typical Mauldin cartoon of G.I. Joe with his big knobby hand curled around a grim .45 automatic pistol. Mauldin has the terrible genius of charging every line of a soldier's body with the tension of the kill. The pistol was pointed at a large rat rearing up vividly in the light of a flash beam focused on it by Willie. Willie is watching, fascinated, and he says in the caption, "Aim between th' eyes, Joe. . . . Sometimes they charge when they're wounded."

The drawing on the opposite page portrayed an Army chaplain with his eyes rolled apprehensively at an unseen plane in the sky and saying, ". . . forever and ever, amen—hit the dirt."

I knew then Mauldin was great, because only his sardonic humor seems able to make these men in constant peril of their lives laugh at the torment of their own existence. And that genius has made him, in a little more than a year, the idol of combat men in North Africa and Italy, Sardinia and Corsica, and now, at last, in France. Even British Tommies are known to laugh; and one of life's funnier moments for me was watching an American soldier in Grenoble, France, try to explain by gestures the inner meaning of one of Bill's cartoons to a perplexed but friendly French poilu.

In the United States, seventy-nine daily newspapers carry Bill's front-line cartoons to millions of Americans. But, apparently, only a few of these readers think he's funny. I had one man say, "It took me some time and study to catch on to Bill's brand of humor, but now I feel I know him and the men over there." Yet, for every such understanding soul, there are scores like the woman who wrote indignantly to Bill, "Our boys don't look like the way you draw them. They're not bearded and horrible-looking. They're clean fine Americans."

In this war and the last, Americans have been conditioned to war humor built around traditional gags that have little relation to war's reality. Bill's drawings and humor portray for the first time the essential truth of front-line life. So a soldier will howl with laughter at two such cartoons as I have described, while the wives stare and say, "What's so funny about that?"

The thousands of veterans of combat who have come home are trying hard to teach their wives and friends how to appreciate Bill Mauldin. If they succeed, a lot of people are going to understand for the first time what the war is really like to the men up there doing the shooting.

The unscraped condition of Joe and Willie caused a lot of us to kid Bill by saying he drew black-bearded guys because of some mental complex occasioned by his own inability to grow a resplendent set of whiskers.

But Bill shook his head. "No, that isn't it at all. I draw our guys that way because that's the way they are. You look at 'em sometime and you'll see."

I had seen them many times, but it took this terrible day for me to see that Bill was right. These tired and worn men not only looked like Bill's characters, they felt like them. And I wondered anew at his uncanny understanding of how combat men look and feel and act.

Bill himself sees no great mystery in it. "They're the little people in peace," he said; "and they're the little people who always have to win a war. I'm a little guy myself. I've been four years in this man's Army, and everything that has happened to them has happened to me, except the final pay-off."

This is literally true. You could print Bill's life story in leaflet form and distribute it to the world as a Horatio Alger epic of the American way of life. On a sunny afternoon at the Anzio beachhead, with our jeep in a revetment where we could safely watch jerry shell hell out of Nettuno, Bill told me about his beginning. That was in Mountain Park, New Mexico, on October 29, 1921; and nobody would have made book on much of a future for Bill.

His father, Sidney, had been badly gassed in the first World War, and afterward always found the going tough. He tried dry-farming, worked as a hired hand, and became a tire changer at a bus station in Phoenix, Arizona. "After he changed two, three thousand tires," Bill said, "he wanted a change back to New Mexico—and who could blame him?"

Bill was a sickly child, plagued by rickets. He spent lots of time in bed, looking out the window at other kids playing. He took out his childish dreams and longings by drawing. He drew pictures of himself riding a roping pony, as a cowboy in chaps and ten-gallon hat. Grandma Callie Bemis—on his mother's side—still has an early Mauldin showing him frantically shoveling coal into a locomotive firebox. Always during those lean years he longed for a horse of his own. When graduation approached at the grammar school, he was promised one if he stood well in his class. Bill made himself valedictorian of the class.

"The damned horse was ready for the glue factory," Bill said, "but I sure rode him."

Commuting eighteen miles to the Alamogordo High School, he sold his first drawing to the La Luz Pottery Company for ten dollars. "The old man promptly borrowed five of it to pay a traffic fine," Bill said. "We were like that—what we had we shared."

In 1938, Bill's parents were divorced. So Bill and his brother Sidney went back to Phoenix. Here, for twenty-nine dollars a month, they got board and a bed on a porch, and went to high school. Bill drew for the school paper, and he joined the ROTC unit, in which he rose to be a corporal. He sold a drawing for five dollars, and instantly invested it as a down payment on a correspondence course in cartooning. He painted posters; he even painted the white sidewalls of aristocratic tires.

All this extracurricular work for chile and beans brought Bill to graduation day lacking a half point for his diploma. He still lacks it. He knew now, to be a real cartoonist, he must have better training, so he just told Grandma Callie Bemis he had to have $300 to attend the Chicago Academy of Fine Arts. And somehow she found it. This was tough going too. He washed dishes for his meals until he found a smart restaurateur who let him illustrate menus for better meals. He worked all day and he worked most of the night, which began the permanent impairment of his eyesight. Even now, in France, he thinks nothing of going two or three days without sleep, and he meets any early-morning-rising problem by staying up all the night.

At the end of the Chicago interlude, he arrived back in Phoenix in the same condition he always arrived—broke. So, in 300 days, he drew 3000 of the gag layouts the big national magazines print to brighten their back pages. He kept accounts on these, sending them out with return postage to all the big publications, and as regularly getting them back. When he ran out of stamp money, he drew cartoons for *Arizona Highways* to buy more. He drew political cartoons for his room and food. At the end of the year he had sold two cartoons nationally.

It was now getting along in September, 1940, and he knew —or rather sensed—that soon the United States would be at war. So he enlisted in the National Guard. The interesting fact about this is that volunteers in the Arizona National Guard, Bill says, do not have to take a physical examination, or at least Bill did not. Five days after he enlisted, the Arizona Guard was Federalized, and Bill found himself in the Army with a physique which any friend of his on *The Stars and Stripes* will give you even money couldn't have passed the first doctor.

"Anyway," Bill said, "I was in this man's Army when it was an infant, and we kinda grew up together—me being only eighteen. All I know—grown-up—is Army life."

He had come up the years the hard way and he took it the hard way now. He drilled and toted a rifle, and skirmished and patrolled, and ran and marched. He rose day after day at 5:30, and after drilling and working all day, spent most of the night in the 45th Division News office, drawing pictures for the paper. Out of all these experiences at Fort Sill, Oklahoma, came his vast understanding of the line soldier.

He also did another thing plenty of soldiers did—he got married. While he was at Camp Barkeley, Texas, he met Norma Jean Humphries, from Toyah, Texas. Norma Jean is a lovely brunette and about 102 pounds in a dirndl. She was a junior at Hardin-Simmons University, studying to be a surgeon.

Bill is pretty proud of that job of wooing. "There was a glamour pilot—a looey, at that—of the Royal Canadian Air Force giving her an awful rush," he said. "And I was a pretty sad sack until she finally broke dates with him for me. Right then, I drew a cartoon and sold it to the *Daily Oklahoman* for the down payment on a diamond ring costing twenty-seven-fifty. If you held it up to the light, you could see the diamond real good—at least, I think it's a diamond."

Nowadays, with more money, when Bill would like to replace that first engagement ring with something rockier from Cartier's, Norma Jean refuses, preferring to wear the chip.

"Girls are sentimental like that," Bill explained admiringly.

Bill now experienced all the trials of supporting a wife on the pay of a private first class. He added another ten a week by drawing cartoons for the *Daily Oklahoman*.

There was little enough home life for the bride and the boy trying to be a soldier and a husband. From camp to camp the division moved, glacierlike, toward its ultimate destiny overseas. An episode at Pine Camp, New York, is typical of their existence. Here Bill rose at 3:30 A.M. each day to catch the bus from Watertown to camp in time to stand reveille. He got back to the cheap room at nine o'clock each night, dead tired.

But he could still draw cartoons of doughboys pitching pup tents beside the bus terminal and setting up housekeeping while waiting for room on the bus.

The division had moved down to Camp Pickett, Virginia, when Norma Jean told him about the coming baby. This was the spring of 1943. The division would sail almost any time. Norma Jean had taught him how to save; they had $200 in the bank. But Bill figured a baby would need more. He arranged for the *Army Times,* a Washington war publication, to bring out a book of cartoons. He got $100 down, and a few days later sailed into the silences of the sea.

He was storming inland in the conquest of Sicily when his son, Bruce Patrick, was born. Like so many other soldiers, he has never seen his child, but he has the greatest galaxy of pin-ups of mother and son ever hung on one wall. The last count was, I think, thirty-four.

This news stirred him to get money for Bruce. He found two lieutenant colonels to guarantee his printing bill, talked a Palermo printer into issuing *Sicily Sketchbook,* a collection of the cartoons that had appeared in the 45th Division News. Bill got 5000 copies and started out personally to sell them. To his amazement, one regiment took the whole load. He finally printed 17,000. Bruce Patrick now had $1800, and Bill could get on with the war. As a result of the book, two things happened—he was promoted from corporal to sergeant, and the editors of *The Stars and Stripes* arranged to have him transferred to their staff as official cartoonist.

Bill met the soldier's greatest enemies, fear and death, on the beaches at Salerno. Here he discovered the "bees in the belly," as he calls the tenseness in face of death that assails all men in jeopardy of their lives.

Since then, he goes regularly to the front to keep the bees well exercised, because this, he thinks, is the direct link between the combat man and himself. On one such trip he earned the Purple Heart.

He had gone up into the Italian mountains around Cassino in that cold and terrible winter of 1943–1944, which, Bill swears, was worse than Valley Forge. The machine-gun nest he visited was perched on a mountain crag like an eagle's nest, and the trail to it was perpendicular and coated with ice and snow. The scene later became the basis for his drawing of several American soldiers clinging to rock outcroppings over a precipitous cliff while a sergeant shouts, "Hit the dirt, men!"

The Yank outpost was within spitting distance of the Germans, and Bill went in cautiously. Coming out, however, he and his companion dislodged some small stones, and these sounds startled the nervous jerries, who promptly hurled some mortar shells in that direction. One of these just missed Bill's head, bounced off his heel, and burst with a terrific blast a few yards below. The brilliant flash of its detonation blinded Bill; the terrific concussion that can kill without wounding paralyzed his body.

"I had that first horrible instant," said Bill, "when you think you're blinded for life. Then, when I could see a little, I had that awful fear of looking down at myself. So many guys do when numbed, and find an arm or leg missing. After a while, I forced myself to look, and I seemed to be all in one piece. Then I policed myself bone by bone, and found blood and traced it. I was lucky—only three barber's nicks, the worst in the shoulder."

That winter changed Bill from a boy to a man. Day after day, he saw the grim courage, the endurance that sent tired-faced men back time and again to the dogged slugging that finally beat the best the Germans had. And, too, he heard their grim laughs, their odd humor, and out of this nadir of suffering, G.I. Joe and Willie, as Bill says, "just growed, like Topsy."

His style hardened, his boyish soldiers became hollow-eyed and bearded and very lethal. His humor became grim and sardonic and often bitter. As an example, take the cartoon he drew for the soldiers to clip and send home on Mother's Day. This portrays G.I. Joe wrapped in the sling of his Garand rifle, every muscle tightened to squeeze the trigger. In front of the rifle's muzzle a stately hen marches, followed by her brood of chicks. Willie, who is watching, says, "Aw, hold it, Joe. Remember, she's a mother."

His humor became even mocking, as when he drew some infantry replacements limp with exhaustion, sleeping with bowed heads on their rifles. In the distance, one officer says to another, "How can you tell they're fresh troops 'til you wake them up and ask?"

Always in war there is an unofficial feud between the front-line troops and the rear-echelon military police. Bill kidded this feud by drawing a picture of G.I. Joe and Willie, as disreputable as ever, staring in open-mouthed amazement at the campaign ribbons and battle stars of a spit-and-polish military policeman in the rear areas. On the background buildings are signs, FOR OFFICERS ONLY; PBS CLUB—a club for base-section troops—and OUT OF BOUNDS TO ENLISTED MEN.

An outcry resounded through Southern Italy. For a time, it appeared Bill would wind up in the hoosegow. Then Lt. Gen. Mark W. Clark, of the 5th Army, asked for the original of this drawing, and Bill's freedom to depict what he liked was assured. Once or twice since, he has made brass hats gasp. One colonel said in my presence, "No sergeant should have such power."

He was referring to a drawing in which bearded, disreputable G.I. Joe and Willie are having their names taken by a spick-and-span base-section lieutenant for not having buttons on their clothing. The caption reads, "I lost them buttons capturing this town."

This was Bill's indignant outburst when he learned that some combat men from Anzio beachhead, sent out for a brief five-day rest, had been picked up at the dock by MP's, kept five days in the hoosegow, and then escorted aboard an LST to return to Anzio. This did not happen often, be it said.

This ardent defense has made Bill the idol of the front-line troops. One incident of that admiration and trust, I shall never forget. Bill and I were leaving Anzio on an LST. While he drove the jeep into the hold, I had to sign the papers to get the vehicle and ourselves aboard. The Germans had just looped in an Anzio Express, a high-velocity 170-mm. shell, that hit on the dockside a hundred yards or so away and tore itself apart with a stunning crash. There was no knowing where the next shell would land or when. Consequently, I was scribbling our names hastily.

"I'm signing also for Bill Mauldin," I said. "He's parking the jeep."

The MP had been paying me little attention, his tense eyes and wary body more concerned with where that next shell might land. But at my words, he suddenly stared hard at me.

"Who'd you say?" he demanded. "Bill Mauldin! You mean the guy that draws Joe and Willie in *The Stars and Stripes?*"

Nodding, I hastily thrust the documents into his hand. He never even looked down at them. "Well, what do you know?" he muttered. "That snub-nosed kid. Why, he ain't old enough to wear long pants." He took a half step toward the darksome bowels of the LST, then stopped. "I wish I'd 'a' known," he said. "I'd like to shake that kid's hand."

I've seen Bill go through a division area with privates yelling, "Hi yuh, Bill!" and chicken colonels shaking hands and saying, "How goes it, Bill, and when do I get that autographed copy?"

This last reference was to Bill's Italian publishing venture that brought out *Mud, Mules and Mountains,* that tells, better than words, the hell of that terrible winter.

Bill later turned over all rights in the edition to the Army Special Services Division, which at last accounts had orders for 125,000 copies.

But despite his adult outlook, Bill remains very much the boy. He yelled for joy when General Clark assigned to him, for his own use, a jeep, so he could get around the front without hitch-hiking rides. That jeep is a traveling pin-up gallery of pictures of Norma Jean and Bruce, jerry rifle and burp gun, blankets and musettes full of clothing, and a complete studio outfit, so Bill can produce pictures wherever he pauses for a time.

Bill has a professional soldier's love for shooting the breeze, and squats for hours with G.I.'s to swap experiences. He works day and night to be accurate. I saw him spend hours sketching new uniforms, equipment and weapons. "The guys eat my tail out if I muff a point," he said.

Sgt. Stanley Meltzoff and the late Sgt. Gregor Duncan, of *The Stars and Stripes* art staff, have said that Bill is in direct line of the great cartoonists who go back to Cruikshank and Tom Nast, and the famous cartoonists of the last war, Wallgren and Bruce Bairnsfather, creator of "The Better 'Ole."

As proof of their statement, they both pointed to Bill's brilliant, original style, which, they said, is extraordinary in one so tender in years.

Bill has a strict sense of good taste. He never puts dead men in his cartoons—even Germans—though you sense they are just outside the edges of the picture.

Yet he can poke fun at the business of killing by drawing an infantryman loaded down with rifle and grenades, bayonet and knife, staring enviously at an engineer who was digging a ditch and saying, "At least you're learning a peacetime trade."

Bill is very glad his cartoon is syndicated in the papers back home, and not only for the money.

"I want the people to know the frontline guys," he said. "We've been away from home a long, long time, and the combat troops don't realize things change. They think they'll find it just like it was and as they remember it. They're going to get a shock—many of the girls married, guys they knew going up in better jobs, towns changing. It's going to be tough on Joe and Willie when they come home. They have to adjust themselves. So, after the parades and the whoopee are over, I hope my cartoons will inspire the people to help these bewildered guys back into peacetime life."

The Paper That Was Tailored to a City

(WILLIAM L. MCLEAN AND THE PHILADELPHIA BULLETIN)

By DAVID G. WITTELS

EDITOR'S PREFACE.—Playing, of course, both on the title of this article and the expression most used by the promotion department of the newspaper herein treated, the *Post* editors made this pertinent comment when the following piece first was published:

"The fit is close to perfect. 'Nearly everybody' in staid Philadelphia reads the staid *Bulletin*. Without crusades or hoopla, it has attained largest evening circulation in U. S."

Since the *Post* also is published in Philadelphia, the word *staid* has added significance.

Because this book will undoubtedly be read by teachers and students of journalism, it should be said here that the *Bulletin* is the newspaper which Fred Fuller Shedd served as editorial writer from 1911 to 1921, and of which he was editor-in-chief from 1921 until his death in 1937.

Mr. Shedd, himself a distinguished teacher of journalism at Pennsylvania State College, during his two years (1930–32) as president of the American Society of Newspaper Editors did much to bring about a closer relationship between instructors and practitioners of journalism, and also to elevate standards of professional education for journalism. In arranging the program for the 1930 Boston convention of the American Association of Teachers of Journalism, the writer, who was president of the Association that year, asked leading editors to explain their expectations of schools of journalism, and prominent teachers, in turn, to tell of the aims and methods of such schools. So mutually helpful was this exchange of points of view that at this meeting Mr. Shedd, one of the speakers, initiated the National Joint Committee, which has since become the American Council on Education for

178

Journalism and which today embraces the American Association of Schools and Departments of Journalism, Southern Newspaper Publishers Association, National Editorial Association, American Society of Newspaper Editors, American Newspaper Publishers Association, and Inland Daily Press Association, all of which are working toward higher standards for education in and for journalism.

Mr. Shedd is therefore very much a part of the story of the *Bulletin* and his contributions both to the paper and to American journalism in a larger way merit special mention here.

April 7, 1945

THE greatest mystery in the newspaper business today is a fat, wealthy paper in Philadelphia called *The Evening Bulletin*. Outside the Quaker City, it is little known to the layman, except perhaps through reiteration of its provocative slogan: "In Philadelphia, Nearly Everybody Reads the *Bulletin*." But among newspapermen the *Bulletin* is the subject of many baffled bull sessions, during which the professionals try to figure out how and why a paper like that should have the biggest evening circulation in the United States, which the *Bulletin* has.

Its slogan is literally true, though in some newspaper circles it is apt to incite agonized remarks such as "but only God knows why," and "it serves them right." The *Bulletin*, with about 675,000 daily circulation, dominates its field perhaps more fully than any other paper in the country. In most newsrooms, certain truths are held to be self-evident and among them are these: that a good newspaper must be well-written, lively, militant, and sophisticated in tone. The *Bulletin* is, broadly speaking, none of these things, and doesn't even try to be.

It is perhaps the most commonplace metropolitan newspaper in the country, it never crusades about anything, some of its editorials require two or three careful readings to determine whether they are pro or con, and it is so reluctant to offend the sensibilities of its readers that it has been known to paint extra clothes on some of the ladies in its comic strips and at least once cut the word "lousy" out of a strip, thereby virtually ruining the punch line. Even that acutely true-to-life small-fry character, "Stinky" Davis, in Fontaine Fox's cartoon, "Toonerville Trolley," was dipped into the sterilization tank and bowdlerized to "Stingy" Davis. Those are some of the reasons why the irreverent refer to it as The Old Lady of Filbert Street.

The *Bulletin's* success, to those of the reporting craft who possibly are more romantic than they should be, seems like a denial of idealism and mediocrity triumphant. The *Bulletin* has ignored not only most of the fascinating sagas of the newsroom but also the supposedly practical, opportunistic tenets of the counting rooms. If no *Bulletin* reporter has ever had the thrill of working on a first-class exposé, neither have the more prosaic departments ever resorted to prizes or premiums to lure new circulation, or cut advertising rates to gain new business. There has arisen a naïve legend that the *Bulletin* is simply a case of dumb luck.

Recently, a hot-shot New York expert came down to look over the Philadelphia newspaper scene. He wrote a forty-page report for his clients; but privately, in the bar of the Pen and Pencil Club, he summed up the *Bulletin* thus: "That's not a newspaper, it's a symptom." At least he was closer to the mark than was General Taylor, creator of the present Boston *Globe,* during a visit some years ago to his good friend, the late William L. McLean, who made the *Bulletin* what it is today.

Taylor went over the paper with expert, professional eye; and the more he studied, the greater his puzzlement grew. The peacetime headlines were small, drab and flat; the news items under them written in commonplace fashion. The whole paper was a monotone; there was no sparkle, no savor, no punch.

"McLean," he demanded at last, "how in hell do you sell this thing? I couldn't get away with something like that in Boston."

McLean, a tall, mild man with a wise, tolerant twinkle behind his spectacles, did not take offense. "Well," he replied, "neither could I. But I wouldn't try to sell the Philadelphia *Bulletin* in Boston."

Therein lies the first clue to the mystery of the *Bulletin*. The largest evening circulation in the United States isn't, of course, dumb luck. The *Bulletin* is the creation of a circulation genius who, though no editor, took the trouble and had the ability to study his public down to its fundamental character and desires. In other words, he learned to understand his market, and fashioned his business in accordance. To pursue that simile further, McLean tried to sell Philadelphia neither a zoot suit nor a frock coat, but made up for it the plain, staid little number it seemed to want. He never argued with his customers, never tried to inculcate into them a taste for better style. Whether this method fulfills the whole function and duty of a newspaper is another matter. McLean deliberately made the *Bulletin* as typical of Philadelphia as its anachronistic City Hall, spraddling obstinately in the path of its two main streets; the quiet dignity of Independence Hall; the monotonous miles of row houses filled with solid, unspectacular workers; the lovely, childlike quality of its Mummers' Parade; the Quaker-garbed statue of Billy Penn, and scrapple.

The things great and the things bad about the *Bulletin* are both products of The Chief, as his staff called him. His hand is still upon it, though now it is run by his two surviving sons, and though both are men of extraordinary ability in their own right. William L., Jr., former All-American tackle at Princeton and now vice-president and treasurer of the paper, still refers to his father, quite simply and reverentially, as The Chief. Robert, who has distinguished himself as president of the Associated Press, in addition to heading the *Bulletin* management and dictating its editorial policy, still sometimes lapses into the present tense in speaking of his father, dead thirteen years. Both served apprenticeships at the bottom, progressing through delivery, composing and newsroom; and Robert still bears marks of those days on two fingers mashed in a stereotyping machine while trying to set a new speed record in turning out a matrix. Both sons have adhered to the formula The Chief taught them.

It is no magic formula; the trick lay in recognizing it and

applying it with painstaking care. Whatever the *Bulletin* does, in its columns or its business structure, it does with consistent thoroughness and minute attention to detail. This solid trait, composed too much of seeming trivia to lend itself readily to illustration, underlies every other factor in the *Bulletin's* success.

The Chief missed no bets, overlooked no angle. Recently, a new executive noted an odd item of $300 in a bill for signs advertising the *Bulletin*. It was for "antiquing." Puzzled as to why brand-new signs should be antiqued, he pursued the mystery until finally, from an old-timer in the circulation department, he got the answer. "The Chief started that," the ancient explained. "The Chief said people in Philadelphia didn't like new things. He didn't want them to think the *Bulletin* was a new paper." The *Bulletin* pursues the same thought today. Most papers, when they modernize their make-up, proudly and loudly proclaim their progress. When the *Bulletin,* a couple of years ago, made thirty changes in its heads and other matters of make-up, it did so at the rate of only one a day, so that readers would not be disturbed by noticing that something new had been added.

It wasn't a new paper when McLean bought it in 1895 for $73,000—largely borrowed—but it might just as well have been. Out of thirteen newspapers in the city then, with a combined circulation of more than 850,000, the *Bulletin* had less than 7000. The record McLean made still stands to the amazement of modern circulation experts. In one year he increased the sales fivefold, to above 33,000 daily. In five years he was crowding 130,000; and on the tenth anniversary of his ownership the *Bulletin* was at the top of the heap with 220,000—a more than thirty-fold increase. It has never been headed in Philadelphia since. Today, not quite fifty years after he bought it, only two of his original competitors remain, and they have changed hands and had injections of new money several times. Estimates of the current value of the *Bulletin* go to $25,000,000 —if the owners were crazy enough to sell. It is entirely a family-held concern.

McLean's background for newspaper ownership consisted of spectacular success as a youthful circulation hustler in Pittsburgh, and seventeen years as business and circulation manager of the old Philadelphia *Press*. Almost immediately after he bought the decrepit *Bulletin,* he plunged himself deeper in debt to increase its press capacity. Scoffed at, he replied, "The paper that gets to the newsstands and homes soonest with the latest news sells the most." To this end, he was a daring innovator in his mechanical and delivery departments, and made them the most modern in the country. This tradition of modernity in plant has persisted. The staid *Bulletin* is put together in streamlined, air-conditioned, soundproofed, scientifically lighted offices which resemble more a Hollywood version of a tycoon's suite than the traditional journalistic warrens.

Only in the news and editorial branches was he cautious; perhaps wisely, but perhaps because, not having had training in those departments, he did not know how to use the spices and condiments of journalism. He liked to pretend that he gave his editors a free hand, and told his sons, "If you always have to tell a managing editor what to do, you might as well be the managing editor yourself." The truth of the matter was that, though he did it by indirection, he laid down very narrow limits for his editors. When once a reporter wrote and the managing editor put on Page 1 an exposé of a gambling house running full tilt, The Chief came into the newsroom and, pointing to the story, quietly asked, "Do you think this is quite the sort of thing the *Bulletin* ought to do?" He said no more, but the executive caught the hint. There were no more exposés or crusades.

If the police raid a place, the *Bulletin* prints that fact. If another paper forces an investigation of graft or other skulduggery, the *Bulletin* gives its readers the bare facts of the progress of the investigation—and of its inevitable demise. It never stirs up trouble on its own. Cleverness and sophisticated writing are taboo in its news columns. Dwight Perrin, the present managing editor, is too wise to attempt to toss a monkey wrench into so successful a set of gears, but he has succeeded in getting a little flavor into the paper, partly by allowing a couple of his abler reporters to show flashes of top-notch newspaper style. Morley Cassidy, for instance, has been turning in one of the greatest jobs of war correspondence being done by any correspondent for a single newspaper.

"The newspaper is a visitor in the home," The Chief declared, "and so there should never be anything in it which conceivably could offend any member of the family." There never is in the *Bulletin*. When Winnie Winkle was about to have her twins a few years ago, the editors decided that the strips for the week prior to the accouchement were too realistic for *Bulletin* readers. Scores of other newspapers printed them without qualm or resultant complaints, but the *Bulletin* made the syndicate cartoonist draw for its readers another, more delicate set.

"If you use big headlines every day," The Chief taught, "you will have nothing in reserve to emphasize the big news when it comes." He preached moderation and understatement, and his sons agree. The penetrating words Robert McLean wrote some time ago to explain the *Bulletin* theory to an advertising agency were his own, but they were also an echo of his father. "Understatement that carries conviction (because the mind of the reader feels in it the sense that it is right) may carry with it a lesser effect . . . at the moment, but it will never subject us to the misfortune of being doubted or discredited. Scrupulous attention to moderation in statement is one of the things which it is our constant effort to maintain in the daily news and editorial contents of the *Bulletin*."

Moderation may have been The Chief's natural inclination, but it was also admirably suited to Philadelphia. Show people hate the town because it is so moderate—though they use harsher, nastier adjectives to describe a populace which "sits on its hands" and never bursts into lusty enthusiasm. Most other cities, if they possessed such a traditional and lovely spectacle as Philadelphia's annual Mummers' Parade, would hoopla and boost it all over the country. Philadelphia prefers to enjoy it quietly by itself, though if any outsider insists on coming, he is welcome. Even its City Hall politicians are moderate. Lincoln Steffens' characterization of Philadelphia as "corrupt and contented" was misleading in one respect; it is not very corrupt.

Someone aptly has said that "Philadelphia is not a city; it is a collection of villages." The Chief phrased it more tactfully, but he realized that size alone does not make a big city. He understood that most Philadelphians, the dwellers in the row houses, do not think of themselves as living in a metropolis of 2,000,000 population, the third largest city in the land. They look upon themselves as inhabitants of communities, of sections, which they call Kensington, Southwark, West Philadelphia, Tioga, Germantown, Frankford, Fishtown, Olney, Overbrook, Nicetown, Hunting Park, Richmond, Grays Ferry, Roxborough, Bustleton, Mt. Airy, Tacony, Manayunk, Eastwick. These are all within the city, with no apparent boundaries, but to most of the inhabitants the distinctions are very real.

The truth of this observation is demonstrated frequently in a *Bulletin* department entitled—how typically!—Ethical Problems. This department, comprised almost entirely of letters from teen-agers begging other readers for advice on matters of social intercourse, is at once an acute finger on the pulse of the generation about to inherit Philadelphia, and one of the most touching and delightful columns in newspaperdom. For a long time, the major issues raging in it were whether West Philadelphia boys were more gentlemanly and "nicer fellows" than Southwark boys, whether Richmond girls were prettier than Frankford girls, and whether the younger set of Germantown were more "stuck-up" than those from other sections. The reality of this neighborhood feeling was tragically emphasized not long ago when a sixteen-year-old boy was beaten to death by South Philadelphia youngsters, resentful because West Philadelphia boys had cut them out with their own South Philadelphia girls.

Other editors and publishers have noted this phenomenon, and paid passing obeisance to these communities in the form of occasional feature stories. Obviously, it would be impossible to cater in the news columns to each section separately or to print all their neighborhood trivia. But The Chief found the answer. He added up the communities and saw the common denominator—small-town interests. And so he gave Philadelphia the biggest and best small-town newspaper in the United States.

Nothing has happened in the years that followed to make his sons doubt the wisdom of this. In the early 20's, a letter came to the Ethical Problems column from a young lady concerning her fiancé. He was a fine, steady, sober young man, she explained, and she was very fond of him. However, he had one habit which disturbed her. When he called upon her in her home, he invariably took off his shoes. Did this show a lack of consideration for her sufficient to make it wise for her to give him up or should she overlook it, in view of the fact that he worked hard and complained that his feet hurt? Some four weeks later, the editors had to put an arbitrary stop to printing the flood of letters which resulted.

In 1926, during the supposedly wild jazz era, a letter arrived from a boy named Rusty Kirschner. He was troubled because, although he was "passing in looks" and had a "pleasing personality," he couldn't get girl friends. He was called "dead" and "slow" because he couldn't dance and didn't dress "collegiate."

George F. Kearney, then in charge of the Ethical Problems column, put this letter at the top of the column. A week later, a nineteen-year-old stenographer named Rose Marie Carney replied that she thought Rusty wasn't "slow," but someone to be admired. She wished there was a way people like themselves, "who do not go to extremes in everything," could meet. Three months later there were twenty-nine chapters and 25,000 members in an organization called, defiantly, the "Slow Club." It was, by definition, for those who "neither jazz nor pet." Flask-toters were barred. Eventually, there were at least 70,000 members. Such incidents have universal roots, but they are especially in the pattern and the flavor of Philadelphia.

Times haven't changed. On June 23, 1942, a letter signed "Thomas McMurters" appeared in the regular letters-to-the-editor section. McMurters anounced that when he caught cats trespassing in his garden, he buried them under his tomato plants and thereby got the finest tomatoes in Overbrook.

Well! The nation was newly in a World War and losing. The City Council had again refused to repeal a city wage tax, unique in this country, which tapped every pay envelope. But the flood of letters was mostly inspired by McMurters. To this day, if you mention McMurters to a Philadelphian, the odds are he will reply: "Oh, the man who kills cats." Some said he ought to have a medal, and one patriot coined a slogan: "A cat in a trap is a slap at the Jap." But mostly they demanded his blood.

All of which is related by this reporter not jeeringly but with respect, even if there is no Thomas McMurters.

The Chief believed, and taught his sons, that what interests newspaper readers most is trivia concerning the haps and mishaps of their neighbors; the kind which could have happened to themselves. Before paper rationing, the *Bulletin* let not a sparrow fall unheeded in Philadelphia. Even now, there is always room on the front page for plenty of local news.

Though traditionally Republican, the *Bulletin* has escaped damage from Philadelphia's recent habit of going Democratic in national elections and coming close to it in local ones. This, too, is no accident. The *Bulletin* never hits its readers over the head with its political viewpoint. Some who knew The Chief quote him as saying, "When a reader buys my paper, he expects news, not advice on how to vote and what is right." He had seen that the circulations of violently partisan newspapers were dangerously vulnerable to shifts of public opinion.

Robert McLean, though a member of the rock-ribbed Union League, is registered as a non-partisan. His charming wife, coming from the South, is a Democrat. This may have something to do with the fact that both parties usually get fairly equal treatment in the news columns. Editorially, the *Bulletin* has been so unsuccessful in picking candidates, even when it switched to the Democratic side in two purely local elections, that some wit has paraphrased its slogan thus: "Nearly Everybody Reads the *Bulletin,* but Nobody Pays Any Attention to It."

Robert McLean is not too disturbed by this, but he tells a story to rebut it. It concerns the days when the sheriff of Philadelphia County collected the fees of his office in lieu of a salary. These might run to $100,000 a year. Of course, under the rules of practical politics, he turned all above a reasonable sum into the chest of the party which put him in office. Some papers more militant than the *Bulletin* had screamed vainly about this for years. One day the *Bulletin* printed a four-line editorial saying in effect that it didn't seem quite right. A few days later, it ran another, similar in tone. The next day the sheriff came into the office. "Well," he said, "I'm licked. I never saw anything wrong with that system, but after your first editorial, my wife said to me: 'Are you sure you're right? The *Bulletin* doesn't seem to like it.' When your second editorial came out, my wife said to me, 'Look, you must be wrong. The *Bulletin* says so.' "

This almost indirect method, this avoidance of the open brawl, is typical of the *Bulletin* in all its dealings. When, in 1938, the standard Philadelphia papers went to three cents, they suffered the inevitable drop in circulation. Two of the other papers countered this by offering free premiums to lure new subscribers. One of them put on the greatest premium drive in American newspaper history, with 300,000 premiums in two years alone, in addition to prize contests and insurance policies. Both these Santa Clauses were morning papers, but a housewife offered a gleaming electric clock or a set of silverware may sometimes not worry overmuch whether it is a morning or evening paper she must buy to get the present. The *Bulletin,* eying its own circulation slump, did not like the picture. Finally, it found a way to stop the spree. It went to the merchants of Philadelphia and pointed out to them that every premium meant the loss of a potential sale to their stores. It also intimated that unless the merchants put the heat on the other papers, the *Bulletin* would be forced—most regretfully, of course—to break its own taboo against premiums and put on the biggest jamboree of all time. That did it, and quickly.

Similarly, when a morning newspaper began encroaching on the *Bulletin's* time territory with earlier editions in the evening and later ones in the morning, in an effort to overhaul it as biggest paper in the area, the *Bulletin* made no crude threats. It merely began shopping for comics and other features for a five-cent Sunday paper. Trade secrets are hard to keep in the newspaper business, and this one was extraordinarily badly kept. The *Bulletin* does not have a Sunday edition, and its entrance into this field, particularly at such a low price, could have raised hob with its morning competitor's cherished Sunday circulation. The hint was enough. The competitor behaved.

The *Bulletin* snapped out of its own circulation slump partly by the standard method of injecting new, top-notch blood into its organization. The Chief was gone and the men he had trained were getting old and unable to adjust his basic principles to the present. Perrin came in as managing editor, knocked some of the stuffiness out, and may yet be able to wangle a bit of sparkle into it.

Whereas previously the *Bulletin* was considered a graveyard for newspaper writing talent, it now began to unleash some any paper might envy. There were, for example, the two new columnists it introduced. One was Paul Jones, who had taught French at the University of Pennsylvania and conducted summer European tours before turning to a writing career. He was already well known as a free lance, having had several fiction stories printed in *The Saturday Evening Post,* when the *Bulletin* got him. There he writes a delightful column called "Candid Shots," in which he manages subtly to spread caviar for sophisticated tastes on the solid bread most Philadelphians like. The other is Ralph W. Page, son of the late Walter Hines Page, World War I diplomat. Page was running the family banking and orchard interests in North Carolina when Robert McLean met him and was intrigued by the clarity and calmness with which he expounded his pro-New Deal ideas in after-dinner conversation. These ideas were mostly counter to Mc-

Lean's, but McLean persuaded him to give up his business and start writing for the *Bulletin*. The result was that the *Bulletin* harbors in its arch-conservative bosom perhaps the most articulate and best-written liberal column in the country. Not only that, but it proudly features and advertises it. Like Jones' column, however, it is known only to *Bulletin* readers. McLean will not permit either to be syndicated.

Howard W. Stodghill, hired away from a job as one of Hearst's general managers, tightened up and streamlined the circulation department. Stodghill also brought the *Bulletin* national publicity and praise as originator of a plan whereby lagging sales of War Savings Stamps were boosted spectacularly by having boy newspaper carriers offer them for sale at subscribers' front doors. Nearly 900 newspapers adopted the plan, which by last November had sold 1,286,707,636 stamps and started many families on bond purchases.

George T. Eager, crack New York advertising-agency executive, was brought in as promotion director and trouble shooter. Richard W. Slocum, transformed from a successful Philadelphia lawyer to general manager of the paper, speaks the language of the newer generation of advertisers and businessmen. These men did not, however, take any real liberties with the basic formula that The Chief had handed down. It was Slocum, for instance, though personally a man of cultivated, sophisticated tastes, who discovered Charles J. Love, the Pigeon Man.

That is as typical a piece of *Bulletin* promotion as if it had been done by The Chief himself. Love is a pigeon fancier, with a troupe of birds bearing such names as Dopey, Happy, Grumpy and Speedy, and a knack for making pigeons fascinating to people who ordinarily wouldn't give a hoot. Today, Love and his birds appear by courtesy of the *Bulletin* and are wowing them at the rate of 30,000 a year. When the Pigeon Man shows up at a school, an assembly of all classes is called and the kids are popeyed with anticipation. The climax of his act begins when he announces that his pets are real homing pigeons, which can find their way, high and straight over the city, to their loft in the *Bulletin*.

"Now," says Love, "if you boys and girls will give me a secret message, we will see if this is true." With much excitement and help from the teachers, themselves fascinated, a committee is chosen to formulate a secret message. Another group is elected to stand by the telephone in the principal's office. Love fastens the message to Speedy's leg and tosses the bird out the window. "In six and one half minutes," he predicts, "the telephone will ring and my assistant at the *Bulletin* will read the secret message over the telephone." The tension generated during those minutes is something any playwright would envy. And if the secret message, as is not infrequently the case, is something like: "Tommy Jones loves Mary Smith," the house is brought down. The total cost to the *Bulletin* is around $5000 a year.

The payoff circulation-wise? This writer's six-year-old daughter came home from school one afternoon wide-eyed with excitement and spilling a tale of a wonderful man with real live pigeons. "Daddy," she demanded, "you must buy the *Bulletin* and read me about the Pigeon Man." That's catching them a trifle young, but the odds are that she will be a devoted *Bulletin* reader, like her mother, when she grows up.

Squire of Washington

(EUGENE MEYER)

By MARQUIS W. CHILDS

EDITOR'S PREFACE.—Much has been said and written about the seductive qualities of printer's ink for young persons of a creative turn of mind. Glenn Frank, formerly editor of *Century Magazine* and president of the University of Wisconsin, once wrote in this connection:

". . . It is not wise to tamper with journalism in your youth unless you want it to haunt you for the rest of your days. The smell of printers' ink is seductive. There is a drug-like something about journalism. It is habit forming. Once the siren clatter of typewriter and printing press has sounded in your ears, you will not be happy until you have discovered by experience that you can or cannot find a satisfactory career in journalism."

The appeal of journalism is not limited, however, to the young who are yet to make a place for themselves in life. It is not unusual for those who have reached the top in business, one of the professions (other than journalism), or government service to turn to journalism to crown their successful careers, to cap the climax, to gild the lily, so to speak, by becoming journalists, with all the honors, privileges, and immunities thereunto appertaining (to use the language employed by college presidents in degree conferring). Even Presidents of the United States so behave. Theodore Roosevelt, it will be remembered, became associate editor of *Outlook* the day after he left the White House. Calvin Coolidge wrote for *Cosmopolitan* and conducted a syndicated column. The few times that Woodrow Wilson was heard from after he left the executive mansion was in the pages of the *Atlantic Monthly* or over the radio. Many think that had Franklin D. Roosevelt lived to leave the White House (what a thought!), he un-

192

doubtedly would have devoted the remainder of his life to writing and the radio. (How many times have his radio voice and personality been the subject of favorable comment, even by his enemies!) As a matter of fact, the International News Service in a news story dated August 18, 1945, quoted Stephen Early, for 12 years a White House secretary, as saying that President Roosevelt planned to invade the New York newspaper field with a non-editorial tabloid at the end of his fourth term. "His plans had advanced to the extent of knowing the format of his paper in size and content," Mr. Early said.

There must be a reason for the attractiveness of journalism to those who have reached the heights in other fields. Journalists themselves, with understandable and pardonable pride, think that it is because there is no other human endeavor which offers so much by way of opportunities for constructive public service, creative self-expression, and legitimate personal recognition for worthy accomplishments. As Glenn Frank, out of his own varied experience, testified: "[Journalism] is the most fascinating, the most challenging, the most varied, the most satisfying career that modern life has to offer." Newspapers, in the language of the Canons of Journalism of the American Society of Newspaper Editors, "communicate to the human race what its members do, feel, and think." Or as Henry Ward Beecher put it, the newspaper is "the parent, school, college, theatre, pulpit, example, counsellor, all in one. Every drop in our blood is colored by it." Which means that the person who writes for the press or who controls a newspaper or magazine cannot be unmindful of the power of his position. This, undoubtedly, is the key to the fascination of journalism for those who, if they wished, could retire or could continue to amass a fortune in other fields. When such power is used wisely, there is no particular reason for being critical as to the motivations that led to an editorial post.

All of which is said by way of comment on the career of Mr. Meyer and introduction to the following sketch. As Mr. Childs reveals, Mr. Meyer became a newspaper publisher late in life, after a highly successful career in business and governmental circles. It is significant to note that from 1933–1940, Mr. Meyer listed himself as publisher of the Washington *Post*. Since 1940, he has been editor and publisher.

June 5, 1943

JUST ten years ago a little group gathered on the steps of the Washington *Post* building to participate in a sad ceremony. One of two morning newspapers in the nation's capital, the Washington *Post,* having sunk to a dolorous state, was about to be sold down the river.

Present was Evalyn Walsh McLean complete with Hope diamond. She wanted, so she told reporters, to try to save the property, part of the once extensive McLean fortune, for her sons. She might even go so far, it was hinted, as to pawn the famous diamond. Present also was Geoffrey Conta, an agent for William Randolph Hearst, who, at that time, had a voracious appetite for stray newspaper properties.

As the bidding started, under order of the Federal Court of the District of Columbia to satisfy a paper bill, a mysterious stranger soon made his presence felt. The pace was fast, $50,000 and $100,000 at a clip.

At $600,000 Mrs. McLean and the Hope diamond dropped out. Conta bid $800,000. The mysterious stranger went to $825,000, and the *Post,* lock, stock and linotypes, was his. He let it be known merely that he was acting as agent for the real purchaser.

Eleven days later the masthead of the *Post* carried the name of Eugene Meyer as president and publisher, with Mrs. Meyer as vice-president. Meyer was a rich Republican, a highly successful financier, who only a few weeks before had resigned as governor of the Federal Reserve Board, an office to which his friend Herbert Hoover had appointed him in 1930.

In the interval between the sale and the announcement, rumor had connected Meyer's name with the paper, and the wise whispered knowingly that this was a Republican device to maintain a critic right on the doorstep while the opposition was in power. This newcomer, Roosevelt, would need watching. To offset such whispers Meyer concluded his initial statement as owner by saying: "I think I should, in this connection, make it clear that, in purchasing the *Post,* I acted entirely on my own behalf, without suggestion from or discussion with any person, group or organization."

The newspaper business being full of unregenerate cynics, the spectacle of a rich man turning publisher late in life is an occasion for the kind of knowing smiles that greet the widower who marries his blond secretary.

But Meyer, despite some early splurging in the reckless honeymoon stage, has refuted the cynics. He has created a lively, stimulating newspaper which is read even by those who disagree with it most violently. Both circulation and advertising revenue have tripled under his ownership. Dissenters have descended on the publisher of the *Post* with everything from lawsuits to fisticuffs.

While Meyer was still an undergraduate at Yale, he planned his entire life. For the first twenty years he would make money. He did. The second twenty years he would devote to public service. He did. The last twenty years he would spend in contemplative retirement. Publishing an outspoken newspaper in the city of Washington, which has meant getting into one fierce scrap after another, hardly comes under the latter heading.

One of Washington's most conspicuous feuds recently involved the publisher of the *Post* with a husky opponent in a battle that made the front pages of every paper in town except Meyer's own. It had its origin in a rivalry going back to the early days of the Reconstruction Finance Corporation in 1931. At President Hoover's bidding Meyer wrote the RFC Act. He began to hire assistants to get the corporation going even before Congress had made the RFC legal.

When the law was passed, Hoover made Meyer chairman of the RFC. One of the directors named by the President was Jesse Jones, a hulking Texan, who owned banks, office buildings, apartments and a newspaper in Houston. Both are strongminded men. Both think well of their own opinion. They did not always see eye to eye on RFC policy nor were they overly considerate of each other's feelings.

Outwardly the two were polite enough in the years that

followed, but, as later events were to show, rancor was there. Beginning in October of 1941 the *Post* had a series of editorials, each sharper than the one that preceded it, in which Jones was accused of procrastination, first, in expanding aluminum and magnesium production, and then, later on, for what the paper charged was his failure to advance the rubber program.

As loan administrator, so the *Post* charged, he had haggled over pennies while the opportunity to build precious stock piles slipped away.

For all his taciturnity and seeming indifference, Jones is acutely sensitive to criticism. His friends reported that he was seething. On the day of an Alfalfa Club dinner, an occasion for mild horseplay at the expense of Washington's bigwigs, the *Post* carried a particularly strong editorial. Both the publisher and the Federal Loan Administrator were to be present at the dinner.

That evening as Meyer approached the banqueting hall, Jones came toward him. After a few well-chosen remarks, the loan administrator opened up with his fists. The astonished Meyer, who must weigh seventy-five pounds less than the Texan, started to come back in kind.

Friends stepped in and separated the two. Meyer's pince-nez were knocked off his nose and broken in the scrap, but that was the only casualty.

The *Post* did not modify its editorial policy toward the Federal Loan Administrator. Meyer says that his editorial writers started the campaign and he let them continue it as they thought fit. The timing of one of the rebukes read out to Jones did, however, hurt a little.

"I don't know whether you know it or not," he said in editorial conference one day, picking up the *Post* of that morning and pointing to a strong Jones editorial, "but this happens to be the night of another Alfalfa dinner."

President Roosevelt, too, was aware of the coincidence. He had been vastly amused by the report of the fisticuffs on the previous occasion. When he discovered that his aide, Maj. Gen.

Edwin M. Watson, was to attend the dinner that night, he sent out for an MP's brassard and stick, which he presented to Watson.

"There," he said, "I instruct you to keep the peace between Jesse and Gene."

Meyer has been engaged in a series of lawsuits with Mrs. Eleanor Patterson, the famous Cissy, his rival in the morning field. Although, like Meyer, Mrs. Patterson brought great wealth in middle life to a publishing venture, she can claim more legitimate accession to the title of editor of her Washington *Times-Herald* by virtue of her connection with the McCormick-Patterson Chicago *Tribune*.

The lawsuits began when Mrs. Patterson took over the *Times-Herald* from Hearst and promptly demanded from Meyer the "Gumps," "Gasoline Alley," and the other *Tribune* comics he was running.

Meyer stood on his contract with the *Tribune* syndicate and refused to give them up. He won in the courts.

When Meyer signed for the reports of the International News Service, Mrs. Patterson sued him again. Through a hot June in Philadelphia the case dragged on.

"Cissy, why do we have to spend so much time suing each other?" Meyer said at the end of a dreary day in court.

"Well, other people sue me and so I decided I'd do a little suing myself," Cissy is said to have replied.

As the shadow of impending war grew darker, the Washington *Post* was not content merely to oppose the isolationist point of view in academic editorials. The paper carried on a running vendetta with the isolationist leaders in Congress and thereby made some powerful enemies. This took the form of a series of exposés of Axis propagandists, both foreign and domestic.

Any good casting director would have recognized the principals immediately. The *Post's* managing editor is Alexander F. (Casey) Jones, a Welshman with a low boiling point, who is one of the reasons the paper is as full of fight as a wildcat.

Dillard Stokes, a reporter in the crusading tradition, pursued the propaganda assignment with unremitting zeal for two and a half years. And certainly Meyer belonged in the picture.

While he took no active part in the campaign, he stood ready to back up his men on any and all occasions, chewing on his unlighted cigar and talking back to the *Post's* enemies with haughty disdain.

When the turmoil of Washington is too great, Meyer slips off to his estate near Mt. Kisco outside New York—referred to as "the farm." It does have a farm attached to it, also an outdoor swimming pool, done in the Pompeian manner, an indoor pool in white marble, a house, built of stone from a quarry opened on the place, together with tennis courts, sunken gardens, stables, greenhouses with growing orchids, and attendant buildings. It is said to have cost more than $2,000,000. Here in the bosom of the family, with, in normal times, a generous complement of guests, Meyer is the busy squire.

Although he is sixty-seven, he looks a bare fifty-five and he still plays a fairly fast game of tennis. This worries his wife, and when there is talk of playing the rubber set she makes frantic gestures to the opposing pair, knowing that, if they signify their willingness to go on, nothing in the world will persuade her husband to stop.

The war and a succession of marriages have greatly reduced the family circle. An only son, Eugene, III, nicknamed Bill, a year out of Johns Hopkins Medical School, is with an Army Air Force unit overseas, a fact in which his father takes inordinate pride. Two of four daughters are married, Florence, the eldest, to Oscar Homolka, a character actor in Hollywood, and Katharine to Philip L. Graham, who was law clerk to Justice Stanley Reed, of the Supreme Court, before he went into the Army. Katharine and Bill in particular have always argued violently with their father, who regards their New Dealish point of view with a parental tolerance.

Katharine and Elizabeth lean toward journalism. The

youngest daughter, Ruth, is a nurses' aide at Bellevue Hospital in New York.

Mrs. Meyer, a Barnard graduate, worked on the old New York *World* briefly, prior to her marriage. The former Agnes Elizabeth Ernst, a noted beauty, she possesses an energy that matches her husband's. Brünnehilde with a typewriter, one of her friends once described her.

Last fall she flew to England and from there wrote a series of articles on how the average English family had adjusted themselves to the terrors of blitz and the hardships of total war.

This spring Mrs. Meyer made a strenuous tour covering war-production centers throughout the country. The articles which she wrote for her husband's newspaper gave a sympathetic picture of the human problems growing out of the war boom.

A woman of strong likes and dislikes, one of her chief enthusiasms is for the work of Thomas Mann, the German novelist. Whenever a new Mann work appears, Mrs. Meyer reviews it at generous length in the columns of the *Post,* and she has translated some of his shorter things into English. When Doctor and Mrs. Mann are in Washington, they customarily stop with the Meyers.

Of a shy, retiring nature, the novelist sometimes appears a little overwhelmed at the tide of energy that surges through the house.

No. 1 on Mrs. Meyer's list of dislikes is probably Eleanor Roosevelt. As women sometimes do, she takes her politics straight, with an intense partisanship, and for her the symbol of all things Democratic and objectionable is the peripatetic First Lady.

In outspokenness Mrs. Meyer can, and often does, rival her husband. On her trip to England, she spent a week end at Clivenden with her old friend, Lady Astor, who expressed concern over the press England had been getting in America and suggested it might be well if she, herself, ran over to give a few lectures and set things right.

"I don't think that would be such a good idea, Nancy, dear," Mrs. Meyer said.

The Meyer town house on Crescent Place in Washington, not far from a colony of embassies and legations on Sixteenth Street, has sometimes been mistaken by the uninitiated for the Library of Congress. Here during the past two years the *Post's* publisher has held a number of off-the-record sessions with leading figures in the war administration, inviting correspondents of out-of-town papers, together with members of the *Post's* staff, to hear the man of the evening.

Under Secretary of State Sumner Welles, at a luncheon in Meyer's office, spoke of the importance of giving American newspapermen background on foreign policy, but added that it was difficult or impossible in ordinary press conferences because of the presence of representatives of Axis newspapers. Meyer promptly volunteered to arrange special conferences in his drawing room.

Officials who come are, of course, Meyer's personal guests, as are the newspapermen, and the rule of secrecy has been scrupulously observed. Not merely foreign policy but the whole course of the war has been expounded by those directly responsible for it in the big handsome room with its Cézannes and Picassos.

Donald Nelson as chairman of the War Production Board was guest star at least twice. Meyer himself has done some expert needling of Nelson on these occasions. In charge of the division of nonferrous metals of the War Industries Board in the last war, he is said to have saved the Government many millions of dollars on copper purchases alone. It was in copper that Meyer made part of his fortune.

"How many men do you have in your copper division?" he asked.

"About two hundred and fifty," the WPB chief replied.

"I had five," Meyer remarked succinctly.

Meyer and his wife bought their Cézannes and Picassos in Paris on their wedding trip in 1910, when such modernists were laughed at by respectable collectors. Edward Steichen, the photographer, a friend of many years, had recommended the French moderns, and Meyer took his advice in spite of cabled warnings from more conventionally minded friends in America.

The Cézannes in particular are as fine as any museum examples in this country. Thinking he had found a base of mutual comradeship with his rather austere employer, a young reporter from the *Post* told Meyer that he had a print of the Cézanne fruit piece over the mantel in the Meyer drawing room.

"Oh, no, you haven't, young man," Meyer said. "There are no copies of that picture."

For one of his extensive resources, Meyer, except for those early years, has been remarkably restrained as a publisher. He began hiring columnists and commentators, high-priced promotion managers and other trained seals, besides starting a syndicate when, in all truth, the paper had little to syndicate.

He did, however, make some fortunate discoveries. One of them was Raymond Clapper, whom he had hired away from the United Press and who was subsequently hired back by Roy Howard, of the Scripps-Howard papers.

"In two and a half years I made all the mistakes of a lifetime," Meyer was to say later of this early phase.

A far more conservative policy was initiated under the prudent direction of Floyd R. Harrison, who for twenty years has been Meyer's "secretary of the treasury." Trained seals were turned off in a general policy of retrenchment. Alexander F. (Casey) Jones came to the paper as managing editor, and circulation, which had been under 50,000 at the time of the sale, had already begun to climb. It is today around 165,000. Advertising revenue has grown during the decade from 4,000,000 lines a year to 12,000,000, as the depression gave way to the war boom.

During the first two years of his ownership, Meyer held the *Post* in a corporation. He then put it in a partnership, the partners being himself and Mrs. Meyers. Publishing a newspaper in Washington is a luxury and the Meyers wanted to be able to deduct their losses from their income for income-tax purposes. Although Meyer hopes eventually to put the *Post* in the black, he now looks upon his losses as a kind of public benefaction. Salaries, however, have been kept so low in relation to the standard for Washington correspondents that many of the paper's bright young men have gone to other publications.

Until three years ago the title of editor was held by Felix Morley, brother of Christopher Morley, the novelist, while Meyer's title was publisher. Morley's trenchant editorial style, directed for the most part at the New Deal, attracted wide attention. He had a free hand in determining policy.

As the war drew close, however, Morley and his employer did not see eye to eye on foreign policy. Meyer was to become an interventionist while Morley was far more reluctant to accept the inevitability of implication in the world quarrel. They made a quick trip to Europe together in the summer of 1937, talking to prime ministers and potentates in most of the European capitals. The publisher and his editor disagreed on the relative strength of Germany and the democracies, Morley having been convinced of the Nazis' great underlying strength.

Complicating the situation was the presence on the paper of Barnet Nover, an old friend whom Morley had brought in in 1936 as a specialist in foreign affairs. Nover, who writes a signed column on the foreign trend as well as editorials, was an interventionist. The result was a split personality which readers of the paper found a little confusing.

Obviously such a situation could not continue indefinitely. In the summer of 1940, Morley informed Meyer he had been offered the presidency of Haverford College, in Pennsylvania. For some months after he left Washington, however, he continued to write articles on the way the world was going. And he has maintained a friendly relationship with his ex-boss. Later these articles appeared in the Washington *Star*.

The search for a successor was long and painstaking. Many candidates were subjected to the Meyer interviewing technique. He has a habit of asking naïve questions that are not so naïve as they seem. One of the candidates briefly, was Elmer Davis, head of the Office of War Information, who was then on his way to radio's upper brackets.

"Why, that fellow makes more than $50,000 a year," Meyer said, a little astonished that anyone should be paid so much for reporting the news.

The candidate finally chosen was Herbert Elliston, who had been foreign correspondent and then financial editor and columnist for *The Christian Science Monitor*. Elliston, who was one of Morley's old friends and warmly recommended by him for the job, was made associate editor, Meyer retaining the titles of publisher and editor.

Meyer's imprint is on the entire institution. The men in the composing room know him and like him. Their name for him, although not to his face, is Butch. He is proud of an embossed scroll which they presented him celebrating the even tenor of their relationship.

The most trival matters connected with the *Post* engage his interest. Now and then certain of his distinguished subscribers call up to make complaints. Justice William O. Douglas, of the Supreme Court, telephoned one day to say that he was not receiving his paper regularly. Thereupon Meyer thoroughly investigated the distribution of the *Post* in suburban Silver Spring, where the Douglases live.

Now and then, either in the news or the editorial columns, the *Post* treads on the feet of Meyer's friends or favorite prejudices. On the occasion of the famous Liberty League dinner in 1936 a reporter for the *Post* wrote a graphic account of the emeralds and the ermine coats that graced that strange political feast. It served as a mine of source material for the New Deal and the left-wing press seeking to discredit the Liberty Leaguers.

"It might have been possible to offend more of my friends, but I don't know how," Meyer said plaintively to one of his editors the next day, praising the story for its obvious merits.

While the bulk of his fortune is of his own making, Meyer did not start from scratch. Of a French-speaking Jewish family in Alsace, his father emigrated as an adventurous young man of sixteen to California. He settled in Los Angeles when it was a frontier town, and, because he had acquired a safe in which miners could keep their gold, he became a banker. Later he formed a connection with Lazard Frères, the European banking house.

Eugene II was sent to Yale and then to Europe for study in the counting-houses of his father's associates in Hamburg, Berlin, Paris and London. Back in America, he served for four years as a clerk in the New York offices of Lazard Frères. Then in 1901 he opened his own investment house, Eugene Meyer, Jr., and Company.

The qualities he possessed were precisely those necessary to accumulate wealth in that expansive era. He was one of the first Wall Street speculators to apply a fact-finding technique. His clinical analysis of United States Steel set a precedent. With a respect for factual detail and a phenomenal memory went a combative boldness essential in the unrestricted warfare of the period.

In 1917 Bernard M. Baruch brought Meyer to Washington to head the nonferrous-metals division of the War Industries Board. From then until 1933, with brief interruptions, he held one Government office after another. Woodrow Wilson in 1918 named him director of the War Finance Corporation, intended to shore up industries "necessary or contributory to prosecution of the war."

Activities of the corporation were suspended in 1920. But when Meyer's prophecy of a business collapse came true in 1921, President Harding recalled him to serve as managing director again. Calvin Coolidge assigned him the task of reorganizing the Federal Farm Loan Board, a job he carried through with so little regard for political sensitivities that he made many enemies.

Often Meyer has as luncheon guests figures in the war organization who have felt themselves wronged by a *Post* editorial.

Telephoning to set the editor or the associate editor right, they not infrequently receive an invitation to lunch. But if they come expecting to find Meyer ready with an apology, they are due for a shock. He believes the best defense is the offensive.

"You know," he often begins, "your whole public-relations policy is entirely wrong. Why, just take——"

Dismayed by this beginning, the guest rarely gets around to delivering the corrective that he had framed for the occasion.

The scriptural warning to the rich, who are said to have as much chance to enter the Kingdom of Heaven as a camel to pass through the needle's eye, applies in a lesser degree to the accessibility of the inner fraternity of the newspaper world to those who would buy their way into it. But Meyer is on the threshold.

As one of the boys in the city room put it, "I kind of have to hang on to myself because I'm getting to like the old man."

Paper Dolls

By STANLEY FRANK AND PAUL SANN

EDITOR'S PREFACE.—The word *paper,* in this instance, refers to newspaper, and the word *dolls* to the many members of the fairer sex who have found a place for themselves in journalism within recent years. This article was written during World War II. Its theme and spirit are suggested by this editorial note which accompanied the original publication:

"What happens when 8,000 reporters march out and 8,000 girls march in? Masculine growls in the city room prove that the ancient prejudice stands—but on a weakening foundation."

Women were making a place for themselves in all types of journalism, especially advertising, magazine, radio, and book publishing circles, before the war. The exodus of men for battle service, however, made possible wider assaults and deeper penetrations on all journalistic fronts, particularly newspapers and press associations, by the feminine brigade. City rooms all over the land have come to resemble a girls' boarding school study hall. Even the copy desk, once as completely masculine as a strip poker game, has been taken over by the ladies. One of the press services announced during the war, not without pride, that nearly a dozen of its bureau managers were women. Possibly the best index to the place of women in journalism today, or the degree of masculine surrender, is the headline which Messrs. Frank and Sann say appeared during the war in *Editor and Publisher*:

"Man Joins Staff."

Lest the men readers of this piece be disheartened, let it be said that there is still a place for the masculine sex in journalism, but the competition is today much keener, largely on account of the school of journalism trained girls, than it once was. As this article brings out, "all

things considered, the recommendations in favor of newspaper women outweigh the objections," and men must,
therefore, face the inevitable—or rather, the reality, because the fair sex is now pretty well entrenched in what
was once almost wholly a masculine domain.

May 20, 1944

THE management of the Shelby (North Carolina) *Daily Star*,
having been given proper pause by the pitfalls lurking in New
York to ensnare a Southern belle fresh out of college, finally
decided the cause of journalism had to be served by sending
Miss Catherine Bailey, the new sports editor, to report the
World Series last October. Miss Bailey was given an expense
account, an admonition to do good, and a warning against
wolves, whereupon the management pointed her northward
and sat back to await its lady expert's interpretation of baseball
and the queer customs of the natives.

A crowd of 68,676, including Shelby's championship Junior
Legion team, presently saw the first series game, but Miss
Bailey sent her paper no dispatch. The following day, Morton
and Walker Cooper, the Cardinals' brother battery, defeated
the Yankees a few hours after they had learned of their father's
death, a dramatic situation supposedly made to order for the
tender touch of a lady chronicler. Still no word from Bailey.

Holt McPherson, managing editor of the *Star*, began to
think of the several fates, some worst than death, that might
have befallen his representative, and got on the long-distance
telephone. After several hours, he finally located Miss Bailey
with unmistakable sounds of revelry in the background. With
the charm and courtesy characteristic of the old South, Mc-
Pherson asked what the hell, what about the stories.

"Why, Mister Mac," Miss Bailey said coyly, "there hasn't
a thing happened worth writing about."

Mr. Mac's reaction was identical to that of Joe Croom,
editor of the Okmulgee (Oklahoma) *Daily Times,* the busy
night he discovered his all-girl staff draped over the office
windows and listening dreamily to a serenading sextet of town
gallants. He made feeble, fluttering passes at the air and mum-

bled wordlessly to himself. This series of related gestures is practically a ritual performed at least once a day in every newspaper shop throughout the country. The war has crumbled old, formidable barriers against women in the newspaper business, thereby confirming the morbid suspicions of editors that it is not man's destiny to be happy.

Editor & Publisher estimates that more than 8,000 men reporters have gone into the armed forces in the last two years, and they have been replaced almost entirely by women. This figure does not include thousands of new copy boys, some of whom have lovely legs and wear peekaboo blouses. Dozens of small dailies and weeklies are staffed by females exclusively; a male addition to a paper has become such a rarity that *Editor & Publisher* ran, in October, the following headline: MAN JOINS STAFF.

Women have invaded such hitherto inviolate masculine precincts on newspapers as finance, politics, sports, and the police beat. Paper dolls are reading copy, working on the rewrite desk, taking pictures. They are covering riots, crimes of purple passion, train wrecks, fires and suicides without swooning. Much to the astonishment of the misogynists who work alongside them, the paper always appears on time, it is reasonably free of errors and there has not yet been a deluge of libel suits or indignant readers canceling their subscriptions.

Some excellent reporting is being done by women and some sisters in the lodge are exercising their right to ask scatter-brained questions and to go native with unprofessional behavior that is embarrassing to colleagues on the same assignment. All things considered, the recommendations in favor of newspaperwomen outweight the objections against them, but the ancient prejudice still holds firm. Managing and city editors are suffering the dames under protest; chivalry impels them to throw the ladies a few words of good cheer and encouragement, but candor compels most editors to admit they will take a dumb man of erratic social habits over a smart gal every time.

The bill of particulars against women reporters is summed

up by Walter Lister, managing editor of the Philadelphia *Record.*

"Sloppiness is the one word that covers everything," Lister says. "Too many (a) can't spell, (b) don't ask the right questions, (c) lack imagination, (d) won't get specific information. In short, the gals are inclined to misfire on just the points you would expect a woman's neat, precise, accurate touch to supplement the work of the supposedly careless male. You hear so much about the wonderful women secretaries without whom the captains of industry simply would be lost. These office wives keep the great man's checkbook, remind him of the due date on the billion-dollar contract, buy off the chorus girls, correct his grammar, and so on. I don't know why we don't get some of these wonders in the newspaper business. Maybe the whole thing is a myth."

These criticisms are subject to the usual sweeping exceptions and, frankly, are colored by the intransigent prejudices veteran newspaper guys hold against dames. Walter Bodin, city editor of the Oakland *Tribune,* swears his beefs concerning the attitude and mannerisms of women are a blanket indictment of the wrecker sex.

"No matter how able they are, all are given to chattering among themselves and with personable male staffmen," Bodin broods. "They are coy and warm by turns; they clutter and clatter endlessly. Every afternoon, just after the home-edition dead line, the local room presents the sight and sound of a meeting of neurotic clubwomen. The atmosphere demoralizes the men. I have to restrain myself violently from installing a samovar and serving tea and ladyfingers at three o'clock. But all I can do is hum "God Bless America" as tears splash into my highball, and pray fervently for the end of this godless war. Just to make sure I am not becoming insensitive to feminine allure, I asked Joe Sheridan, city editor of the San Francisco *Daily News,* how he felt about it. He looked at me through pain-stricken eyes and mumbled, 'This must be the penalty I am paying for the crimes of my youth.' "

The most common complaint from editors is that the ladies

are as irresponsible as an amorous monkey and have absolutely no sense of the urgency of hot news. One young lady—a competent hand on the rewrite desk of the New York *Post*—checked in a half hour late one crowded morning and was pretty nonchalant about it.

"I used a new leg make-up for the first time," she explained casually, "and it took me longer to put it on than I figured."

This same rewrite girl is treasured at the *Post* for a crack she inspired when Ed Flynn, the city editor, asked her to take a story over the phone.

It was a long yarn and meant using the headset gadget.

"Aw, gee," she said petulantly, "I just fixed my hair, and this will spoil it."

"I suppose," a desk man observed morosely, "we'll have to go out and get ourselves bald lady rewrites."

Sometimes editors must have a nostalgic yearning for the classic excuses offered by men who suffered a slight touch of amnesia regarding hours of work and place of employment: The alarm clock didn't go off; a long-lost cousin suddenly turned up and promptly was seized by a mysterious tropical disease; bus service was disrupted by a dreadful accident and the "interests" covered up all traces of same by burying the victims in quicklime; "I have the grandfather of all hangovers and I am about to die." These evasions strike a familiar gong in bosses who have used the same dodge themselves, but the masculine mind is baffled by a woman's inability to disassociate herself from the trivia of private life when there is work to be done.

The girls think nothing of asking for time off to shop or go to the hairdresser during the peak hours of the day's news. A man cannot comprehend why a woman neglects to report for work just because the mean old laundry failed to return a blouse which is the only thing that will go with an ensemble the other girls in the office haven't seen for two weeks. The girl who explains she is late because she couldn't leave home until galoshes had been found to encase her toeless shoes is likely to give the boss the pitying look reserved for idiot children if he asks why in the world she couldn't wear another pair of shoes. The incidence of one-day pneumonia rises sharply when boy friends are home on furlough.

Carl Kesler, of the Chicago *Daily News,* winces when he recalls the time he sent one of his females to cover a convention of beauty operators at a hotel. A few minutes after she left, a press agent dropped into the office with an idea for a story. Kesler had the girl paged at the hotel.

"What is it?" she demanded breathlessly.

"A guy up here has a pretty good angle on that convention——"

"For goodness' sakes!" the girl gasped indignantly. "I was scared to death when I heard the office was calling. I thought something happened to my family. Don't ever frighten me like this again!"

Another bleat heard frequently from editors is that the ladies create bottlenecks in office routine and impede the promotion of deserving men. Editors have to think twice before giving women late-night assignments and stories that involve too much scrambling or hand-to-hand fighting for news. Some public figures are reluctant to confide in women or have any official truck with them. This attitude was expressed succinctly by Judge Kenesaw M. Landis, the commissioner of baseball, at the last World Series, when Ruth Robertson, photographer for Acme Newspictures, asked the old gent to smile, please.

"I never take orders from women," the judge snapped.

The result is that men who are eligible for the greater prestige and pay of the rewrite desk—the brain and nerve center of a newspaper—have to do overtime leg-work on obscure, but indispensable, beats. The men grouse about lost opportunity, the women scream shrilly against the discrimination that keeps them off exciting stories and, in the confusion, the city editor has to step lively to avoid the crossfire of flaming temperaments.

The strangest aspect of the firm prejudice against ladies of the press is that journalism was among the first professions in

America to accept women, who have found steady—and sometimes lucrative—employment in it for more than a century.
The pioneer was the fabulous Anne Royall, an ignorant, vin-
dictive shrew who once forced President John Quincy Adams
to give her an interview by sitting on his clothes while he
bathed in the Potomac. Anne made such a pest of herself with
gossip and invective that she was arrested as a common scold
in 1829. She was found guilty and fined ten dollars, but escaped the ducking stool because she was sixty years old. Un-
daunted, Anne in 1831 began to publish *Paul Pry,* a four-page
paper devoted to violent abuse of public officials, malicious
scandal and indiscriminate charges of corruption, which often
were valid. Five years later, she brought out *The Huntress,* a
less rancorous sheet, but Ishbel Ross, the historian of the
distaff side of journalism, observes "it always retained a flavor
of her strong and eccentric personality." On October 1, 1854,
Anne died penniless, a bitter and unreconstructed rebel
throughout her eighty-five years.

The most vivid personalities in women's journalism were
the Woodhull sisters, Victoria and Tennessee, who launched
Woodhull and Claflin's Weekly in 1870. Their paper was
designed to attract attention by scandal, shock, and scurrility.
Neither had the education or the social-consciousness to run a
newspaper, but they had two smart ghosts in Col. James H.
Blood and Stephen P. Andrews. The sisters caused a sensation
for a time; they invaded Wall Street, and Victoria was nominated for the presidency of the United States by the Equal
Rights Party. She failed to poll a single electoral vote. By
discussing in print such taboos as free love and prostitution, the
circulation of the *Weekly* rose to a healthy 20,000, but public
opinion turned against them when they began to demand
$500 for withholding the private histories of prominent ladies
of New York. The *Weekly* suspended publication in 1872, but
Victoria revived it a few months later for the express purpose
of exposing the affair between Henry Ward Beecher and
Mrs. Theodore Tilton. Anthony Comstock had Victoria put

in jail, and, when she got out, trapped her on a charge of sending obscene matter through the mails. Victoria beat that rap, too, and went to England, where she married John Biddulph Martin, a banker, and Tennessee became Lady Cook. Tennie died in 1923 and left her sister more than a half million dollars. Victoria died in 1927 at the age of eighty-nine.

The first significant jobs of straight news reporting were done by the famous Nellie Bly, the daughter of a judge in Cochran's Mills, Pennsylvania. Nellie's greatest feat was her round-the-world trip for Joseph Pulitzer in 1890. She made it in seventy-two days, six hours and eleven minutes, beating the elapsed time of Jules Verne's literary flight of fantasy by a week. Essentially a stunt reporter, Nellie impersonated beggars, lunatics, shop girls and Salvation Army lassies to gather her material, which was enormously popular.

Miss Bly's competence and circulation appeal were the springboards which gave women acceptance in the business as something more than necessary nuisances for handling fashions, recipes, society news, advice to the lovelorn and the other trifles on the women's pages. Working reporters, both men and women, recognize spot-news assignments as the only hall mark of the genuine pro, and in the last half century a distinguished list of women have earned respect as first-class craftsmen capable of covering any type of story skillfully and intelligently.

Although Ishbel Ross retired from newspaper work more than a decade ago, her copy in the New York *Herald Tribune* still is remembered and admired, a pretty remarkable tribute in a town where reputations have no more permanency than yesterday's paper. Mrs. C. A. Bonfils, whose material was syndicated for many years under her maiden name of Winifred Black, was famous as "Annie Laurie" in the San Francisco *Examiner* at the turn of the century. Another woman who was outstanding in Chicago, Denver, San Francisco and New York was Nellie Revell. In recent years, Dorothy Thompson, Anne O'Hare McCormick and Ruth Finney have written pieces for the ages and, to give the list a once-over-lightly, other expert newspapermen in skirts have been Lorena Hickok, Genevieve Forbes Herrick, Marjorie Driscoll, Grace Robinson, Helen Worden, Maureen McKernan, Emma Bugbee, Irene Kuhn and Julia Harpman, who married Westbrook Pegler.

It still is true, however, that in normal times it was very easy for a newspaper to get along without women on its reportorial staff. The girls write well enough; they have a deft touch on descriptive stories, human-interest yarns and interviews—provided they don't gush over the interviewee. Yet it is rare to see a woman write the lead story on a news break of major importance. Most editors believe women have a constitutional inability to gather up all the loose ends of a complicated story and weave them into a compact, well-rounded piece. In winding up and making with the deathless prose, too many ladies forget the time-proved formula of who-what-when-where-why-how. Their stuff is apt to be another "Johnstown Flood" epic, which is a classic story of the newspaper business, and may even be true.

On the night of May 31, 1889—so the story goes—an editor had no one in the office but a cub reporter when the first flash of the catastrophe at Johnstown came over the wires. The editor immediately sent the cub to Johnstown and routed out other members of the staff, but by the time they could reach the scene, all communication was closed. For several days the cub was isolated on top of the biggest story of the year. When the telegraph wires finally were opened, the editor waited feverishly for the cub's dispatch telling of the number of victims, the property damage, health conditions in the devastated area, plans for rehabilitation and all other vital information. The stuttering wires at last began to tap out the eyewitness account the entire country was awaiting breathlessly. The story began:

"God sits upon a lonely mountaintop tonight and looks down upon a desolate Johnstown" and went on from there, carrying the reader through several hundred high-powered adjectives and verbs before getting down to the simple, arresting facts.

The editor bounced the following wire into the cub's teeth: "Forget flood. Interview God. Rush pictures."

A few words in defense of the girls should be offered at this time. All the faults found with them can be applied to inexperienced men; editors are prone to forget that the majority of their new paper dolls were secretaries, file clerks, telephone operators, receptionists or copy girls a short time ago. They have been thrown into jobs demanding special technique and know-how without the basic training given men reporters in normal times. Veterans had to serve a long apprenticeship of dreary leg work, and they were promoted slowly as their knowledge of the craft expanded. The girls have been plunged into the whirlpool of news without the breaking-in process that teaches them how to keep their heads above water.

Newspaperwomen further are laboring under strains men do not have to contend with. Many are married and some have young children; there are households to maintain and, if husbands are in the service, there is a constant pressure for money. Under the circumstances, it is understandable that women are unable to divorce themselves from outside interests and obligations during working hours.

Still, women are doing good sound jobs in fields entirely new to them. The *Chicago Journal of Commerce* has three girls covering the intricate and multitudinous Government agencies in Washington. Mary B. Smith handles the Reno divorce mill for the Associated Press all by herself. The A. P.'s assistant market editor in Chicago is Charlotte Ingalls, who was a switchboard operator before the war decimated the staff. At least twenty Southern papers claim the first lady sports editor in history.

A genuine precedent smasher is Adelaide Leavy, one of the first girl photographers to make good in New York on a major paper or picture service. Robert P. Dorman, general manager of Acme Newspictures, says twenty-nine-year-old Miss

Leavy is the only woman he ever has known who can take any spot picture with the assurance that it will come out all right. Miss Leavy is an attractive redhead who makes a point of dressing in the height of feminine fashion, although she wears slacks when she knows a job will require kneeling and climbing. News photographers usually are given a strenuous pushing around from the authorities when they attempt to take action shots of accidents, arrests, fires and such, but Miss Leavy was given a regulation raincoat and helmet by a solicitous fireman when she took a shot of a theater fire from the water-flooded balcony. The fireman said she'd spoil her pretty black-and-white-gingham dress if she went into the theater unprotected.

It pains die-hard newshounds to admit it, but the newspapers would have been in an awful jam in the last two years if women had not been ready, willing and sometimes able to step into vacancies on staffs depleted by the draft. The Associated Press, for example, had six girl reporters before Pearl Harbor; it now has sixty-five in its ninety-four bureaus. The United Press has approximately 100 girls, or 20 per cent of the staff, scattered among its sixty-one bureaus.

Those men waiting for the day former colleagues are mustered out of the service and all the Johanna-come-latelys are pitched out on their pink ears are whistling up a blind alley. The girls have got their teeth into the business and will not be dislodged easily.

"The last two years have taught me to give more consideration to a woman applicant for a job than I did before the war," says L. L. Engelking, city editor of the New York *Herald Tribune.* "Women frequently are a lot more difficult to handle than men, but I can't kick. I might have a squawk," he adds thoughtfully, "if I had a staff that was two-thirds female. I'm a tolerant man, but that would be too much."

Deep down in their hard hearts, most editors vibrate on the same wave length with Harry Nason, former managing editor of the New York *Post,* the first time he saw Sylvia Porter, now that paper's financial editor, wearing her Phi Beta Kappa key.

It was a miniature key, the smallest made, but it was, nevertheless, recognizable as the badge of intellect.

Nason grabbed Miss Porter by the arm and glared at the key. "Dames around a newspaper office are bad enough," he yelped, "but smart dames are going to kill me and the business."

Pugnacious Pearson

(DREW PEARSON)

By JACK ALEXANDER

EDITOR'S PREFACE.—Books usually follow, not precede, newspaper publication. In the case of Drew Pearson and *Washington Merry-Go-Round,* however, the book came first and set the pattern for the syndicated column by the same title which followed. As a matter of fact, this book, and another by the title of *More Merry-Go-Round,* made it necessary for Mr. Pearson and his co-author, Robert S. Allen, to start a column, or do something, because indirectly these books and their irreverent pinking of capital personages had caused both Mr. Pearson and Mr. Allen to lose their newspaper connections. So, as Mr. Alexander reports, "the two dischargees set about adapting the sassy style of their books to a newspaper column" and "from the beginning, it treated the capital as if it were a circus and tirelessly taunted the star animals, in the manner of Clyde Beatty."

Mr. Pearson (Mr. Allen took leave from the partnership during the war to accept a commission in the Army) has not limited his journalistic activities to the press and books. He is also a radio news-commentator. The *Post* writer calls him a "columnist-oracle," and says that "he regularly goes out on a limb with his 'predictions of things to come,' approximately 60 per cent of which come true."

Newspaper readers recall that Mr. Pearson and President Franklin D. Roosevelt were often at odds. The President was sharp in his criticism of the writer, and the columnist was equally caustic in his comments. "Among Washington office holders, Pearson is one of the most hated and feared of men," writes Mr. Alexander, "and concern over what he will print or say next has caused more stomach ulcers in high places than any other single source of worry."

Here, then is a portrait of a modern journalism gadfly, a columnist and commentator who, as the *Post* editors say, "wields a tremendous influence, not always wisely."

January 6, 1945

THE only time in American history when conduct of a war was embarrassed in the interest of laxation was on Sunday evening, November 21, 1943. That was the evening on which Drew Pearson, the columnist and radio oracle, breathlessly spoke into a microphone the news that General Patton had slapped an ailing soldier. Pearson's radio sponsor was the company which manufactures and sells Serutan, a proprietary remedy for costive middle-agers, a circumstance which was topped in majestic irrelevance only by the hysterical furor which followed the broadcast.

Although criticized on some editorial pages for dangerously talking out of turn, Pearson was widely commended for what was termed his "courage" and his "scoop." The excitable New York tabloid *PM* spotlighted him in its "Hats Off!" department, which is devoted to the current hero of the day. Senator Pepper, of Florida, favored a court-martial for Patton.

The orgy reached its apex in this passage from Walter Winchell's Broadway gossip column: "I think that General Patton will never live it down. . . . Every mother still must writhe in agony wondering if her son is mistreated by others. . . . Mothers always see their grown sons as little, frightened children, suddenly awakened in the dark, crying 'Mommy!' " Winchell went on to meditate solemnly on the possibility that Patton might be shot by one of his own soldiers. Pearson was a shade more conservative. He contented himself with a prediction that Patton would never be used in combat again and with reviewing in his column subsequently what purported to be earlier misdeeds of the erring general.

Both Pearson's prediction and Winchell's premonition went sour. No soldier murdered Patton; in fact, Patton was cheered by armed units wherever he went. General Eisenhower, withstanding the journalistic heat, preserved Patton for his brilliant armored drive through France, a drive which hastened the invasion of Germany and probably avoided the longer casualty lists which would have resulted from a slower campaign. In sum, Eisenhower, who was backed up by Secretary Stimson and General Marshall, sensibly refused to be diverted from the path of military efficiency by a noisy incident of the crusade for peristaltic efficiency.

What Pearson, Winchell and the other critics ignored, or didn't know, was that Patton, besides being a great leader, was Eisenhower's most valuable piece on the psychological chessboard. The Germans respected him, and Eisenhower shrewdly capitalized on this respect. After Sicily, he sent Patton to Corsica, where he was a threat to Genoa; the Germans sent their 10th Army to Genoa. Patton next appeared in Cairo, and the Germans, reasoning that he might strike through the Balkans, dispatched their 8th Army to Greece. While these crack units were cooling their heels on the wings, Eisenhower invaded at Salerno. Last summer, when the invasion of France was imminent, the Germans stationed their 15th Army, another seasoned outfit, in the Pas-de-Calais, which seemed a logical place for Patton to strike. The 15th didn't pull out of the Pas-de-Calais until after Patton's break-through at Avranches, and by that time its opportunity had vanished.

Pearson's disclosure of the slapping was scarcely an act of courage, in the normal meaning of the word. There was no danger involved in it, except that of adding more readers and listeners to an array of followers already counted in the millions. Nor was the Patton story a "scoop," which is what reporters—at least those of the screen—call a news story which is published before rivals are aware of its existence. For several months, some sixty-odd war correspondents at Algiers had full knowledge of the slapping, but none had tried to send it back home. It was likewise known to many newspapers and magazines in this country. All, except Pearson, voluntarily refrained from making it public.

Pearson, in explaining his act, says simply, "I decided it was time to let loose on him."

In so doing, he was hewing closely to a sure-fire formula for journalistic success. This formula began to come into its own with the advent of the political column which is syndicated, or sold, to large numbers of newspapers. It has reached its present full-blown development with the growth of the radio networks. Its success, on the radio side, stems from a passion for artificially contrived excitement which undeniably exists among large masses of listeners.

By working radio and newspaper syndication together, the exponent of the formula is able to wield a unique double-action influence on public opinion. The chief ingredient of the formula is aggressive indiscretion, and with it go various knacks for making and keeping enemies, preferably big ones; for making one's self, instead of the news, the focus of interest; for highjacking public controversies and creating one when none is boiling at the moment; for investing the most trivial items with a sense of urgency and drama, and, sometimes, for giving gossip the status of established fact. Because all this tends to build up the practitioner into a sort of journalist-politician, his product in print or on the air often takes on the punitive character of political prose of oratory. On the whole, the formula, when literally followed, bears as much resemblance to sober journalism as ax murder does to brain surgery.

Viewed from the standpoint of what Broadway calls the box office, Winchell is the most skillful of the practitioners. As he dispenses presumably hot items from his radio script in a throaty voice or chuckles derisively at knaves he has confounded, he plays a background accompaniment, now on a dummy telegraph key, which makes a clacking noise, now on a dummy wireless sender, which whistles. These stage-prop sounds, which are meaningless to students of any code, help to convey to the listener a feeling of being close to where the big news is breaking.

Theatrically, Pearson's performance falls considerably below Winchell's. Winchell is theatrical by nature and experience—he was once in vaudeville—and even his ordinary conversation has a tense quality about it; Pearson, when detached from his microphone, is a quiet, almost shy man. He is forty-seven and bald, has a sandy mustache and is a little hesitant of speech. What drama he is able to inject into his broadcasting is the fruit of long practice in raising his voice and in speeding up the reading of his script. Despite the blessings of voice culture, his announcement of an opinion or an event of earth-shaking proportions often sounds as flat as the unveiling of a Las Vagas elopement by Louella Parsons. His radio-popularity rating runs well below Winchell's and his column, "Washington Merry-Go-Round," is published in slightly more than 600 newspapers, whereas Winchell's "On Broadway" is published in more than 800.

Yet, possibly because Pearson does not dilute his comments on public affairs with divorce news and café-society chitchat, he is much the more powerful of the two politically. He is, in fact, one of the strongest political influences in the United States today. His colleagues in the capital correspondent corps, most of whom frankly disapprove of his approach to reporting, last October voted him "the Washington correspondent who exerts through his writings the greatest influence on the nation." In the poll, which was conducted by *The Saturday Review of Literature,* Pearson got fifty-six votes, exactly twice as many as his nearest competitor, Walter Lippmann. In another category—that of "the Washington correspondent who does the best all-around job as measured in terms of reliability, fairness, ability to analyze the news"—Pearson got only two votes. This enviable category was led by Thomas L. Stokes and Marquis W. Childs, with twenty-five and twenty-three votes, respectively. Oddly, neither Stokes nor Childs got more than a scattering of votes as a wielder of influence, a paradox which seems to suggest that American newspaper readers have a long way to go before attaining political maturity.

Among Washington officeholders, Pearson is one of the most hated and feared of men, and concern over what he will print or say next has caused more stomach ulcers in high places than any other single source of worry. The concern is felt through all the levels of Government, for Pearson has pipe lines throughout the structure. It hasn't been necessary for him to establish the pipe lines; they seem to establish themselves. As one observer sagely explains it, "For every guy that Pearson wants to get, there is at least one ambitious subordinate in his department who will volunteer the information Pearson needs. Pearson has been in business for a long time, and it is easy for anyone with a grudge to find his number in the telephone book. Besides, Pearson himself knows the location of every grudge in Washington."

A column such as the "Merry-Go-Round" could not exist in England, the only major country in which the leeway accorded the press is as broad as it is here. England has an Official Secrets Act which prohibits a public servant, under pain of punishment, from publishing government secrets, or from letting them out to someone else for publication. No comparable law exists in this country. Government secrets are, in effect, the unofficial property of whoever happens to handle them or overhear private discussion of them, unless they bear directly upon military security. The only brake on the tongue of the public servant is whatever sense of fitness he happens to possess. Since 1933, this sense of fitness has deteriorated in the intense intramural struggle for power, and the brokerage of Government information, frequently in a distorted form, has flourished. Its main outlet is columns such as the "Merry-Go-Round," and government by grudge has become a capital fixture.

In retailing his wares, Pearson is fond of opening with a titillating line which implies that the lid is about to be lifted from a juicy conspiratorial plot. Often, this is mere window dressing for an item of no particular freshness or novelty; at other times it heralds the approach of information which the newspapers haven't printed, because they didn't have it, or have omitted because it was plainly angled for someone's political benefit. Pearson's most over-worked opening line is, "It hasn't leaked out yet, but——" Some of its variants are: "The State Department is trying to hush it up, but——"; "Only those quite close to Prime Minister Churchill know it, but

——"; "The War Department isn't advertising the details, but ——" and "Only insiders know it, but——." There are other gambits, including "This will be denied, but——," which have the effect of setting the reader's mind against any prospective defense by the parties accused. Pearson heightens the effect by occasionally printing a list of his stories which have been met with denial and which, to his own satisfaction, have been proved to be true. A literal-minded reader of the column might easily get the impression that the higher officeholders are constantly engaged in an undercover movement to dynamite the public weal.

So assiduously has Pearson cultivated the use of the word "leak," both as a verb and as a noun, that it has found its way into the everyday vocabularies of exasperated officeholders. The "Merry-Go-Round" is required breakfast-table reading in Washington, and it is a common occurrence for a Cabinet member or bureau chief to rattle the pages of his newspaper over the grapefruit and exclaim, "I wonder who the hell could have leaked that out!" If he waits a few weeks, the chances are that he will find out, for Pearson likes to reward the faithfulness of his leaks by lauding them as progressive, fearless or up-and-coming public men. In the course of time, most of the top men in Washington have succeeded in spotting the more persistent leaks. Unhappily for the top men, nothing effective can be done about them. If a leak is fired or demoted or denied access to private conference circles, he is likely to redouble his efforts to obtain leakable material. So he is kept on the pay roll, and his chances of long tenure are, if anything, enhanced by his superior's lack of confidence in him.

"Before I was suspected of tipping off Pearson," one of them said not long ago, "I was just another Joe in a big department. Now the boss goes out of his way to say 'good morning' to me."

The continued presence of a leak can have a seriously hamstringing effect on Government. Early in 1941, for instance, when it appeared likely that America would be drawn into the war, one department head was charged with organizing a confidential study which had a direct bearing on preparedness.

The subordinate in charge of the section to which the task would normally be assigned happened to be a Pearson leak. The department head was caught on a dilemma. If he went ahead and assigned the secret study to the section, it might become, *in toto,* the property of the "Merry-Go-Round." If he by-passed the section and assigned it to another section, he felt confident that the distrusted subordinate, angry at being by-passed, would dribble out whatever fragments of the secret study he was able to obtain by reason of his presence in the office. He did the only thing possible under the circumstances —he pigeonholed the study. It was begun, belatedly, after Pearl Harbor had been attacked.

Students of the fear complex which Pearson's work has generated in officialdom disagree on the question of whether it has a good or bad influence on the public mind. Some hold that, although Pearson strains the press-freedom privilege to the breaking point and fosters throughout Government the dubious ethical practice of undercutting one's chief, his disclosures, even when inaccurate or slanted, serve the national interest. They argue that the dread of what Pearson may say or write acts as an inhibition upon official chicanery. The other school of thought, which is the more numerous, holds that while the Pearson complex may make a dishonest official more careful, it can never succeed in restraining his impulse to do evil; and that Pearson's one-sided campaigns against, in many instances, honorable officials trying to do an honorable job have helped to create an unjustified distrust of them.

Pearson's own view of the criticism which is heaped upon his head is that it has been the inevitable reward of vigorous political reformers since the time of Tom Paine.

"Naturally," he says cheerily, "I'm damned all over the place sometimes."

Nothing seems to invigorate Pearson more than being damned all over the place, and he is especially pleased when some high-ranking member of the Government accuses him of barefaced mendacity. At a press conference in September, 1943, President Roosevelt called him "a chronic liar" after Pearson had stated on his radio program that Secretary Hull wanted to see Russia "bled white." Afterward, placards appeared on the nation's newsstands exhorting passers-by to "read the man the President called a liar!" Pearson has saved one of the placards as a memento.

In the rough-and-tumble climate of the Senate, McKellar, of Tennessee, once unwound a Philippic in which he called Pearson an infamous liar, a revolving liar, a pusillanimous liar, a lying ass, a natural-born liar, a liar by profession, a liar for a living, a liar in the daytime and a liar in the nighttime. McKellar also used the nouns "crook" and "skunk" and the adjectives "dishonest," "ignorant," "corrupt" and "groveling." Pearson was so delighted that he reprinted the untasty speech in his column.

Pearson's growth into a controversialist and national irritant is another confirmation of the belief that anything can happen in America. His family background is eminently conservative and serene. His father, the late Paul Martin Pearson, was a storekeeper's son who worked his way through Baker University, in Kansas, by selling fruit to train passengers while locomotives were taking on water. Paul Pearson married Edna Wolfe, a classmate, and, after graduation, became a Methodist minister in a small Kansas community. Later he took postgraduate work at Northwestern University, in Evanston, Illinois, where Drew was born and baptized Andrew Russell Pearson. After a year of further study, at Harvard, the elder Pearson joined the faculty of Swarthmore College, a Quaker institution, at Swarthmore, Pennsylvania, where he ultimately became professor of public speaking. He joined the Society of Friends and took his family along with him into the Quaker faith. At family reunions, Drew and his brother and two sisters still use "thee" and "thy" in conversation.

The family income was modest, and Drew, as a youngster, earned money at the usual boyish jobs and at trapping skunks. While he was attending Phillips Academy, at Exeter, New Hampshire, his father founded the Swarthmore Chautauqua, and Drew, during his prep-school vacations and, later, during his Swarthmore College vacations, worked on the Chautauqua circuit. Starting out as a member of a tent crew, he rose to motion-picture operator and advance man, and finally, to the high post of Chautauqua lecturer. By his own estimate, he was a poor lecturer.

Graduating from Swarthmore in 1919, Pearson went abroad for the American Friends Service Committee. He spent two years in the Balkans, helping to rebuild razed villages, and when he came home he had decided that his future lay in diplomacy. Lacking the private income usually deemed necessary for this kind of career, he decided to approach diplomacy through newspaper work, in the optimistic hope that he would be able to save enough money to finance the career he really wanted. Newspaper opportunities were scarce, so he took a job teaching industrial geography at the University of Pennsylvania.

The Washington Disarmament Conference came along in 1922, and with it a chance to rub elbows with the world's leading striped-pants wearers. Pearson enterprisingly manufactured the chance himself. He paid a visit to the editor of the Swarthmore student weekly, *The Phoenix,* of which he had once been editor himself, and suggested that his successor write to Secretary of State Hughes asking that Pearson be allowed to interpret the conference for college men. While in college, Pearson had founded something called the Intercollegiate Press Association and, at his urging, the letter was typed on one of the association's letterheads. Hughes thought the idea a good one, and Pearson got to attend the conference as correspondent for the Swarthmore *Phoenix* and the college-press association. After this coup, he was discussed on the Swarthmore campus, near which he lived, as one of the alumni most likely to succeed.

Soon afterward, Pearson transformed himself into a world traveler. The transformation was accomplished with surprising rapidity. A world-traveler friend of his, who had had some success as a lecturer, lent him a copy of his publicity circular and, with his permission, Pearson converted the text to his own use, largely by substituting his own name for that of his friend. Marked "Confidential—Not For Publication," the circular, under the headline AROUND THE WORLD WITH DREW PEARSON, stated in part: "Asia, Africa and Europe are familiar fields to Drew Pearson. He has visited all three continents. He has an international point of view. . . . As a lecturer on international politics, Pearson is known over most of this country and in England." It went on to describe the mysterious, teeming Orient, which Pearson now proposed to probe into, "traveling by steamship, airplane, ox-cart, automobile, on camel, on horse and on foot."

Instead of mailing the circular to newspaper editors, as a less imaginative young man might have done, Pearson took it to them personally, traversing the continent in day coaches, with stop-overs. Through fast talking, he sold thirty-five editors between Philadelphia and Seattle on the notion of buying dispatches which he proposed to mail back. In Seattle, from which he intended to work his way across the Pacific, his resourcefulness showed itself again. Turned down by the hiring halls because he lacked experience as a seaman, Pearson had his chest tattooed—with the Greek letters of his fraternity, Kappa Sigma—and haunted the halls once more with his shirt front unbuttoned. The ruse worked, and he shipped aboard a passenger vessel as an ordinary seaman, jumping ship at Yokohama.

His travels carried him through the Japanese islands and into Siberia, then down to Australia, where, in addition to sending home his regular dispatches, he made money by lecturing on the Japanese menace, which has always worried the Australians. From Australia, he sailed to India to interview Mahatma Gandhi. Unfortunately, Gandhi was in jail and couldn't be seen. On returning to the United States, Pearson made capital of him anyway; he interviewed Henry Ford, who had Gandhi-like ideas about decentralizing industry, and sold an article on the two decentralizers to the magazine *Asia*. Two years later Pearson went back to India to have another go at the Mahatma. This time the holy man was on a fast and couldn't be bothered, and to this day Pearson has never seen him.

Meanwhile, in 1924, during another voyage, something had happened which had caused him to throw in his lot definitely with journalism and to repress his ambition for a diplomatic career. By some queer psychological process, the repressed ambition was to turn subsequently into something resembling detestation and to make him a self-appointed gadfly of all diplomats, particularly those of the State Department. Still traveling third class, barely making expenses and just about washed up with newspapering, Pearson was crossing the Mediterranean when he received a wireless message from an American syndicate. The message offered him excellent pay if he could obtain interviews with twelve leading politicians and rulers of Europe. Pearson got the interviews and sailed for home, first class, on the Aquitania. It was a triumphal voyage. He ordered rich meals, including lobster at least once a day, and lolled on the soft cushions of the men's lounge.

The syndicate took him on as chief salesman of its newspaper features and, on the side, he did more great-man interviews with giants like Ford, Edison and Burbank. "I also interviewed a lot of people who were not so great," he says reminiscently, "but I pumped them up as if they were." After another trip to the Orient, during which he added the Gobi Desert to the list of exotic places on which he had left his footprint, Pearson was taken on as foreign editor of the newly founded *United States Daily,* of Washington.

The job carried more prestige than pay, but it got him to the Geneva Naval Conference of 1927, and he was able to eke out his slim salary by writing articles on the Geneva doings for *The Japan Advertiser* and *The Tokyo Jiji*. In 1929, he moved to the Washington bureau of the Baltimore *Sun,* where he evolved, gradually this time, from Pearson, the world traveler and salesman, into Pearson, the controversialist.

The *Sun* assigned him to cover the State Department, and Pearson came through with provocative articles which pleased the editors of that liberal sheet for a time, as the Hoover era was in full swing and Washington was a rather stuffy place. The capital scene was vastly enlivened in 1931 with publication of a book written anonymously and titled *Washington Merry-Go-Round*. The book irreverently pinked prominent capital personages—Wrong-Horse Harry, the heading of a chapter on Secretary of State Stimson, suggests the general flavor. Authorship was traced to Pearson and Robert S. Allen, a Washington correspondent for *The Christian Science Monitor*. The *Monitor* fired Allen, who thereupon went to work for Hearst.

With their first book selling well, the pair issued a sequel, *More Merry-Go-Round,* in the following year. In a chapter on bootlegging in the capital, the book took a gratuitous slap at the moral conduct of a prominent matron; or, at least, it seemed gratuitous to the late William E. Moore, managing editor of the *Sun,* and he requested Pearson to come in for a talk. Moore had been getting progressively more angered at some of Pearson's dispatches. One depicted the purported embarrassment of the British ambassador over his failure to be invited to a dinner given by the State Department correspondents; Pearson, Moore learned after the dispatch had been published, had been in charge of sending out the invitations.

Another Pearson dispatch related that when former Secretary of War Newton D. Baker tried to pay a visit to the incumbent, Patrick J. Hurley, he failed to get past the Secretary's anteroom, and walked out. Baker, in a letter written to the *Sun,* protested that there was "not a syllable of truth in the story." He added that he had seen Hurley and that his reception had been marked by "kindness and courtesy."

"The *Sun* isn't a keyhole paper," Moore grumbled around the *Sun* office. "If we wanted Walter Winchell, we'd hire him."

When Pearson reported to Moore, he was handed a month's pay and offered a choice of resigning or of being fired. Pearson said he preferred to be fired, and got his wish.

The reason for his preference soon became apparent. The discharge made Pearson the Dred Scott of a freedom-of-the-press controversy which won national notice. Newspaper stories appeared intimating that Hurley had brought pressure on the *Sun* because of a chapter in *More Merry-Go-Round,* entitled "The Cotillion Leader," in which he was pictured as a socially ambitious fop. Hurley had not communicated with the *Sun* at all, but the hullabaloo was kept alive for a while anyway.

Allen meanwhile had been discharged by Hearst because of some magazine articles he had written, and the two dischargees set about adapting the sassy style of their books to a newspaper column, which they named after the first of their two books. A newspaper feature syndicate which undertook to market it found the going hard. The "Washington Merry-Go-Round" column started off inauspiciously in December, 1932, with only six subscribing newspapers. From the beginning, it treated the capital as if it were a circus, and tirelessly taunted the star animals, in the manner of Clyde Beatty.

Pearson and Allen made an efficient working team. Allen, a hard-boiled ex-cavalryman, covered Capitol Hill mostly, while Pearson, polite and soft-spoken, covered the State, War and Navy departments and played the diplomatic dinners, at which there was much unguarded talk of important matters. When trying to pry a story out of a stubborn legislator, the pair resorted to an ingenious version of the police third degree. Allen would beard the legislator in his office, shouting at him and pounding on his desk. Next day, Pearson would turn up at the office, pour oil on the victim's emotional wounds and apologize for his colleague's impetuousness. Often, the legislator, bruised by Allen's bludgeoning and mollified by Pearson's courtly kindness, would blat out his precious secret, only to experience new pangs when it came out in the "Merry-Go-Round."

For a time, the coauthors netted about twenty-five dollars a month each from the column, and did other writing work in order to preserve their nutritional balance. Then in March, 1933, the New Deal took over Washington, and hatchet-throwing became a recognized adjunct of Government. Pearson and Allen had had plenty of practice in the art. While the bulk of the correspondent corps fumbled around trying to use the scholarly approach in interpreting the new marvel, Pearson and Allen joined in the hatchet-throwing with zest, and the column was well on its way to prosperity. During this period, their relations with the White House were cordial. Their third book, *The Nine Old Men,* published in 1936, was a precursor of President Roosevelt's ill-starred attempt to pack the Supreme Court.

When the United States got into the present war, Allen went back into the Army. In his absence, Pearson, as the announcer for his radio program tersely puts it, "carries on alone." In the old spectacular team tradition, he operates in a welter of libel suits and charges of skul-duggery hurled by lacerated victims.

Even in his private life, the serene Pearson has managed to be spectacular. In 1925, he married into a spectacular family, taking as his bride Countess Felicia Gizycka, the daughter of Mrs. Eleanor M. Patterson, who, in turn, is a granddaughter of Joseph Medill, founder of the Chicago *Tribune.* Mrs. Patterson took a strong fancy to her son-in-law and, when she later became proprietor of the spectacular Washington *Times-Herald,* subscribed to the "Merry-Go-Round" column. After Pearson was divorced from her daughter, the attachment seemed somehow to become closer. And when Pearson was married a second time, in 1936, to another young matron of social standing, Mrs. Patterson installed his bride on the *Times-Herald* staff as a motion-picture reviewer, a calling at which she had had no experience. The event caused some commotion in the city room, as the second Mrs. Pearson had formerly been the wife of George Abell, another member of the staff.

In 1937, Abell took his young son, Tyler, to England, ignoring a split-custody decree which forbade the boy's removal from this country. The Pearsons sailed to England and, with the aid of Scotland Yard, learned that Abell had taken the boy to the Isle of Sark, off the French coast. Pearson chartered an airplane and flew to Sark, where he found his stepson out walking with his nursemaid. Loading him aboard, he flew back to

London, with Abell in hot pursuit in another plane. The upshot of the dramatic chase by air and sea was that full custody was awarded to the boy's mother, Mrs. Pearson. Ellen, Pearson's eighteen-year-old daughter by his first marriage, divides her time between the homes of Pearson and her own mother.

Over a period of years, the idyllic relationship between Pearson and his ex-mother-in-law lost its bloom. Mrs. Patterson fired Mrs. Pearson from the staff and, on expiration of her syndicate contract, announced that the *Times-Herald* was dropping the "Merry-Go-Round." In reply, Pearson and Allen published an advertisement in which they stated that it was they who were dropping the *Times-Herald,* and added that it couldn't have the column back if the publisher came begging for it. There have been no diplomatic relations since then. Not long ago, the *Times-Herald,* which now refers to Pearson as The Headache Boy, took him apart in an unflattering full-page article. Pearson loftily ignored it.

Whatever else may be said of Pearson as a journalist, he is beyond question one of the hardest-working members of his craft. In the hot months, he works in a modernistic house on his 280-acre stock and dairy farm near Gaithersburg, Maryland, and cools himself off in a private swimming pool. The farm operates at a profit, and Pearson gets a wry satisfaction out of naming his bulls after public characters who have called him a liar or some other unfavorable name.

During most of the year he works in the study of his yellow-brick home in the Georgetown section of Washington. He is in his study by nine o'clock in the morning, and he works until noon, reading his mail, which is heavy, and dictating replies. Many telephone calls, offering confidential tips, come to him during the forenoon. If the tipster is an obscure person, such as a Government clerk or a congressman's rejected mistress, Pearson takes down the caller's number and hangs up. Then he goes out to a public pay station and calls the tipster back to arrange a personal interview, if the tip looks good enough. Pearson lives in constant apprehension of wire tapping and is careful about protecting his volunteer informants.

Pearson starts his personal news gathering by lunching downtown with some highly placed man who may know something he wants to know—and who usually wants Pearson to know about it—and he spends the rest of the afternoon in visiting other prospective sources. He entertains a good deal at dinner, his guests often including someone of Cabinet, Supreme Court or boss-bureaucrat rank, and is a familiar figure at dinners of the capital's tail-coat set. Wherever he has dinner, Pearson makes a point of getting back to his study by nine o'clock or shortly thereafter, and dictating notes on what he has learned, to be placed in a file.

Then, using a twenty-year-old portable typewriter, he begins pecking out his "Merry-Go-Round" column, finishing it sometime between midnight and one A.M. His staff consists of three girl secretaries, one of whom works on a night shift, and a reporter, or legman, who spends the day rounding up items, at off-the-record press conferences and in visits to the various departments. According to other correspondents, material dispensed as background information at off-the-record conferences has a recurring habit of turning up as news in the "Merry-Go-Round."

Pearson turns out seven columns a week and, in addition, writes his Sunday radio script and a separate "Merry-Go-Round" for Maryland, which he distributes gratis to weekly papers all over the Free State. He also writes the plot of a comic strip glorifying a mythical Washington correspondent named Hap Hopper, who leads a stormy career resembling Pearson's, and every now and then he lectures before some organization. It is a back-breaking schedule, and his friends are inclined to attribute his errors, in part, at least, to his self-imposed stretch-out system. The rest they attribute to his grudges.

For sheer durability, Pearson's antipathy for Sen. Millard Tydings, of Maryland, occupies the top of the grudge list. The feud dates back to 1933, when Tydings, as a member of a Senate committee, helped bring about the removal of Pearson's father from the governorship of the Virgin Islands, to which

President Hoover had appointed him. A year before the White House's 1938 purge program, in which Tydings was one of the Democrats proscribed, Pearson instituted his Maryland "Merry-Go-Round" and devoted it mostly to attacking Tydings and his own former employer, the Baltimore *Sun,* which was backing Tydings. Pearson joined actively in the purge movements as liaison man for Congressman David J. Lewis, Tydings' opponent. He also swelled Lewis' campaign fund by a $17,000 donation, some of which was contributed by his sisters, neither of whom was a resident of Maryland. The Pearson family donation amounted to half of Lewis' campaign fund. Tydings survived the purge.

In 1939, the expensive Tydings grudge pushed Pearson into an error of fact. Appearing with his colleague, Allen, as a guest on another radio program, Pearson stated, "Well, we suddenly became interested in checking up on Government works and discovered that the senator (Tydings) had put through a very interesting little deal." The "little deal," Pearson went on to say, consisted of using WPA workers to build a road and yacht basin on the Tydings country place in Maryland. What had really happened, as was later established, was that the city of Havre de Grace had built a public yacht basin near some town property owned by Tydings and a farm-to-market road passing by Tydings' country place had been resurfaced. The broadcasting chain which carried the program made a public apology.

Pearson smiles when the incident is recalled to him now. "The funny thing about it," he says, "is that Bob and I didn't write that script. We never saw it until just before we went on the air. The whole thing was just a technical error anyway."

One of Pearson's few excursions into obstetrical gossip likewise kicked back. In July, 1943, Miss Margaret Suckley, of Poughkeepsie, a distant cousin of the President's, spent a few days at the White House. Her Scottie, Heather, was seen gamboling with Fala on the lawn. Pearson, in one of his August broadcasts, announced that Heather was an expectant mother. He repeated the story in his column, and in his broadcast on the following Sunday became even more coyly vehement about it. Heather was only seven months old at the time, and veterinarians say that Scotties don't have puppies that early, at least not in these latitudes. Anyway, the touted litter didn't materialize and, according to Miss Suckley, Heather still retains her spinster standing.

Heather's sufferings at the hands of Pearson are inconsequential when compared to those of Secretary Hull. For years, Pearson gleefully needled and ridiculed Hull, and his severely paternal attitude toward the State Department has expressed itself in criticisms of such intradepartmental matters as the promotions of young diplomats to better jobs and the location of colored messengers' desks. His Hull-baiting reached its zenith, or nadir, last September twentieth, when he wrote that the Secretary had cracked down on Argentina because of an Argentine motion-picture cartoon in which the Secretary was caricatured as a squawking duck. Such a film did exist, but Pearson's conclusion was, necessarily, based upon pure mind-reading, an occult pursuit in which he indulges periodically. When Edward R. Stettinius, Jr., succeeded Hull not long ago, Pearson condescendingly pictured him as an amiable blunderer. His only real diplomatic hero, outside of President Roosevelt and himself, is former Under Secretary Sumner Welles, who has long been a close friend.

Another of Pearson's close friends is Walter Winchell, who also lampoons the State Department, and who once by-passed it and issued what was practically a personal declaration of war on Argentina. The columnists exchange visits and bouquets and sometimes help out with each other's crusades.

After the "chronic-liar" episode, Pearson became more enthusiastic about the President than he had ever been before. He supported the fourth-term candidacy with almost as much fervor as did Secretary Ickes. In one column he intimated that both Dewey and Bricker were draft dodgers. He did this by referring to Dewey's "reported agricultural deferment" and expressing mystification over Bricker's sudden shift from the law to the ministry during the first World War. This was shoddy journalism and shoddy politics, coming, as it did, just four days before the election. Actually, Dewey has never sought any kind of deferment; he is, besides, a public official with three dependents, and is over effective military age. The fact that Bricker was rejected for service during the first war because of an abnormally low pulse rate had long been a matter of public knowledge; so had the fact that he became a minister in order to qualify for duty as an Army chaplain. Pearson's own military record is far from warlike. At the age of twenty, he was a member of the Students' Army Training Corps on the Swarthmore campus. This rugged military experience is described with technical correctness in his Who's Who In America pedigree as, "Served in United States Army, 1918."

To date, the White House, despite his friendly advances, hasn't seen fit to have Pearson over for tea. "The President isn't very keen about me," Pearson says with regret.

The business of forecasting is a risky one at best, but it is a popular one in eras of alarum, and Pearson shines at his aggressive best in the role of oracle. He assumes it each Sunday during the closing minutes of his radio program, when he launches confidently into what he calls redundantly, "my predictions of things to come." Some of his predictions are ambiguous, in the Delphic tradition. Others are predictions of the deadly obvious. For example: last October twenty-second he predicted that our next step in the Pacific would be to isolate Mindanao; this prediction came well after the start of the Leyte invasion, the plain purpose of which was to sever Mindanao from Luzon. On the same evening he predicted that the Red army would go around the Masurian Lakes district, where, in the first World War, the Czar's soldiers were annihilated when the Germans shelled the roads and forced them to leap into the deadly swamps. It didn't take anyone in Marshal Stalin's confidence to make that prediction.

But in many of his bouts with the crystal ball, Pearson takes real chances. He has predicted, for example, that President Roosevelt would not run for a fourth term; that, if he did run, the Southern Democrats would defeat him; that Japan would "stab Russia in the back" before the spring of 1943; that the war with Germany would be over by last September fifteenth, and that Robert E. Sherwood, of the White House advisory staff, would be appointed minister to North Africa.

In one six-month period, according to an independent check, Pearson made 153 predictions. The checker, in trying to arrive at a score, eliminated four predictions as half true, seven as not having come true yet, and nineteen as uncheckable for various reasons. Of the 123 which remained, seventy-four, including some fairly obvious predictions, were listed as having come true, and forty-nine were classified as errors. Roughly, therefore, the Pearson crystal ball appears to give off the right glint 60 per cent of the time.

Pearson sees himself as a gladiator for political rectitude who would like to get away from it all. The pains of his servitude, however, are mitigated to some extent by its financial rewards. He nets about $90,000 a year, before taxes, from radio and his column alone. In view of these financial rewards and his duty to humanity, Pearson is not likely to retire to the farm. If, however, he should, a lot of people would cheer, as he has publicly stated they would, and among them would be a number of newspaper editors. Columns of the shriller type, such as the "Merry-Go-Round," have caused much soul-searching in the past few years on the part of the editors. Some have steadfastly opposed them, in spite of their value as circulation getters, on the ground that they overdo the sensational approach to the facts of life. Others take the bread-and-butter view that the see-all-know-all tone of the columns tends to relegate their own editorial pages to a position of secondary importance.

Next April, at the annual meeting of the American Society of Newspaper Editors, the question of whether to cut out the columns will come up for discussion. If this surgery is carried out, which seems highly improbable, it will be the first hysterectomy on record in which the patient has wielded the knife.

So You Want to Be a Sports Editor?

By DAN PARKER

EDITOR'S PREFACE.—Sports writing and editing, almost as much so as foreign correspondence, has a great fascination for the would-be journalist and is the subject of considerable curiosity on the part of the reading public. It is that part of the journalistic spectrum which is pure adventure and glamour. It is a world of big names, both as to writers and those written about. It is that phase of newspaperdom which, with the possible exception of foreign news coverage, has shown the greatest development during the present century—certainly on a quantitative basis. Silas Bent in his *Ballyhoo,* along with certain criticisms of sports pages, points out that there was a 47 per cent increase in the amount of space devoted to this subject during a brief quarter of a century. Paper restrictions and other restraints of World War II tended to reduce somewhat the mushroom growth of sports pages, but the amount of space devoted to this part of the average newspaper is comparatively large.

It is true, too, that some of our best writers are sports editors or those who have been graduated to other types of creative endeavor by sports departments. Dan Parker, who was sports editor of the New York *Daily Mirror* when the following article was written, would be a good example of the first, whereas among those who have used the sports pages as a stepping stone to column writing, fiction, and other editorial work would be such well known figures as Westbrook Pegler, the late Heywood Broun, Damon Runyon, Paul Gallico, Ralph McGill, Bob Considine, Quentin Reynolds, the late Ring Lardner, and many others.

Mr. Parker's article is a partial explanation of why a sports editor has to be good if he is to succeed. He must, of necessity, write in many moods of many things—and in many differing forms—from the single pithy sentence to

239

several columns. He must report games, he must explain victories and defeats, he must delineate personality, he must champion just causes and crusade against evils in the sports world, and, at all times, he must be attractive and entertaining. To read Mr. Parker's article is to know one sports editor who scores high in all these requirements and also to have a better understanding of the fascination of the sports pages for so many readers and would-be sports writers and editors alike.

May 2, 1942

EVERY sports editor hears over and over again the trite remark: "You don't mean to tell me they pay you fellows for doing this?"

It is all too true that the sports editor's job, examined superficially, seems like a cross between the life of Riley and a Mohammedan's idea of paradise, with which are combined the better features of a Frank Merriwell thriller.

Sports editors sit at ringside at all the big fights. They get stacks of tickets for all sports events. In mid-February they travel South with the baseball clubs. They know all the heroes of the sports world by their first names and hobnob with them. The race track is wide open to them when they want feed-box information. Long before the public hears about it, they have the inside dope on everything. And, to top it all, they are paid for attending events that the average man eagerly scrapes together enough money to witness.

There's another side of the picture the public seldom sees. Soon enough, one who is taken behind the scenes finds out that there's more to the business than slipping a sheet of paper into a typewriter, looking at a pair of stumblebums wrapped in warm embrace and waiting for inspiration to release from its cocoon a literary butterfly that's doomed to flutter around for a day, then perish. But come, come! Before I break down and weep hysterically over our plight, let's get to the facts.

If a sports editor ever found time to keep a diary, this is probably how he'd record the events of a typical working day:

9:05 A.M.: Awakened by phone call from office. Advertising

Department wants better locations for tonight's fight than second row. "Journal got first row, so why can't we?" Promise to call Promoter Mike Jacobs about it, reflecting glumly: "Mike'll be just tickled silly to do this for me, after reading that blast I gave him this morning."

10 A.M.: Arrive at office early, hoping to get some work done before parade of procrastinators starts, only to find five callers waiting. First is ex-fighter who wants job. Next guy has surefire system for beating ponies and doesn't know enough to keep it to himself. Third has something of important personal nature to tell me—an insurance agent. Then comes longwinded fight manager who claims there's plot to keep him and his horizontal hooligan out of heavyweight picture. Last in line is chap who sends in word he has good sports story. Turns out to be press agent for Broadway band leader who, he says, was good amateur boxer at Slobodka University.

11:05 A.M.: A good hour wasted, start opening mail; a patriotic duty in that it makes face turn red, then white, finally blue. Ticket moochers begin to arrive and boys in back room start calling to have their sports arguments settled.

11:45 A.M.: Tilt chair back, concentrate deeply and wait for verbiage volcano to erupt from typewriter. Nothing comes out, but press agent comes in, soliciting publicity for his club's next show. Seeing you staring at typewriter, he thinks you're bored and entertains with a half hour of inane chatter.

12:15 P.M.: A spot of tea and a sandwich, gulped at desk in hope they will awaken inspiration. They awaken indigestion.

1:10 P.M.: Seven false starts and only one paragraph written when phone rings ominously. It's only MacPhail unloading cargo of brimstone for that story about him yesterday.

1:45 P.M.: Fifteen minutes to deadline for column, still only one paragraph written. Maybe decline of wrestling would have been better subject than second-guessing Boxing Commission again. What's this? Giants name Ott to succeed Terry? Lemme at that mill!

2 P.M.: Wow! Another close shave, but another deadline made. Nothing to worry about now only supervising work on

edition, answering queries and fan mail, listening to press agents, attending to demands of ticket customers, locating athletes by phone to wheedle them into appearing at that benefit, and listening politely to small talk of casual visitors who have nothing but time to kill.

3:30 P.M.: Listen to complaint of baseball writer that his best lines are being murdered by "them vultures" on copy desk. Golf expert makes it a wailing duet by demanding to know why by-line was left off his story yesterday. Who's trying to knife him and why?

3:45 P.M.: Cup patient ear to bleat of copyreader that all sports writers should be sent back to night school to learn rudiments of grammar.

4 P.M.: Duck out for swing around sports beat, only to have ear bent into pretzel shape, listening to barefaced lies fight managers tell.

5:15 P.M.: Back to desk to take care of late-afternoon ticket trade and apply to National Sports Alliance Fund for relief check for needy fight manager.

6:10 P.M.: A Mr. Beeswax, sending in card by doorman, says he has story for me—and he has. Story is that he went to school with me and will consider debt squared if I give him carfare to Washington where Cabinet job awaits him.

6:45 P.M.: Slam early edition to press on dot, but call two pages back in panic upon discovering on page proofs that heads on racing story and fish column have been transposed.

7 P.M.: Off to dinner, only to be stopped on way out by wrestling promoter, having in tow a bearded Rooshian who, he claims, is only legitimate champion, other twenty-six claimants to the title being low-lives.

7:45 P.M.: The feed bag at last.

8:30 P.M.: Arrive at Garden and hear latest crop of lobby rumors about fight being bagged for gambling mob. Fight managers, discussing bout, try to cover every possible angle in their predictions without actually committing themselves. On way out they'll be waiting to say: "Well, I gave you the right dope on that one, didn't I?"

9 P.M.: Read newspapers in press row while preliminaries—usually the best fights—are going on. It's considered sign of naïveté to watch prelims.

10 P.M.: Start dictating blow-by-blow story of main bout to telegraph operator, tipping office as to probable outcome as soon as possible, to expedite fight extra. Write new story on fight when it's over—interrupted, if you've picked a loser, by frank criticism from readers who've lost dough on the fight and blame you for it. Then submit badly battered ears to final bending of the day by fight managers who unload a 5000-word version of "I told you so."

11:45 P.M.: And so, as Samivel Pepys would gurgle, to bed, and dreams of a ticketless paradise where sports editors always pick the winners.

To the envious onlooker, the sports-writing profession appears to be one big happy family that never grows up. This is only partly true. The family may remain perpetually juvenile in its outlook but, as is the case with many a barbershop quartet, harmony is often lacking. There are more feuds in the sports-writing craft than in the entire Appalachian chain. Any town large enough to support two sports editors more likely than not harbors a journalistic feud, in which the principals are always running down each other, instead of the latest sports items. Even in the larger cities, few sports columnists can be induced to admit that any of their contemporaries can write.

This trait of the profession is a by-product of the critical nature of the work. It is only natural that young men, called on to review sports events critically, should become highly opinionated and, after they've passed the sophomore stage, cynical almost to a ludicrous degree. A facetious sort of cynicism is the favorite pose of the profession. Crusades aren't popular. Anyone who undertakes them is likely to find himself looked upon with distrust.

Despite the trivial feuds and the petty jealousies, sports writing would still be the Utopian existence outsiders picture, if there were no such things as tickets for sporting events. But alas, between professional pass moochers and kind friends who believe the sports editor will feel slighted if they give their ticket business to the guy on the rival sheet, ye olde ed spends most of his waking moments being tossed by a horrible nightmare. The amount of a newspaper's time wasted on this colossal nuisance is appalling. Publishers would do something about it if they were privy to the brutal statistics.

There is no special social stratum which produces chronic pass addicts. The fraternity embraces the rich as well as the poor, not skipping the middle class. It is an odd trait of human nature that many wealthy sports fans would gladly pay more for a pass than a ticket in the same location would cost them at the box office. Their vanity is tickled when they can show a friend they weigh enough to get passes. That's why some of the ticket agencies do a thriving side-line business bootlegging passes which somehow or other find their way into their hands.

The technique employed by the various types of moochers falls into several main classifications. Good old No. 3-A is the most popular, both with the moocher and his prey. Reduced to the raw, No. 3-A is nothing more than the food of fools, fulsome flattery. It is a poison which pleasantly paralyzes the victim.

"That was a swell column you wrote this morning," the bounder says as he approaches the sports ed. A sucker for any hint that he is being bracketed with Shakespeare by the public, the silly scribbler experiences a warm glow all over. Gratitude shines from his trusting eyes as from those of a cocker spaniel that has been petted by his master. This is the signal for the moocher to move in and deliver the knockout wallop.

"Oh, by the way," he says as a casual afterthought, "there's a fight at the Stadium Thursday night, isn't there? Joe Louis and somebody or other? If you have any trouble getting rid of your tickets, I could use a pair—that is, if you haven't got anyone else to give them to. Of course, I'll be willing to pay the tax myself."

This last magnanimous gesture is what really seals the bargain. The big-hearted fellow is willing to take a pair of passes off your hands, but does not ask you to lay out the five or six dollars in taxes and service charges which a pair of Annie Oakleys for a big boxing contest are assessed.

I know ticket chiselers who have been repeating this formula shamelessly for fifteen years. Nor are they bothered by the coincidence that they never get in touch with the sports editor except on the eve of a big sporting event.

There's another large group of pasteboard panhandlers known as life members. Give these lads a pair of tickets in a moment of thoughtlessness and they're on your neck for the rest of your life, like a carbuncle scar. Rather than face the wrath of a member of this group, I have often surrendered my own tickets and gone out and bought a pair at the box office. A woman scorned is a thing of beauty and a joy forever compared with a moocher neglected.

Still another type is the Greek bearing gifts. This rogue will breeze up to your desk and drop a pair of passes for a flop show that is flooding the house with paper to make it look like a hit. In the most disarming manner, he will ply you with mallarkey about his desire to repay you for all the favors you have done for him. Then, while the blush is still fresh on your cheek, he will strike swiftly with his demand for two ringside seats or a pair for a ball game that's a sellout.

Some of my worst headaches have been caused by those eager to pay for their pasteboards. On the eve of a big sporting event, advertisers will suddenly learn about it—although the whole world has been talking about it for weeks. Nothing but the best seats will do. The fact that by this time the event is a sellout doesn't bother them. They must have tickets in the front row, or none at all. Complications, such as a feud with the promoter staging the event, may make the assignment tougher still for the hapless sports editor. But he must deliver, or risk a loss of caste for his paper with the advertiser in question.

Two weeks before last year's world series, I invited the wrath of Leland Stanford MacPhail, president of the Dodgers, by printing a number of bleats from long-suffering Brooklynites about the ticket situation at Ebbets Field. Each letter contained an implication or two that Mr. MacPhail was neither a genius nor Brooklyn's most popular citizen. All one night at half-hour intervals, after reading my column in the New York *Daily Mirror,* MacPhail called me up to tell me what he thought of my ancestry.

Imagine my predicament, therefore, when the Dodgers clinched the pennant a few days later and my ticket clients, fearful of slighting me, turned over their orders to me for the Brooklyn end of the world series. MacPhail was ignoring me and, like Mr. Goldwyn, I wasn't even ignoring him. What to do? By what was virtually a stroke of genius, I told everyone who asked me to get him tickets to apply for them himself, and, wonder of wonders, every order was filled. The Dodgers' world-series ticket scarcity had been so overplayed that tickets were to be had for each game right up to the time the umpire called "Play ball," even by people who didn't have enough influence to get a pass for a dog track.

For every enemy I have made with an unfavorable notice in my column, I've picked up at least ten for falling down on ticket assignments from people to whom I owe nothing.

People who ask you to buy their tickets for them will often ask you to lay out the money until they have a chance to reimburse you—never thinking that you, perhaps, are trying to scrape up enough to meet an income-tax payment. Almost never does a ticket customer include the cost of registering the letter in which his tickets are mailed to him, or the fee of the errand boy you must send for the tickets, since you have a deadline to meet and can't run the errand yourself.

Expenses of this type can mount up to a fine farthing at the end of the year—and they're not deductible on your income-tax report.

Even so, it isn't the expense that annoys you so much as the never-ending interruptions. A sports editor settles down to a pleasurable session of tearing apart some phony wrestling promoter or high-diving pugilist; before he has had time to split his first infinitive, his train of thought is wrecked on a ticket order from a shameless knave whom he has caught red-handed more than once reading the rival sheet. From this bad beginning, if the eager author is able to set down three words in succession without a ticket interruption, he considers that Fortune is smiling on him.

Another branch of sports writing the envious public never hears about is the free employment bureau conducted by every sports editor. There is a never-ending demand on him to get jobs for broken-down fighters and other athletes who find that last year's headlines won't keep them out of this year's breadlines. There's nothing quite so pathetic as the sight of an athletic star who was on top of the heap a few years back humbly seeking any kind of work. Yesterday's world-conquering hero is now as helpless as a little child, frightened by realities. The callousness of most sports promoters toward their former breadwinners is shocking. For the supreme example of this, stand outside any big fight club on the night of an important match. Among the loiterers, whose eyes convey to every passerby the mute appeal: "Please take me in, I'm broke," will be found several former world's champions. Once they headlined cards that packed this very arena—that was once and this is now.

Another growing nightmare of the sports editor is the guest-star nuisance.

Maybe it's a church smoker or a lodge dinner, and some athletic headliners are required to make what Harry Balogh, eminent authority on redundancy, would call "personal appearances." Instead of doing the dirty work themselves, the members of the committee on entertainment invariably will call up a sports editor—usually an utter stranger—and, by resort to flattery laid on a foot thick—"None of us up this way would think of missing your column"—delegate to the hapless harebrain the task of lining up an array of talent for them.

A fighter probably will agree cheerfully to make an appearance the first time you ask him. But he rebels if imposed on.

Ballplayers are more difficult. They seldom go in for this sort of stuff, because there would be no end to it after a while—such is the chain-letter effect of the habit once it becomes noised about that Joe Doakes is a sucker for a "personal appearance." Every time a sports editor asks an athlete to show up at an affair, he incurs a tacit obligation never thereafter to criticize the young man for a poor performance. Embarrassing complications can develop when the boxer who spread cheer at the church smoker last week "smells out the jernt" on his next professional appearance at the Garden and your public demands the whole truth about it.

Recently I rounded up some talent for the police department of a suburban city which was holding an amateur boxing show. I couldn't drive Lefty Gomez, Lou Nova, Abe Simon and the other "names" I had rounded up, to the arena in my own car—the committee usually expects you not only to furnish the talent but also to transport it—so I delegated that duty to a friend. I'm learning, at last, myself. Wishing to check up on whether they had reached their destination, I wrote a letter to the chairman who had wished the job on me, inquiring if everything had turned out all right. The next day I received a letter I consider a classic.

"Everything turned out fine," he wrote. "You don't have to worry. Hereafter we will let you get all our talent for us whenever we hold a show."

Naturally, a sports editor finally gets around to doing his own work, after he has finished doing everyone else's errands. By then he is likely to be in a most serious mood, eager to save his public from being imposed upon—his own fate. Ah, me! Would that it were possible!

Stark disillusionment is the reward of the sports editor who would save the sap from the sundry traps set for him by sharpsters. This odd fact of life I learned through the extraordinary episode of Theodore Hayes, alias Theodore the Tout.

Theodore Hayes wasn't the bounder's name at all, any more than it was Teddy Hayes'—born Theodore Weinstein, eminently respectable ex-pugilist and one-time trainer of Jack Dempsey—to whom Theodore Hayes the Tout caused no end of pain and embarrassment by adopting his adopted name, without so much as a by-your-leave.

Theodore the Tout flooded the mails several years back with extravagant claims of what he could do on a race track, given an owner's ear, a bit of time and a roll of bills. In his literature, Theodore boldly claimed that he could fix any claiming race at the Saratoga race meeting, then in progress, and would gladly do so to the advantage of the recipient of his form letter upon receipt of one dollar.

One of Theodore's less gullible prospects sent me a copy of his promise-laden prospectus. Donning my knightly armor and reaching for Excalibur, I rushed headlong at Theodore and sliced him thinner than gold leaf, exposing his every fraudulent claim.

"That will teach the knave not to swindle people," I said, giving myself a premature pat on the back.

The morrow's mail was heavy, each letter fat. The first missive I opened told the story repeated several hundred times during the ensuing week. A dollar bill was enclosed. Would I be so kind as to forward it to that nice gentleman, Mr. Hayes, who could fix the races?

Having duly reported the almost unbelievable reaction to my blunt exposé of the thieving tout in the next day's column, I was summoned to the office of my editor, the late Arthur Brisbane.

"Of course, all this about the money being sent in for that tout is sheer imagination on your part, isn't it?"

"May I be excused for a minute?" I asked. Hastening back to my desk, I collected a pile of letters containing money, which I brought back to Mr. Brisbane's office.

He read them curiously; then, half to himself, said, "I was wrong all the time."

"You mean about me making up that stuff about the letters?" I asked.

"No," said the editor. "In my estimate of the mental age of newspaper readers. I always put it at twelve. I guess it's nearer eight."

If Theodore the Tout is still fixing claiming races, he can keep on fixing them, as far as I'm concerned.

Race-track addicts are a hard lot to convince where the truth is concerned. They'll believe anything but it. Occasionally, for want of a better subject, I preach a sermon on the futility of trying to beat the races. This always brings a shower of abusive letters, since nothing hurts a sucker more than to be told he's one. Usually the writer has a pet system, and nothing will satisfy him until he convinces the ignorant sports columnist that playing the races is the shortest road to wealth. One such correspondent wrote so convincingly that, while my guard was low and my spirits high, he argued me into agreeing to let him demonstrate his system's infallibility by means of paper bets. He would record his hypothetical wagers on a slip of paper every day and mail them to me so that they would be postmarked before post time at the track. That was three years ago last July. Every day since then, this wizard, who has confessed to me recently that he has never been at a race track in his life, has sent in a list of selections, usually three, together with a neatly tabulated record of his mental transactions to date. At last accounts, this infallible system for beating the ponies showed a deficit of more than $6000, and in the three and a half years it has been in operation it hasn't been out of the red for more than a few months all together.

One of the sports editor's antidotes for ticket headaches is fan mail. If the moochers give him a chance to read it, his interest in life is renewed immediately. Nor is this necessarily because of the favorable nature of the letters from his beloved public. Chances are that before he gets well into his daily pile of correspondence, his face will have given an imitation of a boiled lobster.

The layman may not be aware of it, but there are probably more experts at large in the field of sports than in any other sphere. Nor is this said sarcastically. A writer may—and hun-

dreds of them do—pretend to a profound knowledge of international affairs, and there are few in a position to dispute him.
But woe unto the sports editor who comes up with a wrongo
in any one of a dozen sports with which the man in the street
is familiar. The morrow's mail is weighted with blistering invective which leaves the hapless expert with a rather low opinion of himself.

Commonest of all fan letters is the type which starts: "You
are my favorite sports columnist" or "I have been reading your
column for years and think it is the best in the world." When
this smooth number rears its sleek head, duck. The author
wants a favor. To attain supersubtlety, he will often close
with: "Whether you do this for me or not, I will still keep
reading you and regard you as my favorite columnist." As if
refusal of the favor could affect one's literary style!

Another common type is the screed that starts: "If you aren't
the yellow dog I think you to be, print this letter in your lousy
column." This number usually winds up: "I dare you to print
this."

Not all sports editors' letters are about sporting subjects.
There are some fans who call on him to settle any argument
that comes up in their street-corner or tavern tongue-wagging
soirees. At least one question out of ten submitted to every
sports editor concerns an election result, the exact location of
the nitroglycerine plants near the Pennsylvania oil fields, the
population of a town in Peru, or some such exotic subject.

Sports queries run in cycles. Although we get a never-ending
variety of questions, there is a certain number of hardy peren-
nials which come and go with the seasons. Year after year, fans
write in to find out how many times Gene Tunney and Harry
Greb fought and the result of each bout; how many times
Firpo knocked Dempsey down; what was the first boxing
match ever broadcast; how many horses started in the Travers
at Saratoga when Jim Dandy beat Gallant Fox; what baseball
team has won the most world series; what Babe Ruth's real
name is—George Herman Ruth, not George Ehrhardt, as
some dispenser of misinformation announced years ago and

some people still believe, despite thousands of printed denials —the lifetime batting averages of the late Lou Gehrig and Bill Terry, and the comparative records of Carl Hubbell and Dizzy Dean in the games they pitched against each other.

Sometimes a sports editor can trace the course of a barroom argument from one end of the city to the other, by the addresses on his fan mail. The boys can certainly get worked up over the silliest subjects. Last summer, for instance, when Joe DiMaggio was in the closing stages of his record-shattering consecutive-hitting streak, a group of fans up in the dear old Bronx took to worrying one night as to what would happen to Joe's streak if some afternoon a pitcher, out of sheer orneriness, walked DiMadge every time he came to the plate. Would his streak be ended or would it be unbroken? The boys don't stop to reason things out. From the Bronx, this barroom argument spread down through Manhattan, and then, finally, like the National League pennant itself, reached that quaint hamlet y-clept Brooklyn. Will Harridge and Ford Frick, presidents of the two major leagues, were quoted at length on the subject, both agreeing that Joe's streak would remain intact, since you can't be charged with going hitless if you haven't been officially at bat. Nevertheless, the letters poured in, day after day, all asking the question that had been answered almost daily for weeks.

Most sports fans are so partisan themselves they think every opinion written by a sports columnist which doesn't agree with their own is prejudiced. New York sports columnists had a most trying time of it just before and during last year's world series. Any honest attempt to analyze the chances of the rival clubs brought down a shower of wrathful epistles on the head of the expert who was straining to be fair to both clubs. If he gave the Yankees the edge, as any expert who studied the facts at hand would have to, he was castigated roundly by Dodger fans, who accused him of being in the pay of the Yankees. If, on the other hand, he honestly thought the Dodgers would win out, Yankee fans heaped coals of abuse on his unhappy noggin for being a Dodger sympathizer. I was called a Yankee fan by

Dodger supporters, a Dodger fan by the minions of the Yanks and a Giant fan by the combined forces of the enemies.

Libel suits are another pain. Yet, considering that sports writers have more latitude than news writers, and take off their kid gloves when they attack a typewriter, there are surprisingly few actions. This may be because of the late Big Tim Sullivan's dictum, "Don't sue the papers or they may prove what they said about you is true." Oddly enough, wrestlers, who by common consent are the most difficult of all classes of athletes to libel because they are the most vulnerable, sue most frequently. This is possibly because one of their number, some years back, recovered damages of $25,000 from a newspaper which had compared him pictorially to a gorilla, to the latter's disadvantage, as many judges of slander thought. This burping beauty has made a career of suing newspapers ever since, but the pickings have been lean of late.

Most of the libel suits I have been a codefendant in were brought by wrestlers with the idea of stopping me from exposing their racket. It costs only about twenty-five dollars to start a suit and isn't a twenty-five-dollar suit a bargain? None of my suits ever got beyond the starting stage. Whenever wrestlers go to court, the public hears some trade secrets that are better left untold.

Dealing, as he does, with well-conditioned athletes whose reaction to unfavorable press notices is more likely than not to be one of red-blooded anger, the sports editor would seem to be in a spot where he would be called upon often to back up his opinions with his fists. It is probably true that sports writers are socked more often than members of the more pacific branches of the newspaper profession. But, on the whole, considering that they speak their minds more freely and deal with the most virile of the nation's manhood, comparatively few sports writers become involved in fisticuffs over their written opinions. An athlete is likely to blow off steam behind his lampooner's back and then greet him as cordially as if nothing had happened, the next time they meet.

Fighters, oddly enough, are the least likely of any class of athletes to take it out of a sports writer's hide with their knuckles. Hardly a day's low-descending sun but witnesses a battle won by some hollow-chested, flabby-muscled sports columnist over a pugilist who could annihilate him with a light left jab. About the only time fighters get sore at a sports writer is when he fails to mention them, even in a derogatory manner.

A ballplayer is more likely to want to fight. Babe Ruth once was on the trail of a New York sports editor for weeks, threatening to lay him low on sight. But that was early in his career. Later, the only request good-natured, thick-skinned Babe made of the press was that the boys spell his name right.

Dizzy Dean, driven to a state bordering on daffiness by Jack Miley's satire a few seasons back, took a belt at the sports columnist in a Tampa hotel. But despite Jack's ample frame, which makes him almost an unmissable target, Dizzy's punch hit two other guys who were minding their own business. When Miley struck a James Figg posture, Dean decided his honor had been avenged.

Letters and phone calls threatening bodily harm are the frequent fare of the sports editor who is outspoken. When Primo Carnera was on his mobster-backed tank tour, I used to get at least one threat a week. Of course, after the chill induced by the first threat has worn off, such stuff is taken in stride. A chap nice enough to warn you he's going to drive a dirk into your left kidney the next time you venture into a certain fight club or pan his ham-donie certainly is too kindhearted to carry out his threat.

Diggers of ditches and hewers of wood can see from all this that the sports editor's job is beset with frightful hardships. But as Tim Hurst once remarked of umpiring, it's better than going to work and you just can't beat the hours!

Dear Mrs. Post

(EMILY POST)

By MARGARET CASE HARRIMAN

EDITOR'S PREFACE.—Best sellers may come and best sellers may go, but there are a few lusty items in the book world that seem to have been best sellers for all time and give promise of so continuing henceforth and forever more—such books as the Bible, the dictionary, Fannie Farmer's *The Boston Cooking School Cook Book,* Dr. L. Emmett Holt's *The Care and Feeding of Children,* and Emily Post's *Etiquette: The Blue Book of Social Usage.*

The last mentioned, especially its author, is the theme of the following article, which is more than a well written biography of a colorful personality. It is a commentary on American manners and, as such, tells the remarkable story of how an ordinary woman, with no special claims to a place of authority in this realm, has become the acknowledged arbiter of what is right and proper in social behavior, simply through the wisdom, practicality, and simplicity of her dicta. "Her word," writes Mrs. Harriman, "is accepted as gospel by millions of readers." Surely the story of Mrs. Post is a case history of democracy at work—a striking example of how, in this great land of ours, the entrepreneur may reap a rich harvest, provided he has something to sell that the public wants and that is regarded to be worth the purchase price.

Since the original publication of this article, Mrs. Post has written another book, *Children Are People and Ideal Parents Are Companions,* a volume in which she develops the not particularly sensational but altogether sound thesis that "as a usual thing, the flowers watched over by a skilled gardener, and the children watched over by skilled parents, have far greater perfection."

Manners, wrote the great Sir Edmund Burke, "are of more importance than laws. Upon them, in a great measure, the laws depend. The law touches us but here and there, and now and then. Manners are what vex or soothe, corrupt or purify, exalt or debase, barbarize or refine us, by a constant, steady, uniform, insensible operation, like that of the air we breathe in."

If this be true—and all those who share the view of Edmund Spenser that "a man is by nothing so well betrayed as by his manners" will likely agree—it follows that Mrs. Post is a kind of unofficial supreme court, reviewing, interpreting, and adapting to a changing society those practices which are as fundamental to social intercourse as English common law is to business life.

May 15, 1937

LAST year, when the forty-first printing of Emily Post's *Etiquette: the Blue Book of Social Usage* was released to the public, some of its readers were a little startled by the touch of lavender that persisted in its pages. "The bachelor girl can, on occasion, go out alone with any unmarried man she knows well, if the theater she goes to, or the restaurant she dines at, be of conventional character," Mrs. Post's book stated tranquilly in 1936. "The strict rules of etiquette demand that the divorced meet as total and unspeaking strangers" it set forth in another chapter, and "A lady having her portrait painted always takes a woman friend, or her maid, who sits in the studio, or at least within sight or hearing."

All over the country, bachelor girls were going out alone with unmarried men they knew only slightly, in the hope, perhaps, of getting to know them better; divorced people were greeting each other, when they met accidentally, with just as much kindliness as though they had never been married; and whatever ladies were having their portraits painted had very few women friends, or maids either, who were content to spend a whole afternoon just sitting within sight or hearing. But Mrs. Post pretty thoroughly ignored the modern trend. The 1936 edition of *Etiquette* also contained an entire chapter devoted to the Chaperon, and, although she was, in fact, referred to as "The Vanishing Chaperon," the reader could hear in those simple words an echo of the author's own wistfulness over the whole hellish situation.

Etiquette in Society, in Business, in Politics and at Home has sold nearly 500,000 copies—at four dollars apiece—since it was first published in 1922, and it has been slightly revised three times, but it was not until this year that Mrs. Post—apparently convinced that people are going to go right on behaving in the unfettered way that has become fashionable and convenient—decided to broaden the standards of behavior she established fifteen years ago. This spring a completely revised and up-to-date version of *Etiquette* is appearing, in which bachelor girls, divorcees, and ladies who like to hang around artists' studios are considered patiently, even perhaps with a twinkle. "The Vanishing Chaperon" almost entirely disappears, and is replaced by a sprightly chapter on "The Modern Man and Girl." The author has named this couple John Strongheart and Louise Lovely, and plans to let them spend a good deal of time just drifting around together, without anybody within sight or hearing. Mrs. Post is a gentlewoman of the old school, and she likes the old ways best, but she is a businesswoman as well. With scarcely a sigh for the decorous past, she has made up her mind to march sturdily abreast of the times.

Although her word is accepted as gospel by millions of readers, Emily Post has always been somehow at the mercy of the public she created when she wrote *Etiquette*. When the publishing firm of Funk & Wagnalls suggested that she write the book, she was skeptical; she disliked the word "etiquette" as being both fancy and phony, and she felt uncomfortable about setting herself up in print as an authority on correct social behavior, which was something she had always taken more or less idly for granted. Richard Duffy, of Funk & Wagnalls, pointed out that, although there were plenty of etiquette books on the market, none had been written by a woman of recognized social position since Mrs. Sherwood—grandmother of Robert Sherwood, the playwright—wrote *Manners and So-*

cial Usages, back in the 80's. He followed up his argument by sending Mrs. Post all the current books about etiquette he could lay his hands on, and a few days later she telephoned him.

"These people," she said, referring to the etiquette writers, "don't seem to know what they're talking about."

"Well, you tell 'em," said Mr. Duffy simply.

Goaded, Mrs. Post sat down on a high stool at the architect's drafting table she likes to write on and, in the next ten months, turned out 250,000 words on etiquette. She wrote about all the problems that occurred to her, and it was scarcely surprising that they were mainly the problems within her own experience or within that of her friends in New York, at Newport or at Tuxedo. The book, when it was published, was a curiously lively and readable work through which the Toploftys, the Eminents, the Bobo Gildings, the Notquites and other characters—all based on real people, as the author confessed in the dedication—moved symbolically, forever preoccupied with the right livery for their footmen, the order of precedence at formal dinners, the duties of a kitchenmaid in a staff of twelve servants, and similar high-toned nuances of the mannered life.

Before it had been out a month, however, Emily Post began getting letters that staggered her. Women readers throughout the country wrote to her, saying, "Dear Mrs. Post, You didn't say in your book whether a widow ought to sign her letters 'Mrs. John Jones' or 'Mrs. Mary Jones,' " and "Dear Mrs. Post, How can I give a formal dinner for eight people without a servant?"

Shocked and puzzled, Mrs. Post informed such correspondents that no lady, whether married, widowed or single, ever signs a letter "Miss" or "Mrs. Anything"—except in parentheses after "Mary Jones"—and that nobody can give a really formal dinner without any servant.

When letters kept coming in, asking whether it was true that bread must be broken into pieces exactly one inch in diameter before it was eaten, and whether, when passing your plate for a second helping, you must hold your knife and fork in your hand, Mrs. Post began to realize that here, in this vast unsuspected throng of seekers after polite behavior, was her real public. In time for the next edition of the book, she wrote a new chapter called "American Neighborhood Customs," dealing with showers, sewing circles, singing circles and all the other cozy activities of outlying America which she was just beginning to learn about. She also invented a new character—a wonder woman named Mrs. Three-in-One who, without any servant whatever, contrived to be cook, waitress, and charming hostess to a dinner party—informal—of eight people, without getting up from the table. To test the system she had thought up for Mrs. Three-in-One before she brought it out in print, Mrs. Post invited six of her own friends—the Toploftys, the Gildings and the Worldlys—to dine with her and her son, Bruce, at her apartment in New York. Seated serenely at the head of her table with a stack of soup plates before her, she served the soup from a hot tureen and put the empty plates, as they were handed back to her, daintily out of sight on the bottom shelf of a tea wagon at her elbow, while Bruce, at his end of the table, ladled out the meat course from a chafing dish. Everything went smoothly without a servant in the place —except the cook, who stayed in the kitchen—and the glittering guests handed plates around from one to another as flawlessly as though they had been doing it all their lives.

Emily Post looks considerably younger than her age, which is sixty-four. In her youth she was a pretty distinguished beauty —portraits and photographs of her were included in all the collections of famous American beauties—and her face still has that fine transparency of line and texture that never quite leaves a woman who has been beautiful. She is tall and compelling, and she might seem formidable if it were not for her rather fluttery way of talking and a nervous habit of moving her hands continuously in small gestures—pleating a fold of her dress, fussing with a cushion or a letter or anything that happens to be within reach. She doesn't smoke or drink, but her hands are as unrelaxed as those of any habitual cigarette smoker or cocktail nurser. She is endlessly careful about her own choice of words in formal conversation, and it makes her faintly uneasy to hear anyone say "phone," for instance, instead of "telephone." During business hours, however, her contacts with the world of industry have conditioned her to a more colorful language. She says "damn" in a definite way when things exasperate her, she describes furniture or clothes she doesn't like as "godawful," and one advertising man who asked her opinion of a layout showing a table set for a formal dinner got it in one word. Mrs. Post said it was lousy. Not long ago, she went to a cocktail party given by one of the younger and giddier couples among her friends at which a newspaper columnist and his wife, who were also guests, got into an argument, intense enough to attract everybody's attention, about what time he had come home the night before. The husband stated flatly that he had been home, in bed and asleep, at midnight. "You're a damn liar, dear," his wife told him casually, out of long habit, and then, with a glance at the quiet lady sitting on the couch, hastily added, "if you'll excuse me, Mrs. Post." Mrs. Post was a little embarrassed, mostly by the silence that suddenly fell around her, but she just smiled.

In her own apartment, on East 79th Street, Emily Post likes to sit on a wide sofa in the window, generally with one foot tucked under her, and talk in a low, rather breathless voice broken by a good deal of laughter. She laughs easily about the jokes that appear about her in magazines and comic papers, about the strange significance her name has come to have for millions of Americans—about everything, in fact, except etiquette itself, which she has come to respect fiercely as a code governing practically all human relationships. She will tell you, with an air of mild astonishment, that nothing ever happened to her until she was nearly fifty, but that is not quite true. Things started happening to her more than thirty years ago, when she became a double-barreled pioneer in New York society by divorcing her husband in New York State—a pretty bold move at the time—and by going to work for a living. Nothing in her life up to that time had promised such unconventional goings-on, and for a little while even her intimate friends were shaken to the core.

She was born in Baltimore, the only child of Bruce Price, an architect who later designed the Château Frontenac in Quebec and most of the buildings in Tuxedo Park, New York. A portrait of her father, looking handsome and almost sensationally distinguished, hangs in Mrs. Post's study now, and she likes to tell about the time he traveled through Canada with the late Duke of Connaught. Every time they arrived in a town the reception committee, alert on the station platform to greet the royal visitor, passed lightly over the Duke and rushed in a body to heap their flowers and speeches of welcome upon the startled Mr. Price. "Never mind, Bruce," said His Royal Highness tolerantly, when this had happened four or five times; "it isn't your fault that God made you in the perfect image of a duke."

The Prices moved to New York when Emily was five, and sometimes her father would take her along with him when he was working on a building and let her climb around on the scaffolding. But apart from these excursions, her childhood moved in a conventional pattern of summers at Bar Harbor, and winters in her family's brownstone house in Tenth Street, with lessons in the mornings with a German governess and a walk in the park in the afternoons.

As a debutante, in 1892, Emily Price was tall, cool, and so dashing that four men were often required to carry her cotillion favors to her carriage after a ball; and at the end of her first season she married Edwin Main Post, a banker, by whom she had two sons, Edwin, Jr., and Bruce. She was peacefully established in the routine of a wife, mother and hostess when Edwin Post abruptly lost all his money following the panic of 1901. Emily Post's father died shortly afterward and, since he was a generous and popular man, left almost nothing to his heirs. Her mother, who had managed to save a little out of what her husband had given her during his lifetime, moved to a small house at Tuxedo. With disaster fresh upon them, the Posts with their two babies went to live with Mrs. Price. If the marriage had lasted Emily Post's career might never have begun.

She was the first divorcee to combine her maiden name with that of her ex-husband, and it was as Mrs. Price Post that she went to work, after the divorce was granted, to earn enough money to buy clothes for Ned and Bruce, and to educate them. She had picked up a considerable knowledge of architecture from her father; so, at first, she tried making cardboard models of houses, mounting them on cigar boxes and decorating each room with papier-mâché furniture and, sometimes, with tiger-skin rugs made of wax and painted in stripes. John Russell Pope and a few other architects bought some of her models, but there was little money in it for Mrs. Post.

One day a literary friend said to her, "Why don't you try writing? You write such marvelous letters!" And those words—which from one person or another, have probably started more pens traveling over paper than any words ever spoken—sent Mrs. Post hurrying up into her mother's attic to dig out the bundles of letters she had written to her father from Europe during a summer she spent there when she was seventeen. With a little editing and the addition of a hero named Lord "Bobby" Kirth, the letters made a lively and frivolous book called *The Flight of a Moth,* which Dodd, Mead and Company published in 1904. Mrs. Post made about $3000 out of it, and followed it rapidly by other novels: *Purple and Fine Linen, The Title Market,* and *The Eagle's Feather*—all of them pretty classy, swarming with easygoing earls and princes, and laid against a dizzy background of high life.

When some of her conservative friends murmured that writing was a pleasant hobby for a woman of gentle birth, but that taking money for it seemed to them not a little crass, Emily Post pointed out that Mrs. Wharton was doing well in a literary way without noticeably losing caste, and that the Duer girls were still asked to decent people's houses, although they gladly accepted pay for whatever they wrote whenever they could get it. The Duer girls were Alice, who later became Alice Duer

Miller, and Caroline, who wrote a book of etiquette of her own a few years ago.

Mrs. Post's novels sold fairly well, and soon she began writing pieces for magazines—mostly "confessions" by imaginary ladies of title surprised in a moment of exaltation or, conversely, in one of extreme fatigue. These articles and her books brought her varying amounts of money in the years that followed, but the small fortune which her mother managed to leave her at her death in 1910 vanished in bad investments; and in 1922, when Funk & Wagnalls began to badger her about writing the *Book of Etiquette,* she was living in a New York hotel, had sent two sons to Harvard, and was working away on her sixth novel, *Parade,* to pay for it all.

After *Etiquette* was published, the question of whether Emily Post should take money for what she wrote was lost forever in the newer problem of how much money it would take to get her to write anything at all. It was not that she was temperamental about writing—she likes to work, and is always ready to plunge into prodigious chores at the slightest rustle of a contract—but she was in terrific demand. When a ginger-ale company asked her for a testimonial to advertise its product, Mrs. Post wrote pleasantly that ginger ale was a refreshing drink to serve at parties, and avoided the taint of commercialism attached to most testimonials by declining to mention any particular brand. The ginger-ale people said that that would be quite all right, and paid her $3000 for the use of her name. Linen, silver and glass manufacturers paid her as much as $5000 for each pamphlet she wrote for them, describing the correct use of linen, silver or glass.

In 1929, she was given her first radio audition. "There's scarcely any use in my doing this," she said into the microphone, while seven potential sponsors listened critically in another room. "My son tells me that my voice is too thin and too feminine to be any good on the air, and I'm quite sure myself that it isn't very good, so I really don't know why you bother to listen. I guess that will be enough about my voice.

Thank you." Her voice was so good, it turned out, that all seven sponsors rushed in, afire to sign her up for their programs, and asked her to name her price.

"Well," Mrs. Post said placidly, "what do Amos and Andy get?" She didn't get as much as Amos and Andy, but the sponsor with whom she finally signed did pay her $500 a broadcast.

In addition to her income from various side lines, Mrs. Post's royalties from the book of *Etiquette,* which has sold steadily throughout the years, have, since 1922, seldom fallen below $300 a week.

By 1931, she was broadcasting daily over a national network, she had written *The Personality of a House*—a book about architecture and decorating which is used as a textbook in several schools and colleges, although it has never attained the freakish popularity of *Etiquette*—and she had joined a syndicate which now publishes her column of questions and answers about etiquette in 150 newspapers throughout the United States and Canada. On the radio, Emily Post was originally presented as The First Lady of the Air, but her sponsors had to renounce that title when Vaughn De Leath, a female crooner, insisted pretty violently that, if it belonged to anybody, it belonged to her, since she had been crooning over the air since radio began. Vaughn De Leath became The First Lady of the Air after that, and Emily Post was announced simply as "Emily Post."

Radio engineers, announcers, musicians and other studio technicians, who have come to accept delays, mistakes in timing, and a general unremitting panic as their portion, have always revered Mrs. Post because she carried a stop watch to every broadcast, timed herself every fifteen seconds, and never failed to finish courteously on the nose. She seemed to infect her radio listeners, too, with a sudden, Old-World punctiliousness. One woman wrote to her, saying that, the day before, she had called to her sister in the kitchen to come and listen to Mrs. Post, who had just come on the air; the sister hurried into the room, taking off her apron as she came. "Do you think," she replied proudly to the other's glance of inquiry, "that I would dream of receiving a visit from Mrs. Post with my apron on?" Another woman, living alone somewhere in Westchester, wrote that she usually had her tea at five o'clock but she had changed the tea hour to half past four, so that she could listen to Mrs. Post at the same time. "I sit by the fire, with my Persian cat and my Scotty dozing on the hearth," wrote this one, who appears to have been notably carried away by her feelings, "and I pour fragrant China tea into thin yellow cups. One cup for me, and one cup always, dear Mrs. Post, for you."

Mrs. Post liked getting letters like these, and she misses them. Last year, four operations were performed in fairly rapid succession on her eyes, and although she has entirely recovered from them and sees well with the aid of special glasses, she has had to give up the strenuous routine of daily broadcasting for a while. When she was in the hospital, Walter Winchell broadcast the news of her illness one Sunday night. Within an hour, Mrs. Post had received 100 telegrams and a roomful of flowers from people who had heard Winchell—mostly strangers to her. Her acknowledgment to Mr. Winchell startled him, for he had never got around to thinking of Emily Post as a reader familiar with his column and the phrases he uses in it. She sent him an orchid.

Letters from the readers of Mrs. Post's own newspaper column are less intimate and more urgent than those she used to get from her radio fans, and there are more of them. Some 26,000 letters a year, addressed to Emily Post, come in to the syndicate in New York, in addition to the letters received by individual newspapers in other cities. One year, a Detroit paper got 33,000 letters addressed to her column—people in Detroit, it seems, are great hands at writing letters to the papers. Most of the correspondents are women, and about half of them want to know details of etiquette for weddings. Letters from affianced brides almost invariably begin, "Dear Mrs. Post, I plan to be married," and there is a certain blunt quality to this phrase that faintly depresses Mrs. Post; she wishes sometimes that the girls would find a softer, a tenderer way of re-

ferring to the holy event. Occasionally the plans stated in full
by these dewy brides-to-be include strange whimsies. "My intended has a lovely voice," wrote one. "Would it be all right
for him to sing at our wedding, and if so, when and what?"
Another woman—not a bride, this time, but a troubled hostess
—wrote that she had recently given a formal dinner at which
everything had gone well until a cake was passed and served
first to the guest of honor, an old lady whose eyesight was poor;
she took a slice and was tranquilly eating it, when "to our
horror," the hostess wrote, "we saw that it was simply crawling
with ants. She had already eaten quite a lot, and we didn't like
to say anything. Mrs. Post, what would you have done in a
situation like this?" Mrs. Post replied coldly, "I would have
seen to it, in the first place, that the servants in my kitchen had
better eyesight."

Almost all the letters from her readers are addressed to "Mrs.
Emily Post," which is incorrect. Her name on the fly-leaf of
Etiquette is followed by "Mrs. Price Post" in parentheses, but
she realizes that to those readers of her column who haven't
bought the book, she is known by no other name than Emily
Post. It still gives her a slight turn, however, to see "Mrs. Emily
Post" on an envelope. She is not fussy about small matters of
behavior, beyond the occasional mild recoil in the face of bad
manners that is instinctive to any woman of taste, and she likes
to think, and to impress upon her readers, that "etiquette" is
a question of common sense and consideration rather than a
study of how to speak to a visiting prince or eat an ear of corn
on the cob. "No rule of etiquette is of less importance," she has
written patiently, time and time again, "than which fork we
use." And once, when she got fifteen letters in one day, asking
which fork the writers should use when confronted with several,
she answered all fifteen grimly in four words: "Oh, use any
one."

Her only fierce campaign connected with table manners is
against the practice of serving the hostess first, which Mrs. Post
has branded as the Great American Rudeness. There is no excuse for it, she says, unless the food is apt to have been poi-

soned—which is unlikely in a well-ordered house—or unless the guests are such louts that they don't know how to serve themselves—in which case it would be impolite, anyway, for the hostess to call attention to it by showing them how. Mrs. Post's followers, docile in other respects, definitely decline to string along with her on this question. American hostesses are accustomed to being served first, and servants in America are used to serving them first; they get stumble-footed and sullen if they are asked to begin with the guest of honor and come around to the hostess last, and some of them have been known to quit rather than give in to such a notion.

In connection with this determination of servants to attend to the lady of the house before taking any notice of her guests, Mrs. Post brings to light a fairly deep psychological point. She says that investigation has proved it to be based on the fact that it is generally the lady of the house who hands out the wages.

Whatever the reason, Mrs. Post's stanch fight against the Great American Rudeness has been a losing battle for fifteen years.

Questions that cannot be answered by mailing correspondents one of the hundreds of "slips," or pamphlets, written by Mrs. Post on "Wedding Details," "Small Afternoon Teas," "Cards and Visits," and other departments of etiquette, are sent by messenger from the syndicate and mailed from out-of-town papers to Mrs. Post's apartment in New York. Most of these letters, with her answers, go into her daily column, but she dictates about forty personal replies a day, as well, to people who enclose stamped envelopes with the request that their dilemmas be kept out of the newspapers. Their problems are seldom sensational, but the writers are shy. Mrs. Post's secretary, Miss Kent, works in a small morning room, charming with chintz and sunlight; Miss Kent's name is really Miss Keppner, but, feeling that Keppner was not, perhaps, just the right name for Emily Post's secretary, Mrs. Post changed it to Kent, and Miss Keppner doesn't mind. The business of etiquette extends down to the ground floor of the apartment house where, in an office off the entrance hall, two dark, pretty girls whom Mrs. Post gaily addresses as "darlings" take care of the overflow. Shelves around the office walls hold piles of "slips," each pile labeled with a square of white paper thumb-tacked to the shelf and lettered in black initials such as "W. S." or "Z. E."; and Mrs. Post, wandering into the office, is endlessly taken aback by this clear-cut evidence of efficiency. "Darlings, what is 'W. S.'?" she will say, and the girls reply, " 'Widows' Signatures,' Mrs. Post." (Here, the ill-advised Mrs. Mary Jones crops up again.) Or, "What is 'Z. E.'?" Mrs. Post wants to know, and the darlings look shocked. "Why, Mrs. Post," they murmur, "you remember 'Zigzag Eating'?" (Zigzag Eating is the practice—condemned in the Post litany—of shifting the fork from left hand to the right before raising it to the mouth.)

• Mrs. Post's apartment is in a building at the corner of Madison Avenue and 79th Street, leased twelve years ago under a co-operative arrangement by herself and seventeen of her friends who were united by the common complaint that nowhere in New York could they find a medium-sized apartment with big closets, wide windows and a servants' dining room. Once the lease was signed, Mrs. Post and her son, Bruce, who was beginning to be a successful architect, were assigned to re-model the building, and they went happily to work tearing down walls, installing great windows, putting in closets as big as rooms. Mrs. Post's own apartment is cheerful, comfortable and feminine, and it is run without any great formality. Sometimes a parlor-maid opens the door for a visitor; sometimes, if she is busy in another room, the door is left open and people who want to see Mrs. Post come up in the elevator—without being announced a good deal of the time—and simply walk in.

She makes no secret of her address or telephone number, both of which are listed in the Manhattan telephone directory, and she will see almost anybody at almost any time. It may be a boy from Dartmouth who has stated passionately on the telephone that he will lose his job on the college paper unless he can get an interview with Mrs. Post on the question of whether girls ought to wear shorts—or it may be someone with an even more personal problem.

One man, a hearty fellow from the West, brought her a letter of introduction from an acquaintance and laid his trouble before her in a shaken voice. This was his first trip to New York, he said, and, on account of his business connections in the West, he had been invited to a dinner to be given the following night at a great Fifth Avenue house. His hosts were people of staggering social importance. He had to go to the dinner, he wanted to go, but he was terrified for fear he wouldn't know how to behave.

"My dear man, stop worrying," Mrs. Post advised him. "Just be natural."

"Do you really mean that?" he asked eagerly.

"I certainly do," she said.

Two days later Mrs. Post heard, from some other people who had been at the party, that her Westerner had taken the advice so joyfully to heart that he had greeted ancient and distinguished gentlemen throughout the evening by slapping them on the back and shouting "Hello, old pops!" and that he had, more than once, left bruises on the arms of delicately nurtured women in an unaffected effort to be chummy. "In the end, I believe, he was unobtrusively thrown out on his ear," Mrs. Post says reminiscently, when she tells about this.

In 1927 Mrs. Post's younger son, Bruce Post, died. From that time until last year, when she was obliged to follow a little less arduous routine, she worked with a furious concentration, taking on whatever jobs came along, until they often occupied sixteen hours out of twenty-four. Because of her knowledge and love of architecture and design, and because Bruce had been an architect, she somehow found her greatest comfort in fiercely remodeling old farmhouses, or even shacks, into charming country houses. In the last ten years she has designed and decorated twenty-three houses for friends, who are asked to pay her no fee, or for strangers, who pay her plenty, especially if she has to travel to whatever part of the country they live in, in order to do the job. People who want their houses designed by Emily Post are seldom daunted by the question of money, and sometimes they contentedly pay her just for staying in New York and giving them long-distance advice.

One man, who was settling down in Memphis, Tennessee, had the plans for his house drawn up by a local architect, but refused to accept them until the architect had brought them to New York and submitted them to Emily Post. The architect was pretty sore about the whole thing, but he came to New York just the same and had such a pleasant time with Mrs. Post that he swept doorways, mantels and staircases around into the position and form that she suggested in a kind of dizzy fascination, and all without a whimper. Mrs. Post has a sure-fire method of talking to people. She tells them what she thinks and what she wants, quickly, in a level voice; and then, before even the most embattled antagonist has time to argue with her, she says "You see, don't you?" leaning forward a little and speaking in a tone so suddenly warm and winning that there is no possible answer except "Yes, Mrs. Post."

She often gives in easily, however, to whatever notions her clients have about their houses, and she is a notoriously peaceful architect, especially when dealing with fretful chatelaines. "But I want the side door, not the front door, to give onto the garden," some woman will complain, bristling in preparation for a long argument about it. "All right," says Mrs. Post, "we'll have the side door facing on the garden," and with a stroke of her pencil on the plan, she shifts the side door around to where the client wants it. She is genuinely amenable about such things, but frequently her instant submission frightens people more than the iciest resistance on her part could do. They think that she is just being gracious, and it worries them.

In spite of the restrictions put upon it in the past year, Mrs. Post's daily routine continues to be a considerable whirl. She wakes up regularly at half past five in the morning and has her breakfast—coffee in a percolator which she plugs into an electric-light socket in the early dawn, and a slice of zwieback —from a tray arranged beside her bed the night before. After breakfast she works, lying in bed in a flurry of pencils, paper and galley proofs, until half past seven, when her servants get up. She writes fluently, and has no difficulty in thinking of the right word; and her passion for writing so often overflows after she has finished her daily stint that she always carries a fountain pen and notepaper with her during the day, and dashes off notes to friends and acquaintances, generally three or four pages long, while she is riding from one place to another in a taxi. When she is writing for publication, however, she is seldom satisfied with the first frenzied burst of prose that occurs to her, and she revises so endlessly that once, after she had rewritten the first chapter of *Etiquette* thirty-eight times for a new edition, her publishers waggishly sent her a slate and a sponge for Christmas, with a card saying, "Many happy revisions."

By eight o'clock the Post household is wide awake, secretaries begin running in and out, and the telephone starts ringing. Hilda, the dour and devoted woman who has been Mrs. Post's housekeeper and personal maid for thirty-five years, sets out on her daily, faintly suspicious and apparently never-ending tour of the apartment. Hilda is not, in appearance or manner, the perfect maid. "I suppose you'll be wanting me to go to the movies again tonight?" she is apt to say, pausing somberly in the doorway of her employer's room. This remark refers to Hilda's long losing fight against the motion pictures. She hates them, but Mrs. Post likes to go occasionally, and she would rather have Hilda go with her than anybody else. Like most people who are resigned to what life has brought them, Hilda is a fine restful companion. Mrs. Post's cook has been with her almost as long as Hilda, but the parlormaid waitress, who came to work only five years ago, is referred to dryly by the other two as the "new" girl.

Mrs. Post spends the morning dictating letters and her column—since the trouble with her eyes she has been forbidden to type it herself, as she used to do—and generally lunches at home, sometimes with her son, Ned. Except for the sound advice which he regularly gives her about the chapters in the book of *Etiquette* dealing with correct clothes for gentlemen, Ned is an almost completely silent young man, tall, dark and graceful. His mother speaks of him as her "beautiful black swan." Frequently she invites business associates for lunch—burly, cigar-smoking live wires who have built Emily Post's career in radio, books or newspapers, and who are almost always startled into a fawnlike timidity by the idea of lunching with her.

One man who had helped syndicate her column in newspapers all over the country was so alarmed at the thought of lunching for the first time in her apartment that he stopped at a bar on the way, and had a couple of old-fashioneds to give him poise. To his surprise, he found a shaker half full of Martinis waiting for him when he arrived and, feeling poised as anything by that time, he drank three. It was in a pleasant haze that he finally sat down at the luncheon table. The table was highly polished and set with little doilies, but he just stared at it, thinking that he was as good as it was any day, until the nightmare moment came when he cut into an English mutton chop on his plate, saw the plate skid under his knife and fork, and the chop leap into the air and come to rest, greasily and finally, on the edge of the table. Still in his nightmare he rescued it, put it back on his plate and said, "Good God, Mrs. Post, you wrote the book! What do I do now?"

Mrs. Post looked at him thoughtfully over her own fork. "I think you did the best thing," she said. "Just pick it up and begin all over again."

When people are shy with her, Mrs. Post gets, inwardly, just as nervous as they are. But when any vast national question of taste is at stake, her own poise can best be described as immeasurable. A few years ago, when the battle concerning precedence between Alice Roosevelt Longworth and Dolly Gann put Washington into a turmoil, reporters clamored at Mrs. Post's door for a statement for their papers. She gave them a statement of several thousand words, in favor of Alice Longworth, and later sent eight copies of it to diplomats of her acquaintance, and four to the Department of State in Washington. She never got any official reply, but, unofficially, a rather tired letter came from Washington. "If Mrs. Post will settle the precedence question," the letter said, "the State Department will be most grateful."

Every spring in the face of possible contracts that would keep her in town, of thousands of potential dollars waiting to be earned, Mrs. Post declines all work except her daily column and sets out, with Hilda and the rest of her staff, for her house at Edgartown, Massachusetts. She stays there until autumn, spending most of her time with her fifteen-year-old grandson, Billy, the son of Ned Post and his former wife, Barbara Loew Post. Some of Billy's activities are pretty brisk for her, but she stops at nothing where he is concerned, and the other summer people have learned not to be startled by the sight of Mrs. Post whizzing around the bay like a water bug in Billy's outboard motorboat, obviously terrified, but game.

Her curious prestige follows her to Edgartown. Whenever the young people in the colony organize a scavenger party— that daft pursuit in which the players are sent off in all directions with orders to bring back unlikely and difficult loot— Mrs. Post can hear them pounding down the road to her door with urgent pleas for her autograph, a sheet of her notepaper, or maybe as intimate a token as a pair of her bedroom slippers. She gives them whatever they want with the graciousness that carefully marks all of her dealings with her public. Sometimes she wishes, a little plaintively, that she were celebrated as an architect and designer of houses rather than as an etiquette expert, but she has no quarrel with the kind of fame the years have brought her. When she thinks of etiquette in its larger aspects, she becomes reverent. She says, sincerely and often, that the future of America is bright with promise; for no harm, no widening flame of revolution, according to Emily Post, can come to a land where millions of people are forever cozily intent upon the right fork to use for an avocado, and how to remove grape seeds inconspicuously from the mouth.

The Hoosier Letter-Writer

(ERNIE PYLE)

By FREDERICK C. PAINTON

EDITOR'S PREFACE.—Sometimes the emphasis placed on an ordinary word gives special meaning to a statement. Such was the case when President Harry S. Truman used the word *again* in his comment on the death of Ernie Pyle. The President, undoubtedly mindful of the fact that Franklin D. Roosevelt had died only a week previously, issued the following statement when informed that Mr. Pyle had been killed in the Pacific:

"The nation is quickly saddened again by the death of Ernie Pyle. No man in this war has so well told the story of the American fighting man as American fighting men wanted it told. He deserves the gratitude of all his countrymen."

The word *again,* and also *quickly,* indicated that President Truman placed the nation's loss of Mr. Pyle in the same category with that of President Roosevelt. A headline in a Chicago newspaper carried the same implication. The *Herald-American* bannered the Ernie Pyle story with two eight-column lines: "G.I. Joe, You've Lost Another Friend" in red, followed by "Ernie Pyle Killed" in heavy black type. The word *another* undoubtedly referred to Mr. Roosevelt.

Mr. Pyle's death was reported in press dispatches dated April 18. That by the Associated Press read in part:

> The luck of Ernie Pyle, who twice escaped death while reporting the European war, ran out today when an ambushed Japanese machine gunner cut down the famous columnist on Ie Jima with a quick burst from his hidden weapon.
>
> Pyle was killed instantly at 10:15 A.M. (9:15 P.M. Tuesday, EWT.)

The wiry little columnist, beloved by G.I.'s throughout the world, was standing with a regimental commanding officer of headquarters troop 77th Division U. S. Army.

Only yesterday it was reported that enemy resistance on Ie Jima, a 10-square mile island west of Okinawa, had nearly ended.

(A Blue network broadcast from Guam by Jack Hooley gave a somewhat different version. Hooley's broadcast, heard in San Francisco, said Pyle was en route to a sector where there was heavy fighting when he was killed.

(The reporter was with Lt. Col. Joseph Coolidge of Arkansas, Hooley said, and a Japanese machine gun opened fire as their jeep rounded a corner.

(The broadcast said Pyle and Coolidge dived into a ditch. But a few minutes later they peered over the edge. There was another burst of fire and Pyle was struck three times in the temple.

(Coolidge crawled to cover and reported the death, but Pyle's body was inaccessible for some time. Volunteers in three tanks were pinned down by heavy fire but Cpl. Alexander Roberts of New York City went alone and found Pyle peaceful in death. His face was covered with his helmet and his left hand clutched a Marine fatigue cap. Corporal Roberts led a chaplain and a litter bearer to the scene and the body was returned to American lines four hours later.)

Pyle, who hated war, once told a friend that he tried "not to take any foolish chances, but there's just no way to play it completely safe and still do your job."

"The front does get into your blood," he said, "and you miss it and want to be back. Life up there is very simple, very uncomplicated, devoid of all the jealousy and meanness that float around a headquarters city, and time passes so fast it's unbelievable."

So Pyle, who returned from the European war deadly tired, got back into harness, was accredited to the Navy, and went to the Pacific war theater.

And it was on tiny Ie, where he was with the foot soldiers he worshipped, that death came at last to the famous reporter.

In addition to President Truman, others in high places paid tribute to Mr. Pyle and pointed to the unique position which he occupied in the affections of servicemen and civilians alike.

The Secretary of the Navy, James Forrestal, noting that Mr. Pyle's war reports "had endeared him to the men of the armed forces throughout the world and to their families at home," added:

"Mr. Pyle will live in the hearts of all servicemen who revered him as a comrade and spokesman. More than anyone else, he helped America to understand the heroism and sacrifices of her fighting men. For that achievement, the nation owes him its unending gratitude."

The Secretary of War, Henry L. Stimson, said:

"I feel great distress. He has been one of our outstanding correspondents. I'm so sorry."

Several members of the Congress, on learning of Mr. Pyle's death, immediately and spontaneously expressed similar sentiments. Senator Carl A. Hatch of New Mexico, the state in which Mr. Pyle maintained his home with "that girl," his wife, said:

"Ernie Pyle will not die. No Japanese bullet can kill the spirit which will live in his writings."

Senator Dennis Chavez, also of New Mexico, declared that Mr. Pyle's neighbors in Albuquerque loved him as did all Americans. Senator Raymond E. Willis of Indiana said that his state was proud to claim Pyle as a son.

Lt. General Patch said "his great courage and deep patriotism were unsurpassed by our nation's purest heroes. Frontline fighting soldiers everywhere will mourn him as a personal friend. In him they have lost perhaps their greatest and most useful champion."

Following Mr. Pyle's death, George A. Carlin, general manager of the United Feature Syndicate, who handled the Pyle copy, revealed that the correspondent was frightened by his last assignment, but went through with it "because there was a war on and he was a part of it." The Carlin statement follows:

"What all of us dreaded has happened. Before he left on this last trip to the war fronts, Ernie Pyle confessed he was scared to death. He wrote he was going simply because there was a war on and he was part of it. He was going simply because he had to and he hated it.

"We all hated the thought of the risks he ran. He had

been through so much from the beginning of the North African invasion up to the time after the liberation of Paris when he wrote in his last column from Europe:

" 'I am not leaving because of a whim, or even especially because I'm homesick. I am leaving for one reason only—because I have just got to stop. I've had it, as they say in the Army. I have had all I can take for a while. I have been 29 months overseas since this war started; have written about 700,000 words about it; have totaled nearly a year in the front lines . . . my spirit is wobbly and my mind is confused. The hurt has finally become too great. All of a sudden it seemed to me that if I heard one more shot or saw one more dead man, I would go off my nut. And if I had to write one more column I'd collapse. So I am on my way.'

"There are several more columns written from Okinawa before Ernie was killed. This will be the end of a feature that I believe was the most widely read column in newspaper history. There were more than 400 daily and 300 weekly subscribers and new orders were coming in steadily. Only this morning I signed another new contract for the feature. The ABC circulation of his subscribing newspapers was about 14,000,000. All of those readers looked upon Ernie as a personal friend and feel a sense of personal loss. To those of us who knew him personally, the loss is nearly unbearable."

Mr. Pyle was an alumnus of Indiana University—he studied journalism there, and was the recipient of an honorary degree shortly before his death.

His alma mater proposes to keep this Pulitzer prize-winner's memory alive. There has been established on the Bloomington campus the Pyle Memorial Fund. It will provide scholarships in journalism—the first going to returning soldiers.

For some months following his death, first place in the national non-fiction best-seller list was occupied by Ernie Pyle's *Brave Men* (Grosset) . The movie, *Ernie Pyle's Story of G.I. Joe,* which had its premiere in Indianapolis in July, 1945, undoubtedly stimulated additional interest in the book.

Not only was *Brave Men* the leader in the non-fiction group, but in the abridged *Omnibook* version, it was voted the most popular title in this series for a 15-months period. Mr. Pyle's *Here Is Your War,* which also was a

onal best-seller, and which was abridged by *Omnibook*
anuary, 1944, likewise scored high.

October 2, 1943
SOMEWHERE IN AFRICA.

ERNIE PYLE is five feet, eight inches tall and weighs 110
pounds when he's not suffering from what he calls Pyle's pallid
pains. He's lost most of his reddish hair on top, and what's left
is well salted with gray. He wears a faded pair of Army dunga-
rees, big serviceable shoes, and an issue wool cap that makes
him look like a retired jockey. His thin, rather gentle face, in
repose, has the melancholy cast of a sad gnome. In short, he
looks like neither a soldier nor a newspaperman, and bears no
resemblance whatsoever to the dashing storybook war correspondents.

Ernie Pyle was probably the most prayed-for man with the
American troops in North Africa. If the basketfuls of letters
he receives at the rate of 5000 a year can be believed, thousands
of women nightly in the States get down on their knees and
pray that he survives this war unscathed. Hundreds of men
wish him luck and caution him to duck fast. So have many,
many soldiers.

All this has come about because little Ernie Pyle, eight years
ago, began writing a travel column about himself and what
interested him. He wrote about the people he met; he wrote
about a rainy day and how to spend it, a tussle with the zippers
on his pants, an old man with a wooden leg. He poked fun at
his own frailties and eccentricities. And in doing so he made
of himself a character who lived in a daily installment of a
serial adventure which people read smilingly to see "what
Ernie's up to now."

Then Ernie came to North Africa. He still wrote about the
people he met, the sights he saw. But now they were soldiers
in war and he was looking at battlefields. He still wrote about
himself and how he lived, but since he lived like a soldier, and
with them, he was describing how men fight and endure in
battle. Women with sons, husbands and brothers in North

Africa have said his columns are like vivid letters from the ones they love. Lt. Gen. Jacob Devers, in talking to officers at the Command and General Staff School at Fort Leavenworth, Kansas, mentioned Ernie's column as carrying the breath of war realism. The *Infantry Journal* has also praised his reporting. Oddly enough, even soldiers within sound of the guns have learned about the war at their door from the hundreds of Pyle's columns clipped and mailed to them.

Everywhere he went, soldiers waved them under his nose. He came to know a thousand soldiers by name, thousands more by sight. Overnight, as it were, the skinny guy of the column has become known to millions of Americans. As the cheerful, droll character in the column he has lived in foxholes with the advanced infantry, with the gunners of the big 155's, in the desert with bomber commands, swapped gossip with soldiers from one end of North Africa to the other. Always Ernie Pyle, the Midwest farm boy, darting around a battlefield like a curious bird. That's the character you meet in the column.

Actually, the real Ernie Pyle is not that gregarious, easy-talking character at all. He is a shy, extremely sensitive man of forty-three, who has been tortured for years by acute self-consciousness. He likes people enormously, but he is so timid that the prospect of meeting just one sets his heart to pounding.

"I suffer agony in anticipation of meeting anybody, for fear they won't like me," he says. "Once I'm past the meeting I'm all right."

He is very quiet and seldom says much. One day, before his return to the States for a vacation, we were riding together over the old battlefield east of Ferryville. We came to an Arab farmhouse where some 5000 Germans waited around patiently to be captured. We turned in and presently were surrounded by Germans who could speak English and who asked many questions. Ernie said little, but darted glances everywhere. Finally, he saw on the tail of a modern windmill, FLINT & WALLING MANUFACTURING CO., KENDALLVILLE, IND. "Why," he exclaimed joyously, "that was made in my home state. Imagine finding an American windmill on an Arab farm that's chockful of Germans. It's worth a note in the column." The Germans had interested him, but this homespun Americana interested him more.

Ernie doesn't quite understand why he has become the world's leading roamer. He certainly inherited no gypsy urge. His grandfather was born, lived and died on a farm three miles from Dana, Indiana. His father was a farmhand who acquired thirty acres only a short distance away, married Maria Taylor and in a lifetime rounded out a 110-acre farm that he has seldom left. And here, an only child, Ernie was born on August 3, 1900. As a boy, Ernie went once or twice to a circus at Terre Haute, to a state fair at Indianapolis, and a few times to Chicago. He never felt the urge to travel then.

What drove him away, he insists, was dislike of horses. He had to ride a narrow-backed nag three miles daily to school. He figures he rode 5000 miles on that protruding spine. He followed other horses behind the plow. "I decided anything was better than looking at the south end of a horse going north," he says.

His mother encouraged him to pioneer. His father, though regretting his son's desire to leave the farm, cheerfully acquiesced. So that home life and his mother and father became background and characters, later, in the column, and the farm probably the best known in America.

The torturing timidity that still afflicts him was a nightmare to the quiet shy youth. He was thin, small, retiring. He never played in the grade-school games. "I always sat under a tree and ate my apple," he says. He never learned to swim, and even today knows few games. He picked up a skill with darts while sweating out the blitz of 1940 in London—he's good, so don't bet—"snooker" pool acquired in the basement of a London hotel; tennis, which he gave up, after getting good. He plays solitaire and rummy. Queerly enough, he is quick and graceful, and, but for the shyness, might have been a real athlete.

He never had a date with a girl until he was eighteen. Then he went away to the Naval Reserve, and she later married another youth. The only other girl in his life, Geraldine Siebolds, of Hastings, Minnesota, he met and married in Washington, and made famous as "that girl who rides beside me." Jerry's ridden many hundreds of thousands of miles beside him, and but for the fact that women aren't allowed at the front in war, would have accompanied him there.

Ernie also insists that he felt no deep craving to be a newspaperman. He read very few books. "I took journalism at Indiana University because it was a cinch course and offered an escape from a farm life and farm animals. But my mind was small, completely undeveloped—a kid off the farm who knew nothing, had been nowhere."

He made two trips away during this college period; one cautious, the other bold. One summer vacation he and another lad went to Bowling Green, Kentucky, to get a job in the oil field. The job did not appear and their money gave out. After being two days hungry, Ernie took a job unloading bricks from a freight car. He was too proud to send home for money. Then he got a job erecting 500-gallon storage tanks. The thing he likes to remember is that before the summer was over he was foreman of the gang, the kid boss.

In those days, Japan's Waseda University invited a team from an American college to play baseball. Ernie decided he had to take this in. So he shipped as a bellhop on the Keystone State and paid his first visit to the Orient. He almost made another in 1941. But Pearl Harbor changed his plans.

After returning from the Japan junket the urge to be a good newspaperman assailed him. In 1921 he was working on the Indiana University daily which obtained a "pony," or telephoned, report of world news from the Associated Press bureau in Indianapolis. Ernie's job was to don headphones, and as the stories were dictated, copy them on the typewriter in the hunt-and-peck system he still uses. One story was Kirke Simpson's classic report of the burial of the Unknown Soldier in Arlington Cemetery. It won Simpson the Pulitzer Prize; it moved Ernie to tears and gave him a goal to aim at. He can still quote parts of the story.

He left the university a skip and a hop from graduation—always intending, even yet, to go back and get a degree—and there seemed open to him only a routine newspaper career. A brief apprenticeship on the La Porte (Indiana) *Herald* was followed by a job on the Washington *Daily News*. Then, like any farm boy, he had to try his hand at New York, and did a stint on the *Evening World* and the *Evening Post*. He remembers this chiefly because he saved $1000, spent it to take himself and Jerry around the rim of the nation in a model-T Ford, and then came back to have his wife take a day job and himself a night trick. For a year they met on the City Hall steps each day and exchanged greetings.

Then he went to Washington just as commercial air lines were getting well under way. The city editor thought a daily listing of arrivals and departures—this was 1928 and it was news to ride airplanes—would be interesting. Along with his other chores, Ernie took it on. But instead of a mere listing of names, he wrote a chatty, breezy column. Soon he was aviation editor and growing up with the industry. He knew everybody in aviation, rode everywhere. The *News* is a Scripps-Howard paper and Ernie became aviation editor for the Scripps-Howard chain.

So it was one of the heart-searching periods of his life when he was offered the managing editorship of the *News*. It meant giving up his friends and the planes that he loved. But he did so, and thus, accidentally, started toward the column. He was still matchstick thin, still an intense worker, and he overdid it and caught influenza, which hung on and would not be shaken off. Early in 1935 the doctor told him to take three months' leave.

He and "that girl" went to Arizona. When they got back to Washington, the late Heywood Broun happened to be taking a vacation, so Ernie, whose conscience bothered him about having been idle for so long, wrote a dozen or so columns about his vacation experiences, to fill Broun's space in the *News*. They were trivial but interesting, and his employers suggested he have a tryout as roving reporter for the Scripps-Howard papers. Ernie, who had been on the verge of suggesting the same thing himself, accepted with delight. His first column, under a Flemington, New Jersey, date line, appeared on August 8, 1935.

Ernie's travels thereafter took him thirty-five times across the continent and into every state of the Union at least three times. He wore out three typewriters and three automobiles, but never wore out a reader. He traveled by train, plane, boat, on horseback and muleback and by truck, but when he could, he stuck to his convertible coupé. Once, after interviewing the Dionne quintuplets in Ontario, he fled to Mexico to get warm, and got laid up with dengue fever. He says he has been sick in more hotels than any other man.

In 1938 the United Feature Syndicate tried to sell the column to papers outside the Scripps-Howard chain. It wasn't easy to sell. After six months, only three new papers had taken it on. But since Ernie has gone to war, his list of newspapers has run up close to 150, and new clients come in at the rate of about one a week. His real popularity began with his reporting of the London blitz in 1940. His stories caught that "most hateful, most beautiful" sight so cleverly that portions of his dispatches were cabled back to England to give the bomb victims a chance to see how they looked under the ordeal.

Ernie loathes cold weather. At the front he wears a wool cap when he sleeps, but there was that time in 1936 when he was hot enough for once. That was the drought year, and he wrote about it in the Dakotas and Montana. The temperature was above a hundred every night, and he spent the nights taking baths.

War corresponding was not his first bout with danger. In 1937 he went to Alaska—in the spring, of course; he'd never go there in winter—and went a thousand miles down the Yukon, and rode the 375 miles of highway from Fairbanks to Valdez on what he still considers the roughest trip he ever had. He made the trip standing up in the back end of a truck for twenty-three hours. In a dilapidated plane that seemed momentarily about to lose its wings, he flew over the Alaska range to Goodnews Bay on the Bering Sea just because he wanted to find out how platinum is mined. He toured Arctica on a Coast Guard cutter from Siberia to the Aleutians to Dutch Harbor.

In 1937 he visited the leper colony at Molokai, where he stayed five days and nights with lepers, and found the experience spiritually beautiful instead of revolting. By now his routine was to spend eight months in the States and four months in a foreign country, preferably tropic. So, in 1938, he flew around South America by air, and discovered one city as beautiful as the prospectus—Rio de Janeiro.

Ernie could never pass up anything as legendary as Devil's Island in French Guiana, and the famous penal colony was as revolting and horrible as his imagination had painted it. Just for amusement, on his arrival back in the States, he rode a freight truck, day and night, from Denver to Los Angeles, and later took a bus from New York to San Francisco. These series were as popular as anything he had written up to that time.

He was in Portland, Oregon, when war was declared in Europe in 1939. He and Jerry sat up most of the night talking about it. Even then, Ernie felt that we should be in, never dreaming he was to be a latter-day Richard Harding Davis when we did get in.

In 1940 he dropped automobiles to make a trip from San Francisco to New York on the last trip the liner Washington took before becoming a troopship. Perhaps it was the unease in the air, but in 1940 he took time out from traveling to go to Albuquerque and see an architect. He drew on paper an idea of a house he wanted, some place to come back to, some sense of security in a changing world. He never saw the house until a year later, because he went to England and endured the blitz of 1940.

This was a big sacrifice for Ernie, who usually, like a pert bird, went south when the snow flew. He remembers even now the terrible cold of Lisbon as he waited two weeks for a plane seat. Then and even earlier during the boat trip to Lisbon, he suffered sleepless nights, fearing for his life, dreaming of dive bombers smashing him to bits. That left him the first time he heard a bomb crump, and he has not felt it since.

There is a curious aspect to these fears that seize Ernie. Recently, resting after a column, he picked up *Beau Geste*, a Foreign Legion novel about North Africa by P. C. Wren. Ernie has flown from the Congo and Gold Coast to Khartoum and the Niger, and criss crossed Africa everywhere except in the south. This he did in his usual cheerful fashion. But lying on his cot and reading *Beau Geste*, he was seized with a terrible fear of Africa.

"Think what would have happened to me," he moans, "if I'd known all these dangers exist."

During this trip to England his mother died. All during the years of hegira Ernie returned annually to the Dana farm. He wrote about it, and his mother and father. When she died with him far away, he wrote a column that expressed his grief. Letters poured in to sympathize, for they, too, had been characters in Ernie's adventure serial of life. They and Aunt Mary.

All this he reported in a simple, chatty style, like a letter to people he knows and likes. His readers have called it "down to earth" and "folksy." In those days hundreds of letters came to him, beginning, "I never get to go anywhere, and the next best thing is to travel with you."

Ernie says, "That's what I did— traveled for other people and wrote their letters home. I'm really a letter writer." He feels this responsibility greatly, and struggles to be accurate in detail, as well as interesting. And it was these years of training, he thinks, that have enabled him to report war and battle and soldiers, so the folks back home can see it the way it is.

His accuracy has lost him only one dissatisfied reader. This occurred during the Tunisian campaign. As part of his informal style, Ernie frequently uses "damn" and "hell." One day he wrote about a sergeant and a chaplain in an air raid on a bomber 'drome. They raced for a slit trench.

The sergeant yelled, "Are you with me, chaplain?"

And the chaplain replied, "Right behind you, sergeant."

Then the German planes strafed the spot where they lay, and they had to go elsewhere.

Finally the sergeant plunged into an irrigation ditch and sank down in mud and water. He called, "Are you with me, chaplain?"

And the chaplain's muffled voice replied, "With you? Hell, I'm under you!"

An old lady, a grandmother, wrote coldly that she thought it was all right for Ernie to cuss a little. In fact, it was cute. But to make a chaplain cuss was going too far, the story wasn't true anyway, and she'd never read his column again as long as she lived. As far as Ernie knows, she never has.

"And the funny thing is," Ernie says, "the story is gospel truth."

Ernie has several idiosyncrasies. For instance, rough Army food never gets a growl out of him, for he has never enjoyed eating—though he eats plenty despite his lightweight size. He's left-handed in everything except writing, and along with his dislike for horses, he also loathes snakes. One time he had taken his blanket roll and gone into the front line with an infantry company of the 1st Division. The Germans machine-gunned, they strafed, they lobbed over mortar shells. Ernie stayed on. But one afternoon, waking out of a cat nap, he saw a North African adder coiled on the edge of his foxhole. He let out a yell and started to pack his blankets.

"I can stand German bullets," he says, "but snakes curl my hair—what's left of it, I mean."

Ernie's method of work is to select an outfit—artillery, dough-boys, air service—live with them ten days to two weeks, then return to the advanced public-relations base, hole up and write about what he saw and whom he met. Here he lives in a tent immediately recognized as his by its neatness. He has such a passion for orderliness that we'd sometimes have fun with him by deliberately disarranging his gear and watching him quietly put everything back precisely where it had been. Though he may wear the most amazing collection of Army garments ever assembled on one sparse frame, those clothes are neat and clean, and he somehow looks well tubbed even when miles from the nearest bath.

He is also an excellent putterer. He's puttering when he's trying to begin writing. He putters when his mind is busy—as it always is—with his column. In telling the details of his life to me, he was puttering around a German *Volkswagon,* an enemy command car that an admiring provost marshal of military police had given him. He cleaned out the trash, he swept it with a whisk broom. He sat down and sewed a button on a faded pair of coveralls. Then he rearranged the seats in the *Volkswagon* and examined the tires. It was shining with cleanliness.

The next day the military police took the car away for use by the French army. Ernie didn't mind; he had managed to putter a whole day.

This puttering comes from his complete and constant devotion to his column. He does nothing but think about it, work for it. He has been deluged with requests to write a book, magazine articles, make radio speeches and lectures. He has refused them all. His only book, *Ernie Pyle in England,* is simply a reprint of Pyle columns on the London blitz.

"I know guys who have taken the stuff that belonged in their stories and sold it someplace else, and then wondered why people lost interest in them. Not me. Everything I know, see, feel, hear, think, read or even dream about goes into the column. That's why I think you've got a hell of a job trying to find something to say about me that I haven't said myself."

Ernie has pulled no punches in his column. One doughboy remarked that there were lots of hints in it for newcomers at the front—yet he has had little censor trouble.

Despite his timidity, he possesses that ineffable thing called charm, and people instantly like him. All of them. He has an elfin grin that puts humor even into unhumorous remarks. One time, during his blitz period in England, he was riding to Burford in a third-class coach. He was intently talking to a friend. A child in the compartment took to him immediately and gave him a lovely smile. Hardly interrupting a sentence, Ernie reached into his pocket and gave her a bar of sweet chocolate. It was done instinctively, but it was a great sacrifice for Ernie. For he has a queer belief in the necessity of sugar for the human body, and always carries it in some form wherever he goes. This particular bar of chocolate was all the sugar he had—and no ration card.

This charm that makes people like him gets into his writing. Hundreds of his fan letters begin: "Dear Ernie: You don't know me, but I feel I know you quite well." If he complains of a cold, women send him special home remedies. Many letters gossip about local news as if, as one letter said, "you are part of the family." Hundreds of the letters speak of a son, husband or brother in North Africa, and add, "if you're near APO blank-blank, please look him up and say we have his letters, and give him all our love."

The letter writers all worry about Ernie's safety and urge him to be careful. These letters cannot be classified as to groups; they come from farmers and laborers, businessmen and children, officers and enlisted men. And there are many, many mothers, almost two to one.

Most of these say, "Reading your column is like getting a letter from my beloved son." Ernie takes that seriously, and thinks of himself as the amanuensis of hundreds of thousands of soldiers overseas. So he jumps like a gray little fox terrier from Casablanca to Tunis, from Gabes to Gafsa, peering, studying—never taking a note except names—and then holes up and writes, day and night, until he has exhausted his material and himself.

One nice human item that probably will never appear in a Pyle column concerns Ernie and "that girl who rides beside me." A year or so ago they were divorced. But after Ernie had been in Africa for a while, they decided that the divorce had been a mistake. After an exchange of cablegrams, they were remarried, by proxy—Ernie at the front, Jerry in Albuquerque.

Queen Helen

(MRS. OGDEN [HELEN ROGERS] REID)

By Mona Gardner

EDITOR'S PREFACE.—There was a time—and meas-
ured against the long span of recorded history, it was not so
long ago—when women had little, if any, place in journalism. The same situation existed in a measure for college
men. Horace Greeley is credited with saying that of all the
horned cattle that have no place in a newspaper office, the
college graduate is the worst. As for the fair sex in journalism, Stanley Walker, in his introduction to Isabel Ross'
*Ladies of the Press: The Story of Women in Journalism
by an Insider* (Harper's), written in 1936, says that "from
the first, the woman who sought to make a place for herself
in newspaper work has found editors prejudiced against
her."

Today the situation as regards both college graduates
and women is wholly different from that suggested by these
two statements. A high percentage of our practising journalists is college men. Many of them are school of journalism graduates. And women, in great numbers, are to be
found in various phases of journalism—newspapers, daily
and weekly, community and metropolitan; press associations and syndicates; magazines and trade journals; advertising and promotion; and radio and the cinema. They are
reporters, feature writers, copy editors, script writers, and
departmental editors. In a word, they now do almost everything of a journalistic character that men do, with one possible exception. And that exception serves to introduce the
subject of the following sketch: "Queen Helen"—Helen
Rogers Reid (Mrs. Ogden Mills Reid), vice-president of
the *New York Tribune, Inc.,* since 1922, and virtually generalissimo of the New York *Herald Tribune,* of which her
husband is editor.

There are few women who occupy positions of high

executive authority on large metropolitan newspapers. In other words, there are few women publishers. This is not wholly a matter of sex, however. After all, there is but a limited number of such positions in the whole industry, and it is but natural that most of these should be filled by men. Which makes all the more interesting the personality of a woman who through her own ability, her flair for journalistic leadership and management, is able to steer the course of one of the country's largest, oldest, most influential, and most highly respected newspapers.

I

May 6 and 13, 1944

EVEN in a land where the outward forms of nobility are barred, an informal aristocracy inevitably develops, loosely composed of the wealthy, the talented, the famous, the socially prominent. A reigning queen of this unofficial upper set in the United States is Helen Rogers Reid, mistress of one of the country's oldest fortunes and an important publishing executive in her own right.

Visiting statesmen and notables put up at Mrs. Reid's when in New York. In banquet hall and drawing room, she holds court for the actors, writers, artists, political personages, and other public figures of the day. She has a house off Fifth Avenue, a summer place in the Adirondacks, and a hunting lodge in North Carolina.

This exalted existence revolves around Mrs. Reid's role as wife and business associate of Ogden Reid, owner of the respected and influential New York *Herald Tribune*. Dozens of her sex—notably in the entertainment field—are better known to the public at large than Helen Reid is, but few wield such power. Through the newspaper, and through its annual Current Events Forum, which forms the basis of 40,000 to 50,000 women's-club programs each year, she can and does affect the thinking of millions of Americans. There is a cult of Helen Reid worshipers who consider her one of the truly great women of her era, on a plane with Madame Chiang Kai-shek as a shaper of destiny, and the one woman above all others who should be given a seat at the peace-conference table.

Helen Reid is a self-made queen—a small-town girl who worked her way through school, became social secretary to the majestic Mrs. Whitelaw Reid, married the Reid scion, one of the matrimonial catches of two continents, and went on to carve out a career for herself in the newspaper business.

Without doubt Mrs. Reid is equipped with the requisite mental machinery for just such a course. She has a literal, orderly and direct mind. She is easily and eagerly absorbed by all relevant minutiae. She is never deflected for a moment by an inconvenient or unruly sense of humor. She has no secret misgivings, little or big. Applied together, such coefficients have a way of translating any ordinary course of action into a full-sized campaign, and from campaign it is only a short step to crusade—minus, of course, any emotionalism.

Thus Helen Reid's life has been a succession of skillful and competently waged crusades. She has tackled such widely different objectives as learning Greek, making a college yearbook pay dividends, the suffragist movement, sailing a racing sloop, turning a showy estate into an assembly-line farm, and has attained each as per calculation.

For some time now the *Herald Tribune* has been Mrs. Reid's crusade. She is listed on the masthead as vice-president.

In her whole triumphant march through life, she has never indulged in overt aggressiveness. Quiet purposefulness and tenacity compose her method. Her manner is controlled and pleasant, her conversation a series of questions. To the average woman she volunteers nothing, never chatting spontaneously about her children, her home, the play she saw last week. Only a mention of the *Herald Tribune* does she become smilingly communicative.

If Helen Reid is somewhat unfeminine in her personal reticence, she is ultrafeminine in appearance. Sixty-one years old, she looks much younger. Only five feet one, she has retained the figure of a high-school girl though Spartan avoidance of rich dishes. Even her gray hair is youthful looking—a fine, soft fuzz curling close to her head. Her skin clings tightly to her firm, square jaw with no obvious wrinkles. She wears a light rouge on her lips which softens their rather thin and incisive appearance.

Her eyes are altogether another thing. Gray-green, large, alert, they produce an uncomfortable and upsetting effect upon some. The women who work for her consider them decorative and lovely. Men around the plant compare them to the hard glint of steel. Several advertising salesmen—not exactly a diffident or neurotic race—have reported themselves as completely unnerved after a first encounter with little Mrs. Reid's eyes. She likes bright colors in her clothes—especially the varying shades of purple. She makes no pretense of wearing creations, nor has she a favorite *couturier* who designs her whole wardrobe. When she feels the urge for a frock, she simply starts shopping, and keeps going from shoppe to shop, and even to department stores, until she finds what she wants.

About hats, however, she has as settled a conviction as Queen Mary, although the one model in which she places her faith is somewhat less heroic. A beret, Mrs. Reid has decided, is *her* hat. She comes walking into the shop of the swank New York hat stylist, John Frederics, six or eight times a year, and asks for a new beret. Whereupon Mr. Fred puckers his amiable face, walks thrice around Mrs. Reid, and evolves still another beret; it may be entirely of feathers this time; it may be velvet with pearls, flower petals, sequins on net, or a plain black satin to which Mrs. Reid can affix a little clip she rather likes. The clip has dozens of diamonds in it.

But even on this feminine errand, her business sense is not necessarily relaxed. With Mr. Fred she discusses the practicability of turning the former Whitelaw Reid home on Madison Avenue into a plushy shopping center, with leading designers of dresses, hats, shoes and the like scattered about in its many ornate rooms. It irks Mrs. Reid to be connected in any way with a white elephant, even by inheritance.

Her partner in business and marriage is quite her opposite.

Tall, broad-shouldered, placid, genial, Ogden Reid is thoroughly bored by business machinations. In his very evident friendliness toward everyone, whether significant or not, there is nothing to indicate that he was born with The Comstock Lode in his mouth. He likes his reporters, linotype operators, and others around the plant to call him "Oggie," even if he isn't always sure about their names.

When he comes to grips with any question, he wants to examine each pro and each con. He gives over hours of an editorial conference deliberating, via Robert's *Rules of Order,* whether a partition on the fifth floor should or should not be removed. This indifference to time makes him anywhere from an hour to three days late for most appointments. Away from the office, his preoccupation with detail leaves him, and he is gregarious and convivial. Over a highball he likes to talk journalism, or else discuss his favorite theory that the forward pass has ruined football. In summer, if he isn't actually in the water or in a racing sloop, he wants to talk swimming and sailing. A water-polo game has him beating the rails and shouting.

The exact division of authority between Mrs. Reid and her husband is difficult to pin down. Women satellites insist that Mrs. Reid sticks to her official domain, the advertising department, and never interferes in any editorial matter. Their favorite and perhaps apocryphal story is that Mrs. Reid once hurried to her husband's office to protest an item in the paper, and Ogden said, "Helen, will you get the hell back to your department and run it while I run mine?" Mrs. Reid is reported to have left meekly. Asked about this, she denies the whole episode with, "In the first place, my husband wouldn't speak to me that way. In the second, I wouldn't leave meekly. Besides, nothing like that ever happened."

Whatever this may prove, the trade has concluded that there isn't a department on the paper that doesn't come under Mrs. Reid's close scrutiny, and that she never misses a trick in any of them. For instance, she has as circulation director Kenelm Winslow, the son of one of her sisters. Together they chuckle

over the fact old Mr. Ochs had to get his morning's news from
the *Herald Tribune* at his summer home because, routed by
special truck over the mountains, it reached that area some two
or three hours before his *Times* did. During a normal winter
in Florida, the sun followers at Fort Lauderdale, Miami and
such points read the *Herald Tribune* hours ahead of its competitor, because the edition was flown to Richmond, Virginia,
and there transferred to the Orange Blossom Special, which
had left New York four hours before the edition went to press.
Dartmouth's eight-o'clock journalism classes use the same day's
Herald Tribune as a textbook because Circulation—needled
by Mrs. Reid—thought of a way to get them there by truck.

One of the *Herald Tribune's* circulation strong points, which
the trade credits to Mrs. Reid's influence, is its hold on the
substantial citizenry of the suburbs. Although the *Herald
Tribune* trails its archcompetitor, the New York *Times,* in
total circulation—419,000 to 296,000 week days, 806,000 to
548,000 Sundays—it actually leads the *Times* in the New York
suburban area. This phenomenon is generally attributed to a
country-weekly principle in the *Tribune's* women's and society
pages. Where the *Times* is fussy about such items, almost any
respectable women's club or wedding announcement can win
a place in the *Tribune*.

But Helen Reid is best known in her special field, the sale of
advertising space. Advertising men generally acknowledge her
to be a remarkable business getter. There are those who knew
her when she was just Helen Rogers who say that she was only
a cut above average in ability and personality, that the Reid
wealth and prestige were the basis of her business success. But
even in lukewarm quarters it is conceded that she capitalized
expertly on her advantages. Whatever the relative weight of
her talents and her personal position, there is no disputing her
effectiveness.

The *Tribune's* yearly advertising linage was 5,750,000 when
she went to work there. It doubled her first year. In several
more it was approaching that of the *Times*. Each year the
margin was pared still further, until now the *Tribune's* linage

reaches 15,000,000 and sometimes 18,000,000 a year, while the *Times'* runs around 23,000,000.

Helen Reid entices and captures advertising accounts with a relentlessness that astounds and occasionally frightens competitors. "She has the persistence of gravity," one former associate says admiringly. "If she can't reach a goal one way, she will do it another. If not this year, then next, or maybe five years from now."

Her methods with clients vary. She may go directly to the office of a space buyer, wrapped securely in mink and the Ogden Reid name. The space buyer soon finds, however, that this is not a mere application of the personal equation. Instead he is being buffeted by precise, voluminous and incontrovertible facts.

If a space buyer cuts down or cancels his *Tribune* advertising, Mrs. Reid may pat her beret into place and hurry over to his office to find out why. "Tell her I'm out!" one harried ad man shouted to his secretary "I suppose if I leave a want ad out of the *Journal-American,* Mrs. Hearst will be in here next!"

The intimate chat is another method Mrs. Reid uses very effectively. Say a dealer in men's clothing is still obdurate, despite the best efforts of one of her advertising solicitors. In the course of a week or so, the balky prospect picks up the phone to hear Mrs. Reid herself on the wire, asking him to take lunch with her. Somewhat flustered by this social attention from one so prominent, the man in trade accepts readily enough. He finds the luncheon is on the eighth floor in the *Herald Tribune's* private dining room—called by irreverent reporters "Helen's Chophouse." The guests about the fine old table on a typical day might well include a visiting advertising mogul from Seattle, a best-selling author, a Hollywood actor, and, inconspicuously behind the gladiolus, a couple of the *Herald Tribune* advertising executives.

With Mrs. Reid unobtrusively supplying the cues, conversation skips about nimbly over the weather, politics, the author's latest book, the actor's best role, until the clothing merchant finds they're actually talking about his line too.

Banter and deft flattery eddy about him, up to the time when he either capitulates in a warm glow or decides to go through an uncomfortable hour saying no. It takes a very resolute dealer in men's clothing to stick to his negatives.

Some years ago, in his Broadway column, Walter Winchell aimed a series of sharp barbs at Mrs. Reid. Roundabout, through mutual friends, Winchell learned that Mrs. Reid was always saying she'd like to know him. He dropped in for a quick hello one night at her office. Two hours later he forced himself to stop telling her about his life, even though Mrs. Reid was pressing him to go on. Later, he exclaimed to friends, "I never dreamed she was such a charming woman. She's wonderful." Mrs. Reid has been a darling of the column ever since.

Instances of her failure to gain her point are few. One case was her lack of success in trying to make the paper dry during prohibition days. This wasn't because she herself believed in prohibition, but because it was the law of the land. However, her husband steadfastly opposed her in this, and throughout the arid period the *Herald Tribune* was obstreperously wet.

But most objectives succumb to Helen Reid's unremitting effort and persistency. Her activities, both inside and outside the office, fit into a single broad pattern of tireless, unending application. She entertains continually, both informally and formally. The informal half revolved around her two sons, Whitelaw and Ogden—more generally called Whitey and Brownie—until recently. Now Whitey is a lieutenant (j.g.) in the ferry division of the United States Naval Reserve. Brownie, just eighteen, is in the Army. By now she has so unified her personal life with furthering the prosperity and prestige of the paper that whatever formal entertaining she does automatically satisfies both ends. Thus: Anthony Eden, on the trip before his last, stayed at the British embassy in Washington and with the Ogden Reids in New York.

Helen Reid didn't build up this tradition of the Reid home being the unofficial capital for distinguished visitors from abroad; that was amply set by the hospitality of her mother-in-law, who entertained lavishly at Ophir Hall, a vast Castle in White Plains filled with Van Dycks, Raeburns, Venetian velvets, Coromandel screens, genuine Tudor ceilings, and floors of rose marble. Helen Reid is just continuing the tradition on a somewhat simpler scale. Across the road from the boarded-up old-world castle, she maintains what she modestly calls Ophir Cottage—a house of some thirty-odd rooms.

Unlike Mrs. Whitelaw Reid, however, Helen Reid makes a habit of including her editors and columnists at the luncheons, dinners, and week-end affairs for the distinguished foreigners. Unquestionably, she finds pleasure in the company of these staff members, but she is also coolly aware that such meetings are likely to broaden their insight into international affairs and the value of their subsequent writings.

Frequently, Mrs. Reid gives what might be called significant dinners. A sample gathering might include Wendell Willkie, a New Deal author, a Republican congressman, a top-flight columnist and a sprinkling of couples from the East Seventies. Comes dessert, the hostess—stirring her champagne with a bread crust the while—poses a question on current affairs and calls upon the diners, one by one, to give their views about it. Some deliver their opinions seated, but others feel impelled to stand, as though addressing a public assemblage. "You don't dare come unprepared," one woman remarked who had been a guest and found the experience "so stimulating!"

Helen Reid has come a long way from Appleton, Wisconsin, where she was born Helen Rogers, the eleventh child of Benjamin Talbot Rogers and his wife, Sarah. Rogers, a native of Pennsylvania, had made some money running a store in the copper-mining district of Michigan. He had then moved to Appleton, so his growing children could go to Lawrence College there, and had put his savings into a hotel. It was a money loser. When Helen was three, he died, leaving very little for the large family. Mrs. Reid describes her girlhood as a thoroughly normal, happy and imaginative one. Her sisters say that even as a tot she was curiously fastidious—always making beds without being reminded, always making them just so, always straightening the bureau drawers of the whole family. They can't remember her ever having a brattish moment.

She cooked, washed dishes, waited on table, scrubbed, cleaned and gardened with her sisters, and made over their outgrown dresses for herself. Canoeing picnics on the river, nature walks and popcorn sessions around the fireplace were Appleton's diversions. For pets she had a dog, a cat, a chicken, several birds and a raccoon that played the mouth organ. She also cherished June bugs, and used to take them to bed with her, putting them—without benefit of box—under her pillow. She still regards them as beautiful, shiny creatures, and can't for the life of her understand the aversion others feel for them.

She was the devoted slave of her elder sister Florence—always called Sally—for whom she used to fetch and carry endlessly, even to the point of docilely getting out of bed at midnight to scramble eggs for Sally and the beaus Sally was entertaining on the front porch. The relationship is somewhat reversed now. Sally, now Mrs. Ferguson, has lived with Mrs. Reid for many years, and, until recently, helped look after the multiple housekeeping duties of the various Reid ménages.

By the time she was out of grade school, Helen's elder brother was headmaster of Grafton Hall, a preparatory school for girls at Fond du Lac. She went there, paying her way through by tutoring. From this school she came east to Barnard College in New York City, bent on becoming a Latin teacher. There she found herself irresistibly drawn to the study of zoology. She has written glowingly since in the Barnard alumnae magazine of the courses where "the love life of an earthworm became beautiful and exciting" and "the nervous system of the dogfish integrated the history of the world into a rational pattern."

Meanwhile she kept up a stiff regimen of Greek and Latin, ran a typewriter in the bursar's office, tutored, and helped manage a dormitory. She also sang in a choral club and went in for dramatics—not before the footlights but as stage manager. In her senior year she took on the job of business manager of the *Mortarboard,* the student yearbook, and astonished every-one by ending up with a sizable profit instead of the usual red ink. In this book, the senior-class poet wrote:

> *We love little Helen, her heart is so warm,*   3
> *And if you don't cross her, she'll do you no harm.*
> *So don't contradict her, or else if you do,*
> *Get under the table and wait till she's through.*

Commencement week, word came to Helen from a friend that Mrs. Whitelaw Reid was looking for a social secretary. Mrs. Reid, the informant let it be known, was a woman of majestic whimsey and of many moods. She would brook stupidity only once; demanded, and would pay munificently for, quiet perfection. Helen Rogers decided she was the neces-sary paragon, saw Mrs. Reid, and came back with the job.

The girl from Appleton went to work in the famous Floren-tine palace on Madison Avenue which, art critics agreed, con-tained a greater quantity and variety of art treasures than any other private dwelling of the period. By the light of its silver chandeliers, little Miss Rogers memorized the Social Register and familiarized herself with the social certainties of that gen-eration. Summers she accompanied Mrs. Reid to the intimi-dating elegance of Ophir Hall.

Her employer was a unique personality of the time. The daughter of Darius Ogden Mills, the eminent California finan-cier, she had come blazing into New York and proceeded to spend her father's millions with cheery and startling abandon. Abhorring a social vacuum, she had a dinner table seating eighty. When none of New York's discomfited shops could provide her with damask in one continuous piece to cover such a board, she sent to Ireland and had two woven that would.

Behind their napkins, guests used to speculate whether Cen-tral Park wasn't the only place in the city big enough for the cloths to be laundered and hung out to dry.

Stout, resplendent, Malapropian at times, and utterly candid, Elizabeth Mills Reid had a way of making a guest's scalp tingle with some such remark as, "My husband likes you so much. I could never understand why." The next moment she was being breath-takingly generous to anyone in her path—a writer, a musician, a store clerk, or a Republican candidate. It was a constant source of satisfaction to her that she had been born a Republican, and she shouldered the responsibility conscientiously.

In 1905, President Theodore Roosevelt named Whitelaw Reid ambassador to Great Britain. Miss Rogers, by now an indispensable part of Mrs. Reid's life, journeyed to London. Here, with her usual fine diligence, she soon probed the mystery of diplomatic entertaining, mastered the intricacies of protocol and became intimate with Burke's *Peerage and Landed Gentry*. She watched the morning newspaper lists of arriving Americans; by ten A.M. she had made a list of the ones worth entertaining and, after checking with Mrs. Reid, had invitations on the way to them.

The Reids' only son, Ogden, who was the same age as Miss Rogers, had just graduated from Yale, and was studying law. Usually, he spent his summers with the family in London. Handsome, genial, not too formidably intellectual, co-heir to the Mills millions, and in line for the editorship of the *Tribune,* he was a matrimonial catch not to be overlooked. Many an aspiring mother on both sides of the Atlantic had her hopes dashed when it was announced that young Ogden was marrying an unknown Miss Rogers. It was not a sudden romance; the engagement was announced in 1911, eight years after Miss Rogers had gone to work for his mother.

Privately, the ambassador—who hadn't been born a Brahmin, but had become one by inclination and hard work—was disturbed. His wife, however, took the romantic viewpoint, stressed Miss Rogers' brains and talent for management. Miss Rogers, despite the Reid millions, insisted that a wedding should be at the bride's home, and took herself off to Racine, Wisconsin. Not wishing it to appear that they didn't sanction the nuptials, the ambassador and his lady journeyed to Racine for the wedding. It was a stirring time for Racine, with newspaper headlines all over the country, the Reid private car on the railroad siding, and a live ambassador riding up the main street.

Ogden's interests in swimming, tennis, shooting, and sailing became Helen Reid's interests. But she didn't acquire any of them casually. She marshaled her forces and conquered them, technical bit by technical bit, until she was an accomplished swimmer, a first-rate tennis player, a crack wing shot and had won a pleasant collection of yachting cups. Friends call Ogden a natural yachtsman who has the feel of sails and winds and tides in his bones. He sails by instinct, and it's a devilishly exciting interlude doing it with him, they say. Whereas Mrs. Reid's sailing is a triumph of mathematics. When she comes aboard her sloop, she comes with an armload of charts—on tides, wind drift, plotted course, and so on. She stations someone with binoculars watching to loo'ard, another watching off the port side for any close-tacking competitors who might take the wind from her. Oh, she wins the race in fine style—but it's work, every minute of it.

With leisure time to fill, and her natural penchant for campaigns, young Mrs. Reid soon became an ardent woman suffragist. She found New York rated a hopeless state; organization lagged, money was tight. She volunteered to raise funds, training her sights on wealthy women who were lukewarm to suffrage, but not to the Reid name. She had them to lunch in small groups and passed the fountain pen with dessert. The $500,000 she raised this way helped swing the state into the suffrage column.

When more farm crops were urged during World War I, Helen Reid turned her managerial talents to Ophir Hall's 800 decorative but unproductive acres. Plows ripped through the green sod; wheat, corn, and oats went in. The aristocratic languor of the Guernseys and Holsteins departed overnight when they found themselves up against Helen Reid's charts on milk and butter expectation. As for the blooded Hampshire Down sheep—it was as though the Ford assembly line had struck them. Whereas Ophir Hall had bought its broilers and eggs heretofore, now the laggard Leghorns and Rhode Island

Reds began laying it on the line, or off with their heads. The farm paid, and paid handsomely.

Fresh from these tidy conquests, young Mrs. Reid was asked by her mother-in-law and by her husband—who had succeeded to the editorship on the death of his father in 1912—to focus her dollar magic on the ailing *Tribune*. She rolled up her lacy sleeves and started on the advertising department. It was a portentous event for all concerned. Without her publishing role, Helen Reid would not have attained so full-bodied an eminence; without Helen Reid, it is doubtful if the paper would be in the hands of the Reid family today.

II

TWENTY-FIVE years ago Helen Reid, a self-made princess, went to work on the New York *Tribune,* a tottering old-line aristocrat. The results have been mutually broadening. Today, Mrs. Reid is a full-blown queen, presiding as hostess for the great figures of the day. The newspaper, now the *Herald Tribune,* is an established institution of the upper-income and social brackets.

Fifteen million dollars had been pumped into the palsied *Tribune* by the Whitelaw Reids in the two decades before Helen stepped in. But, paradoxically, the Reid dynasty was saved, and what has now become the *Herald Tribune* was achieved less by this largess than by the inexorable and chronic business vein in the girl from Appleton, Wisconsin, who had become the wife of the Reids' son, Ogden, after eight years as social secretary to his mother.

Today she rejoices as composedly as any born Reid that the family tradition as the oldest continuous newspaper proprietorship in New York has been preserved and that the *Herald Tribune* is respectably solvent. As a closely held corporation—Ogden Reid inherited all but a scattering of its 200 shares—the paper does not make its balance sheet public. However, it may be said to stay consistently on the profit side of the ledger, with proceeds in the best years running to $1,000,000 and even $1,500,000.

Although her influence has been felt in all departments, Helen Reid's special contribution to the *Tribune's* rise has been in the sale of advertising space. She has preached the *Tribune's* message to unbelieving advertisers with all the unremitting zeal of a missionary going into head-hunter country. The analogy is imperfect, however. For in her conversions Helen Reid has never resorted to dramatic emotionalism. Instead she has applied her own special blend of facts, strategic artlessness and a persistence akin to sandpaper.

The Appleton girl had been Mrs. Ogden Reid seven years when her husband suggested that she might be the one to cure the paralysis which had overtaken the *Tribune's* advertising department. He himself was less than fascinated by such business details. But he knew it was time somebody became fascinated with that side of the business if "the Old Lady of Park Row"—as newspapermen about town were calling the *Tribune* then—was going to survive much longer. Even his mother—a woman who spent her money gloriously, rapturously—was beginning to feel a little less glow in this prospect. She, too, added her persuasions. Wasn't little Helen a born manager? Hadn't she raised money at her own luncheon table for the woman suffragists, turned the Reid estate's gentlemanly park into a humming farm factory? Founded by Horace Greeley, the *Tribune* had come into Reid hands unexpectedly when Greeley, who had a passion for running unsuccessfully for office, did it again. This time he made the error of thinking he could run for President and defeat Grant, who, in 1872, was up for re-election. Retiring—temporarily, so he thought—to conduct his campaign, Greeley left the running of the paper to his razor-witted, thirty-five-year-old managing editor, Whitelaw Reid. Greeley was swamped by Grant. Coming back to resume his job as editor, he was taken ill and died within a month.

Reid, a farm boy from Xenia, Ohio, had peddled ink, apple trees and kitchen utensils to pay his way through Miami University, and owned a country newspaper by the time he was twenty-one. He traded advertising space for beeswax, feathers, tallow, sugar, and made a good thing out of it. He had the basic instinct for good newspaper writing, though, and left to become one of the crack Civil War correspondents.

He became a very successful *Tribune* editor. In an era of personal journalism, he changed over from "What Horace Greeley would say" to "What the *Tribune* would say." He stopped the paper's swashbuckling and soapbox thumping, substituted the lofty moral and intellectual issues, and managed to impart a literary tone to each page. It became a daily encyclopedia for the solid, genteel, cultured folk of New York, and for many years was one of the most respected papers in the country.

It lost vigor under absentee treatment, however, when Reid grew a Vandyke and committed himself to diplomacy. He served as minister to France, as special envoy to London at Queen Victoria's Jubilee and again at the coronation of Edward VII. Finally, he was made ambassador to Great Britain. He held that post for seven years, until his death in 1912. Ogden inherited a dull, stodgy, outdated sheet that was a distinct commercial liability.

Thirty, and full of eagerness, Ogden gave it a transfusion of new blood. News coverage became lively and impartial. He changed the format to a modern eight-column page, put in a more cheerful type face, used bigger headlines, more photographs, and included a four-page comic with the Sunday edition. He acquired entertainment features his father had thought undignified: hiring the columnists F. P. A.—Franklin P. Adams—and Grantland Rice; putting Clare Briggs' cartoons, "Mr. and Mrs." and "When a Feller Needs a Friend," on the sports page; turning Heywood Broun into a baseball reporter and then a drama critic; making the editor of *Puck,* Arthur Folwell, editor of the Sunday edition.

To popularize this rejuvenation, the Reids contracted for $250,000 worth of billboard advertising. As an indication that

Helen Reid, although not yet officially connected with the *Tribune,* was already taking an interest in it and offering suggestions, the campaign took the form of a crusade. Its cause was clean advertising. Piously, the *Tribune* threw out its patent-medicine ads, and began exposing various sharp practices by department stores and automobile dealers, pledging itself to refund purchase money to any reader who felt misled by a *Tribune* ad, whether for a necktie or a town car. The crusade continued for three years, brought considerable prestige, new advertisers, and helped boost circulation from 25,000 to 90,000. But the ink was still red on the *Tribune* ledgers. It was at this point that Ogden appealed to his wife to try her hand on the advertising department.

Leaving her home each day to work at the paper's offices wasn't going into foreign territory. But going out on the street was. Her first objective was the department stores. Her name got her past the reception clerks; if the advertising manager was indifferent, she arranged to have some social acquaintance— or maybe half a dozen of them—present her to the president. From there on, it was a slow siege. Rodman Wanamaker held out six months, then surrendered. DePinna, Macy's and Gimbel Bros. capitulated, one by one. There was no dramatic swordplay to mark these passages; just the inch-by-inch, never-give-up stuff that sieges are made of. Today, the *Herald Tribune* is one of the country's leading newspapers in department-store advertising.

After her groundwork with the department stores, Helen Reid turned to the automobile advertisers in Detroit. This was harder, because doorsteps weren't handy for daily dropping in. On her first trips to the motor capital, her name failed to impress the motor executives. But she went back regularly, relentlessly, to rap on these same Detroit doors. Again, persistence sandpapered through; again, contracts were duly executed.

Tribune advertising receipts grew with each year, to the point where, in 1922, the dowager Mrs. Reid gave a celebration dinner for department heads. As the brandy and cigars were passed, she rose and announced with great elation, "It has been a glorious year. We've only lost one hundred and fifty thousand dollars."

All this while the *Tribune's* most irritating rival was Frank Munsey's *Herald*. There was a striking similarity between the two newspapers—both appealed to the higher-income level; both were morning papers; both were prime money losers. It seemed obvious to many that they should join forces.

One March night in 1924, Munsey, a matchless horse trader in newspaper properties, came to dinner at Mrs. Whitelaw Reid's. He gave Mrs. Reid and daughter-in-law Helen to understand that he proposed to buy the *Tribune*. Some students of newspaper history think that this may conceivably have been a master stroke of reverse salesmanship on Munsey's part. At any rate, whether or not he had planned it that way, Munsey had agreed by dessert time to sell his *Herald* to the Reids instead.

Thrown in with this deal was the Paris *Herald,* which, started as a clearinghouse for Continental news for its New York parent, had by this time become a small-town social sheet for the American colony in Paris, as well as a haven for all itinerant American reporters bent on getting on, or off, their feet. A substantial portion of its tidy revenue came from the German and Italian governments for steamship advertisements.

On May 22, 1932, it carried an amazing editorial recommending Fascism for the United States, which Helen Reid characterized as "shocking" when it was brought to her attention. However, the Paris editor remained at his job. The German and Italian ads continued. The Paris *Herald* finally fell, unmourned in substantial newspaper circles, to the Germans in 1940.

Helen Reid's advertising zeal caused another hullabaloo in 1937, when the *Herald Tribune* splashed out with a special forty-page glorification of Fulgencio Batista's dictatorship in Cuba. Bought by "friends of Cuba" and paid for with $32,000, all forty pages were commercial announcements without the label "Advertisement" to distinguish them from editorial material. It was widely condemned as being "perilously close to the ethical line."

When Helen Reid started at the *Tribune,* there were ten salesmen of display advertising space. Now she needles seven times that number. "What miracles today?" she hails solicitors when she meets them about the plant. "You get so you sneak up the back stairs five days a week," says one solicitor, "rather than confess you're not a wonder boy."

But on the sixth day, the salesman knows he must rise to his feet before his coworkers and give a public accounting of his miracles. Regularly on Monday mornings at nine o'clock sharp, with or without hang-over, he attends a staff meeting that has at times been a cross between Kiwanis and the Montessori system. At one period Mrs. Reid presided from a platform with an apple tree decorated with bright red cardboard apples beside her. Each apple was a symbol of an account the *Herald Tribune* was soliciting. One by one, Mrs. Reid called on the solicitors. When a new account was announced, she ceremoniously removed an apple from the tree. This was the cue for everyone to clap hands, cheer, listen to the play-by-play tactics used on the account, and cock his ear for the next miracle.

Should a space seller show up sans miracle, Mrs. Reid knows how to take care of that too. "We're going to pass over Mr. Martin's report today," she explains gently. "He's been slowed up a little. But we've analyzed it together. So next week Mr. Martin will have something really splendid to tell us. . . . Won't you, Mr. Martin?" Mr. Martin gives his earnest word that he will, he certainly will.

The apple tree has not been the only symbol. For a while, fine fat cardboard ducks, pinned up on the walls, indicated accounts which "our contemporary on Forty-third Street"— the *Times*—had, and which Mrs. Reid regarded as fair game for the *Herald Tribune* bag. A huge cardboard thermometer recorded advertising temperatures during another period. Once the sales staff found itself converted into a choral society. The *Herald Tribune* was trying, along with other morning dailies, to persuade department stores out of the habit of advertising a big sale in the evening papers of the preceding day. One Monday morning the solicitors arrived to find a professional song writer seated at a piano, and a lyricist handing out copies of a little torch number entitled *Tell 'Em in the Morning If You Want Them in at Night.*

While the melody didn't exactly offer the fullest scope for barbershop harmony, the impromptu tenors, baritones and basso profundos insist they gave it their all, especially when they heard Mrs. Reid leading them with the words:

> *Tell 'em in the morning, if you want them in at night.*
> *Tell 'em at the breakfast table, when the world seems bright,*
> *And as the husband's munchin' bacon while he's takin' in the news,*
> *She knows he'll see a million little things the house can use—*
> *Coats and hats and bric-a-bracs and household things and such.*
> *Breakfast time when dad is fine's the time to make a touch;*
> *With his hat in one hand, his umbrella in the other,*
> *They make a date to meet at eight and shop with one another.*
> *They feel like millionaires because their day has started right,*
> *So tell 'em in the morning if you want them in at night.*

Mrs. Reid's folksy touch is not confined to sales meetings. She is interested in everything that affects the staff. She has engaged couples to the house for dinner, and likes to have a hand in planning their weddings. When Kay Vincent, the fashion editor, and Howard Barnes, the present drama critic, slipped away to White Sulphur Springs to be married quietly, Mrs. Reid's one-word congratulatory telegram indicated her frustration. It said: "Pigs!"

When there's an illness in any department, she wants to know about it. On minor ailments her secretary makes sympathetic daily telephone inquiries. Perhaps flowers go out or a basket of fruit with Mrs. Reid's card. But let anything major happen and Mrs. Reid snaps into the same immediate and competent action that she does over an ailing account.

One of the men in the advertising department tells about the time he pulled up to the *Herald Tribune* entrance in a newly acquired Rolls-Royce—how he got it is another story— and saw Mrs. Reid waving to him from the foyer. "I've got to get to Jamaica the quickest way," she said, commandeering him and the car. On the sprint out to Long Island she explained that one of their foreign correspondents, just back from Europe, had deposited himself out there in a rented room and now was reported to have come down with something that sounded like pneumonia.

Pneumonia it was. While Mrs. Reid rolled up her sleeves and went to work in the sickroom, she dispatched the advertising man to fetch ice, a nurse, a doctor. "Immediately" Mrs. Reid said. "Immediately!" The nurse and doctor got there under their own power. But, knowing the grim standard for Mrs. Reid's "immediately," the *Tribune* man took no chances on the ice plant's truck. In 200-pound cakes, the ice journeyed from one end of the suburb to the other on the back seat of the Rolls.

Traditionally, the editorial and the business offices of a newspaper save their best invectives for one another—editorial workers calling the men of the business office money-grubbers, the business-office men calling the writers mere parasites who do nothing toward meeting the weekly pay roll. This does not hold true at the *Herald Tribune*. The two sects tolerate each other, and frequently are seen fraternizing together. No one knows just why this is; some say it is Mrs. Reid's influence in exposing department heads to each other so often in her home; others are inclined to attribute it to the institution known as Bleeck's.

This is a reformed speak-easy on West 40th Street adjacent to the delivery entrance of the *Herald Tribune*—so adjacent, in fact, that these plant doors are invariably spoken of as "the

Bleeck entrance." Noisy and lively, it is the staff's unofficial clubhouse from noon until the last edition in put to bed at three-thirty in the morning. They come drifting in—editors, business managers, columnists, men off the slot, reporters, circulation experts, sports writers, foreign correspondents, the boss, and even Mrs. Reid herself now and then, to yarn away over a drink at the old oaken bar or over some of Jack Bleeck's prime beef in the back rooms. Everyone is on cozy terms with everyone else, and there isn't a last name in the place. All this is in direct contrast to the *Times,* where one department corresponds distantly with another. The *Herald Tribune* hearties maintain that now and then a *Times* spy—easily identified by his wan, intellectual face—comes creeping into Bleeck's to watch them at their antic camaraderie from behind a menu. They never molest him, they say, knowing he has been lured from the cold camphorated realm of journalism by sheer need of human warmth.

Certainly this solid family feeling is not a thing engendered by money. Although the Ogden Reids inherited half of a fortune estimated at $20,000,000—the other half going to Ogden's sister Jean, wife of Sir John Ward—the *Herald Tribune* has never been noted for high salaries. There are isolated cases where the Reids have paid a man or a woman seventy-five dollars a week more than the individual expected, or where they suddenly jumped another $5000 a year without his asking for it, but general editorial salaries are skimpy. The Newspaper Guild's contract with the *Herald Tribune* got somewhat higher minimums, which, for lack of subsequent raises, also have become maximums for any number of the jobs.

Many graduates of the Ivy League colleges have been happy to go to work for the *Herald Tribune* at twenty-five dollars a week, and to take the rest out in glamour and prestige. The college man knows that if he writes moderately well his stories may carry his name on the pages of what is generally conceded to be a superior newspaper. Going on duty at noon, he can depart at six if he has finished his assignment, whereas his higher-paid *Times* colleague probably would be held until ten or eleven, just in case. Occasionally he may be asked to fill in at white-tie dinners at the Reid home. On the purely monetary side, he can take heart from the example of the numerous eminent writers in the Hollywood, Broadway, magazine and book fields who have put in stints at the *Herald Tribune*. The roster includes such stellar names as George S. Kaufman, J. P. Marquand, Joseph W. Alsop, Jr., Forrest Davis, Nunnally Johnson, St. Clair McKelway, John O'Hara, Alva Johnston, Boyden Sparkes, Ernest K. Lindley, and Deems Taylor.

The *Herald Tribune* has also been distinguished, editorially, for some curious style taboos, generally attributed to the feminine touch upstairs. The word "blood" could be used only in scientific articles, which led to such strange substitutions as "a stained coat found near the dead man" or "a sanguinary encounter." When Mrs. Whitelaw Reid died abroad in 1931, a difficulty in nicety of phrasing cropped up. Her daughter-in-law felt such words as "body" or "remains" were lacking in dignity. Subsequent obituary articles said Mrs. Whitelaw Reid had left a Riviera villa for Paris, had been put aboard a liner at Cherbourg, had arrived in New York, and so on. Obituary writers struggled with such circumlocutions until, a year or two later, the body of Texas Guinan arrived in New York from Vancouver, where the night-club hostess had died, and was met at the Pennsylvania Station by a group of friends who hadn't realized, from the delicate phraseology in the paper, that their favorite, instead of being a passenger, was moribund. Now "body" creeps into print, especially in cases of suicide.

When China's First Lady arrived last spring, she appeared in *Herald Tribune* columns as Madame Chiang Kai-shek. Someone called attention to the ruling against foreign titles; "Mrs." was hastily substituted until, readers roundly objecting to this indignity, the American spelling of "Madam" was adopted.

Helen Reid champions women for all jobs. Decidedly in favor of the compulsory drafting of women today, she says, "I'm glad to see women in industry. Their families will be the better for it. I want to see fathers back in the home, a more equal division of work and sharing of domestic responsibility."

News stories about women's achievements receive generous space in the *Herald Tribune;* so do women's professional societies and garden groups. Helen Reid mothered the *Herald Tribune* Home Institute, sponsor of the first experimental newspaper kitchen in America, which puts on career courses, food shows, and such, in an auditorium in the *Herald Tribune* building each winter.

In the *Herald Tribune* organization itself women hold down many positions which, on most other metropolitan dailies, are held by men. There have been woman promotion managers, women heading the travel-advertising department, and since 1926, *Books,* the Sunday literary supplement, has been edited by Mrs. Irita Van Doren. Adjoining Mrs. Reid's office is that of Mrs. Helen Leavitt, whose title is assistant advertising director, but whose job has become a combination of right-hand woman and official frightener of timid souls trying to get a word with Mrs. Reid. Their friendship dates from the suffragist campaign. When Mrs. Reid went into the *Tribune's* advertising department she convinced her friend that the *Tribune* was an even bigger crusade, and a life-long one. Mrs. Leavitt moved down from Albany, and has worked so faithfully for the cause that she is now a director of The New York Tribune, Inc.

Mrs. Reid is impatient with lack of ambition in any of the woman employees. If they raise families in addition to their work, it pleases her vastly. One of her phrases in inducing women to take on new jobs is, "Why not take a sporting chance with Fate?"

It is generally agreed that Mrs. Reid's annual Forum on Current Problems is one of the smartest newspaper-promotion stunts ever devised. It also serves to underscore Helen Reid's queenly stature. At this event she is the unobtrusive ringmaster for a dazzling galaxy of world notables. At last year's forum, 16,000 men and women elbowed their way into the five sessions in the Waldorf-Astoria ballroom, having come from forty-eight states, Alaska and Canada. This was only a nucleus of the total audience. Speeches were broadcast on all major coast-to-coast networks, translated into twenty-two foreign languages and rebroadcast by short wave all over the world. Franklin D. Roosevelt's speech closed the final session.

Helen Reid picks the subjects, plans each session of the entire forum, and goes out herself and gets the speakers she wants. In all this she hews to the creed she and her husband have now imposed on the *Herald Tribune's* editorial and news pages—that of "providing the public with arguments for and against a given subject or political candidate and letting the people make up their own minds." More Democrats may speak than Republicans. She is careful to lard significance with glamour. Her speaker lists include such names as Sir Stafford Cripps, Charles Boyer, James F. Byrnes, Clare Boothe Luce, Wendell Willkie, Robert Montgomery, and Queen Wilhelmina.

It is not by accident that the *Herald Tribune* has won several national awards for typographical excellence. It is Helen Reid's infinite capacity for detail finding expression again. She encouraged her husband to have stop-watch tests made of various type faces to find the one most quickly read and the one producing the least eyestrain. Their linotype machines are fed with a special metal formula which gives sharp clear edges. To make sure the quality remains constant, lead samples are analyzed weekly. The ink used is mixed with a special volatile ester which gives it its bright black finish.

With all this inexhaustible efficiency, she yet does not seem to rob the menfolks in her family of their masculinity or pride in doing things their way. Young Whitelaw sailed a forty-foot schooner across the Atlantic after he was graduated from Yale. Week ends he rode in steeplechase meets, and the rest of the week worked in blue jeans in the composing room. He was one of the paper's correspondents in London during the blitz days, and left to come home and take private flying lessons, so he could get into the Navy's ferry command.

When it comes to Christmas, birthdays and other present-giving times, the Reid men spend as much time hunting up surprises for Helen as another man spends on a helpless doll of a woman. Mr. Reid, who conceivably might telephone Tiffany's to send over a quart of diamonds, goes out combing the town to get just the muff he fancies for his wife, and for not one, not two, but five hats he's sure will be dashing on her. Last Christmas, Whitelaw decided he'd give his mother a lounging robe made like a Chinese dress. He searched the town over for Chinese silk in the particular shade of vermilion he knew she liked. Unable to get it, he retraced his steps, bought a length of white silk and made a round of dyeing establishments looking over color charts. He finally found the coveted shade on a railway poster, tore it down and took it triumphantly to a dyeing plant. That was only the halfway mark; after that, he tackled the job of finding a dressmaker in New York City who could whip up a Chinese gown.

Outside her immediate family, however, men look at this woman on the forum platform, contemplate the *Herald Tribune's* advertising totals and the achievements wrought with and on its pages, and feel Disraeli's remark about Queen Victoria is equally applicable to Helen Reid. They mutter it in awe, admiration and apprehension: "She's not a woman; she's an institution."

How to Get Your Name in Who's Who

(WHEELER SAMMONS)

By HENRY F. PRINGLE

EDITOR'S PREFACE.—There is no publication on the periphery of journalism in which there is more journalistic and other kinds of interest than *Who's Who in America*. It is the one reference work, with the possible exception of *The World Almanac* and encyclopedias, which is consulted more frequently by more writers in more places than any other. It is also the book about which the layman asks more questions than any other. How do you get your name in *Who's Who*? How much does it cost to get in? Do you write your own sketch? As the *Post* editors pointed out when Mr. Pringle's article first appeared, "you can't buy or chisel your way into the big red book; you have to be tapped for the honor." But this fact does not keep a lot of persons from trying none the less by devious routes to make the grade. Wheeler Sammons, fallible but honest arbiter of who belongs in *Who's Who*, could, as the *Post* editors said, "take bribes and retire to Tahiti, but his job is too much fun." Why? How? That is Mr. Pringle's story, and it has more adventure than one would at first associate with a publication such as *Who's Who*. This piece has the same enduring qualities as the book about which it is written, and the current *Who's Who* in 1947 celebrates its fiftieth year.

April 6, 1946

AMONG the 33,893 "notable living men and women" listed in the current edition of *Who's Who in America* is a gentleman, identified as an author, named Harold Edward Kelly. His address is given as 1928 West 102nd Street, Chicago.

Mr. Kelly, according to his biography, has had a colorful career. Born in Ireland in 1874, he has been a newsboy, type-

315

setter, editor and war correspondent. Among his published books are *The Wanderers in Darkest Africa, The Wanderers Sail Around the World,* and *Yellow versus White.*

Some 700 pages further along in this well-known reference book of current biography is a less vivid character, Alexander John Sargent, a mining engineer. He lives at 1504 Forest Avenue, Evanston, Illinois. The sketch about him says that he studied at the Massachusetts Institute of Technology, but does not give the date. Thereafter he studied in London, Paris and Berlin at unnamed institutions and practiced his profession with "various corporations."

Neither Author Kelly nor Engineer Sargent exists anywhere except thus in the otherwise solemn and factual pages of *Who's Who.* This has no relation to the unfortunate incident a few years back when the editors were appalled to learn that they had tapped a former convict for immortality. The fictitious pair are what Mr. Wheeler Sammons, now owner and publisher of *Who's Who,* has described as "burglar alarms." The Chicago addresses are real. Mail to either of them swiftly reaches Mr. Sammons or his staff. Thus he can spot phony sales or promotion schemes in which *Who's Who* is used as a mailing list. Even more important, he can keep tab on publishers of rival *Who's Who* volumes, honest and dishonest, who circularize his bona fide inmates for inclusion in regional volumes.

Scotching spurious Halls of Fame is a holy cause with Mr. Sammons, who is otherwise an extremely amiable grayhaired gentleman in his middle fifties. He has some reason to be concerned. A Who's Who of local residents has been published in almost every American city, sometimes for the sole purpose of selling copies to the citizens listed.

Who's-whoing is a popular form of book publishing, and it is highly specialized. A glance at the catalogue in the Library of Congress discloses the following more unusual and perfectly respectable volumes: *Who's Who in Jazz Collecting, Who's Who in Music and Dance in Southern California, Who's Who in Music and Dramatic Art in the Twin Cities, Minneapolis and St. Paul, Who's Who in Cocker Spaniels.*

The crooked publishers for whom Mr. Sammons is gunning might have been warned against soliciting Messrs. Kelly and Sargent if they had read the imaginative biographies more carefully. They would then have noted that Kelly, a newsboy at thirteen, was married to "Mabel Alice Rankin" in 1889— which would have made the happy groom a mere fifteen. They might have been made suspicious, too, by the vagueness surrounding Sargent's education and corporate connections. But the "burglar alarms" have been of great assistance to Mr. Sammons in litigation against publishers infringing on his rights. Doubtless others, about which he obviously says nothing, lurk in the 7200 columns of closely packed type. No imaginary cocker spaniels, though.

Mr. Sammons' zeal in prosecuting imitators may be a touch illogical. Albert N. Marquis, who published the first edition of *Who's Who in America* back in 1899, baldly lifted the title from the English work, *Who's Who.* But on the eve of the fiftieth anniversary of the founding of the company, no doubt exists that this is the outstanding reference work on living Americans, and on foreigners, relatively small in number, of interest in this country. It is far from perfect, but the system of selecting names now used is vastly better than the hit-or-miss procedure of the old days. Mr. Marquis ran the book rather like a club of which he was a one-man committee on admissions. Most of the suggestions for membership came from people already elected.

Mr. Sammons and his staff have substituted two main standards. The first is "prominence in creditable lines of effort." The second consists of public officials, heads of certain private organizations, Army and Navy officers who attain stated ranks, and leading churchmen. Inclusion through the second standard is arbitrary, and this is one of the weaknesses of *Who's Who.* All members of Congress are listed, but are bounced if defeated unless they have other claims to distinction. Ambas-

sadors and ministers plenipotentiary are automatically elevated. But so are the heads of all Federal Government departments, even the heads of bureaus within departments. So are
the attorneys general of all the states—many of them non-
entities or political hacks. Others included by rote are Federal
judges and judges of the highest state courts.

Who's Who lists too many obscure officeholders, ministers
and educators. It has a goodly number of men, and women,
too, whose principal claim to fame is that they have joined
innumerable organizations. Mr. Sammons has labored dili-
gently to draw up categories by which admissions are judged,
but mere size is often the principal factor. If a company is
capitalized at five million dollars or more, for example, its
president goes into *Who's Who*. So do comparable bankers.
The presidents of all colleges with endowments of two million
dollars are automatically listed. So are deans if the endowment
is five million dollars and there are at least one thousand
students. Similar categories include also superintendents of
schools in the twenty-five largest cities, presidents of state
normal schools, head librarians in cities of over three hundred
thousand, and many such types.

The chief weakness of *Who's Who*, probably, lies in its
method of selecting painters, sculptors and writers. The editors
keep reiterating that the people in *Who's Who* are not necessarily the best in their field; they are merely the best known.
Yet they frequently fail, even by this standard. Specialists in
all fields including medicine—their identities are closely
guarded—are called upon for advice. Among the ones who
have given it in the past are Henry L. Mencken and the late
Hendrik van Loon. Librarians, who usually know all the dirt
in their communities, are consulted. But the main reliance is
upon such public awards as the Pulitzer prizes, elevation to
academies, and quantity rather than quality production. The
pedant who does a two-volume work on ichthyology is fairly
certain to get in.

The integrity, if not the infallibility of its editors, of *Who's
Who in America* is unassailable. Not long ago some deluded

egocentric sent in an application with a $100 bill attached to it. Mr. Marquis, the founder, once received a letter saying that $2500 in securities would quietly be transferred to his account in return for a write-up. No sketch has ever been paid for, of course, and buying a copy means nothing, either. Social, political or business pressures caused Mr. Marquis, a gentleman of the old school, to make rejections forthwith. Mr. Sammons gets more amused than angry. He likes to tell about a lecturer, probably a mental case, who invented learned societies and had stationery printed on which these extolled his accomplishments. The present publisher of *Who's Who* finds entertainment in the foibles and vanities of his fellowmen, about which he knows a great deal.

"One very prominent American," he confides, "wired us to hold his sketch for revision—he'd just been elected a member of the National Geographic Society."

On occasion, as law-abiding citizens sometimes do, Mr. Sammons indulges in mild criminal ponderings. He estimates that he could clear a million dollars at least on each of two crooked editions and then rapidly retire to Tahiti.

However, his temptations are slight indeed. A. N. Marquis Company is not incorporated, but is a partnership, wholly owned by Mr. and Mrs. Sammons. An edition of *Who's Who*, published every two years, runs to more than 60,000 copies. Reliable estimates put the cost, exclusive of overhead, at about $250,000 per volume. If the net revenue to the company— after selling costs are deducted—is $7.50 per copy, and it is possibly more than that, the take is $450,000 per biennium.

The A. N. Marquis Company also publishes a *Who's Who in Commerce and Industry,* a directory of medical specialists and several of the regional and city volumes which Mr. Sammons views with a fishy eye when brought out by other concerns. *Who Was Who in America,* first published in 1943, reprints unchanged the biographies of nonliving Americans published from 1897 to 1942, and will be brought up to date from time to time. Mr. Sammons is planning a book to be called *Who Knows—the Book of Authorities,* which will attempt the staggering job of listing all the specialists in all fields of endeavor in the United States.

Some of the material for this rests in the *Who's Who in America* archives. When the War Department faced the necessity of running the railroads in Persia and appealed to Sammons for an expert, he readily turned up a man who had long known all about the subject. Most of the material for the book of experts will come, however, from a monthly supplement to *Who's Who* which was started five years ago. This lists people currently in the public eye and gives brief sketches about them. The supplement is much broader in scope than the parent, biennial volume. Being nominated for it in no way assures inclusion in *Who's Who*.

Compiling biographies of hundreds of thousands of famous folk, living or dead or temporary, might seem a degree confining, if not downright crushing, to creative spirits. No frustrations are discernible at the *Who's Who* Building on East Ohio Street in Chicago, though. It is a small organization of about forty full-time employees. To them should be added a dozen or more outside writers familiar with the strange jargon and abbreviations which mark the undeviating style of the books. They are the world's most anonymous biographers.

Mr. Sammons has the final word and is the supreme arbiter on the exclusion of dubious celebrities. His son, Wheeler Sammons, Jr., specializes in revising the categories which are the main basis for new names. Fred Ek is managing editor; Mrs. Joyce Teskey, an extremely pretty girl, is a kind of all-around handy man who knows everything about the business. Mr. Sammons leans heavily on her and on Charles Walker, the general manager, who spends most of his time these days sadly informing people that Volume 23 has long been out of print and that Volume 24 won't be ready until spring.

The growth of the war government brought astonishing demands from Washington for copies; no Government press agent, obviously, could carry on without the big red book at his elbow. Only a fraction of the Government orders were filled. The edition was already exhausted when a War Department demand for two thousand copies for overseas came in. Sammons was puzzling over their possible use one day when his telephone rang. A colonel in Jersey City said that he had been notified that there were no copies. But the order for them, he barked, had come "from the field!" Sammons protested mildly that none was left.

"Would you deny our boys at the front!" the colonel demanded.

The head of *Who's Who* had occasional qualms when he thought of G. I. Joe yearning for a copy of *Who's Who* in some foxhole. It later developed that Army public-relations officers desperately needed *Who's Who* as a guide in rating Very Important Persons who passed through their domains. The 2000 copies, however, simply were not to be had. But such crises, military or other, are rare at the A. N. Marquis Company. When the founder of *Who's Who* died in 1943, the Baltimore *Sun* took editorial note of how happy had been his lot.

"Celebrated authors who could command fancy prices per word," it said, "gladly gave him all he sought and, if they complained at all, complained only that he would not take more."

By attempting to standardize the selection of names, and in other ways, the Sammons regime has increased the efficiency of the company, but some of the old flavor lingers on. Aside from his interest in *Who's Who,* which overshadowed everything else, Marquis was devoted to the church, the Republican Party, American genealogy, and campaigns against cigarettes. Many an obscure preacher is still glorified in *Who's Who* merely because old Mr. Marquis regarded him as worthy. Today Sammons and his staff struggle against the knowledge that a good many such old gentlemen, including a number of educators, should be eliminated as no longer of interest to anybody. But they haven't the heart; anyway, the antiques will soon pass on.

Mr. Marquis, who had been a small Chicago publisher, held sternly to his conviction that no individual of uncertain morals could be listed. So he barred, for years, a world-renowned architect who had been married several times. The founder was not always consistent, on the other hand. Lillian Russell, then a beauty of thirty-eight, was allowed to name in Volume 1 all the gentlemen to whom she had been married, even to add flippantly, "divorced from all three."

Volume I had only 8602 names and 840 pages, including a few college and publishers' advertisements. In a preface, Marquis admitted that the book's name came from the British *Who's Who,* but added that he had made many improvements. This was true. The British edition was, in 1899, much more of a bluebook, naming the socially elite, and without much biographical data. Marquis selected his worthies as best he could and sent them questionnaires on which he based the sketches.

The question of age was a baffler from the start and has not been wholly solved yet. Men as well as women balked stubbornly at telling the truth, and they still do. Maude Adams, appearing in Volume 1, was among the exceptions. She said then she was born in 1872 and gives the same date in Volume 23. But Charles Francis Adams, the historian, reported in the first edition that he was born in 1833. By Volume 3 he claimed 1835, and is so listed in the official histories today. Elbert H. Gary, of the United States Steel Corporation, admitted in Volume 1 that he was born in 1846. In the 1926–27 edition he wrote only "b. on father's farm." In Volume 10 Andrew Mellon, who would become Secretary of the Treasury, said he was born in 1852. Four years later he claimed 1854, and six years after that insisted that he was born in 1855.

This was distinctly embarrassing to A. N. Marquis. In Volume 3—the book had grown to 1800 pages with 14,443 sketches —he presented a statistical study of the ages of his flock. The average of the men, this showed, was 53.38 years; that of the women, 50.57. But these statistics, Mr. Marquis mourned, would be more accurate if 29.46 per cent of the women and 2.35 per cent of the men had not concealed their ages.

He noted that the girls were more culpable than the men and concluded that, although men offended too, it was a primary female trait. Then he decided to forget the matter because it was insoluble. In the 1908–09 edition he noted that a controversy had arisen during the 1904 Presidential campaign over the true age of Judge Alton B. Parker, the Democratic candidate. It had ben settled, he remarked, by reference to *Who's Who.*

"Always data may be relied upon," said Mr. Marquis smugly, "which are gained, as in this publication, directly from the fountainheads."

By now *Who's Who* was a publishing success. Mr. Marquis, by all standards, including his own, was fully qualified for listing. But he waited for years, then modesty fell before a natural yearning. He included himself. He told how he had been born in Brown County, Ohio, had been left an orphan, had worked in a country store and had achieved eminence. But he failed to specify, by day, year or month, when he had been born.

The fact is that the autobiographical data in *Who's Who* are checked only rarely. Philip Musica, the fantastic ex-convict who assumed the name of F. Donald Coster and became head of McKesson and Robbins, the drug house, automatically qualified as a big corporation executive. He filled out the usual questionnaire, giving imaginary facts on his birth, education and career. These were published just as he submitted them. At that, Musica fooled the entire drug industry, the press and the financial world until his exposure, arrest and suicide in December, 1938.

Mr. Marquis, who continued as editor and as an adviser long after selling the company, would tolerate no flippancies after Miss Russell's matrimonial one. One day at a Chicago club his successor as owner of *Who's Who* met Orlando Clinton Harn, counsel to the Audit Bureau of Circulations, the agency which audits and verifies magazine and newspaper circulations. Mr. Harn delicately worked the conversation around to *Who's Who.* He had once been approached and had filled out all the forms, he said. But nothing had happened.

Returning to his office, Sammons looked up the papers and found "Disapproved, A.N.M." written across Harn's sketch. He stepped into the Marquis sanctum and asked why this had been done. Harn was a prominent Chicagoan, wholly eligible. Old Marquis studied the attached biographical sketch carefully and handed it back.

"See!" he said severely. "Mr. Harn gives his wife's name as Merry Christmas. Rubbish!"

But Mrs. Harn's maiden name had, indeed, been Merry Christmas Williams. Mr. Harn was immediately put into the book and dwells happily there today.

Mr. Marquis' own sketch—if birthdayless—is as modest as any in all the volumes of *Who's Who*. So was his life. He had a small office on the south side of Chicago, a solitary elderly assistant and a clerk or two. He drew, for himself, only $3600 a year. After the first volume or two had appeared, the relationship of the publisher to his "biographees," as he called them, grew very close. The prefaces in each volume took on the flavor of a pastoral from a benign cleric.

He told his readers about the "amusing incidents" in the day's work, of the "grotesque side views of various idiosyncrasies" it afforded. Several actors, Mr. Marquis chuckled, "asked to have extracts from especially favorable press notices appended to their sketches." He also told with gentle pleasure about "one gentleman of distinguished antebellum record" who mailed in an autobiographical installment of eight thousand words which carried his history up to the Mexican War. Further installments of equal length were promised, and received.

A few years later Mr. Marquis concluded that *Who's Who* was much more than a reference work for librarians and for obituary editors trying frantically to make a dead line. It was, he felt, an influence for good in America, and he concluded all of his pastoral letters as follows:

> Many deeds of noble and beneficent achievement are recorded in these life histories; and here also are chronicled thousands of activities which might be emulated with profit, not only by the youth of the country, but by all classes of American citizenship.

By 1926 Mr. Marquis began to worry over the fate of *Who's Who* in the event of his death. He was seventy-one. He was terrified over the chance that his cherished book might get into unscrupulous hands, so he arranged to sell it to a reputable Eastern publishing house. At this time Wheeler Sammons was president of the A. W. Shaw Co., of Chicago, publishers of business magazines. He heard about the pending deal, realized that this meant Chicago would lose *Who's Who,* and called on Mr. Marquis. Considerable argument convinced the father of *Who's Who* that he could entrust his child to Sammons. A down payment of $150,000 was made. Mr. Sammons was about to install his staff when Mrs. Marquis called on him.

"Albert will die," she said, "unless he keeps on editing *Who's Who.*"

So he was installed as a kind of editor emeritus and puttered about happily for an additional seventeen years.

Like his predecessor, Mr. Sammons gets a grandstand seat at the parade of human peculiarities. Outside nominations for *Who's Who* have much less weight than in the old days. But letters of recommendation are still carefully read. The publisher of *Who's Who* noted a few years ago that members of the medical profession were the most frequent subjects of such communications. He discovered that the American who had just been operated upon was inclined to regard his doctor as the best in the world and impulsively sent his name to *Who's Who.* New mothers similarly sought to reward their obstetricians. Sammons has also learned that people will never fully understand that innate virtue, unrelated to national prominence, does not in itself qualify for admission.

"You are most remiss," said a rebuking letter from a judge in a small Oklahoma town, "in not listing the owner of our bookstore. She has done more to advance reading in our community than anybody else."

Mr. Sammons is amused when his staff must occasionally cut sketches. Authors will sometimes list every article they have written. Poets will name every poem. Actors will list every

part. Yet cuts are infrequent. For many years Samuel Unter-
myer, the New York lawyer, was the champion for length, with
Pres. Nicholas Murray Butler, of Columbia, a close second.
On Untermyer's death, Doctor Butler wore the crown. But to-
day Thomas J. Watson of the International Business Machines
Corporation, is well in front.

Being a businessman, Mr. Sammons regards *Who's Who in
America* and his other publications as a business proposition.
He keeps faith with Marquis' scrupulous honesty, of course.
But he enlarges *Who's Who* as much as this will permit. Athletes are now listed if they appear to have some degree of lasting reputation. Sammons bars nobody because of his private
life. But any biographee who lands in prison is promptly ban-
ished and does not even appear in *Who Was Who*.

Mr. Marquis, with his single editorial assistant, had been
content to obtain new names by reading the newspapers and
considering recommendations. Sammons, with an eye on his
growing circulation, watches all possible sources for candidates. He knows that about 20 per cent of those in the book—
mostly new names—will buy a copy. But this is a minor consideration. He wants *Who's Who* to be so complete that every
library and every newspaper will buy at least one copy.

He was, in consequence, mildly irritated when Volume 23
went to press without a biography of Marshal Stalin. Requests
for the necessary data remained unanswered by the Soviet Embassy. Mr. Sammons, on a trip to Washington, decided to try,
himself. He telephoned the embassy and was told to call a second number. At this, a pleasant Russian voice suggested that
the owner of *Who's Who* should present himself in person.
The address given was not the embassy; it was in the remote
outskirts of Washington. Sammons and his taxi driver found it
after prolonged difficulty. The attaché who received him appeared to know all about *Who's Who,* however. He agreed
that the Marshal should be listed.

"You will be able to get me the material, then?" Sammons
asked.

The Soviet official looked a little surprised. "You don't seem to know what this place is," he said. "This is the Soviet listening post. We are in direct, two-way radio communication with Moscow."

The necessary facts about Uncle Joe reached Chicago a day or two later, and he will be written up in Volume 24, now on the presses. The run will be in excess of 60,000. But this will be small, compared with future editions of *Who's Who in America,* if what might seem a fantastic idea of its publisher takes concrete shape. Just before the war, on a trip to Europe, Sammons was told by his London banker that they often used the book to establish the identity of Americans seeking to cash checks.

"If they say they're in *Who's Who,*" the banker said, "we ask them to give added facts which would be in the sketch. Then we look it up."

Sammons was stunned by the idea which then hit him. He went to Lloyds and asked whether it was conceivable that any member would consider the idea of insuring checks written by Americans listed in *Who's Who.* To his considerable surprise, he was told that it probably could be arranged, even that the cost would not be great. The war halted a tentative offer by Lloyds to insure the checks of everybody in *Who's Who,* whoever and wherever they may be, for a premium of about five thousand dollars a year. A ceiling will be placed on the amount of the checks, of course, but it will easily allow any traveling American of sufficient distinction to obtain adequate funds anywhere in the world. He will no longer need to carry a letter of credit or buy travelers' checks. Now that the war is over, Mr. Sammons can't wait to resume negotiations with Lloyds. He has visions of copies of *Who's Who* in every hotel on earth, at every ship and railroad ticket office.

For the first time, except possibly to ladies'-club lecturers and college professors, it will be worth real cash to dwell among the great.

Bible of Baseball

(TAYLOR SPINK)

By STANLEY FRANK

EDITOR'S PREFACE.—This article is about *The Sporting News* and its editor, Taylor Spink. It is interesting and worth while not only for what it reveals about this particular publication and its editor, but as a commentary on a type of publication which is much more extensive than many realize.

The Sporting News is a specialized publication, of which there are some six thousand in this country (whereas there are less than two thousand daily newspapers and only some two hundred general magazines). The magnitude of the trade journalism field is a fact which comes in the nature of a discovery, even to veteran newspaper men and to students of journalism. Some express no little amazement when told that for every letter in the alphabet, or for every trade, profession, or hobby, there are literally dozens and scores of publications, largely unknown to all but those whose vocations or avocations bring them in touch with such magazines. To pick a few figures at random, a recent N. W. Ayer and Son *Directory* reveals that there are 751 religious journals, 463 agricultural, 230 educational, 285 devoted to the interests of labor, 118 legal, 229 concerned with automobiles and accessories, 94 grocery and general merchandise, 63 medicine, 189 medicine and surgery, 89 railroad, etc. Some of these exert an influence far out of proportion to their circulations or prominence (or should it be *obscurity?*). Morris Fishbein and the *Journal of the American Medical Association* would be a case in point. The cocker spaniel editor of *Dog World* or the collie editor of *Dog News* would be another. And Mr. Spink and *The Sporting News* are yet another.

Readers of specialized publications are a selected circulation. They have a common interest. They speak a common language. They read their publications under the best possible circumstances—in the office, at home, on the train and with the concentration that grows out of genuine interest. Little wonder, therefore, that the editors of the *Post* chose *Bible* as the key word for the title to this piece. There is something approximating religious devotion to the publication among the 100,000 baseball loving Americans—players, executives, scouts, and fans—who every Tuesday put fifteen cents on the barrel head for the new issue which they devour with absorption down to the last comma, and which, for many, is the only reading-matter, other than the newspaper, that they ever see. In the language of the *Post* editors—

"Wrapped in the history of *The Sporting News* is the saga of our national game—its punks, its heroes, its loyal fans. Taylor Spink is its bellowing Boswell, Mr. Baseball himself."

June 20, 1942

IT SOUNDS screwy today, but in 1885 the St. Louis Browns actually won a pennant. This was in the old American Association, and it was a warm summer, with the beer and *Schmierkäse* gardens doing a heavy business. Gaseous praises to Manager Charlie Comiskey's heroes rose from stein-laden tables as the fans debated how to capitalize culturally on the new eminence that had come to the brewing capital. Only one citizen did anything constructive, a fellow named Al Spink, who was a sports and theatrical promoter. In 1886, as the second season of glory got under way, Spink began publication of something called *The Sporting News*. With the new paper hobbling along obscurely, the Browns that season won the pennant a second time, taking the postseason interleague duel from the Chicago National League team, and in 1887 and 1888 ran their pennant string to four in a row.

When the American League opened in 1901, the Browns graduated to it, and since 1888 the only honor they have acquired has been a negative one—they are the only club in either circuit which has never won a major-league pennant. *The Sporting News* proved to be of tougher stuff. Its circulation spread beyond the confines of the beer barony and in

time it became the national paper of baseball. It has come
down to our own era a solid and unique weekly of full newspaper size, a bible and handbook of the great American game
and an institution rivaling in power that of Judge Landis
himself.

Throughout its fifty-six-year career, *The Sporting News* has
been strictly a Spink family enterprise. The present publisher,
J. G. Taylor Spink, is a nephew of the founder. Born when
The Sporting News was in its second year, Spink today is an
energetic, plumpish, bull-voiced man of excellent digestion,
and his furious labors in behalf of his favorite sport have
earned for him the nickname of Mr. Baseball, a tag he likes
so well he will probably have it chiseled on his tombstone.
Spink is the game's unofficial conscience, historian, watchdog,
and worshiper; and, happily, he has made a nice piece of
change in these public-spirited roles. The fans begrudge him
this no more than they begrudged Babe Ruth the immense income he got from the diamond.

To fix Spink's true position in the baseball cosmos, it is
necessary first to comprehend the scope of *The Sporting News'*
truly remarkable influence. Every Thursday more than 100,000
fans pay fifteen cents for its latest number.

Although its sixteen pages are awesome masses of fine type
containing up to 100,000 English and semi-English words, *The
Sporting News* is devoured by the fans with religious absorption, down to the last comma. Players read it for ammunition
which can be used on the firing line when the dugout jockeys
are unloading. Baseball executives watch it for trends. Managers and scouts study it to trace the progress of rookies in the
deepest bush. It is the only organ that carries percentages, box
scores and weekly reviews of every team in every loop from
the Class D, leaky-roof leagues, with their sixty-five-dollars-a-
month salary limit, to the plushy majors. For a great many
baseball-loving Americans, *The Sporting News* is their only
extracurricular reading material.

Before the present war, *The Sporting News* was sold in virtually every foreign land, with Japan and, surprisingly, South Africa, among the larger overseas centers of distribution.

Despite the loss of its foreign market due to the war, *The Sporting News* sends more copies abroad than ever. Virtually every convoy carries copies of *The Sporting News* which are handed out, free, among the members of the A.E.F.'s. Spink and the major-league club owners share the cost. In the same way, servicemen still in this country get their *Sporting Newses*. *The Sporting News* is a prime morale booster for men cut off from their beloved ball parks.

With Spink this is a sentimental as well as a patriotic gesture, since the first World War saved his baby when it was close to failure. Baseball was classified as a nonessential occupation, and interest in the game dwindled. Circulation fell off to 5000 copies. In France, Capt. Tillinghast L'Hommedieu Huston, co-owner of the Yankees, saw that the boys were starved for baseball news, and he persuaded the American League to buy 150,000 copies of *The Sporting News* for free distribution. It proved to be the most popular publication in the A.E.F., except for *The Stars and Stripes,* even outdrawing *La Vie Parisienne.*

The Spink masterpiece never backs away from a crusade, and in 1890 the National League, annoyed by the fledgling paper's militant sniping and fearless exposure of "the interests," attempted to break the Spinks by bank-rolling an opposition sheet, *The Sporting Times.* The venture cost the league a young fortune, and the *Times,* like all other competitors of the Spinks, folded quickly. Today the National and American Leagues would dip into the sinking fund to subsidize Spink, in the extremely unlikely event he should need assistance. The owners recognize the value of *The Sporting News* in promoting the game, sustaining interest during the off season and, above all, as a barometer of cash-customer opinion. *Sporting News* readers are inveterate letter writers and devoted partisans, and Spink editorially reflects their anxiety for the welfare of the game.

Last winter, Ted Williams' application for draft deferment threatened to start a cause *célèbre* that might have ruined the good will acquired by professional baseball during the course of a century. Before Spink could get an editorial into print on the Williams case, he received more than 300 letters from fans defending Williams' right to appeal for deferment. This flood of unsolicited letters was the earliest and most encouraging assurance given the club owners that they would not have to suspend operations for the duration of the war.

Although Spink is the big shot of the sports publishing business, he counts a sixteen-hour trick a normal working day. For years he has opened up his office at Tenth and Olive streets in St. Louis at seven o'clock, seven days a week. When he is not on the road drumming up advertising or plugging a scheme to promote baseball, he reads every line of the galley proofs and struggles with the composition of gaggy, breezy headlines. They are his particular pride and joy, and the punnier they are the louder he laughs at them.

Like most old-time baseball men, Spink has a passion for accuracy. He loathes sloppy reporting and will drop everything to track down the score, date, pitchers and circumstances of ball games played forty years ago.

It has been suggested to Spink that the customers would derive more pleasure from *The Sporting News* if the paper were sprinkled carefully with factual errors. Dyed-in-the-wool fans are statistical hounds who dearly love to catch the experts in a bobble, but Spink seldom gives them the opportunity.

The most indefatigable user of the telephone and telegraph since Ziegfield, Spink thinks nothing of phoning his correspondents in San Francisco or New York when he rises at five A.M., just to pass the time of night. He seems unable to understand why the party at the other end of the line is not on top of the ball and ready to greet the new day with an idea for the ages. It is not unusual for him to send one man six wires a day, adding up to a thousand words. The tenor of his remarks ordinarily can be confined to five words: How's your local club doing? Spink's telegraph toll runs to about $10,000 a year and his telephone bill averages $6500. Western Union long ago installed a branch office at *The Sporting News* in order to have some messenger boys available for other duties in Greater St. Louis.

Spink's brief vacations from baseball always find him in a sporting atmosphere. He likes to invest an occasional two bucks on a horse race, to scout the talent in the night clubs and to cut up old touches with the mob, but in general he has a constitutional inability to relax in anything but work. In addition to his duties as publisher, salesman and bright-idea man for the paper, he writes two long columns a week under the titles of "Looping the Loops" and "Three and One." In his spare time he appears on the radio—on the average of twice a week during the season—and writes the scripts for three other fifteen-minute broadcasts which are furnished free to 250 stations throughout the country.

The Sporting News is not Spink's only enterprise. He publishes the *Sporting Goods Dealer,* a monthly magazine for the trade; the official record book, formerly issued by the Reach and Spalding companies; the *Baseball Register,* an elaborate compendium of the records of current players and old stars; and *The Sporting News Dope Book.* He has printed scores of pamphlets on how to play the various positions, how to bat and how to score, as well as booklets containing biographical sketches and a welter of valuable historical data on baseball.

The chief characteristic of a volume issued under the Spink imprimatur is its size. A Spink opus expands with each successive issue until it can serve splendidly as the doorstop for a bank vault. If a competing firm puts out a product rivaling a Spink publication in heft, he sees to it that his next edition tops it in the number of pages and wordage. His first *Baseball Register,* in 1940, carried 224 pages; this year it has 288 pages and has sold 100,000 at one dollar the copy. The official record book is a 588-page affair and has fractured all previous records with a circulation of half a million.

The staggering impact of Spink's weight-by-pound baseball literature has led people to suspect it is a manifestation of an

inferiority complex springing from his short stature. The amateur psychologists don't know Spink, who is completely without inhibitions, or the fans' insatiable appetite for figures and
words in bulk. Spink was the first to discover that you can
choke a horse, but never a baseball fan.

He must be right, for *The Sporting News* is the only non-
fiction periodical devoted exclusively to sports, apart from racing sheets, that has ever made important money. It has survived
longer than any other straight sport publication, and it dominates the field so completely that no attempt to invade the
lucrative territory has been made in a quarter of a century.

A typical Spink service that helps to promote baseball interest is the awarding of fifteen trophies to the most valuable
players in the various leagues. Years ago, before he took it over,
much wire pulling verging on scandal was mixed up with the
designation, and for a time it was abandoned.

During the 1920's each league had a rather hit-and-miss system for selecting the outstanding players. In 1930 *The Sporting News,* in conjunction with the baseball writers, took over
the Most Valuable Player award and put an abrupt end to
suspicions of skulduggery.

The Sporting News started off as a combination sports and
theatrical paper. It was the second publication that gave the
up-and-coming game more than casual attention, a paper called
Sporting Life having preceded it by three years.

Uncle Al, the founder, was an inveterate promoter, and in
his zeal to get rich in a hurry he ignored the one potential
meal ticket he had ever launched, and rushed to establish the
St. Louis *World,* a daily newspaper that rolled over and played
dead dog after a year and a half. He also organized the South
Side race track and made the first attempt to popularize night
racing. The ruination of Uncle Al, however, was a misbegotten
inspiration which prompted him to write *The Derby Winner,*
a throbbing melodrama of the race track. It was a turkey by
any standard and even the home town gave it a lukewarm
reception.

But, fascinated by the glamour of the theater, Al decided

to take his epic on tour. Unable to leave the struggling *Sporting News* high and dry, Al offered his younger brother, Charlie —Taylor's father—fifty dollars a week to become business manager of the paper. Charlie, who was then homesteading in the Dakotas, blew a kiss to the prairie dogs and took a train for St. Louis. Al met Charlie at the station and promptly promoted a ten-dollar touch from him with which to celebrate the partnership at the best restaurant in town. The playwright then took his production on the road, and it proceeded to splatter omelets over the surrounding countryside.

The Sporting News was no howler either. Its subsequent growth was due to Charlie's acumen. From the beginning, Charlie perceived that *The Sporting News* could survive only as a straight baseball paper. He dropped the racing, boxing and theatrical news and threw out the patent-medicine ads. The paper plucked feebly at the coverlet and circulation fell below 3000 a week. Baseball was gaining in popularity, but it was regarded as a disreputable, back-alley form of entertainment frequented only by low, coarse characters. It was impossible to get advertising, and more than once Charlie Spink's diamond ring was hocked to meet the paper's slim pay roll.

The future looked dark, but Spink was determined to make the paper go—possibly to avoid a return to homesteading— and he did it in a tried old journalistic way—by attacking "the interests." His first target was Chris Von der Ahe, the president of the Browns, who was then baseball's most powerful figure as a result of his club's great showing in the 1880's. Von der Ahe was a vaudeville-type burgher, who liked to speak of himself as "der poss bresident," and his love for baseball seemed to stem largely from an intense desire to sell lots of beer. Von der Ahe owned a saloon on the North Side, and when Sportsman's Park was built he saw to it that it was located near his establishment. The fans, after paying at the turnstile to cheer his team, flocked to his saloon to slake their thirsts, to celebrate the victory or to drown the memory of a defeat. Von der Ahe pulled considerable political weight locally and it seemed suicidal when Charlie Spink took out after him. But *The Sport-*

ing News chased Von der Ahe out of baseball, then ran a benefit for him which raised $6000. During his happier days, Von der Ahe had taken care that posterity would not forget him by having a life-size statue of himself, in frock coat and statesmanlike pose, hewn out of marble. The image of der poss bresident still adorns his grave in Bellefontaine Cemetery.

Charlie Spink next turned to a campaign against syndicate baseball, or control of more than one team in a league by the same individual. This was a pernicious evil, and Spink alone realized it had to be stamped out if the game was ever to gain the confidence of the public.

The success of these crusades, combined with the changing nature of baseball, helped to consolidate the paper's position. Circulation rose slowly but steadily, and baseball men were beginning to recognize *The Sporting News* as the clearinghouse for authentic news of the business.

For a time, the paper served as an intermediary between players and owners, but ceased to do so after a harrowing experience with Mike Donlin, who had been plugged extravagantly by the Pacific Coast operative. Stanley Robison, owner of the Cardinals, asked Spink to arrange for a state signing of Donlin in St. Louis after the conclusion of the season. Donlin came on from the Coast, made a grand entrance into *The Sporting News* office, observed the pictures of famous players on the walls and flew into a terrible rage.

"Where the hell is my picture?" he cried dramatically.

Donlin deigned to favor St. Louis with his presence after the signing and Charlie Spink more or less adopted him as a protégé. The relationship was hurriedly disavowed when Donlin, filled with Christmas cheer, playfully set fire to an elderly citizen's whiskers in a public place. A bystander, who resented Donlin's sense of humor, pulled a knife and inflicted a permanent scar upon the fun-loving fellow. Donlin was an actor at heart and later became one.

The Sporting News was catching on with the public, yet as late as 1896 Charlie Spink was doing odd jobs around Brother Al's South Side race track to make ends meet. His connection with racing terminated only when the St. Louis cyclone of '96 leveled the track. And then Charlie went overboard for the radical idea put forward by a newspaperman from Cincinnati who was to make baseball and its bible big business.

That man was Ban Johnson, the founder of the American League and the moving spirit in the game until he was superseded by Judge Landis. They laughed when Johnson sat down and tried to prove that baseball was ready for a second major league. They smiled indulgently when Johnson got up and went out to raise financial backing for eight teams which were to compete against the well-established National League.

Johnson organized his league, forced the haughty Nationals to meet his champions in a post-season set of games which, as the World Series, was to become America's premier sporting event. He lived to see his ridiculed scheme surpass the National League in popularity, and *The Sporting News* was an indispensable weapon of support. Johnson always acknowledged his debt to the Spinks, admitting he would have been unable to establish the American League if the paper had not been on his side.

The Sporting News' prestige was given tremendous impetus when the warring factions asked Editor Flanner to write the national agreement, the pact which ended the war and served as the foundation of organized baseball as it is known today. This historic document was set in type by hand in the Spink composing room and submitted to Harry Pulliam, president of the National League. Pulliam was so impressed with its fairness that Flanner's document was adopted without a change.

An aftermath of the bitter struggle, almost as enduring as the American League itself, was the friendship between Johnson and the Spinks. In the case of Taylor Spink, it practically amounted to idolatry. It was only recently that Taylor broke down and confessed that Judge Landis, rather than Johnson, was the first-ranking benefactor of baseball, and he still feels uncomfortable about it, as though he has betrayed a sacred trust or something. Spink refuses to make appointments which will prevent him from going to Spencer, Indiana, on March twenty-eighth each year to lay a wreath on the grave of Johnson, who died in 1931. His son, now in the Coast Guard, was christened Charles C. Johnson Spink, but the only name by which he ever has been called by his father is Johnson. In important issues of editorial policy, Spink tries to shape his course in accordance with Ban Johnson's ideas and philosophy.

Taylor was twenty when he went to work alongside his father on *The Sporting News*. He had left high school in his second year to take a job sweeping out a local sporting-goods store and then, through his father's influence, had got a place on the St. Louis *Post-Dispatch* sports staff. When a *Sporting News* office boy resigned, Taylor quit the *Post-Dispatch* and took his place.

He was an office boy with unusually exalted ideas which, at the time, encompassed a broader world than the family property. One day he sent a telegram to Ban Johnson asking to be appointed official scorer for the 1910 World Series. Every baseball writer in the country wanted the plum, and our hero, who was only twenty-one, had never scored a game in his life, but that did not deter him. He bombarded Johnson with so many telegrams that the league president gave him the assignment in self-defense.

That was the beginning of Taylor's passion for telegrams and his worshipful admiration of Johnson. Just for the record, he was so satisfactory as a scorer that he held the post for eight years, when he voluntarily withdrew to give a baseball writer a crack at the fee which went with it.

At about the same time Taylor was making Johnson's life miserable with wires, Charlie Spink was shopping for an editor to succeed old Joe Flanner, who was resigning to accept an important position with the National Commission. In September, 1910, on Hugh Fullerton's recommendation, Spink hired a solemn young baseball writer out of Chicago. The new editor lasted less than a year, but while he was with *The Sporting News* he gave his first evidence of possessing a talent which was to make an imperishable contribution to American letters.

The solemn, sometimes morose editor was Ring Lardner.

He never was particularly happy working for Charlie Spink; he chafed under the confinement of handling copy and he missed the excitement of the daily baseball beat. Taylor, who was familiar with the editor's work as a traveling correspondent with the Chicago teams, suggested that Lardner do a series of humorous articles dealing with the off-field activities of ballplayers. Lardner wrote the series under the heading of "Pullman Pastimes." This was the genesis of the "You Know Me, Al" yarns which established Lardner as a master of the short story.

Strangely, nobody but Taylor Spink and a few baseball writers thought Lardner's stuff was good at that time. There was increasing friction between Charlie Spink and his editor, and Lardner quit to take a job in Boston.

During Lardner's regime the paper slumped badly, but Taylor believed that the publisher, not the editor, was at fault. He agitated for a drastic reorganization of the paper, and Charlie Spink finally gave in when circulation fell to 22,-000 in 1912.

Until that time the paper had only two staff correspondents —W. M. Rankin, who rewrote the major-league news from New York, and H. G. Merrill, who covered the minors from Wilkes-Barre. *The Sporting News* was at least ten days behind developments and Taylor realized that its copy was stodgy, run-of-the-mine stuff, sadly lacking in originality and freshness. He instituted the system of lining up a correspondent in each city which had a team in organized baseball, and the paper soon came out of its coma. Circulation doubled and for the first time in a quarter of a century the paper assumed the scope of a national publication. Spink, who claims to know more sports writers than any other man, today has more than 300 correspondents and carries the occasional contributions of perhaps fifty free-lances.

Mounting differences between father and son came to an angry boil in 1914 with the formation of the Federal League. Old Charlie Spink believed baseball was ready to embrace a third major circuit. Taylor opposed the Federals on the ground that the prospective owners were backing the teams only to cash in on publicity for other activities in which they were financially interested. With Taylor rooting ardently from the side line, Joe Vila satirized the Federals as the "Lunch-Room League," a nickname inspired by Charles Weeghman, owner of the Chicago franchise, who ran a chain of restaurants. The entire affair became something more serious than a family dispute. It was turned into a fight for survival when the paper's strongest competitor, *Sporting Life,* of Philadelphia, came out in strong support of the Feds.

At the height of the intrafamily controversy, Taylor got married and left on his honeymoon. He was recalled hurriedly on April 22, 1914. Charlie Spink had died suddenly after attending the Federal League inaugural in Chicago. Taylor, now in complete control of *The Sporting News,* blasted the Feds unmercifully. The outlaw league dissolved after the close of the 1915 season when the National and American leagues agreed to pay the backers $700,000. Robert B. Ward, who financed the Brooklyn Feds, is reputed to have lost more than $3,000,000 on the venture. Spink came off handsomely, though. *Sporting Life* collapsed with the Federal League and the Spink paper dominated the field.

Taylor Spink was rapidly gaining recognition as a smart young baseball man, and in 1917 Ban Johnson entrusted him with a delicate diplomatic mission. Johnson wanted to place Miller Huggins, then managing the Cardinals, in New York to build up the Yankees, a chronic second-division team. The Cardinals were in a precarious financial position and Johnson believed Huggins could be induced to shift to the American League, but it was hardly cricket for Johnson to negotiate personally with a manager of the rival organization.

Both Johnson and Jake Ruppert, owner of the Yankees, agreed on Spink as the man to approach Huggins and sound him out. Huggins expressed interest. Spink arranged for a secret meeting between Ruppert and Huggins when the Cardinals were playing in New York, but nothing came of it. Huggins was eager to sign on the spot, but Ruppert, mysteriously evasive, said he would withhold his decision until the end of the season. Johnson invited Huggins to New York as his guest at the Giants-White Sox World Series. Huggins accepted and was considerably embarrassed to find Branch Rickey, general manager of the Cardinals, on the same train.

"When Huggins, in response to Rickey's question, said he was going to take in the World Series, Branch's sensitive nose immediately smelled a rat," Spink relates. "Rickey knew it was highly improbable that Huggins, who was canny with a dollar, would spend a dime to see the coronation of the King of England and the eruption of Mount Vesuvius if both were billed on the same program."

A good deal of comic-opera hocus-pocus followed. Spink registered Huggins at a hotel under an assumed name and led him through devious back alleys to clandestine meetings with Ruppert. Johnson thoughtlessly spoiled Spink's stratagem by giving Huggins a World Series ticket in a section of the Polo Grounds occupied by the American League delegation, and the supposedly secret deal got to be common gossip.

Huggins finally was appointed to the Yankee job in January, 1918, and then Ruppert revealed to Spink his reason for stalling so long. It seems that Huggins had appeared at interviews wearing a cap, and the colonel, an urbane gent who was fond of the amenities, frowned upon grown men who wore caps. Huggins bought himself a proper hat and went on to establish the Yankee dynasty with the help of Babe Ruth, who wore caps when the colonel was paying him more than the President of the United States was getting.

The 1918–1920 period was a critical one for Spink and *The Sporting News*. Saved from extinction during the war by the American League's free distribution of the sheet in France, the paper suffered, along with the sport, from the Black Sox scandal. Public confidence in baseball was at a low ebb and, worst of all—in Spink's view—Ban Johnson was through as the dominating personality of baseball.

The downfall of Johnson was the Carl Mays case. In 1919, Harry Frazee, owner of the Red Sox, was deep in debt and he began to sell his stars to Ruppert, who was spending fabulous sums in his effort to build the Yankees into a winning team. Johnson denounced the ruinous raid on the Boston club, then the best franchise in the league, and refused to sanction the sale of Mays, a Frazee star, to the Yankees. That was the final straw for the club owners, who had been showing increasing resentment of Johnson's autocratic control of the league.

On November 18, 1920, eleven club owners met in secret at Chicago. Their intention was to adopt the Lasker plan, which provided for the formation of a new, twelve-club league. The eight National League teams already had agreed to the proposal and the Yankees, Red Sox and White Sox were ready to secede from the American League. Tipped off to the meeting, Spink belabored the insurgents so vigorously that the scheme was abandoned, but the opposition to Johnson mounted steadily. A new National Commission, designed to curb his powers, undoubtedly would have been proposed even if the Black Sox scandal had not precipitated the appointment of Judge Landis.

The sellout to the gamblers was a blow from which Johnson never recovered. The shock of learning that a ballplayer, and particularly an American Leaguer, could actually be dishonest broke the old man. He ruthlessly explored every clue of crookedness and demanded a public trial of the seven accused players. Serving as Johnson's special investigator, Spink unearthed much of the evidence which later barred some of the players for life.

With baseball a model of honesty for the past couple of decades, *The Sporting News* seldom has occasion these days to pick up its old crusading cudgel. Its chief function for years has been to enlighten and amuse rather than to agitate and excoriate. But Spink insists that the old cudgel is still in his office and will be used in the near future on a few issues. One is the perennially hopeless state of clubs like the Phillies, Athletics, Braves and Browns, who, Spink says, are ruining the essentially competitive nature of the sport. The owners, he says, have got to cure this condition or face increased apathy.

Another is the down-at-the-heel facilities which are provided for the minor-league fans.

And something will be done, for Spink's gripes are the fans' gripes. Hearing him talk about baseball, you can't doubt his authenticity or his sincerity as a spokesman.

"Baseball is the American success story," he says with pious intensity. "It is the only avenue of escape for thousands of boys born into a dreary environment of poverty. It is, moreover, a great common ground on which bartenders and bishops, clergymen and bosses, bankers and laborers meet with true equality and understanding. The game has proved in everyday language that democracy works."

160 Miles of Words

By WARNER OLIVIER

EDITOR'S PREFACE.—In view of the frequency and constancy with which the *Encyclopædia Britannica* is consulted in newspaper, magazine, radio, and book publishing offices, an article about this great reference work would merit a place in this book, even though its editor were not an ex-newspaperman. It so happens, however, that Mr. Yust can qualify as a journalist, both past and present. The *ex,* in his case, is applicable only when used as a prefix to the word *newspaperman.* Mr. Yust is still very much an editor. He has dead lines to meet, makes assignments not unlike a city editor, and has one of the largest and most colorful staff of writers to be found associated with any publication anywhere. Some 3,700 assorted experts, including such diverse types as Gene Tunney, Lord Macaulay, and Henry Ford, were required to produce this "160 miles of words," and new names are constantly being added as new topics are treated and old ones are brought up to date. Mr. Yust and his associates have production problems (and during the war, paper headaches), and they must be concerned with such things as circulation, promotion, and advertising.

One may not think of the editing and publishing of an encyclopedia as an exciting business, but to read this article by Mr. Olivier is to be shown that there is no little adventure and humor associated with such an enterprise.

Older than the United States of America, and almost as widely known, the *Encyclopædia Britannica* contains much (some would say *most*) of the learning and lore that man has accumulated, and is a work the influence of which is in proportion to its physical size—and, as Mr. Olivier notes, it is a huge compendium of knowledge. There are 35,000,000 words in its 24 volumes, and, so far as is known, only three persons have ever read the work in its entirety.

344

The editor, Mr. Yust, oddly enough, is not one of these. He and his associates, as the author of this article explains, "could never, for lack of time, cover this vast amount of literary territory and still read the millions of new words which go into the *Britannica* . . . every year."

I

July 21 and 28, 1945

OLD friends of his newspaper days who drop in to see Walter Yust, editor of the *Encyclopædia Britannica,* usually remark with a conspiratorial smile in the first five minutes of their visit, "It must be pretty soft not to have to meet a dead line but once every ten years or so."

Mr. Yust, who has learned the fine qualities of patience and amassed a store of it in his lifetime, draws upon it at this point to smile forgivingly, though his eyes may be a little grim. The question is a partial but typical summation of public misinformation about the book which, more than any other in the English language, is designed to make an end of misinformation.

Very few metropolitan newspapers have as many as ten dead lines a day. But old "E. B.," as its editors and other servants affectionately call the *Britannica,* has thousands of dead lines to meet a year—frequently twenty or more a day. True, it doesn't meet them in the madhouse spirit of the average newspaper city room. It does it with the decorous poise you would expect of such a Jekyll of ancient wisdom and Hyde of modernity. But it meets them on time and as the result of infinite labor which may have started halfway around the world.

The *Encyclopædia Britannica* today, two years past its 175th-anniversary year, is at an all-time peak of giantism. Each year from 1937 to 1944 it sold in greater numbers than ever before in its history. Sales will level off this year, owing to the paper shortage. With its offspring, the *Britannica Junior,* the *Year Book,* the *Five-Year Omnibus Year Book* and the *Atlas,* it makes its publishers the largest publishers in volume of case-bound—that is, stiff-backed—books in the world. Its influence is profound and incalculable. "Terry and the Pirates" set the course of their adventures by the E. B. The State Department gets the jitters when it publishes new maps, and watches the text of its every printing like a hawk with the collywobbles.

Not long ago one of the loftiest State Department officials summoned editors and executives of the *Britannica* to Washington and petulantly paced the floor while he reprimanded them in choleric terms for printing a fact, known to virtually every literate American, with which the State Department, for reasons of its own, preferred to play ostrich.

The *Britannica* men listened to his scolding and, failing to see that it made much sense, reminded him that there is in this country a constitutionally guaranteed freedom of the press and, by extension, freedom of the encyclopedia.

"But can't you understand," the diplomat asked them aggrievedly, "that whatever appears in the *Britannica* has, in the eyes of foreigners, the authority of a statement by the United States Government?"

The gentlemen of the *Britannica* smiled wanly at this official recognition of the *Encyclopædia's* American citizenship. Though it has been American-owned and printed for the better part of half a century, the *Britannica* is still trying to live down the widely held public misapprehension that it is English to the core, reflecting the beliefs of the Archbishop of Canterbury and the philosophy of Balliol.

The *Britannica* emigrated to this country around the turn of the century. It is not English, and never has been. In all its century and three quarters' existence, no new edition of E. B. has ever been brought out by an English publishing house or edited by an Englishman. The publishers have either been Scots or Americans, and of the eleven editors of new editions, eight have been Scotsmen, one an Irishman and the last two Americans. All of them, barring one lone scholar, have been journalists or newspapermen.

The Nazis, too, apparently were, or assumed to be, under the delusion that the *Britannica* was at one time English owned.

Two years ago, when the *Britannica* was presented as a profitable and going concern to the University of Chicago by Sears, Roebuck & Company, which had saved it from extinction and nurtured it from the financial doldrums into sound prosperity, the Nazi-inspired Spanish radio hailed the gift as a "significant" event of history in the making.

"The encyclopedia forms the mind of a people," the Goebbels broadcaster said, "and the British mind will henceforth be molded by Chicago University. It must be said that Chicago has been better known for its slaughterhouses than for its contribution to science."

The fact is that the University of Chicago, though keeping a benevolent eye on its windfall, leaves the making and editing of the *Britannica* wholly in the hands of its editors and business managers.

Many of the contributors to the *Encyclopædia,* at one time the great majority of them, have been English. But more than half of today's 3700-odd contributors are American. The remainder are from sixty-one different countries. Sold all over the world, the *Britannica* has been printed and bound since 1911 by the Lakeside Press in Chicago. Copies sold in this country carry the President's name first in the dedication. Those sold in the British Empire carry King George's name first, a gesture of publishing diplomacy which ought to endear the old book to the State Department's heart.

Near the close of the eighteenth century a new shah, Futteh Ali, ascended the throne of Persia. Great Britain wanted the new shah's friendship, and the British ambassador, on his long voyage out to Persia, carried with him as a gift for the shah a set of the *Britannica.* Futteh Ali, delighted with the gift, read the entire work from beginning to end. To his list of titles, including "Most Exalted and Generous Prince; Brilliant as the Moon, Resplendent as the Sun; The Jewel of the World; the Center of Beauty, of Musselmen and of the True Faith; Shadow of God; Mirror of Justice; Most Generous King of Kings; Master of the Constellations Whose Throne is the

Stirrup Cup of Heaven," the shah caused to be added "and Most Formidable Lord and Master of the *Encyclopædia Britannica.*"

Times and the *Britannica* have changed since the eighteenth century, and the shah would have a far more difficult time today earning his last title. The 177-year-old patriarch, fat with the lore of the centuries, has grown in the course of its fourteen editions and subsequent revised printings to be a twenty-four-volume giant of 35,000,000 or so words.

Only three persons, so far as is known, have read the present-day *Britannica* in its entirety. One was a retired minister who had to travel for his health and carried the *Encyclopædia* along for bedtime reading, and another was a lad of fourteen who just youthfully read it. The third marathon reader is the novelist, C. S. Forester, who is said to have read it twice.

Each line of type in the *Britannica* runs to about three inches and there are 144 lines to the page. The twenty-four volumes would give you 10,368,000 inches of words, or 864,000 feet of words, or 160 miles. The mere physical task of traveling that road is considerable. The job of seeing that all those words tell the truth is appalling.

Most editors consider it essential to read the publication they edit. Yust and his staff are resigned to the fact that they will never read in its entirety the book they edit, for they will never have the time. The *Britannica* keeps its editors too busy making and editing it to give them an opportunity to read it, except in patches. As it is, Yust reads manuscripts until two and three o'clock in the morning at home. After he goes to bed he reads paper-bound detective stories for relaxation. The sandman usually beats the detective to the gun.

When the first American office of the *Britannica* was opened in 1899 by Franklin H. Hooper, later to become editor in chief, proofs of articles written abroad were sent to Mr. Hooper in New York. One of these dealt with Algebraic Forms, and he submitted it for a report to Dr. Edward S. Holden, a leading American astronomer, for a report. An hour later, Holden reported that it was an important contribution written by the greatest authority on mathematics in the world and that he would like further time to study it.

Three days later he reported that the article was beyond him, and advised that Simon Newcomb, then recently retired from Johns Hopkins University, was probably the only man in the country who would be able to understand it.

"But," he said, "it is a magnificent article!" Hooper made up his mind on the spot that "magnificent articles" which only one man in the United States could understand would be barred from future editions of the *Britannica*. Today's editors continue that policy, their goal being to make the *Encyclopædia* a useful tool rather than a repository of recondite matter.

It was nearly half a century ago, 1897, that American interests first turned to the *Britannica*. But already the *Britannica* had lived a couple of men's lifetimes and it had soaked up the diverse talents of many brilliant men who had sweated and sometimes alcoholized their brains to write and edit it. Yust, when he becomes philosophical about the E. B., says he likes to think of it as an instrument which has been important in the development of democracy. He points out that, when the *Britannica* was launched in 1768, people were stirring restlessly and beginning to do something about democracy. The eccentric George III was on the throne of England, Louis XV ruled France, Frederick the War Lord held sway in Prussia, Catharine in Russia, and Maria Theresa in Austria. In America, the Stamp Act had been fomenting revolution, and invitations to the Boston Tea Party were all but in the mail. The forgotten man of his day was beginning vigorously to call himself to mind. His heart was troubled, and wherever he looked he found things to trouble it the more.

It was against such a global background that the *Britannica* was launched when three men—Colin Macfarquhar, a printer; Andrew Bell, an engraver; and William Smellie—met in Edinburgh, formed "a society of gentlemen" and planned publica-

tion of the *Encyclopædia Britannica* to bring information
to English-speaking people—hence the name *Britannica*—of
whom there were then some 14,000,000 in the world.

"Utility ought to be the principal intention of every publication," the founders wrote in the preface to their first edition. "Wherever this intention does not plainly appear, neither
the books nor their authors have the slightest claim to the
approbation of mankind."

That statement in itself was revolutionary. Learning at that
time was not for the masses, and the young *Britannica* was
leading with its chin. Though Edinburgh was by way of being
an eighteenth century Athens, with a renowned university and
a group of scholars respected throughout the limited world of
scholarship, of the three *Britannica* founders, only Smellie, the
editor, had any claim to scholarship. He had written a number
of books, was a Fellow of the Royal Society and officer of the
Society of Antiquaries of Scotland. In the polite language of
his day, Mr. Smellie was a gentleman "of convivial habits," a
fellow member of Bobby Burns in a club called the Crochallen
Fencibles. Burns wrote of his friend in premature *Time*-style:

> *Shrewd Willie Smellie to Crochallen came,*
> *The old cock'd hat, the gray surtout, the same;*
> *His bristling beard just rising to its might,*
> *'Twas four long nights and days to shaving night;*
> *His uncomb'd grizzly locks, wild staring, thatch'd*
> *A head for thought profound and clear unmatch'd;*
> *Yet though his caustic wit was biting, rude,*
> *His heart was warm, benevolent, and good.*

Not much is known of Macfarquhar, except that he was a
printer and bookseller in Edinburgh. He was sued in 1770 by
His Majesty's printer for issuing a Bible, and five years later he
had to pay some $6000 to two rival booksellers for pirating an
edition of Lord Chesterfield's Letters to His Son.

Bell began his career humbly enough as an engraver of
names and crests on dog collars, and rose to become Edinburgh's leading engraver. For the first edition of the *Britannica*
he engraved 160 full-page copperplate illustrations, and for the

second edition 340. They have been called superb examples of
the art. Bell was notable for the smallness of his stature, an
immense nose and a deformity of the legs. He alone of the
partners made any real money from their venture. The plates
reverted to him in the end, possibly because Macfarquhar was
unable to pay him for the illustrations he made, and he died,
at the age of eighty-three, a wealthy man.

Poor Willie Smellie received the customary editorial pit-
tance—200 pounds for his three years' work on the three
volumes which comprised the first edition. Smellie did all the
work himself, reading books from which he drew his material
and writing the *Encyclopædia*—some 2,000,000 words. The
first edition was completed in 1771 and sold 3000 sets.

James Tytler, the editor of the second edition, was also a
"convivial" man and a friend of Burns, whose lasting affection
Tytler won by writing a defense of Mary Queen of Scots.
Burns, deeply moved, dashed off a Poetical Address to Mr.
James Tytler, one stanza of which read:

> *I send you a trifle, a head of a bard,*
> *A trifle scarce worthy your care;*
> *But accept it, good sir, as a mark of regard,*
> *Sincere as a saint's dying prayer.*

An M.A. who began his life's work as a druggist, Tytler became a free-lance writer and pamphleteer, and was known for
his scientific interests. For more than seven years he labored at
seventeen shillings a week to bring out the second edition of
the *Britannica* in ten volumes. He kept his editorial awareness
warm in various ways, once by making a balloon ascent—the
first person in Great Britain to do so. He constructed a fire
balloon—one in which the air was heated, to lighten it, by a
bucket of burning coals—and succeeded in soaring to the incredible height of 350 feet over Edinburgh.

Tytler was a warm-hearted crusader, a sort of eighteenth-
century Pearl Buck, and he was finally forced to flee the country to escape the government's ire over pamphlets which he
had written to expose current abuses. He came to America and

edited a newspaper in Salem, Massachusetts, where, like many a good newspaperman before and since, he cooled his boiling anger at stuffed shirts of his day in taprooms, until one night he fell into a pit in Salem and died.

Of all his predecessors, Yust confesses to a peculiar fondness for Tytler, possibly the attraction of near opposites. It is true that contemporary poets also like Yust—Carl Sandburg has been his friend for years—but Bobby Burns would have found him too objective for boon companionship. His crusades are *sotto voce* and the stars in his eyes are well charted. He is, for example, a definitely gentle Republican and an outspoken non-admirer of New Deal philosophy. He rationalizes that on the ground that he doesn't consider it necessary to subsidize democracy, a wholly tenable stand, but also he was born and reared in Philadelphia at a time when a young Philadelphian became a Republican as naturally as a young Roman becomes a Christian.

Yust takes his job seriously, but not himself. A tall, slim, quiet-spoken, youngish man, with an inner excitement which rarely bubbles over into anything overt, he has prematurely gray hair, which gives him a distinction fitting to a comparatively young man whom the *Britannica's* promotion brochures describe as an "eminent encyclopedist." Yust laughs that off with the iconoclastic observation that encyclopedists are so darned rare that "eminence" is an occupational adjunct, if not disease. He was too long a newspaperman to accept "eminence" at its type-face value or to refrain from picking at a pedestal with a jackknife.

It was his critical picking at the *Britannica's* pedestal which got him his present job. As a staff member and literary editor of the Philadelphia *Evening Public Ledger,* he reviewed the fourteenth edition of the *Britannica* when it first came off the presses. It was a frank review, uninhibited by any false sense of sacrilege to ancient and established authority.

Franklin H. Hooper, the *Britannica's* editor for that edition, read the review, and on the occasion of his next visit to Philadelphia invited Critic Yust to lunch. The eventual result of this was that Yust became Hooper's associate editor and succeeded him when he retired in 1938—a refreshing example of the rise of a no-man to eminence.

Yust's patience and tact are unquestionably eminent because he successfully handles more prima donnas than any other editor in the world. The words "prima donnas" are not used inadvisedly. The nearly 4000 contributors to the *Britannica* are, by selection, the leading specialists in their fields. There is probably no severer critic in the world than one specialist about an article written by another in the same field. If Anthropologist A writes a piece on anthropology, it automatically has two strikes on it in the eyes of Anthropologist B. That goes for every special field.

The *Britannica* editors were not greatly surprised, therefore, when they sent a historical article which had been in the book for a good many years, to the head of the history department of a Western university for scrutiny and possible revision, to get it back from the history man with the caustic comment that it was "badly disorganized, inaccurate and full of errors of both omission and commission." The professor added helpfully that he would be glad to undertake the job of writing a substitute piece. That was all right with the editors, but they were curious to see who had written such a "disorganized" and "inaccurate" article for them originally, and checked with their files. They were amusedly flabbergasted to find out that the article had been written by the professor himself—so many years before that he had forgotten it. He wrote another piece on the same subject—not noticeably better, either, in the editorial view.

None of the contributors writes for the E. B. with the primary object of increasing his worldly wealth. Its monetary pay is the same as that of some of the pulp magazines—two cents a word—whether the contributor is George Bernard Shaw, who got $68.50 for his article on Socialism, or Albert Einstein, paid $86.40 for his article on Space-Time.

The pay in prestige, of course, is enormous, and the *Britannica* has little trouble commanding the services of the most eminent scientists, scholars and writers. Well-known contributors, living and dead, are numerous—Orville Wright, Gene Tunney, Leon Trotsky, Henry Ford, Charles Evans Hughes, Bernard M. Baruch, Gen. Archibald Wavell, T. E. Lawrence, and hundreds of others equally familiar.

Still carried in the *Britannica* are articles, originally written for it, which have become classics of the language: Lord Macaulay's famous Essay on Samuel Johnson; Julian Huxley's article on the Courtship of Animals; G. K. Chesterton's article on Charles Dickens; articles by James Mill, Malthus, Hazlitt, Robert Louis Stevenson, and many other famed writers.

These include pieces by Sir Walter Scott written to help pay off the heavy indebtedness he assumed because of the failure of a publishing house in which he was interested.

Yust knows relatively few of his contributors personally, and his contacts with them are largely by mail. Despite the fact that every contributor is told, before he accepts an assignment, that the pay is two cents a word, one of them occasionally beefs after the job is done and writes to Yust that he could have got far more money had he sold the article elsewhere. Yust asks him what he feels the work was worth, pays the sum named and blacklists him as a future contributor. Though the blacklist is slim, it also includes those who make themselves habitual nuisances to the editors and those who have proved incorrigible in failing to turn in their manuscripts on time.

Most contributors, with or without the use of the editorial needle, manage to get their pieces in before the dead line. If they don't, the *Britannica* has a "dilatory-domicile" technique of handling delayed copy. When the famous and much-pirated ninth edition was in the works, more than half century ago, the editor asked Lord Rayleigh, the discoverer of argon, Nobel-prize winner and outstanding physicist of his day, to write the article on Light. When Volume 14, in which the Light article should have appeared, was ready to go to press, Rayleigh hadn't written the piece, asked for more time and suggested that it could be printed under the title Optics in the O volume. When that volume was reached, the distinguished scientist still hadn't finished the article, and asked that it be postponed to the U volume and titled Undulatory Theory of Light. The bedeviled editors acquiesced, but were not surprised when Rayleigh again disappointed them. He finally staggered under the wire in the W volume, with the article titled Wave Theory of Light. The same technique is occasionally used today under the spur of necessity.

The influence of a great encyclopedia is like the waves from a pebble dropped in still water. You cannot tell where it will spread. A century or more ago, a man named Timothy Dewey lived in East Hartford, Connecticut. Mr. Dewey was both a prolific man and an admirer of great people and great things. He named his eleven children George Roberts, Anna Diadama, Philander Seabury, Franklin Jefferson, Armenius Philadelphus, Almira Melpomena, Marcus Bonaparte, Pleiades Arastarcus, Victor Millenius, Octavia Ammonia, and Encyclopædia Britannica. Little Encyclopædia lived with her name for more than eighty years, but it must have frightened suitors away, for she was never married.

Adm. Richard E. Byrd took the *Britannica* with him when he left all the rest of his party in Little America and spent the winter alone in Antarctica. Subsequently he wrote of the comfort it had given him in his solitude.

Michael Faraday first became interested in chemistry, a field in which he was to become pre-eminent, when, as a bookbinder's apprentice, he took home with him and read at night volumes of the *Britannica* which had come in for rebinding.

Innumerable authors, famous and obscure, write unsolicited letters to tell how the *Britannica* helps shape their work. Milton Caniff, pen-and-ink father of "Terry and the Pirates," consults the *Britannica* before sending Terry on a new adventure abroad. The framers of the Irish Free State's constitution worked with the *Encyclopædia* constantly within reach.

George Washington purchased a set after failing to win one in a lottery, and Alexander Hamilton also owned and relied on the *Britannica.*

The editors never cease to be amazed by the innumerable uses to which their book is put. Sir Wilfred Grenfell, the noted medical missionary to Labrador, wrote to the editor to tell of an incident in the far north. Sir Wilfred wanted to build a hospital, but in winter the ground was frozen too hard for digging, and as soon as spring came every male inhabitant left home for the fishing. Some sticks of frozen dynamite were found and it was decided to blast the ground. The question was how to thaw the dynamite. One incautious soul tried to heat a stick of the dynamite on a stove, and a few minutes later took his departure for a better world. Someone thought of the *Britannica.* Would it tell how to thaw dynamite? It did. The hospital was built.

A department head at Macy's heard a customer ask a new salesgirl what made silk rustle.

To his amazement the young woman gave the correct explanation. She got a raise forthwith, and wrote to the *Britannica* to thank it for being responsible for the raise.

"When I went to work," she wrote, "I read up on silk in the *Encyclopædia.*"

A couple, visiting friends for a week end, were asked by their host, on their arrival, if they played bridge. They told him they knew nothing about it. He suggested that, inasmuch as a bridge party was planned for the evening, they read the *Britannica's* article on bridge. They did and played that night. The husband became intensely interested in the game and went on to become an expert and widely read bridge writer. He was Shepard Barclay.

Several years ago the Yusts found it necessary to install a new refrigerating unit, but were troubled about the type to get, for certain technical reasons. Yust returned home one day to be assured by Mrs. Yust that she had determined what kind of refrigerator they should have.

"How did you settle it?" he asked.

"I looked it up in the *Encyclopædia*," Mrs. Yust told him. "Gosh," said the *Encyclopædia's* editor, "I never thought of that." The refrigerator didn't work any too well, either, he says.

But for Sears, Roebuck & Company, there would probably be no *Encyclopædia Britannica* today. The book got to Sears in a roundabout way. The first Americans to become interested in the *Britannica* were Horace Hooper, who had been with the Century Company, and his partner, Walter Jackson. They went to London in 1897 when they heard that *The London Times* had on hand thousands of remainder sets which it was unable to sell. Hooper, a dynamic salesman of the the modern school, took over the books, advertised them in a way no Briton had ever seen books advertised—in newspapers, by letter, on the backs of sandwich men walking up and down the Strand.

Hooper and Jackson eventually bought control of the *Britannica* and brought its plates to this country, where the eleventh, twelfth, thirteenth and fourteenth editions were published. After a period of ups and downs, the *Encyclopædia* was finally taken over in 1920 by Sears, Roebuck, largely because of Julius Rosenwald's interest in the project. But even the skilled merchandising of Sears failed, in the beginning, to establish the *Britannica* as a sound commercial venture. There were, as there had always been, periods of famine.

During Hooper's high-pressure selling of the *Encyclopædia* in Great Britain and its Dominons, a number of the usual form sales letters were sent over a period of time to a farmer in the backwoods of Australia.

The letters, each more urgent than the last, told him that a set of the *Britannica* was being reserved for him in Sydney and urged him to place his order immediately.

Finally he received a telegram warning him that only two days remained for him to pick up his reserved *Britannica* in Sydney "at a ridiculously low cost." That got action from the bewildered Australian. Deciding he could afford to wait no longer, he hitched up his buggy and drove two nights and days without a rest, until he reached Sydney.

Rushing breathlessly into the office, he demanded, "Where is my *Britannica?*" When the salesman pointed to a set standing in the corner, the farmer put his head in his hands, groaning with amazement and no little despair, "My God! Books!"

Sears, Roebuck, saddled with the *Britannica* giant and seeming to get nowhere toward making it pay its own way, must have been sorely tempted to cry at times, "My God! Books!"

II

FORTUNES had been made and lost in the publication of the *Encyclopædia Britannica* when the book was taken over in 1920 by Sears, Roebuck & Company because of Julius Rosenwald's desire to preserve it for the English-speaking world. In 1932, Sears, Roebuck gave its then secretary and treasurer, E. Harrison Powell, the assignment of taking over the *Britannica* and putting it on a sound financial basis—if he could, for already Sears had spooned several million dollars into the financially ailing *Britannica* without any notable results.

Like most successful American businessmen, Mr. Powell had come up the business escalator from scratch. A native of a small Ohio town, he had attended the University of Chicago, played semipro football and been advertising manager for Sears, Roebuck. Powell started one of Chicago's radio stations, WLS—which originally stood for World's Largest Store—and designed and built the first building without windows for display at the Chicago Century of Progress World's Fair.

A quiet-spoken man—though he insists he can bellow like a foghorn—keen-eyed and deeply interested in many things, he eschews political arguments because they usually get nowhere and are, he feels, a waste of energy. A fine photographer, he does his own developing and printing. He also paints, dabbles in architecture, and designed and built a servantless ranch house in Colorado and a wing of his home in Winnetka.

When Powell took over the *Britannica,* he knew it was a sound and salable commodity, that there was a need as well as market for it. The fact remained that it wasn't paying its way. Powell determined to make two far-reaching changes. One was to institute direct instead of mail-order sales. The other was to abandon the plan of bringing out new editions of the *Britannica* spaced at intervals of years and to substitute for it a revised printing once or twice a year.

At the time Powell took over, so completely was the *Britannica* committed to mail-order sales that there were hardly a dozen outside salesmen in the organization. Half of these were in New York. Powell started from scratch to build an outside sales organization and establish branch sales offices in key cities of the country. Sales began to go up. But strange letters of complaint also began to come into the *Britannica* home offices in Chicago. Being inexperienced in the field of direct sales, Powell had hired a number of men known to the trade as "old book" salesmen. These were oldtimers, some of them trained and skilled in all the shyster tricks of bookselling.

One of their favorite methods was the give-away, or "you-have-been selected" trick. They would visit a prospect and tell him: "The *Encyclopædia Britannica* is initiating a new advertising campaign, and as one of the most prominent citizens of your community, we have selected you to receive a set of the *Britannica* free—absolutely without any cost to you."

This is almost sure-fire. Rare, indeed, is the man who cannot find some rational justification in his heart for being considered one of the most prominent citizens of his community. When a prospect would modestly tell the salesman that he was not a prominent citizen and ask why he had been selected, the wily salesman had little trouble in overcoming his scruples of modesty.

"Now, Mr. Jones," he would say, "there are no strings attached to this gift whatever. It is absolutely free. But I am sure that you will want to keep this magnificent set of the *Encyclopædia* up to date. There is a way to do that, by subscribing for the *Britannica Year Book*. The *Year Book* for the next ten years will cost you, at the special price I am able to make to you——" He would then name the sum which was the actual price of the full set of the *Encyclopædia* including the *Year Book*.

Oftener than you would think, Mr. Jones would be hooked. As one of the most prominent citizens of his community, he had no desire to prove himself stingy. He would sign the contract. If he didn't, of course, the salesman merely left and never went back. Needless to say, in that case Mr. Jones never received his "free set" either. The salesman would use the same technique on fifty or a hundred prospects in the same community.

Powell was appalled to discover that this traditional sharp practice was being used to sell the book, and he instituted a cleanout of the sales organization. He called in Louis C. Schoenewald as sales manager. Schoenewald at the time was general retail sales manager of the New York office. Mr. Schoenewald, before he begins to sell you on a proposition, has the melancholy look of a great tragedian in the fifth act. He appears disinterested and disapproving. All this is a God-given smoke screen for a born salesman. Salesmanship, Schoenewald says, is a great art, and, as he practices it, it is. For twenty years he was with the Aeolian American Corporation in New York, in charge of retail sales. In the 1930's he faced the fact, he says, that the piano business had slipped badly and that it showed no prospect of ever returning to the volume of sales it once had.

It was not the radio, as you might suppose, which put the piano business on the skids, but the automobile, in Lou Schoenewald's book. A practical cynic, Mr. Schoenewald did not and does not believe that the great majority of American piano buyers bought pianos because of a love of music which would not be denied. They bought them, he says, to keep up with or forge ahead of the Joneses. A piano in the living room was a tangible, highly visible and impressive sign of prosperity. If somebody could and did play it, of course, that was so much velvet.

Came the automobile and the dawn of a new era, but the melancholy twilight of the piano. In order to impress anyone with your piano, you had to get them into your living room. Since you couldn't go out into the streets and drag in perfect strangers with an invitation to come in and look at the piano, this confined your list of potential impressees to friends, neighbors, visiting cousins, the laundryman and house-to-house canvassers, the last a group you'd just as soon not impress.

With a new automobile, the possibilities were limitless. Between rides you could leave it sitting in front of the house for the neighbors to envy. With the advent of the automobile, pianos were bought only by people who actually wanted them, and sales fell sharply. When this became clear to Schoenewald, he began to look for a new job. He conducted a four-month survey before attempting to make any connection.

"I took a classified telephone directory," he says, "and went through it. For each possible classification I came to, I asked myself two questions: 'What have I got that can be used in that business?' and 'What has it got for me?'"

Advertising, he decided, was a good bet, and he wrote letters to twelve advertising agencies. He interviewed George Eager, then with Batten, Barton, Durstine & Osborn, who told him of reorganization plans of the *Britannica* and suggested that he look into that.

Schoenewald then made a survey of the *Britannica's* business and field, and completely sold himself on it.

"It looked so favorable even then (1933) that I determined that was what I wanted to go into," he said. "I didn't regard the *Britannica* then, and I haven't regarded it since, as books, but as an educational tool which people seeking to get ahead need."

Schoenewald found five salesmen in New York when he

went to head that office. He built up the New York sales force, advertising for salesmen and training them. In 1939, when Schoenewald was made general sales manager, he applied on a national scale, in the twenty-four sales offices, the methods he had successfully used in New York. Salesmen were bonded and "shopped" to insure the company against the use of shyster methods of selling.

Lou Schoenewald has developed a formula which salesmen are trained to use in selling the *Britannica*. "We know that when it is followed, a given number of calls on prospects will produce a given number of sales," he says. "The *Britannica* is sold with shoe leather. It doesn't matter in what section of the country you may be selling. People in any part of the country buy a product for the same reasons, whether it is a vacuum cleaner or the *Britannica*. The technique of selling is the same. In the South we talk a little slower and we visit a little longer. But we say the same things."

There is no cold-turkey canvassing. Appointments are made by telephone, either in the prospect's office or in his home. If it is a home appointment, the salesman makes it clear to Mrs. Prospect that he wants to see her when Mr. Prospect is at home, so that he may talk to both of them together. This reassures her and is part of a careful build-up designed to convince the Prospects that they are not going to be high-pressured. They will be, of course, but so skillfully they will never know it.

Most of the *Britannica's* buyers are in the $3500-or-less income group. Californians buy more sets than residents of any other state.

When "Information, Please" began giving out sets of the *Britannica* to those who submitted questions the experts failed to answer, the number of questions submitted to the program jumped from 6000 to 21,000 weekly. Salesmen occasionally have difficulty selling a set because the prospective customer is convinced that he will soon win a set from "Information, Please." To such customers the *Britannica* promises a full refund if the customer wins a set of the *Encyclopædia* from

"Information, Please" within ninety days. It has had to pay only twice.

Though the *Britannica's* branch sales offices have been reduced from thirty-five to twenty-four since the war started, sales have mounted because of increased public interest in reference works which will help them to understand what is going on. The 700 salesmen sell an average of better than one set a week each. After the war it is planned to double the number of branch offices in this country and to reopen offices in England and other foreign countries which were closed by hostilities.

Last December the *Britannica* purchased the ERPI Classroom Films from Electric Research Products, Inc., which will be expanded after the war for the selling or renting of films to schools or county school organizations. Other projects are being considered for after the war, but have not taken definite shape.

Schoenewald has four cardinal points in his sales program:. continuous recruiting of salesmen through sharply worded newspaper advertisements—for there is a large turnover in direct selling—selective hiring; strong field training; and a daily program for each salesman, directing him where to go, what to do and how to do it.

He has prepared a sales-manager's manual which is the envy and despair of all sales organizations which have seen it. The manual, furnished to all branch managers, has the answer to every question of policy which can arise, and is cross-indexed. This saves days of querying the home office.

In the past, an edition of the *Britannica* lived from twenty years to a quarter of a century. The books were printed over and over again without revision until a new numbered edition appeared. It meant no editorial department during the years the old edition was selling, no sales department during the three to fifteen years it required to make a new edition. It would seem obvious that this was uneconomical, yet the thought had occurred to no one until Powell became president of the *Britannica* and devised the plan of continuous revision with abandonment of the numbered editions.

Powell asked the editors if it would be possible to schedule revisions so that all editorial matter in the *Britannica* subject to revision could be brought up to date at least once every ten years. The editors knew from experience that approximately 75 per cent of the material in the *Britannica* is more or less fixed, that it remains true from year to year. The other 25 per cent invited revision, some of it infrequently, some more often. When costs were worked out, it was found that the *Encyclopædia* could be printed every eight months with revision at each printing of at least 10 per cent of the revisable material.

After consultation with specialists in various fields, a schedule was worked out for a ten-year period, so that each classification would be scrutinized and, if necessary, revised at least twice in that period. From 1933 to 1939 was a period of experimentation to learn whether Mr. Powell's proposed policy of continuous revision was the sound one which he hoped it would be and which, in fact, it proved to be. During that period also were launched the *Britannica Junior*—1934—a fascinating encyclopædia for children, and the *Britannica Year Book*—1938. *The Five-Year Omnibus* was started three years ago, as was the *Atlas*. The first step in carrying out the revision plan obviously was to get a clear picture of what was in the book. To do this, the editors had the 41,000 articles in the *Britannica* classified in a dual-card-index system. Each article is represented by two cards, one filed in the alphabetical listing and one under a general subject classification, of which there are thirty.

The first classifiers had to learn their job from doing it, and in the learning process the results were not infrequently amusing. Green little girls classified Virginia Reel under biography, Defense Mechanism under military, Gallstones under geology, Incest under business and industry, and Pope Innocent under law. There were worse bugs than this in the new continuous-revision system, but bug by bug they were and are still being strained out.

In two years the *Britannica* was financially breaking even. The third year it began to make money, and has been a paying business ever since.

There are some 35,000,000 words in the twenty-four volumes of the *Britannica,* type which in a single line would stretch for an incredible 160 miles. Since it is obvious that Walter Yust, editor in chief, and his associates could never, for lack of time, cover this vast amount of literary territory and still read the millions of new words which go into the *Britannica* and its other publications every year, a plan was devised to get the book read by competent men. To this end, thirty fellowships, paying $1000 to $2000, have been established at the University of Chicago, which two years ago was presented with the now profitable Encyclopædia Britannica Company by Sears, Roebuck & Company. Recipients of the fellowships are assigned one of the general-subject classifications, and it is their duty to read everything printed in the *Britannica* under this classification and call the attention of the editors to anything which needs revision. This plan insures constant scrutiny of the entire work.

The permanent editorial staff of the *Britannica* is small. Actually only forty-four are employed at the home offices in Chicago's Civic Opera Building. Mr. Yust is advised by a staff of about fifty contributing editors. These men are specialists in their fields and are scattered over the world. To them are sent articles which need scrutiny and possible revision, and they advise what man in their general field is best qualified to write on a specific subject in that field. All the articles on this specific subject are then sent to the recommended specialist. He must read the articles, decide whether they need revision or rewriting, or whether they can stand as they are. He is paid five dollars a page for the reading and two cents a word for whatever he rewrites or revises. If he pleases, he, in turn, may farm out some of the writing to other specialists whom he may believe better qualified than he is to deal with certain aspects of the subject. The *Britannica* has more than 3700 contributors. The *Year Book* has about 575. In the E. B. itself, 3000 pages are revised with each printing at a cost of eighteen dollars a page.

The war has, of course, cut down the number of articles written by foreign contributors.

Three weeks after the attack on Pearl Harbor, the captain of one of the American warships sunk by the Japanese mailed Mr. Yust his manuscript for the *Britannica's* article on Blockade. In his accompanying letter he wrote:

"I wrote a little too much and cut it with a pencil. Please excuse this, but, in as much as I lost all my personal possessions, my typewriter and my ship in the —— attack, you will understand. It may interest you to know that in one of the files rescued was a water-soaked letter from you and my rough notes for the article."

As a result of the sweeping continuous-revision program, thousands of errors that probably would have run for another quarter of a century were discovered and corrected.

No work of the *Britannica's* scope can ever be errorless. During the printing of one revision, former Attorney General Frank Murphy became an associate justice of the United States Supreme Court. In articles appearing in volumes already run off the presses, Mr. Justice Murphy was referred to as Attorney General. In volumes still to be printed, he was given his new title. The *Britannica* received complaints about this, but its editor's contention is that it is better to be inconsistent and 50 per cent right than consistent and 100 per cent wrong.

Only those who must pursue facts for a living know how elusive and deceptive they can be. Walter Yust regards facts with the gravest suspicion and with reason.

"Facts are among the most difficult things in the world to catch," he says. "Some time ago, a correspondent wrote in to say that the length of an artificial river of the Ozarks was incorrectly given in the *Britannica*. I wrote to five different authorities, local, state and national, and each authority gave a different length for the river. I had to shut my eyes, choose one of them and stick to it."

A revised printing of the *Britannica* appears about every eight months. Since, under war conditions, it requires fourteen months to prepare, edit and print an edition, the staff usually is working on three different printings simultaneously. This in addition to working on the *Year Book* and the other publications. The *Britannica* printings are denominated by letters of the alphabet.

Whether you work on a newspaper, magazine or encyclopædia, the biggest current story in the world is, of course, the war. How does the *Encyclopædia* handle such a story? To a layman, it might appear relatively simple. You want an article on the war in the *Encyclopædia?* All right, just put it in. But "putting it in" is a vastly complex business. First you have to get your authority, a man equipped with the mentality, training and experience to write on such a difficult subject and do it a measure of justice. When the war broke out, the *Britannica* had to get somebody in a terrific hurry to write pieces for the *Year Book* as well as for the E. B. It made a quick grab and came up with Maj. George Fielding Eliot. The M printing of the *Encyclopædia* was in the works at the time. It was impossible to get into it an article entitled "European War," because there was nothing in the E volume which could be eliminated to make space for it. Eliot's article, therefore, was put into the W volume under the title "War in Europe (1939)." To make a place for it, the editors killed the article on War Guilt—of the First World War—and reduced the article entitled War Graves—also referring to the 1914–18 World War. This still did not give sufficient space, and it was necessary to add to the volume what are known as A and B pages, a frequently used device. For example, suppose you are replacing an old article with a new and longer article and the old article ends on Page 397. When you have used as much space for your new article as the deleted article required, you then start numbering pages 397-A, 397-B, and so on. To plug holes which may result, there is a vast file of carefully prepared filler pieces.

The M printing appeared in July, 1940; for the N printing,

which appeared the following April, Eliot revised his article. For the O printing the Eliot article was killed and an entirely new one, titled "World War II" was written by Gen. Hugh A. Drum, of the United States Army. To plug the hole left by eliminating the Eliot War in Europe article, the editors put in an article on War Organizations, written by Henry A. Wallace, Donald Nelson, Edward Stettinius, Leon Henderson, George W. Cronyn and C. A. Dykstra.

When the war is over, there will be a complete revision of the World War II article. When the peace is agreed upon, there will be another complete revision. This will probably be carried for several years, and will then be dropped to make way for what the editors hope will be a definitive revision.

Not even the wisest editor can tell, in the midst of such rapidly eruptive events, what will have permanent significance. What of the German massacre of the citizens of Lidice, for example? Will that have significance for the future? Lidice, in the shadow of such earth-shaking battles, was a small-scale, however brutal, tragedy. As a symbol, however, Lidice may rise like a spire in history. The story of Lidice was put into the *Britannica*—on sufferance. If, after the war, it is a descriptive mosaic of history, it will become a permanent part of the pattern of human knowledge which is bound in the *Britannica* to stay.

The *Britannica,* like every publication which has readers, has its troubles and its critics. The matter of biographies— those which are included and those which are not—produces many howls of anguish from E. B. customers. If a reader's particular hero is not included among the *Britannica's* biographies, the editors are very likely to receive a letter from Mr. Reader asking where they think they get off. The Florida legislature several years ago drew up a document in the form of a legal petition for a writ of mandamus to have a biography of John Gorrie, inventor of a process for artificial production of ice, printed in the *Encyclopædia*. The editors smilingly granted the writ. Obviously, though, the number of biographies which can be printed is limited unless the book is doubled in size.

The best friend, on the basis of being its severest critic, that the *Britannica* ever had was the late Willard Huntingdon Wright—S. S. Van Dine—who in 1917 wrote a book of blistering criticism of the *Britannica* called *Misinforming a Nation*. Most of the things of which he complained have long since been rectified. Another critic was Mary Beard, wife of the historian, Charles A. Beard, whose complaint was that the *Britannica* discriminated against women in its biographies. Yust, after a count showed that of the 13,000 biographies printed, only 600 were of women, asked Mrs. Beard to take charge of preparing the biographies of outstanding women.

Since 1936, every *Britannica* purchaser receives, when he buys his set, a book somewhat similar to a ration book, in which there are fifty stamps. Each of these stamps entitles him to enlist the services of the *Britannica's* Library Research Service to report on any subject he requests within ten years from the date of his purchase. Last year, the Research Service made 10,000 reports to *Britannica* owners, many of them papers running twenty to thirty pages of single-spaced typing, with complete bibliographies. Subjects on which reports are requested run the gamut from history of price control, rubber die presses and sheet-metal extrusion, history of railroad breaking and installation, and functions of voice tubing on ships to sex education for children and how to butcher a hog.

Questions which cannot be answered are those which would involve invasion of professional fields. The Research Service, for example, will not provide, as it is not infrequently requested to do, plans and specifications "for a nice six-room house." That's a job for architects. But it can and does tell how to raise rabbits or goats.

A few years ago, a small city, largely dependent upon a single manufactory, faced ruin when the estate of a factory employee sued the industry for a large sum, alleging that a chemical used at the plant caused the man's death. If the suit was lost, the factory would be compelled to shut down. The lawyer for the defendant obtained a report from the Research Service showing the chemical was harmless. On the basis of this the suit was thrown out of court. Many such things occur. Not only lawyers but businessmen and industrialists, governors and congressmen, writers and cartoonists, policemen, students and club-women desirous of making non-Hokinson speeches appeal to the bureau.

Recently a *Britannica* salesman sold a set to a man in New York State, promising delivery shortly. In due time the customer received his copy of the *Year Book* and his Research Service stamps. Weeks went by, however, and for some reason or other, his set of the *Britannica* did not arrive. The Research Service had a real problem on its hands when it got a letter from the gentleman, enclosing his first stamp, and asking: "Where the hell is my *Encyclopædia?*"

Not infrequently, the problems laid in the bureau's lap are intensely human ones, as was that of a young Southern boy.

"My dad and I," he wrote, "bought a set of your *Encyclopædia* and I want to know all I can about jujetso. Like the wressling holds, throws, defence from a gun and etc. So if you send me a booklet on jujetso I will be pleased. If I need to send any money for it, I will gladly send it. Theres some boys biger than I am and bully me around and I don't like it. I'm a Boy Scout from Troop 70 of Old Hickory, Tennessee."

He got a full report on "jujetso," and the bullies of Old Hickory have probably had their eyes opened—or perhaps closed. At least we may hope so.

Heading the service since it was started has been Aimee C. Buchanan, whom no question, however abstruse, appears to faze. Not that she knows all the answers herself or pretends to. But she knows where to send her staff to find the answers.

Mrs. Buchanan is a native of Denver and a graduate of Denver University. Upon the insistence of her mother, who believed that schoolteaching was the only fit occupation for a young woman, she started her career as a schoolmarm. It probably wasn't just as her mother had pictured it though. Mrs. Buchanan's first school was in a copper-mining camp in Nevada. Extracurricularly she coached high-school plays in a deserted saloon. She doesn't remember just what caused the saloon to be deserted.

Her next teaching stop was a coal-mining town in Montana. "There wasn't a bathtub in the town," she says. "We got one bucket of hot water and one bucket of cold water from the mine mouth each day. That was the water ration. I would go to Great Falls every Friday and stay at a hotel in order to get a bath."

The remainder of Mrs. Buchanan's seven years of teaching was put in at Clarkston, Washington, across the Snake River from Lewiston, Idaho—which was the metropolis—and in Kentucky, where she, like the immortalized Mr. Scopes, was also fired for teaching evolution. After a stint at Macy's, "putting Size 52 ladies into Size 16 dresses," she went to the *Britannica*, with which she has worked for seventeen years. Deeply interested in the position of women in business and industry, she has devoted considerable study to the question and recently published a book on the subject, *The Lady Means Business*—Simon & Schuster. There is a chapter in the book on Men Executives which the *Britannica's* men executives regard in about the same light as they would the Communist Manifesto—for different reasons, of course. Mrs. Buchanan has a staff of college graduates who work in Chicago, New York and at the Congressional Library in Washington.

The history of the *Britannica* since it was founded in Edinburgh 177 years ago by the little "society of gentlemen" has virtually paralleled in many respects the history of the English-speaking world. Sets of it have followed these people into all parts of the world, in war and in peace. And today, the *Britannica* can be frequently found within reach of the men who plan the United Nations strategy. The Nazi radio spoke a measure of truth for once, when it said that "the encyclopædia forms the mind of a people." But it also reflects a people's philosophy and ideals. It might have been well if the war lords of the world, plotting global conquest, had taken the time to consult the *Britannica*.

Headlines in Celluloid

By T. F. Woods

EDITOR'S PREFACE.—The history of American journalism is to some extent an account of trends. Around the middle of the nineteenth century the literary magazines, such as *Harper's* and *Atlantic Monthly* came into being, and some, including the two mentioned, gained a foothold sufficient to keep them going to the present. The latter part of the past century saw the rise of the popular magazines—*McClure's, Munsey's,* and *Cosmopolitan.* Next was the period of what Theodore Roosevelt called the "muckrakers." The 1920's saw the rise and tremendous influence of H. L. Mencken, George Jean Nathan, *The American Mercury,* and all those who gave expression to the post-World-War-I cynicism. Today, and for some ten years or more, two dominant trends have been noticeable in contemporary journalism: (1) condensation of text as reflected in the multiplication of digest magazines, and (2) the greater and more intelligent use of pictures by all types of media. An important phase of the latter trend, and one which must necessarily continue if we are to have television, is the newsreel, the theme of the significant article which follows. Once regarded as the stepchild of both the theatre and journalism, and treated accordingly by both, the newsreel is no longer considered a kiss of death at the box office, but rather is proving an astonishingly popular form of journalism—the kind of offspring in which both theatre and journalism can (and do) take pride.

August 11, 1945

AS A newsreel unfolded the battle of Iwo Jima on a small screen set up in the darkened hospital ward, a wounded veteran of that campaign observed a shadowy figure move into the picture, stumble, and fall face down as a Jap slug found its mark. Suddenly he found his voice in a cry of astonishment. That figure had been himself and this was the first recorded instance of a man bearing witness to his own shooting.

Less spectacular perhaps, but laden with pathos, has been the four-year trek to newsreels by wives, parents and sweethearts on the off-chance they might catch a fleeting glimpse of servicemen alive and well. Impetus was given to this movement back in the early dark days of the war; a handful of Americans landed at Port Moresby in the midst of a hail of enemy bombs. When the celluloid record of that historic event appeared at the Telenews Theatre in San Francisco, a distraught middle-aged man walked purposefully into the manager's office. "I want you to run the picture slower," he announced.

"Sorry, it can't be done," said the manager.

"Yes, it can," the other declared. "I used to be an operator myself, and I know you can crank those machines any speed you want."

Patiently the manager pointed out that standard projection machines are now driven by electricity. His caller produced a card, introduced himself and then explained. He thought he had just seen his son in the newsreel, but the picture had gone by so quickly that he couldn't be sure. It was months since he had heard from his son. Peter was a good boy, he added, but just a boy. He had sat through the film four times. If only he could be sure.

That was easy, the manager told him with a sigh of relief. He escorted the man to the projection room, where the film was slowly run off through an editing machine. Crying unashamedly, the visitor identified his son. A few frames of the film were removed and an enlargement was made and presented to the grateful parent. Thus began one of the greatest boons to an already-booming newsreel industry.

Local papers played up the story, with names, and copies went out over the press wires. Everywhere, managers and press agents for the Telenews chain turned out copy to this effect: "Identify a relative in the newsreel and receive a free enlarged photo taken from the film." People all over the nation recognized or thought they recognized their friends or relatives in the armed forces, and alert advertising men beat the drums of publicity. Shrewd newsreel editors began selecting the shots which showed the greatest number of American troops.

Before the reconquest of the Philippines, captured Jap films of the fall of Bataan provided some of the most pathetic cases of identification. Because of the lack of Japanese co-operation with the Red Cross, these motion pictures provided many with the first inkling of the fate of relatives who had participated in that immortal stand. One mother, after tentatively identifying her son among the prisoners of war, finally refused either to take the film or to accept an enlargement. So terribly drawn and emaciated was the figure she believed to be her boy that she preferred the uncertainty of not knowing whether he was alive.

When Maj. Ed Larner, of San Francisco, a hero of almost legendary proportions in the South Pacific battle zone, appeared in a newsreel speaking a few lines, his wife and parents were invited to a private showing of the film by the local newsreel-theater manager. With them came the major's two-year-old daughter, who, from the vantage point of her mother's lap, gazed with wide-eyed wonder at the handsome man on the screen described to her as "daddy." The films were run off many times and publicity pictures were duly taken for the evening papers. Several weeks later, those pictures were republished, a group of smiling people looking fondly upon a tiny piece of film. And, for once, a manager sincerely regretted his publicity. News had been released that Major Larner had met his death in a plane crash. However, a child who had never known him will have at least a living, talking record of a gallant father, thanks to a newsreel company which provided her with the film.

As the attendance of newsreels grew to be a personalized experience for millions, a kind of search among shadows with all the odds of Bank Night, many theater owners were forced to reverse a long-held contention that motion pictures are an escapist's medium exclusively. In the light of a persistent stream of telephone calls asking for newsreels by their trade numbers, theater owners no longer eliminated the newsreel in order to shorten shows, heretofore a common way of facilitating audience turnover on crowded nights. Today, the lowly newsreel has come into its own. The dowdiest grind-house on Skid Row features in the lobby a stock one-sheet listing the news items to be seen inside.

Long before this tide of relative seekers engulfed them, however, theater managers might have taken a cue from the newsreel theater. But the idea of people paying for mere information via the screen proved to be a bitter pill for dyed-in-the-wool showmen to swallow. Even while the line-ups continued to grow in front of those theaters devoted entirely to films of current events, many exhibitors continued to advertise: "No War News Shown Here."

Yet the fact remains that a new form of journalism has quietly emerged from this war. The motion-picture industry and even the public itself have been scarcely conscious of its development, so natural has been their acceptance of the newsreel and its corollary, the documentary film, only a few short years ago considered by showmen to be the kiss of death so far as box-office receipts were concerned.

Probably the first motion pictures were newsreels in the sense that they developed no plot. The Spanish-American War was covered by a motion-picture camera in 1898, but it was not until 1909 that a Frenchman, Charles Pathé, presented films of current events to the people of France. Pathé, a circus performer by profession, had invested his life's savings in a raw film-stock enterprise and hit upon newsreels as a manner of stimulating sales. For a time he actually sold his news by the foot, measuring it out as a notion salesman vends pink ribbons. And woe betide the cameraman who did not drag the footage out, covering a story down to the most minute detail! However, the idea of visual news immediately captured public fancy, and a year later was introduced to American audiences. Today, in this country alone, more than 100,000,000 persons each week view newsreels.

There are five major American newsreels—Metro-Goldwyn-Mayer's News of the Day, Paramount, Universal, 20th Century-Fox Movietone and Pathe, still active, but under the aegis of RKO. All American, a newsreel devoted to Negro activities, has broken into the field and is being well received by mixed audiences everywhere.

The original Pathe News was a weekly. In England daily issues were once attempted experimentally, but proved impractical. Present-day newsreel companies, with make-up headquarters in New York, each release two issues per week. The reels are shipped by plane to distant accounts, so that Wednesday and Friday are simultaneous release dates from California to Maine.

The first newsreel subject filmed in sound was Lindbergh's transatlantic take-off in May of 1927. In the ensuing years, much time and effort were spent vainly attempting to persuade him to talk for theater audiences. Ironically, later films of Lindbergh's isolationist speeches created so much disturbance that many theater managers were forced to clip his appearance out to forestall further demonstrations.

Rodman Law, who narrowly escaped death in parachuting from the Statue of Liberty, made newsreel history with this first stunt subject. One of the most spectacular items in the field was the Tacoma Bridge crash, caught on film by a scientist who at that precise moment happened to be filming the antics of the structure for future study. The assassination of King Alexander was another dramatic smash caught by routine coverage.

It is surprising how newsreels taken a few years ago can work on the emotions when seen today. For example, one of the most naturally dramatic scenes ever put between sprocket holes is bearded Haile Selassie's appeal to the League of Nations for aid against Mussolini's Italy. Attempts of the motion picture *Mission to Moscow* to reconstruct this scene were ill-advised in the eyes of those who remember the news shots, for no actor could possibly portray the heartfelt anguish welling out of the little man's dark face as, with tragic dignity, he faces his audience and waits for the jeers to cease, so that he may continue what is obviously a hopeless gesture. Nor does the return of Neville Chamberlain from the Munich conference lack in sad irony. Pity somehow has replaced bitterness as one looks upon the man jubilantly waving a scrap of paper to the cheering crowds and proclaiming "Peace in our time!" Films of Roosevelt's return from Yalta are so patently the portrait of a man doomed that one wonders how that fact escaped when the pictures were originally released.

Films of historic importance are preserved by the New York Museum of Modern Art Film Library and the Library of Congress, whose vaults contain scenes from the first World War, shots of Czar Nicholas and Rasputin, Theodore Roosevelt, Queen Victoria, the flight of the Wright Brothers, and much else of inestimable value.

Cameramen would guffaw at the suggestion that they are emissaries of history. But they can never be certain that destiny will not take a hand in some prosaic assignment. On the evening of May 6, 1937, a newsreel cameraman was dispatched to cover the arrival of the Hindenburg at Lakehurst, New Jersey. To pleas that he had tickets for a Broadway play, that it would be just another assignment, that it had been done before, the editor turned a deaf ear. So, considerably disgruntled, the cameraman did some plotting: If he took his date along, which incidentally could not fail to impress the lady, perhaps he could cover the assignment in time to make the opening curtain.

Setting up his camera at the scheduled time of the Zeppelin's arrival, he and the girl chatted for long, nervous moments. The giant airship was late. At last they could wait no longer. As the Hindenburg came out of the darkness over the edge of the field, they drove madly off.

"It was just another routine flight," the cameraman consoled himself.

Fortunately, however, other cameramen were without romantic entanglements; and we have in existence one of the
most startling newsreel sequences ever filmed.

In this country it was in 1929 that the newsreel graduated
from a novelty dependent upon good features into genuine
pictorial journalism. That was the year Fox Film Company
introduced into the Embassy Theater in New York a successful
policy of exhibiting newsreels and shorts exclusively. Trans-
Lux Corporation later added rear projection, turnstiles and
other features of low-cost operation.

Showmen, who at the beginning had been skeptical of these
enterprises, grudgingly admitted their limited success. But
they predicted that such a policy could never be possible in
cities with less population than New York, Chicago, Philadelphia, Detroit or Los Angeles. In their opinion, newsreel
theaters were freaks. The shortness of the program—an hour
to ninety minutes—was the attraction, drawing salesmen,
shoppers and other persons with limited time. Put a newsreel
theater where thousands of tired people did not pass the
door every hour, they jeered, and that theater would cease to
exist. This upstart, the old guard insisted, was only a con-
venience—and newsreel-theater owners, strangely enough,
were inclined to agree. That great new frontiers were being
opened did not immediately occur to them.

On September 1, 1939, a group of New York businessmen
headed by Alfred G. Burger and Herbert L. Sheftel opened
the Telenews Theater in the city of San Francisco. On that
same day, Germany marched into Poland, a coincidence which
theatermen still speak of as the luckiest break ever accorded
any venture in the history of show business. But managing
editors—as those in charge of newsreel houses affect to call
themselves—disclaim any relationship to show business and
maintain that pictorial journalism would eventually have
come into its own without the aid of the horrors of war.

Attendance at newsreels is more or less habit-forming. Long
association of films with entertainment is a natural barrier to

immediate acceptance of this medium as a serious source of information. Once this prejudice is broken down, however, the skeptic is often converted into a rabid supporter. Some of these patrons write fan letters in phrases which even a press agent would hesitate to use. "Your theater," gushes one enthusiast, "with its informative up-to-the-minute world news, is a college of firsthand education playing a big part in awakening and arousing the American public to a greater understanding and responsibility." But not all reactions are couched in such appreciative language.

Regular devotees are quick to spot a faked shot and are loud in their denunciation. And the building up of synthetic stories in lieu of on-the-spot films—a practice editors resort to in order to keep on top of the headlines—is equally irritating to the newsreel fan.

Discriminating patrons are also hypercritical of the manner in which a program is edited. Actually, there is much duplication in all newsreels from every company. The job of the newsreel-theater editor is to select the best story in each instance and remove the duplication from the other reels, so that only the exclusive sequences remain. These are combined into a smoothly flowing whole. A story which, in the single version, was only two or three minutes in length often can be built up to ten minutes on the screen. Pace is considered of utmost importance. Occasionally the editor tries for effect by contrast, such as following up a particularly bloody battle scene with shots of strikers on the home front.

Managing a newsreel theater calls for the most vigorous features of journalism plus old-time, drag-'em-in showmanship. As in a newspaper, a dead line must be met. The new show must follow on the heels of the old one, so that a thrifty patron may see both programs for a single admission. Since his film is flown from New York, the vagaries of wartime transportation give the manager some anxious moments. If he uses all five news services, he must screen and edit between 8000 and 10,000 feet, often within a few hours of his dead line. Air-line and mail officials are alternately bullied, wheedled and cultivated in the hope of gaining a few precious moments in delivery.

One of the major headaches of the celluloid editor is the shortage of material related to a spectacular news break. Obviously, the camera version and the "hot" headline cannot be released simultaneously. Consequently, motion-picture distributors are sometimes driven to distraction by newsreel managers clamoring to get into their vaults any time of the day or night in search of some long-forgotten film subject, however slight its relevancy to the news of the moment. Within an hour after the Allies landed in France, nearly every news theater in America was showing some suitable subject on its screen, with marquee and lobby posters screaming their "scoop" to the world. Prepared "rehashes" are usually kept on hand, anticipating such expected headlines as Germany's surrender, although the flood of rumors before that event called for almost superhuman restraint.

Cameramen are the forgotten men of this war, victims of illusion. Audiences watching a newsreel are prone to forget that beside a flame thrower flushing slant-eyed quarry a cameraman stood, armed only with an Eyemo. And few recognize from the angle of the "shot" that as brave G. I.'s rise from their foxholes to assault a pillbox it was a cameraman, his eye glued to a viewer, that first exposed himself. Casualties among members of the Signal Corps and newsreel correspondents have been heavy. But these men have not only provided a military record from which enemy weaknesses and strengths may be studied; they have given to the world a moving document which might well prove of lasting benefit for mankind in years to come.

Newsreels and Government-released films of Okinawa, Iwo Jima, Tarawa, and others will, according to present plans, supplement history textbooks in future classrooms. But above all, they have brought home to Americans the terrible price they must pay for total victory. They have provided Americans with the most graphic coverage of any war.

No amount of words written on the subject could compete with that now famous newsreel picture of a tiny Chinese baby crying his heart out as he sits beside his dead mother in a bomb-shattered railway station. During the Battle of Britain, newsreels of the destruction wrought by the German Luftwaffe raised the average American's respect for the citizens of that country to a pinnacle never before attained. And, although the whole world applauded the Russian people for stopping the Nazi Juggernaut, it remained for such documentary pictures as *Moscow Strikes Back, Our Russian Front,* and March of Time's *One Day of War* to remind millions of Americans that the grief of a woman over her child transcends all political beliefs.

It is a far cry, indeed, from the first flickering newsreel of Pathe, valued in terms of its physical proportions, to films of Nazi murder camps as witnessed by a group of German prisoners.

Meanwhile, because the same people that buy his tickets also buy the papers, our celluloid editor must scramble to keep on top of the headlines . . . an antic which occasionally results in woeful repercussions. When the world was waiting breathlessly to hear of V-E Day, a newsboy making his daily sale to a theater manager gibed, "What do you want with this? You'll have the surrender before we will!" He was right.

Biographical Sketches of Contributors

JACK ALEXANDER.—Associate editor of *The Saturday Evening Post*, Mr. Alexander during World War II was on foreign assignment. Versatile reporter, good on almost any kind of story, this former St. Louis newspaper man is particularly adept at biographical writing. An examination of the *Reader's Guide to Periodical Literature* will reveal that he has told the life stories of a long and varied list of distinguished Americans through the pages of the *Post* and other periodicals. Mr. Alexander was educated in his home city—at St. Louis University. Before going east in 1931, he worked for both the St. Louis *Star* and the St. Louis *Post-Dispatch*. He did a little of everything: he was reporter, sports writer, substitute columnist, and movie reviewer. In New York, he was with the New York City News Association for three years, the *Daily News* for two years, and *The New Yorker* for two years.

MARQUIS W. CHILDS.—Winner of the 1944 Sigma Delta Chi distinguished service award for Washington correspondence, Mr. Childs has achieved renown both as a correspondent and as an author. A teacher of English, a United Press bureau man (1923 and 1925–26), and a roving reporter for the St. Louis *Post-Dispatch* (since 1926) before he became a syndicated columnist, Mr. Childs was selected by Sigma Delta Chi for the Washington correspondence award "for sustained insight in national affairs, first-hand reporting, and effective writing." Born in the Mississippi river town of Clinton, Iowa (March 17, 1903), Mr. Childs received the A.B. degree from the University of Wisconsin (1923) and the A.M. from the University of Iowa (1925). Upsala College conferred the honorary LL.D. degree on him in 1943. On leave of absence from the *Post-Dispatch*, he visited Sweden in 1930 and returned to Europe several times before the publication of his widely read *Sweden—The Middle Way* in 1936. Other books by Mr. Childs are *They Hate Roosevelt, Washington Calling, This Is Democracy, Toward a Dynamic America* (with William T. Stone), *This Is Your War*, and *I Write from Washington*.

STANLEY FRANK.—Author of the piece, "Bible of Baseball," and co-author (with Paul Sann) of the article, "Paper Dolls," Mr. Frank has long been a newspaper and magazine writer. With the New York *Post* for 18 years, he has been sports columnist and war correspondent (he was with the AEF from D-Day until the defeat of Germany). In 1945 he left newspaperdom to devote all his time to magazine work. He has written articles and fiction for thirty national magazines, including, in addition to the *Post, Collier's, Liberty, American,* and *This Week*. Mr. Frank edited *Sports Extra,* a collection of outstanding sports articles from newspapers and periodicals. He was born in New York City on April 22, 1908, and was graduated from City College of New York in 1930.

OTTO FUERBRINGER.—This writer of the piece, "Average Man's Columnist" (Raymond Clapper) , was born in St. Louis on September 27, 1910. In the language of the "Keeping Posted" section of the *Post*, he "took after an ancestor who wasn't a Lutheran minister. Just who this lay character in the Fuerbringer family tree was, our author can't remember. Otto is the son of a Lutheran minister. Both his grandfathers were Lutheran ministers. Three of his uncles are Lutheran ministers. His brother and two brothers-in-law are Lutheran ministers. An ex-newspaperman, Otto now works for *Time* magazine. No pastor he.

"After attending Lutheran parochial school and Cleveland High School in his native St. Louis, Mr. Fuerbringer went to Harvard, to which he'd won a scholarship, and put in ten to twelve hours a day as a reporter and editor of the *Crimson*.

In 1932, upon graduation, he returned to St. Louis and conferred with City Editor Ben Reese, of the *Post-Dispatch*. Mr. Reese said the man who wrote the Boy Scout news once a week was quitting and that Mr. Fuerbringer could have his job with the fourteen dollars a week it paid, and if he wanted to come to work the other five days a week, he could have six dollars more. Mr. Fuerbringer plumped for the full-time job.

"His third day on the paper brought Cub Fuerbringer an assignment to beg, borrow, or otherwise get hold of a photograph of a young woman who had sat down in front of the kitchen range, turned on the gas and died, scribbling away for dear life her final thoughts of this world on a piece of paper.

" 'I spent the day having doors slammed in my face and went back to the office to report no success,' Mr. Fuerbringer says. 'Ben Reese gave me a look which clearly said he was wasting that extra six bucks a week and informed me that when he wanted a picture he wanted it; even if it took a reporter a week or a month, he wanted it, and a reporter had better not come back until he had it.'

"Mr. Fuerbringer's success in getting the picture the next day has given him a never-failing topic for conversation with young reporters breaking into the game. 'There is no experience,' he tells them solemnly, 'like picture chasing. It is the best possible training for a reporter. If a young cub can wheedle a picture of a suicide out of a bereaved family, he can worm a story out of anybody.'

"After doing rewrite and general assignments for the *Post-Dispatch,* Mr. Fuerbringer went to Europe and wrote a series of articles on Germany. He now lives in New York with his wife and two children, who, with the world what it is today, will probably grow up to be Lutheran ministers."

MONA GARDNER.—Born of English parents in Seattle, Washington, Mona Gardner majored in English at Stanford University. Upon graduation, she began newspaper work on the San Francisco *Call-Bulletin*. Later she decided to combine writing with travel—a decision which took her to Japan where she lived for some 12 years, making various trips from Japan to Formosa, head-hunter country, and China. When the Sino-Japanese war broke out, Miss Gardner began doing feature articles for the North American Newspaper Alliance. Among these were interviews with Generalissimo and Madam Chiang Kai-shek and Madam Soong. Miss Gardner was in Shanghai during the bombardment and siege, then went on to Hong Kong. She moved from China down into Indo-China and Siam, through Malaya to Singapore, and went on to Java, Sumatra, Bali, Ceylon, and Bombay. While in India, she became interested in "the Indian problem" and did stories on Gandhi and several Nationalist Congress leaders. From the Orient her writing trail led to Italy and then to Paris. A stop-off in England delayed her return home to the United States in 1938. One result of Miss Gardner's Far Eastern experiences was a book, *The Menacing Sun,* published in 1941. This was a collection of profiles of the personalities she had interviewed for NANA, plus her impressions of peoples in the Orient. National groups and profiles are her major interests. In addition to personality sketches, she has written fiction with Far Eastern backgrounds for American magazines.

MARGARET CASE HARRIMAN.—Just as the *Post* is an institution among magazines, so is the Algonquin distinctive among American hotels. It is the literary inn of the nation. Not only is it the New York home of many nationally known writers, but its late proprietor was himself an author of no mean skill. Frank Case wrote two books, *Tales of a Wayward Inn* and *Do Not Disturb,* which attracted much favorable notice and sold widely. All of which is said by way of introduction of the writer of the piece about Emily Post. Margaret Case Harriman is the daughter of Frank Case. She was reared among the celebrities of the Algonquin. She is, therefore, an author both by heredity and environment. Recalling some of the high points in her journalistic past, Mrs. Harriman has written:

"I was born in New York and grew up in my father's hotel, the Algonquin, in a kind of nest of writing and acting celebs.

Frank Ward O'Malley used to take me to the circus every spring; Joseph Hergesheimer gave me my first autographed books, and when I was twelve, Douglas Fairbanks (Senior) once dared me to follow him up an iron ladder on the outside wall of the hotel, thirteen stories above the street. (I did, and this is the first father will have heard of it.) As further education, I went to Gardner School in New York and to the pension at Morel de Fos in France. When I came home I got a job writing feature stories for a newspaper, at space rates of ten dollars a column. Pretty soon *Vanity Fair* took me on as dramatic editor and, a year later, as associate editor. Clare Luce—who was then Clare Brokaw—and I had an office together, and they do say we were an eyeful. I left *Vanity Fair* about five years ago and started writing profiles for the *New Yorker;* been writing them ever since, also other pieces for various magazines, including *The Saturday Evening Post.* I have a son . . . who likes swimming, ice skating, boats, the funny papers and Topper, my cocker spaniel, as much as I do; where we split is that he likes arithmetic too."

Matthew Josephson.—For two years (1924–26) with the New York Stock Exchange, following his graduation from Columbia University (A.B., 1920), Mr. Josephson has more recently devoted his time and talents to authorship and editorial work. His books include *Zola and His Time* (1928), *Portrait of the Artist as an American* (1930), *Jean-Jacques Rousseau* (1932) , and *The Robber Barons* (1934). He has been contributing editor, *Transition* (1928–29), and book editor of the Macaulay Company (1929). Mr. Josephson was born in Brooklyn, New York, February 15, 1899, and is a member of the Authors' League of America.

Tom (Thomas) Mahoney.—Born in Dallas, Texas, December 3, 1905, Mr. Mahoney was educated in the University of Missouri's School of Journalism (B.J., 1927), and has had a variety of newspaper, press association, and magazine experience. He has been editor, *Modern Mechanix;* Sunday editor, Buffalo (New York) *Times;* bureau manager, United Press, Dallas and Kansas City; city editor, El Paso (Texas) *Post;* and reporter, Dallas *News.* At present associate editor of *Look* Magazine, Mr. Mahoney is a past national vice-president, Sigma Delta Chi, professional journalistic fraternity; is a member of the Mexican Pilgrims, and contributes to a variety of magazines, including, in addition to the *Post* and *Look,* such journals as *Esquire, New Yorker,* and *Southwest Review.*

MARK MURPHY.—On leave from *The New Yorker* for military service during World War II (enlisted combat correspondent, Army Air Forces), Mr. Murphy, like many others, used newspaper work as a stepping stone to periodical journalism. He was a reporter for three Ohio newspapers (Toledo *News-Bee,* Akron *Times-Press,* and Columbus *Citizen*) and the New York *Post* before becoming a staff writer for *The New Yorker.* Born in Chicago, July 31, 1912, Mr. Murphy attended school in Minot, North Dakota; Monmouth, Illinois; and Davenport, Iowa. He received the A.B. degree from the University of Michigan in 1936. He is the author of *83 Days.*

MARY ELLEN MURPHY.—The wife of Mark Murphy (they were married February 10, 1940). Born in Watertown, Wisconsin, Mrs. Murphy attended school in Toledo, Ohio, and graduated from Smith College in 1938 and the Columbia School of Journalism in 1939. Presently connected with *Fortune Magazine,* she has been associated with the New York *Post,* the Office of War Information, and has done free lance work for the Condé Nast publications and *The Saturday Evening Post.*

WARNER OLIVIER.—The writer of the article about the *Encyclopaedia Britannica,* "160 Miles of Words," was born in Staunton, Virginia, August 14, 1900. He attended public school in Staunton and Episcopal High in Alexandria and began newspaper work when but 16 years old by working summers on the Staunton *Daily News* (now the *News-Leader*). Mr. Olivier says that he "fought the first World War for 70 days from the campus at Charlottesville, Virginia, and *mis*attended the University of Virginia the following year." He has worked on a score of newspapers in Baltimore, New York, Philadelphia, Paris, and in other cities. Mr. Olivier was associate editor of the *Post* for two years, but resigned in 1945 to devote all his time to free-lance writing. He is a member of the Pen and Pencil Club, Philadelphia, and at this writing his address is Makoma Inn, Laporte, Pennsylvania.

FREDERICK C. PAINTON.—The writer of the article, "Up Front with Bill Mauldin" and "The Hoosier Letter-Writer," as might well be suspected, was a war correspondent. In fact, he devoted his journalistic talents to both World War I and II. Born July 15, 1895 in Elmira, New York, and a graduate of Columbia University, he was on *Stars and Stripes* during the first conflict. Between wars he was on the New York *Tribune*, was national publicity director for the American Legion, and did free lance writing. A correspondent for *Reader's Digest*, Mr. Painton was overseas for two years in the European theatre, beginning with the Tunisian campaign. He was in the D-Day Sicilian landing, July 10, 1943, and the D-Day landing in Southern France, August 15, 1944. He left for the Pacific in January, 1945, and died on Guam March 31, 1945.

DAN(IEL FRANCIS) PARKER.—In his article, "So You Want to Be a Sports Editor?," Mr. Parker is largely autobiographical. A few facts and dates are appropriate here, however. This sports editor and columnist was born in Waterbury, Connecticut (July 1, 1893), and was educated at the local Crosby High School. He was a reporter on the Waterbury *Republican* (1912–13); reporter, Waterbury *American* (1913–20) and sports writer of the same paper (1920–24); sports writer, New York *Daily Mirror* (1924–26), and sports editor and columnist since 1926. Mr. Parker served as a sergeant with the Headquarters Company, 354th Infantry, 87th Division, with the American Expeditionary Force in 1918. He is a member of the Baseball

Writers' Association of America and the Lambs Club, writes articles for the popular magazines, and is the author of *Racing Primer*.

HENRY F. PRINGLE.—The person who did the article "How to Get Your Name in Who's Who" is a newspaper man, author, and teacher of much distinction. Winner of the Pulitzer prize in biography in 1931, he has a long list of outstanding books to his credit—*Alfred E. Smith—A Critical Study, Big Frogs, Industrial Explorers* (with Maurice Holland), *Theodore Roosevelt—A Biography,* and *The Life and Times of William Howard Taft*. Born in New York City and educated at Cornell University (A.B. 1920), Mr. Pringle has been reporter on the New York *Sun* (1920–22), New York *Globe* (1922–24), and New York *World* (1924–27); associate editor, *The Outlook* (1929–31); associate in journalism (1932–36) and professor of journalism (1936–43), Columbia University; chief, Division of Publications, Office of War Information (February, 1942–April, 1943), and a free-lance writer since 1927. He has contributed to many magazines—*Harper's, The New Yorker, Collier's* and *The American Mercury*. He was a Guggenheim Fellow, 1944–45, and at this writing is at work on a new book with his wife (Katharine Douglas Pringle)—*America at War*.

WALLIS M. REEF.—The man responsible for "She Didn't Write It for Money, She Says" is a third generation Coloradan. He was born in Denver, January 2, 1895. His mother's parents (she too is Denver born), Mr. and Mrs. John M. Melvin, crossed the plains by ox-team in 1859 to found the town of Melvin, which is 12 miles south of Denver. (The middle initial in Mr. Reef's name is for Melvin). Mr. Reef sold his first story (to *The Bellman Magazine* in 1913) while a student in high school. He attended the University of Colorado but left to become a reporter on the old Denver *Post* in 1915. During World War I he served as battalion sergeant major of engineers and second lieutenant of infantry. Mr. Reef joined the *Rocky*

Mountain News in 1921 and remained until 1935, serving as special assignment reporter (mostly crime), promotion editor, and city editor. It was during this period that Mary Coyle Chase (about whom Mr. Reef writes in this collection) was on the *News,* as were Clyde Brion Davis, author of *The Great American Novel;* John P. Lewis, editor, *PM;* and Glenn T. Neville, executive editor, New York *Daily Mirror.* Mr. Reef served as special investigator for the U. S. Senate committee investigating the munitions industry until its work ended in 1935 when he became editor in charge of special events for Radio Station KFEL. He ran for mayor of Denver in 1939 and, as he phrases the result, "limped in fourth in a field of nine." Mr. Reef left the radio station in 1944 to devote his time to magazine writing. He is a member of the Denver Press Club, American Legion, and Masons.

PAUL SANN.—Co-author (with Stanley Frank) of "Paper Dolls," Mr. Sann was born in Brooklyn, New York (March 7, 1914) and was educated at Morris High School, The Bronx, and New York Preparatory School, Park Avenue. He began work on the New York *Post* in 1931 as a copy boy and later served successively as city desk clerk, operator of city desk switchboard, lobster rewrite man, police headquarters, Criminal Courts, and general assignment reporter. He next specialized in housing–slum clearance problems and home relief–WPA assignments. He was next night city editor and then assistant city editor. In September, 1944, Mr. Sann went to the New York *Journal-American* as reporter–rewrite man, but returned to the *Post* (Washington bureau) January 15, 1945. During the United Nations Conference in San Francisco (April to June, 1945), he served as news editor of the *Post's* special conference edition which was distributed in San Francisco. At this writing (early 1946) Mr. Sann is assistant to the executive editor of the *Bronx Home News,* New York (owned by the *Post*), on leave from the *Post.* He has written for a variety of magazines, including *Nation, Common Sense, This Month, B'nai B'rith,* and *Magazine Digest;* is the author (with Malcolm Logan) of

Must We Have Slums?; and is a member of the National Press Club, White House Correspondents Association, and the Senate and House Press Galleries.

DAVID G. WITTELS.—Born in New York City, April 22, 1905, the man who wrote the piece about the Philadelphia *Bulletin* was reared in Philadelphia and its environs. He spent 17 years as a reporter and editor on newspapers—Camden (N. J.) *Courier-Post,* Lancaster (Pa.) *New Era,* Brooklyn *Eagle,* Philadelphia *Inquirer,* Philadelphia *Record,* and New York *Post.* He is the author (with Leon G. Turrow, a G-man) of *Nazi Spies in America.* With the late Elsie Finn, he wrote the original screen play for Lily Pons' first starring picture, *I Dream Too Much.* Mr. Wittels became a professional magazine writer in November, 1941, and has written some fifty articles and one fiction piece for *The Saturday Evening Post.* He has also contributed to *Liberty, Esquire, Coronet* and *Catholic Digest;* has been reprinted in English publications; and is represented in at least three anthologies. Ten months a war correspondent in the South-West Pacific and China-Burma-India theatres, he literally circled the globe, going west from Philadelphia and returning from the East. Mr. Wittels is married to the former Tana Graitcer, painter and fashion artist, and has three children. He is a member of the Pen and Pencil Club, Philadelphia, and the National Press Club, Washington.

T. F. WOODS.—This author of "Headlines in Celluloid" was born March 19, 1910, in San Francisco and provides the following autobiographical note:

"Attended San Francisco State Teachers' College for a short period, until after prolonged introspection, the ideal of inculcating knowledge into young heads became increasingly hopeless. Became convinced of the wisdom of this decision after siring two children. Beat my head for a time against the Hemingway school for hacks. Then, as the necessity for keeping the chops on the table grew more evident, became alternately a publicity man, tennis bum, and theatre manager, which I am the first to admit is another kind of a bum. I recently became more respectable. Am at present General Manager for the Robert L. Lippert Theatres, a chain of twenty movie houses, and am currently engaged in writing a book about screen journalism."

CONCERNING THE FOURTH ESTATE

By John E. Drewry

"Here is a book of interest to the prospective journalism student seeking information on the opportunities offered and preparation needed for newspaper work. It likewise holds an equal interest for the professional newspaper man and the thoughtful freedom loving American citizen."

—Franklin Banner, Director, Department of Journalism, Pennsylvania State College

"... *Concerning the Fourth Estate,* published in such attractive format, will be a valuable reference for journalism teachers, newspaper men, journalism students and alumni, and others interested in the press and schools of journalism. It is not only pleasant reading, but an interesting source of factual material and pertinent quotations. It gives an enlightening picture of the best current thought concerning the newspaper press and the newly achieved position of the schools of journalism in relation to it."

—Grant M. Hyde, Director, School of Journalism, University of Wisconsin